Dear
                                            1997

love

Tom + Jan-Willem

THE THEATRE OF DEATH
THE RITUAL MANAGEMENT OF ROYAL FUNERALS
IN RENAISSANCE ENGLAND, 1570–1625

THE THEATRE OF DEATH

THE RITUAL MANAGEMENT OF ROYAL FUNERALS IN RENAISSANCE ENGLAND 1570–1625

Jennifer Woodward

THE BOYDELL PRESS

© Jennifer Woodward 1997

All Rights Reserved. Except as permitted under current legislation
no part of this work may be photocopied, stored in a retrieval system,
published, performed in public, adapted, broadcast,
transmitted, recorded or reproduced in any form or by any means,
without the prior permission of the copyright owner

First published 1997
The Boydell Press, Woodbridge

ISBN 0 85115 704 1

The Boydell Press is an imprint of Boydell and Brewer Ltd
PO Box 9, Woodbridge, Suffolk IP12 3DF, UK
and of Boydell and Brewer Inc.
PO Box 41026, Rochester, NY 14604–4126, USA

A catalogue record for this book is available
from the British Library

Library of Congress Cataloging-in-Publication Data
Woodward, Jennifer, 1966–
 The theatre of death : the ritual management of royal funerals in
Renaissance England, 1570–1625 / Jennifer Woodward.
   p.   cm.
 Originally published, 1997.
 Includes bibliographical references and index.
 ISBN 0–85115–704–1 (hardback :alk. paper)
  1. Funeral rites and ceremonies – England – History – 16th century.
 2. Funeral rites and ceremonies – England – History – 17th century.
 3. England – Kings and rulers – Death and burial. 4. Nobility –
England – Heraldry. 5. Renaissance – England. 6. Reformation –
England. 7. England – Social life and customs. I. Title.
GT3244.W66 1998
393'.08621 – dc21   97–15603

This publication is printed on acid-free paper

Printed in Great Britain by
St Edmundsbury Press Ltd, Bury St Edmunds, Suffolk

CONTENTS

List of Illustrations	ix
Acknowledgements	xi
Abbreviations	xii
The English Succession 1485–1625	xiii
The French Succession 1515–1610	xiv

The Theatre of Death: An Introduction   1
Power and ceremony: preliminaries 2; Histories of death and death rituals 3; Context and performance: an approach to the study of royal funerals in Renaissance England 5; Power and ceremony: the relationship refined 9

1 **The Heraldic Funeral in Renaissance England**   15
The form and functions of the heraldic funeral procession 15; Participant and observer motivation 23; The Form and Functions of the Heraldic Funeral Church Service 28: The church setting 28; The offering ceremony and ritual succession 30; The funeral feast 35

2 **Funeral Ritual and the Reformation**   37
Church interiors and ritual accessibility 37; Funeral ritual and iconomachy 39; The abolition of purgatory and prayers for the dead 40; The burial liturgy 42; Priests, incense, candles and torches: the fabric of intercession 44; The funeral offering ritual and intercessionary practices 46; Funerals, chivalry and 'secularization' 50; Royal appropriation and the resilience of funeral ritual 52

3 **The Renaissance Royal Funeral and Succession Rituals: England and France**   61
Succession and the royal offering ritual in England 61; Succession rituals in the French royal funeral: 1422–1574 62; The royal funeral effigy in England and France: ritual cross-fertilization 65

4 **The 1587 Funerals of Mary Queen of Scots**   67
The political implications of Mary's execution: domestic and foreign 68; The ceremonial response to Mary's death: France, Spain and Scotland 71; The Peterborough Funeral: 1 August 1587 74: The funeral procession 79; The church service 81; Alternative versions of the Peterborough funeral 83

5   **The Royal Funeral of Elizabeth I (1603)**   87
    Elizabeth's Funeral and the Jacobean Succession 87: The effigy and
    the funeral procession 87; Succession theories and the display of
    the royal person 93; James and Elizabeth's royal funeral: the
    exploitation of tradition 97; The vulnerability of the royal funeral:
    threats to the ritual demonstration of order 100. The Royal
    Funeral Effigy and the Reformation 103: Funeral effigies, tomb
    effigies and Elizabethan iconophobia 103; Iconoclasm and the
    official protection of tombs 104; Tomb and funeral effigy design:
    functionalism vs. naturalism 106; Royal appropriation of religious
    symbols and symbolism 111; English awareness of the French
    lying-in-state ritual 113; Idolatry and Elizabeth's lying-in-state
    ritual 115

6   **Religion and Culture under the Early Stuarts**   118
    Cultural developments under James and Charles 118; Religion and
    art 121; Jacobean religious policy and the rise of Arminianism 123;
    Charles, Arminianism and the development of a ceremonial
    Religion Royale 127

7   **Playing with Death: The Exploitation and Subversion of**   129
    Funeral Ritual (1603–1625)
    Elizabeth's funeral effigy 129; Elizabeth's tomb effigy 131; Mary
    Stuart's tomb effigy 134; A second funeral for Mary Queen of Scots
    138; Night-burials and the re-legitimization of torchlight 140; The
    non-homogeneity of Jacobean funeral ritual 144

8   **The Funeral of Prince Henry Stuart (1612)**   148
    The magnificence of the prince's funeral 149; Motives behind the
    magnificence of the funeral: the management of public grief and
    political loss 152; Posthumous glory: James, Henry and a conflict
    resolved 157; The funeral effigy as monument 162

9   **The Funeral of Anne of Denmark (1619)**   166
    The vulnerability of ritual: Anne's lying-in-state and funeral
    procession 166; The funeral effigy and the burial of the viscera: a
    shift towards Catholic ritual forms? 170

10 **The Funeral of King James I (1625)**   175
    The Church Service 175: The image of the king: sermon, effigy and
    hearse 175; The offering ritual: the adaptation of royal funeral
    ritual to divine right kingship 180; An alternative solution:
    funerals, *Lits de Justice* and absolutism in France (1563–1610) 184.
    The Lying-in-State Ritual 186: The funeral of Ludovick Stuart,

Duke of Richmond and Lennox (1624) 187; The lying-in-state of James I's funeral effigy 190. The funeral processions of James I 196; 'Royal' funerals post-1625 198; Posthumous images of King James 202

Epilogue 204

Appendix I: The Funeral Procession of Elizabeth I (1603) 210
Appendix II: The Funeral Rites of Charles IX of France (1574) 214
Bibliography
   Manuscript Sources 221
   Primary Sources: Printed 221
   Secondary Sources 228
Index 243

ILLUSTRATIONS

Illustrations appear between pages 114 and 115

1. Sir Philip Sidney's spurs and gauntlets borne at his funeral by officers at arms (1587).
2. Chief mourner with two escorts (1578).
3. Structure of the hearse for the funeral of William Paulet, Marquis of Winchester (1572).
4. 'The figure of the hearse' for the funeral of a Countess (c. 1576).
5. Hearse design for the funeral of William Paulet, Marquis of Winchester (1572).
6. Elizabeth I's arms painted over the medieval Last Judgement in St Margaret's Church, Tivetshall, Norfolk.
7. Chasuble for Requiem Mass, velvet embroidered in silks and metal thread.
8. The 'chapelle ardente' enclosing the effigy of Anne of Brittany at the Notre-Dame (1514).
9. The embalmed body borne in the funeral procession of Jeanne de Bourbon (1378).
10. Funeral procession of Charles VI (1422).
11. The funeral hearse and the high altar at the obsequies of Abbot Islip, Westminster Abbey, from the 'Obituary Roll of John Islip' (1532).
12. Head of effigy of Anne of Bohemia (d. 1394), Undercroft Museum, Westminster Abbey.
13. The reconstituted effigy head of Henry VII, Undercroft Museum, Westminster Abbey.
14. The funeral effigies of Mary I (d. 1558) and Anne of Denmark (d. 1619).
15. The chariot and funeral effigy of Queen Elizabeth I (1603).
16. Effigy of Mary Queen of Scots (1587).
17. Sir Robert Cecil in the funeral procession of Elizabeth I (1603).
18. Monument to Raphe and Elizabeth Wyseman, alabaster and imported 'marbles', after 1594. St Mary and All Saints, Rivenhall, Essex.

Illustrations

19. Detail of the monument for the Catholic Sir Thomas Hawkins, Boughton-under-Blean, Kent.
20. The tomb of Mary Queen of Scots, Westminster Abbey.
21. Hearse of James I with funeral effigy (1625).
22. Hearse and funeral effigy of Prince Henry Stuart (1612).
23. Effigy of Henry IV on the bed of state (1610).

ACKNOWLEDGEMENTS

This book has grown out of my doctoral thesis and is the product of research undertaken in the Centre for the Study of the Renaissance at the University of Warwick. I am extremely grateful to the Chairman of the Centre, Professor Ronnie Mulryne, for all his help, guidance and encouragement. I am also indebted to the British Academy for the grant which has facilitated my study. My research at the Bibliothèque Nationale was made possible by grants from the ERASMUS programme and the Centre for the Study of the Renaissance and I would like to thank them for their contributions.

Publication has been made possible by a grant from The Scouloudi Foundation in association with the Institute of Historical Research at the University of London and I would like to express my gratitude for their support.

Various other academic staff at Warwick University have assisted me during the course of my study. In particular I would like to thank Jack Scarisbrick for his critical reading of my chapter on the Reformation. In addition I am indebted to Bernard Capp, Peter Davidson, Malcolm Lowry, Richard Morris and Margaret Shewring. Charmaine Witherall, the secretary of the research centre, has also been invaluable in helping with administrative issues.

I am also grateful to Graham Parry, Glynne Wickham, Christopher Hill and Jennifer Loach for responding helpfully to queries and to Graham Parry and Peter Davidson for encouraging me to seek publication.

My research has taken me to the British Library, the Public Records Office, the Bodleian Library, the libraries at Westminster Abbey and the College of Arms, and the Bibliothèque Nationale. I am very grateful to the staff of all these institutions for their advice and aid. I would also like to thank Mme Marie-Therèse Jones-Davies of the Sorbonne for helping me to gain admission to the various libraries of Paris.

The following institutions have kindly granted permission for illustrations to be reproduced in the text: the Bibliothèque Nationale de France, Paris; the Bodleian, Oxford; the British Library, London; the National Monuments Record; the Victoria and Albert Museum, London; and Westminster Abbey Library, London.

Finally, I would like to thank those friends and colleagues who have given me the opportunity to discuss my ideas. Among them Glen Mynott deserves a special mention for his invaluable criticism and many helpful suggestions. I would also like to thank Peter Moore, Christine Orton, Tom Wilde and Noel Woodward for proof-reading sections of the original thesis. Finally I would like to thank Peter Moore and my parents, Kate and Noel Woodward, for continued support during the long and often frustrating process of writing a book.

ABBREVIATIONS

Primary Sources
CSPD	Calendar of State Papers, Domestic Series
CSPF	Calendar of State Papers, Foreign Series
CSPSc	Calendar of State Papers, Scotland
CSPS	Calendar of State Papers, Spain
CSPV	Calendar of State Papers, Venice

Secondary Sources
DNB	*Dictionary of National Biography*

Libraries
Bod.	Bodleian Library, Oxford
BL	British Library, London
CA	College of Arms, London
PRO	Public Records Office, London
WA	Westminster Abbey Library, London
BN	Bibliothèque Nationale, Paris

Others
OED	*Oxford English Dictionary*

THE ENGLISH SUCCESSION 1485–1625

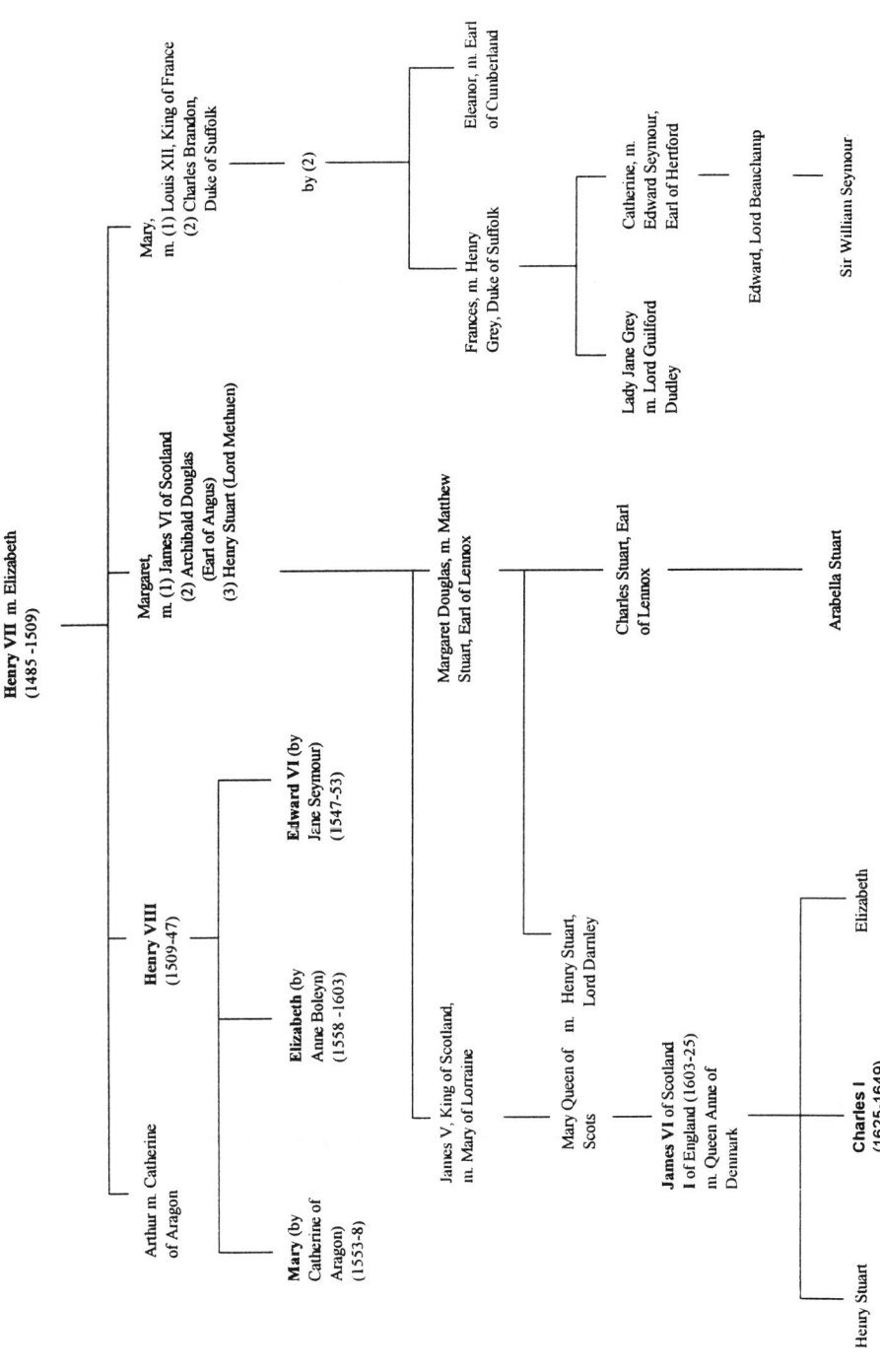

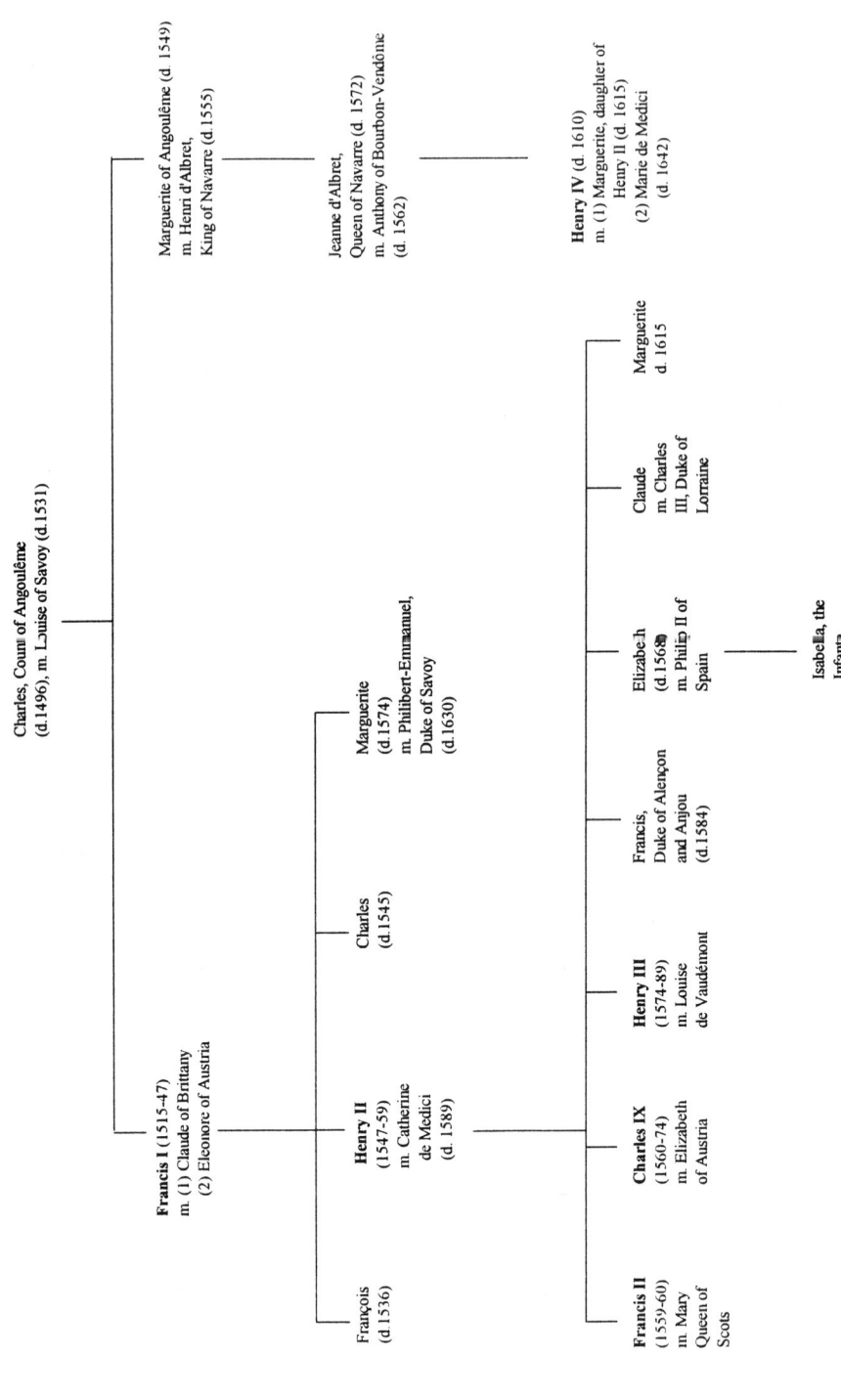

The Theatre of Death: An Introduction

The English Renaissance stage saw many representations of royal funeral ceremonies: the obsequies of Henry V, marred by the factional behaviour of the nobility, and the 'maimed rites' of Ophelia being two instances still well-known today. The theatre of death created by Shakespeare and his contemporaries was a stage-mirroring of the state funerals staged for members of the Tudor and early Stuart royal families. The ritual devices of this royal theatre of death reached their apotheosis with the funeral of James I in 1625, as the following contemporary accounts illustrate.

> After arranging the house where the remains of the late king [. . . were] laid, they put life-like figures there, and they observe[d] the customary vigil, thirty to forty noblemen and cavaliers being always present day and night.[1]

> A representation of his Matie [King James I] was layd upon the said Pall over ye body in his robes of Estate and Royall Diademe and so it contynewed until the funerall. All Kinge James his Servants removynge from Whyte-hall to Denmarke House and King Charles his Servants from St. James to Whyte-hall. The Service contynewed in all poyntes as if his Maite had byn lyvinge.[2]

> All the officers are to attend and the state of the house to be kept as in the kinges life tyme.[3]

A life-sized and life-like effigy of the dead monarch, dressed and served by the King's entourage as if he were still alive: such was the drama enacted by the Renaissance royal funeral. Medieval, Tudor and Stuart royal effigies can still be seen in the Undercroft Museum at Westminster Abbey. That of James I, however, is in a highly fragile state and is not on display to the public.[4]

---

[1] CSPV, XIX (1625–6), 19–20.
[2] College of Arms, Nayler (Press 20F/ Royal Funerals): 1618–1738, p. 28. See also Bodleian Library, Ashmole MS 818 fol. 51, 'when the body is reported here at Whitehall [?], all the officers are to attend and the state of the house to be kept as in the kinges life tyme'.
[3] Bod., Ashmole MS 818 fol. 51.
[4] Considerable damage was done to some of the effigies, notably Elizabeth of York and Henry VII, during the Second World War as a result of flooding at the Abbey see Anthony Harvey and Richard Mortimer, eds, *The Funeral Effigies of Westminster Abbey* (Woodbridge: The Boydell Press, 1994).

Power and Ceremony: Preliminaries

The need to mark royal death with elaborate ritual or ceremony, terms used interchangeably throughout this book, has persisted well into the twentieth century. The death of any individual represents a breach of the normal order of the society in which he or she had operated. The death of a ruler tears at the very fabric of the nation. Funeral ritual has always been a necessary part of the process of reintegrating the disturbed social group, whether a parish or a kingdom.[5] When the political future of a Renaissance dynasty was at stake, the funeral rite played a crucial role in smoothing the transfer of power from the defunct monarch to his heir. The royal theatre of death enacted the succession process and thus it functioned as a manifestation of political power.

Regarding Renaissance royal funeral ritual as a political tool in this way does not constitute an anachronistic imposition of a late twentieth-century intellectual construct onto early modern ceremonial forms. Shakespeare's *Henry V* (1599) makes it clear that contemporaries were not unaware of the relationship between power and ceremony.

> And what art thou, thou idol ceremony?
> What kind of god art thou, that suffer'st more
> Of mortal griefs than do thy worshippers?
> What are thy rents? What are thy comings in?
> O ceremony, show me but thy worth!
> What? Is thy soul of adoration?
> Art thou ought else but place, degree and form,
> Creating awe and fear in other men
> Wherein thou art less happy being feared
> Than they in fearing?[6]   (*Henry V*, IV, i, 213–220)

A similar consciousness is evident in Henry Wotton's comments on the Venetian Corpus Christi procession of May 1606:

> The reasons for this extraordinary solemnity were two, as I conceive it. First to contain the people in good order with superstition, the foolish band of

---

5   The terms 'breach' and 'reintegration' are derived from Victor Turner's model of the ritual process first expounded in his *Drama, Fields and Metaphors* (London: Cornell University Press, 1974), pp. 38–42. The model comprises four main phases of public action: (i) *breach* of the regular norm-governed social relations; (ii) *crisis*, during which there is a tendency for the breach to widen; (iii) *redressive action*, the performance of public ritual, and (iv) *reintegration* of the disturbed social group. The whole ritual process is characterised by what Turner calls liminality, the *limen* being the threshold between more or less stable phases of social process. See Victor Turner, *The Anthropology of Performance* (New York: P. A. J. Publications, 1987). Turner's model is an elaboration of the Van Gennepian tripartite model of separation, marginal period and reincorporation. Similarly, Turner's *limen* equates with Van Gennep's *marges de transition*. See Arnold Van Gennep, *The Rites of Passage*, trans. by Monika B. Vizedom and Gabrielle L. Caffee (London: Routledge, 1960), pp. 15–26.
6   Andrew Gurr, ed., *King Henry V* (Cambridge: Cambridge University Press, 1992).

An Introduction

obedience. Secondly, to let the Pope know (who wanteth not intelligencers) that notwithstanding his interdict, they had friars enough and clergymen to furnish the day.[7]

Both Shakespeare and Wotton thus display the same clear-sighted recognition of the significance of ceremony as an instrument of power that has been central to ritual criticism in recent years, particularly since the publication of Clifford Geertz's highly influential *Negara: the Theater State in Nineteenth Century Bali* (1980).[8] Geertz identified ritual and pageantry as the core of the Balinese power structure and the Geertzian legacy is clear in the work of Jonathan Goldberg who, with others, has established that, in the late sixteenth and early seventeenth centuries, 'power [was] manifested in spectacle'.[9] The recognition of the centrality of ceremony in the power structure of the period has led to a recent fascination with the interaction of Renaissance court ritual and court politics, demonstrated, for example, by such works as Peter Burke's *The Fabrication of Louis XIV* (1992) and Roy Strong's *Henry, Prince of Wales: England's Lost Renaissance* (1986). The current climate of interest makes the study of Renaissance royal funeral ritual undertaken here particularly timely.[10]

Histories of Death and Death Rituals

The Theatre of Death has also been influenced by and builds upon work published in the field of social history over the last two decades.

It was Philippe Ariès's ambitious studies of western attitudes towards death, in particular *L'Homme devant la mort* (1977), that sparked off much of the recent interest in the history of death. His wide-ranging text answered the call made in France in the late 1940s by the influential *Annales* School for historians to recreate 'la vie affective' of the past.[11] In striving to satisfy this aim, Ariès

---

7   L. P. Smith, ed., *The Life and Letters of Sir Henry Wotton*, 2 vols (Oxford: Clarendon Press, 1907), I, 350, cited by James Knowles, 'The Spectacle of the Realm: civic consciousness, rhetoric and ritual in early modern London', in *Theatre and Government Under the Early Stuarts*, ed. by J. R. Mulryne and Margaret Shewring (Cambridge: Cambridge University Press, 1993), p. 157.
8   Clifford Geertz, *Negara: the Theater State in Nineteenth Century Bali* (Princeton, NJ: Princeton University Press, 1980).
9   Jonathan Goldberg, *James I and the Politics of English Literature* (Baltimore: John Hopkins University Press, 1983), p. 149. There are many recent studies concerned with the relationship between power and ceremony; see, for example, David Cannadine and Simon Price, eds, *Rituals of Royalty: Power and Ceremonial in Traditional Societies* (Cambridge: Cambridge University Press, 1987).
10 Peter Burke, *The Fabrication of Louis XIV* (London: Yale University Press, 1992), pp. 5–6; Roy Strong, *The Cult of Elizabeth* (London: Thames & Hudson, 1977; repr. 1987); Roy Strong, *Henry, Prince of Wales: England's Lost Renaissance* (London: Thames & Hudson, 1986).
11 John McManners, 'Death and the French Historians', in *Mirrors of Mortality: Studies in*

identifies the degree of awareness of the individual in human society as a key contributor to changes in historical attitudes towards death.[12]

Ariès's discursive and highly provocative work contrasts markedly with the approaches of main-stream French historians such as Michelle Vovelle, Pierre Chaunu and François Lebrun whose research is solidly rooted in the statistical analysis of death and burial records, population figures and wills.[13]

Lawrence Stone rekindled scholarly interest in the social history of death in England with his essay on elite funerals in *The Crisis of the Aristocracy* (1965). Stone's focus is on expenditure on funerals and he identifies a decline in the incidence of elaborate funeral ritual from about the 1580s, attributing it to 'a profound change in the accepted forms of symbolic justification'. According to Stone, the cost of elaborate funerals came to be considered out of proportion to the prestige earned.[14]

Clare Gittings's *Death, Burial and the Individual in Early Modern England* (1984) was the first comprehensive English social history of death to deal with the Renaissance period.[15] Her book shows the influence of Ariès and also of Stone in looking at the decline in the incidence of elaborate funeral ritual in early modern England. She explains this decline in terms of the development of the nuclear family and the parallel growth of affective individualism in an argument which draws heavily on another work by Lawrence Stone, *The Family, Sex and Marriage*.[16] In the late Middle Ages the funeral ritual is seen as a manifestation of increased individualism. Later, however, the same ritual became, according to Gittings, a suppressant of individualism. Thus elaborate funerals declined in the seventeenth century and became virtually extinct in the eighteenth.

While Gittings's book is a source of much invaluable factual material, her theoretical approach appears inherently flawed. As she herself admits, her use of the term 'individualism' is anachronistic. It superimposes a twentieth-century intellectual construct onto Renaissance funeral rituals. Further, 'individualism'

---

    the Social History of Death, ed. by Joachim Whaley (London: Europa Publications, 1981), pp. 106–130.

12 Philippe Ariès, *The Hour of Our Death*, trans. by Helen Weaver (London: Allen Lane, 1981) first published as *L'Homme Devant la Mort* (Paris: Editions du Seuil, 1977).

13 Michel Vovelle, *Mourir Autrefois: Attitudes Collectives devant la mort aux XVIIe et XVIIIe siècles* ([Paris (?)]: Editions Gallimore/ Julliard, 1974); François Lebrun, *Les Hommes et la mort en Anjou aux XVIIe et XVIIIe siècles* (Paris: Mouton, 1971); Pierre Chaunu, 'Mourir à Paris, XVe, XVIIe, XVIIIe siècles', *Annales E. S. C.*, 31 (1976), 29–50.

14 Lawrence Stone, *The Crisis of the Aristocracy 1558–1641* (Oxford: Clarendon Press, 1965), pp. 572–81 (p. 578). Mervyn James's essay on Tudor funerals in his *Society, Politics and Culture: Studies in Early Modern England* (Cambridge: Cambridge University Press, 1986) is discussed in chapter 2, pp. 81–7.

15 Clare Gittings, *Death, Burial and the Individual in Early Modern England* (London: Routledge, 1984).

16 Lawrence Stone, *The Family, Sex and Marriage in England 1500–1800*, 2nd edn (Harmondsworth: Penguin Books, 1979).

An Introduction

is a development in western philosophy which is difficult to locate in any particular period. Alan Macfarlane has provoked considerable debate of this issue by arguing that the origins of individualism can be pushed back as far as the early Middle Ages.[17] 'Individualism' does not seem, therefore, to be a useful concept in terms of the study of funeral ritual.

The approach taken in this book builds more directly on a different study, one that concentrates on the royal funeral ritual of another European country: Ralph Giesey's *The Royal Funeral Ceremony in Renaissance France* (1960).[18] Giesey was the first historian to deal specifically with elite funeral rituals. He identifies the funeral of Francis I (d. 1547) as the apotheosis of French royal death ritual and concentrates on tracing its development up to that point. Francis I's funeral is seen as a ritual manifestation of the sixteenth-century politico-legal theory of the king's two bodies, which has been so eloquently expounded by Giesey's mentor, Ernst Kantorowicz. The only other study of French royal funerals rejects the *néo-cérémonialism* that regards ritual as a legitimate field for political analysis.[19]

Until now there has been no detailed study of English royal funerals in the Renaissance. Paul Fritz has discussed English royal obsequies in terms of the distinction between 'public' and 'private' funerals, demonstrating the shift from the elaborate, ostentatious pre-Restoration funerals to more restrained post-Restoration practices, but concentrates on the latter.[20] There has remained a need for a comprehensive analysis of royal funeral ritual in the English Renaissance.

Context and Performance: An Approach to the Study of Royal Funerals in Renaissance England

My interest in royal funeral ritual was engendered by Giesey's book. His analysis of the French obsequies of the fifteenth and sixteenth centuries always endeavours to take account of the interaction between ritual forms and historical context. My own research began with an examination of a later French royal funeral, that of Charles IX (1574). My approach was to accept that ritual occasions, like the staging of a play, are dependent on the conditions of their performance, political, social and cultural.[21] Funeral ritual is seen not as a static

---

[17] Alan Macfarlane, *The Origins of English Individualism: The Family, Property and Social Transition* (Oxford: Basil Blackwell, 1978).
[18] Ralph Giesey, *The Royal Funeral Ceremony in Renaissance France* (Geneva: Droz, 1960).
[19] See Alain Boureau, *Le simple corps du roi: L'impossible sacralité des souverains français XVe – XVIIIe siècles* (Paris: Les Editions de Paris, 1988).
[20] Paul S. Fritz, 'From "Public" to "Private": the Royal Funerals in England, 1500–1830', in *Mirrors of Mortality: Studies in the Social History of Death*, ed. by Joachim Whaley (London: Europa Publications, 1981), pp. 61–79. His emphasis on decline may owe something to Lawrence Stone.
[21] Turner (1987), p. 85. In this respect my method is in disagreement with the belief that

vehicle for ideological propaganda but as a performance process through which its organisers endeavour to enact and thereby effect the reintegration of the community and the smooth transfer of power. Thus, my focus in the study of Charles IX's funeral was on the impact of the political turmoil surrounding the Wars of Religion on French royal funeral ritual.[22]

The performative nature of Renaissance royal funeral ritual provides the theoretical frame for this book. The method of analysis is substantive, a thorough investigation of all the available source material. The connections made and the conclusions drawn grow out of an assessment of the historical evidence.

During the Renaissance, funeral ritual in both England and France was an extended process. A striking visual representation of the English elite funeral in Renaissance England, incorporating a number of its distinct performance arenas, survives in the form of the *Henry Unton Memorial* portrait (1596).[23] The painting simultaneously celebrates the life and commemorates the death of Sir Henry Unton who represented England on two embassies to France, the second of which (1595–6) culminated in his death. The black-draped ship that carried his corpse across the English Channel is depicted in the top right-hand portion of the painting. The funeral cortege with its horse-drawn chariot bearing the coffin covered with a black pall and mourners on horseback are shown leaving the coast. To the left of the painting is the church where Unton's funeral took place. The funeral procession moves across the foreground of the painting, from right to left, before a crowd of onlookers, some, the poor, cripples and the blind, beneficiaries of Unton's charity. Mourners are crowded inside the church for the burial service, which took place four months after Unton's death. In the lower left section of the portrait is the Unton monument, perhaps a representation of that finally erected at Faringdon in 1606, complete with a stone effigy reclining on a tomb. The coffin and viscera chest are visible in the grave below.[24] The Unton portrait thus presents an overall scheme for the elite, or heraldic, funeral: embalming; funeral journey; procession; church services;

---

ritual is acted outside time; see Mary Gluckman and Max Gluckman, 'On Drama, Games and Athletic Contests', in Sally F. Moore and Barbara G. Myherhoff, eds, *Secular Ritual* (Amsterdam: Van Gorcum, 1977), p. 236. On the important distinction between the 'dramatic text' and the 'performance text' in recent literary criticism, see Kier Elam, *The Semiotics of Theatre and Drama* (London: Methuen, 1980), pp. 2–3, 208. The view that stage drama, and literature in general, is dependent upon its historical context, is the mark of cultural materialism or New Historicism, see, for example, Jonathan Dollimore, *Radical Tragedy: Religion, Ideology and Power in the Drama of Shakespeare and his Contemporaries* (London: Harvester Wheatsheaf, 1984).

22 Jennifer K. A. Woodward, 'The Theatre of Death: Politics, Ritual and Ideology in the Royal Funeral of Charles IX' (unpublished master's thesis, University of Warwick, 1992).

23 The *Henry Unton Memorial* portrait is at the National Portrait Gallery, London.

24 The accuracy in the rendition of the funeral complete with its numerous and complex coats of arms suggest that the picture may well have been the work of a herald. See Roy Strong, 'Sir Henry Unton and His Portrait: An Elizabethan Memorial Picture and Its History', *Archaeologia*, xcix (1965), pp. 53–76; and Strong (1977), pp. 84–110. For a

An Introduction

and the construction of a permanent memorial. To these it is only necessary to add the lying-in-state that often preceded the funeral procession and the feast that followed the church services to complete the performance process. The royal funeral followed the same basic form as this, the heraldic funeral of a member of the ruling elite.

The royal funeral rituals discussed in *The Theatre of Death* are those staged for Mary Queen of Scots (1587), Elizabeth I (1603), Henry, Prince of Wales (1612), Queen Anne of Denmark (1619) and James I (1625). In each case the whole discourse of funeral ritual is considered including, where appropriate, tombs, engravings and funeral effigies as well as funeral processions and church services. The performance conditions pertaining to each funeral are examined in an attempt to place them within a wider political and cultural context and to reconstruct the contemporary significance of the rituals enacted.

Detailed discussion of specific royal obsequies is, however, postponed until later chapters. Introductory chapters furnish the reader with a good understanding of the basic forms, symbolism and functions of the elite funeral, rendering the analysis of the royal funerals that follows more accessible.

There are practical difficulties with basing an introductory chapter on the evidence of royal funerals. Source material relating to royal funeral church services is limited with no extant account of the services at the funeral of Elizabeth and Edward VI, and restricted material relating to those of Mary Tudor, Henry VII and Henry VIII. For a more detailed account we need to go right back to Edward IV. Further, while we possess a detailed account of the church services held at the funeral of James I, there are crucial features of this occasion which can only be understood in relation to non-royal heraldic funeral practice. It is necessary, therefore, to establish the non-royal form first.

Chapter 1 thus offers a descriptive account of the two main performance arenas of the heraldic funeral, the funeral procession and the church services. In the interests of clarity and coherence the non-royal heraldic funeral discussed is presented in its entirety. The funeral selected is that of Edward, Earl of Derby, both because detailed records survive and because it occurred in 1572, before the royal funerals that will be discussed but after the Reformation. The Derby funeral serves as the basis for an analysis of the form and functions of elite funeral processions and church services. The discussion is supplemented by wide-ranging reference to other funerals of the period. Embalming, funeral journeys and monument construction are relatively unproblematic areas and will be discussed in relation to specific examples in the chapters that follow. In contrast, the royal lying-in-state ritual is complex but since it is central to much of the discussion of royal funeral rituals, in particular those of Elizabeth and James, it is not dealt with until those chapters.

The differences that exist between royal and non-royal heraldic funerals are

---

contemporary description of the stages of the heraldic funeral, see Sir William Segar, *Honour Military and Civill* (London, [n. pub.], 1602), p. 242.

largely differences of degree rather than kind. Crucial differences in procession composition are highlighted in the course of discussion and a transcript of Elizabeth's funeral procession is provided in Appendix I. The most significant way that the royal funeral differed from its heraldic counterpart was in the use of life-like effigies of the defunct. The distinctive royal effigy rituals will constitute a major part of the discussion of individual funerals undertaken in later chapters.

Chapter 2 looks at the other important model for the analysis of English royal funeral practice: French royal funerals. The survey is necessarily brief but provides useful material for comparison with English practice and establishes the ground for subsequent discussions of possible cross-fertilization. During the Renaissance period the major European powers, France, Spain and England, indulged in the reciprocal celebration of royal funerals.[25] In 1558, for example, Queen Mary's hearse was re-used for the obsequies of Charles V while, in 1574, obsequies were celebrated at St Paul's for the French King, Charles IX. The implications of this practice are considered in the chapters on the individual funerals, and are particularly significant in the chapter that deals with the funeral of Mary Stuart.[26] English royal funeral ritual is thus seen within its wider European context.

The temporal scope of this book, 1570–1625, has been set with various considerations in mind: the incidence of royal funerals; the potential for comparative analysis with French royal funeral rituals; and the availability of source material. The period has particular significance for a study of funeral ritual because of the great religious upheaval and change undergone, change which impacted on ritual forms just as it did on the visual and performative arts.

It is my belief that the iconophobic impulses of the Reformation had profound implications for Renaissance royal funeral rituals because of their heavy reliance on the operation of symbols. It is impossible to comprehend fully these ceremonies without placing them within the context of Reformation and post-Reformation attitudes to ritual and images. My belief reflects the now generally accepted view by historians that the Reformation was more than a mid-sixteenth-century phenomenon. No recent scholarship has claimed that England was Protestant pre-1558. It was with the accession of Elizabeth that Protestantism became firmly institutionalised and that a coherent programme

---

[25] J. G. Nichols, ed., *The Diary of Henry Machyn* (London: Camden Society, 1848), p. 184. For other examples, see CA, I Series MS III fol. 11: Louis XII of France; fol. 12: Ferdinand, King of Aragon; fol. 13: Maximilian; and CA, I Series MS XIII fol. 8: Henry II of France. See also British Library, Additional MS 45131 fols 6, 33.

[26] The funeral of Charles V (d. 1558) was celebrated in Brussels but obsequies were also held at Westminster Abbey. See CA, I Series MS XIV fols 3–6b; CSPD, I (1558–59), 35, 38, 40–1, 49, 66; William Camden, *The Historie of the most renowned and victorious Princesse Elizabeth, late Queene of England* (London: Benjamin Fisher, 1630), p. 16.

An Introduction

of Protestantism was worked out and adopted by Church and government.[27] The programme of changes, including those relating to religious ceremony, introduced by the reformed Church extended well into the 1570s and 1580s. In the light of this it is, perhaps, unsurprising that Jennifer Loach, in her recently published essay, 'The Function of Ceremonial in the Reign of Henry VIII', concludes that contemporary politico-religious issues had a negligible impact on the funeral ceremony of Henry VIII.[28] It is later that the Reformation makes its mark upon funeral ritual and it is in the later Tudor royal funerals that one might expect to see evidence of its influence. Thus, although the temporal parameters of this study, as far as the detailed discussion of specific royal funerals is concerned, are 1570–1625, chapter 3 deals with the impact of the Reformation on Renaissance funeral ritual.

Once the Anglican church had achieved an established coherence, its position on ceremony continued to have implications for the development of funeral ritual well into the seventeenth century.[29] Chapter 6 looks at cultural change under the early Stuarts, focusing on the relationship between art and religion, and the rise of Arminianism in a European context. These developments in religious and cultural sensibility are shown to interact with changes made to the royal theatre of death.

Power and Ceremony: the Relationship Refined

The key role played by symbols in the staging of royal funeral ritual, and its consequent potential vulnerability to reform, is central to the analysis carried out in this book. At the same time my focus on the politics of symbolism has something to add to the current academic debate concerning the relationship between power and ceremony. A brief discussion of my approach in the context of the main issues and theoretical positions of this debate is included here. The intention is to place the contribution made by this study within the field of contemporary ritual criticism and care is taken to minimize and clarify the academic jargon necessarily introduced to fulfill this purpose.

Throughout the book consideration is given to the observers of royal funerals, their audience. The performative approach to ritual acknowledges a complicity between the actors, directors and audience of ceremonial occasions,

---

[27] A survey conducted by bishops in 1564 to test the religious sympathies of Justices of the Peace found that, out of 850, barely half could be characterised as Protestant, while fifty were strong adherents of the old faith; see Wallace MacCaffrey, *Elizabeth I* (London: Edward Arnold, 1993), pp. 87, 445 n. 16.

[28] Jennifer Loach, 'The Function of Ceremonial in the Reign of Henry VIII', *Past and Present*, 142 (February, 1994), 43–68.

[29] Rosemary O'Day, *The Debate on the English Reformation* (London: Methuen, 1986), pp. 2, 153.

mirroring that required for the staging of a play.[30] The nature and source of this complicity are probed in the introductory chapters. The visual codes and choreography employed in the funeral processions and church service are seen as the means of manufacturing the required complicity.

Onlookers at funeral ritual occasions are sometimes simply viewed as pawns exploited by their rulers, unwittingly or unwillingly contributing to the performance of a smooth transition of political power from one monarch to the next. This simplistic attitude has been prevalent amongst literary critics who have turned their attention to ritual criticism in recent years. These critics have tended to focus solely on the political dimensions of ritual and there has been a tendency, particularly amongst cultural materialists, to see the relationship between power and pageantry simply in terms of processes of 'mystification', a term employed to describe the use of ritual by the ruling elite to exploit and manipulate the lower classes.[31]

In my view many materialist critics ignore the questions of 'how' ritual operates and of what induces or attracts people to take part. Why do people permit or submit themselves to the act of complicity required by participating in or observing the ritual performance?[32]

Some functional analysts have drawn on sociological models in an attempt to answer these questions, seeing ritual as paradigmatic of the sociologist Emile Durkheim's concept of 'collective effervescence'. This refers to the need felt by each society to uphold and reaffirm at regular intervals the collective sentiments and collective ideas which make up its personality and give rise to its unity. People consciously agree to ignore their differences for the time being in favour of a display of togetherness. Thus ritual is seen as a consensual manifestation of cultural and political identity.[33] Durkheim's model recognises psychological motives for involvement in ritual and that there is a two-way exchange involved in power relations, but over-simplifies and homogenizes ritual experience.

Both Burke, in *The Fabrication of Louis XIV*, and Geertz, in his essay, 'Centers, Kings and Charisma: Reflections on the Symbolics of Power', have investigated how ceremonial can confer charisma on a ruler.[34] Their work begins to take account of the fact that participants and spectators respond to ritual experience

---

[30] Gilbert Lewis, *Day of Shining Red: An Essay on Understanding Ritual* (Cambridge: Cambridge University Press, 1980), p. 8.
[31] Dollimore, pp. xx–xii.
[32] Cannadine (1987), p. 19.
[33] E. Durkheim, *Elementary Forms of the Religious Life*, trans. by J. W. Swain (London: George Allen & Unwin, 1915), p. 375; Steven Lukes, *Essays in Social Theory* (London: [n. pub.], 1987), pp. 292–3.
[34] Clifford Geertz, 'Centers, Kings and Charisma: Reflections on the Symbolics of Power', in *Culture and Its Creators: Essays in Honor of Edward Shils*, ed. by Joseph Ben-David and Terry Nichols Clark (London: University of Chicago Press, 1977), pp. 150–71 (p. 151); Burke (1992), pp. 11–13.

An Introduction

in a variety of ways, and that these responses are not confined to the political and ideological arenas.

My own analysis similarly recognises that the power of ritual lies in its multivocality and identifies the use of symbols as the means of achieving it. Symbols, whether visual or choreographic, operate through multivalency, multivocality and ambiguity, qualities that enable them to draw together the multifarious experiences of individuals, emotional and intellectual, shaping them into the homogeneity that is required on ritual occasions.[35] Symbols function by engaging the imagination of the observer and transforming his experience in what may be a very physical way. Max Gluckman's term 'sublimation' may be useful here. It refers to the physical energy that is 'evoked by a set of symbolical physiological referents and transposed to strengthen social and moral values which are simultaneously exhibited in [...] symbols'.[36] A modern example might be the involuntary but unifying emotion evoked by hearing the opening bars of *Land of Hope and Glory* at the last night of the Promenade concerts at the Royal Albert Hall. Symbols thus permit an order to be imposed onto human experience, a function that is of particular value in the face of the inner disturbance engendered by the individual's encounter with transience and death.

Because symbols do not mean the same things to different people and no one meaning is either explicitly included or excluded, all meanings, conscious and unconscious, can be embraced. Many of these meanings, even those pertaining to one individual, will be conflictual. An open grave can symbolise both death and resurrection. Thus symbols often embody paradox. Elizabeth Tonkin suggests that it is paradox which makes symbols so compelling. I prefer to replace the term 'paradox' with 'ambiguity' since it has a broader application to symbolic meaning, including the non-conflictual as well as the conflictual. Through ambiguity ritual transcends the specific meanings and motives, and generates the impression of consensus. The manifestation of ambiguity in the ritual context is a creative act which both expresses and is power.[37] As Geertz puts it, 'the trappings of rule and its substance are like mass and energy continually being transformed into each other'. Imagined power creates power: 'The real is as imagined as the imaginary.'[38]

The evocative presentational style of ritual with its symbols and sensory

---

[35] Stanley Tambiah has argued that through symbols, ritual creates 'heightened, intensified and fused communication' and labels the result 'higher-order experiences'. See S. J. Tambiah, *Culture, Thought and Social Action* (Cambridge, MA: Harvard University Press, 1985), p. 243.

[36] Moore and Myerhoff, p. 234.

[37] Elizabeth Tonkin, 'Masks and Powers', *Man*, n. s. 14 (1979), 237–48. Goldberg agrees that it is 'precisely in ambiguity that power resides', pp. 11–12. See also D. Kertzer, *Ritual, Politics and Power* (London: Yale University Press, 1988), p. 10.

[38] Clifford Geertz, *Local Knowledge: Further Essays in Interpretative Anthropology* (New York: Basic Books, 1983), p. 124. See also Geertz (1980), p. 104.

stimuli, multivalence and patterning underlines the fact that the generation of political power through ritual is an inherently theatrical act. The centrality of symbolism reaffirms the aptness of both the performative approach taken in this book and of the importance accorded to issues of iconography.[39] Thus analysis of the heraldic funeral undertaken in the opening chapter also draws heavily on semiotics, the theory of sign symbols developed in the field of drama and theatre criticism.[40]

Ritual symbolism fuses the emotional and political implications of the Renaissance royal funeral. As Stanley Tambiah observes, symbols operate on both the ideological or cosmological level, where they satisfy human cravings for 'truth' and order, and in the real political world where they directly affect the participants, 'creating, affirming or legitimating their social positions and power'.[41]

Ultimately, however, the affective is subsumed by the political, since, for the organisers of ritual, it is the impression of consensus that is important and not the feelings or beliefs of the individuals taking part. The very fact that attendance at a ritual can have many motivations other than political support is of value to its organisers. While political support is not a necessary corollary of attendance, the very presence of an observer, nonetheless, functions as a demonstration of political consensus in the eyes of others.[42] Royal funerals, as I shall demonstrate, can thus be used as a vehicle for political propaganda.

Here I am in agreement with Stephen Lukes who calls this propagandistic functionality of ritual on behalf of a particular value system or systems the 'mobilisation of bias'.[43] The 'bias' may not just be on the side of the funeral organisers, however. The breach of social order caused by royal death gives rise to a potential for subversion. Thus ritual can be a medium for factional activity.[44] Occasionally, such as, for example, at the funeral of Queen Anne of Denmark, funeral ritual is subject to disruption. The impression of consensus

---

[39] Goldberg, p. xiii. Michael Neill calls funerals 'political theater' in his ' "Exeunt with a Dead March": Funeral Pageantry on the Shakespearean Stage', in *Pageantry in the Shakespearean Theatre*, ed. by David M. Bergeron (Atlanta: University of Georgia Press, 1985), pp. 154–61 (p. 161).

[40] On semiotics, see Elam (1980).

[41] Tambiah uses the term 'indexical symbols', p. 156. He acknowledges a debt to A. W. Burks's 'Icon, Index and Symbol', *Philosophy and Phenomenological Research*, 9 (4) (1949), 673–89. See also Max Gluckman on 'sublimation' in Moore and Myerhoff, p. 234.

[42] As Goldberg puts it, 'the spectacle of state combines deception and display, both the show of participation and genuine participation', p. 30.

[43] Lukes, pp. 62, 68–9. For an example of ritual analysis using the 'mobilisation of bias' model, see D. N. Cannadine, 'Conflict and Consensus on a Ceremonial Occasion: The Diamond Jubilee in Cambridge in 1897', *Historical Journal*, 24 (1981), 111–46.

[44] Linda Woodbridge and Edward Berry, eds, *True Rites and Maimed Rites: Ritual and Anti-Ritual in Shakespeare and His Age* (Urbana: University of Illinois Press, 1992), p. 22. See also David McMullen, 'Bureaucrats and Cosmology: the Ritual code of T'ang China', in Cannadine (1987), pp. 181–236 (p. 238).

An Introduction

can be lost by the deliberate disruptive behaviour of participants.[45] Yet the propensity to engage in such disruptive behaviour will be small because the complicity of participants and observers in ritual is rooted in deep human desires for order, stability and predictability: desires which create inertia against social disruption and change, even where participants are in a manifestly oppressive situation.[46] Further, taking part in a ritual, even for the lower social groups, always involves the conferment of status and identity, increasing its attraction for participants.[47] Ritual thus has a strong collective dimension and functions by linking the individual to society in a process which generates order.

My analysis of royal funerals thus leads to a refinement of the relationship between power and ceremony outlined at the beginning of this introduction. The organisers manipulate funeral ritual, moulding its form and symbolism to suit the political needs of the moment. They are, however, also constrained by ritual, compelled to stage performances that will meet the expectations of the funeral's participants and observers and forced to employ symbolism that is sufficient in quantity and affective quality to ensure the homogeneity of behavioural response required for the manifestation of order. Power is not confined to the ruling elite that organizes the royal funeral.

The above constraints appear to represent an impulse towards stasis. Perhaps they are to be equated with the natural propensity that ritual displays have towards tradition, a restraining influence that circumscribes the organisers' wish to adapt the ceremony to deliver their own political message. Yet audience and participant expectations cannot themselves be distinct from cultural context. Tradition, as Raymond Williams has observed, is not static but rather, ' [a] selective version of a shaping past and a pre-shaped present, which is then powerfully operative in the process of social and cultural definition and identification'.[48] The desire to comply with tradition can itself be a shaping force that leads to the modification of ritual forms and symbols. As Sally F. Moore has pointed out, sometimes the organisers of a ritual are not clear about the details of its precedents and put the performance together in accordance with their arbitrary views of what is appropriate. This process, which Moore terms 'regularisation', may be behind changes in ritual form effected at the funeral of Charles IX, as discussed in chapter 3. Moore contrasts 'regularisation' with the deliberate alteration, or 'situational adjustment' of ritual forms.[49] These complementary processes ensure the inherent flexibility of ritual in spite of its generally accepted tendency towards order and harmony.

---

45 Jack Goody, 'Against "Ritual": Loosely Structured Thoughts on a Loosely Defined Topic', in Moore and Myerhoff, pp. 25–35 (p. 33). See also Kertzer, p. 11.
46 Woodbridge, p. 16.
47 Lewis, p. 12.
48 Raymond Williams, *Marxism and Literature* (Oxford: Oxford University Press, 1977), p. 115.
49 Sally Falk Moore, *Law as Process: An Anthropological Approach* (London: Routledge and Kegan Paul, 1978), pp. 48–53. See also Woodbridge, p. 18.

The Theatre of Death makes a valuable contribution not only as the first detailed study of the royal funerals that took place in Renaissance England, but also as an important extension of the debate surrounding the relationship between power and ceremony. As this book illustrates, the persistence of funeral ritual forms in spite of the Reformation underlines the crucial role played by symbolism in the achievement of their political function.

CHAPTER ONE

The Heraldic Funeral in Renaissance England

The Form and Functions of the Heraldic Funeral Procession

In this chapter I seek to establish the basic forms and functions of the Elizabethan funeral, together with the motivations that lay behind participation in and observation of funeral occasions. Much of the analysis focuses on the funeral of Edward Stanley, Earl of Derby, Privy Councillor and Knight of the Garter (d. 1572), a funeral for which detailed records survive, although other funerals will be referred to in order to broaden the overall picture.[1] The Derby funeral took six weeks to organize and there were around nine hundred participants. The procession escorted the body of the late Earl from Latham House, where he had died, to the parish church at Ormskirk, Lancashire, a distance of two miles.[2]

At the head of the procession came two yeomen conductors dressed in black coats and bearing black staves, leading the way for a group of one hundred poor men wearing gowns of coarse cloth, marching two by two. Next strode the forty boys and men of the choir dressed in their surplices. There followed an esquire, mounted on horseback, bearing the standard. His horse was trapped 'to the ground' and decorated with a shaffron (the frontlet of a barbed horse) of the defunct's arms in garter and four escutcheons of buckram and metal, two on each side.[3] The horses of the other esquires and heralds, and those that drew the chariot bearing the coffin were similarly trapped and garnished.

The first part of the procession was all on foot but the core of the convoy rode on horseback, beginning with eighty of the Earl's gentlemen mounted 'on

---

[1] The account of Derby's funeral is given in Bod., Ashmole MS 836 fols 215–223; Arthur Collins, *The Peerage of England*, 8 vols (London: [n. pub.], 1779), III, 55–62 which, in turn, was taken from a manuscript in the library of John Anstis, Esq., Garter King of Arms. It is referred to in Stone (1965), pp. 573–4; and also Cunnington and Lucas, *Costume for Births, Marriages and Deaths* (London: Adam and Charles Black, 1972), p. 219 and Appendix 5.

[2] Latham was the Earl's seat, Christopher Haigh, *Reformation and Resistance in Tudor Lancashire* (London: Cambridge University Press, 1975), p. 133.

[3] 'Shaffrons' are described by J. Coats in his *Dict. Her.* (1739), p. 73, as, 'those little Shields, containing Death's Heads, and other Funeral Devices, plac'd upon the Foreheads of the Horses, that draw Hearses at Pompous Funerals vulgarly now call'd, by Corruption "Chaperoons", or "Shafferoons" ', see *OED* (earlier instances are cited).

comely geldings'. There followed the Earl's two secretaries, fifty knights and esquires, riding two abreast, the two chaplains of the defunct, the preacher, who was the Dean of Chester, and the three chief officers of the Earl's household, the Steward, Treasurer and Comptroller, bearing their white staves of office.[4]

The central section of the procession came next, led by an esquire on horseback, trapped as above, and carrying the late Earl's great banner. There followed four mounted heralds bearing the dead Earl's achievements, the gorgeous colouring of their tabards strikingly set off by the jet black of their full-length mourning gowns and hoods.[5] First came Lancaster carrying the Earl's parcel gilt steel helmet and, on an heraldic 'wreath or torce of his colours', his crest 'carved, painted, and wrought in gold and silver'.[6] Norroy followed with the Earl's shield of arms within a garter surmounted by a coronet. Then came Clarenceux with the Earl's sword, carried pommel upwards. Its hilt and chape were finely gilt, the scabbard was made of velvet.[7] (All weapons borne in the obsequies were reversed, as they would be in token of truce on the battlefield. He who offered the sword in the church, for example, would be 'holding the poynte thereof in both his handes, the pomell . . . upwards'.) Finally came Garter bearing another coat of arms 'wrought as the other'. Lancaster, a Herald at Arms, wore the Earl's coat of arms in damask while the remaining three heralds, each of them a King of Arms, wore the coat of arms of England (figure 1). A gentleman usher, white rod in hand, rode on Garter's left.

The heralds directly preceded the coffin, which was borne on a chariot draped with a large black velvet pall and drawn by four horses, each mounted by a page. Another gentleman usher, carrying a white rod, sat on the fore-seat. The chariot was surrounded by hooded esquires on horseback, four escorting the coffin and six more, outside them, carrying bannerols.

Behind the chariot rode the chief mourner, the heir of the defunct, wearing the mourning robes of an earl. He was flanked by two gentleman ushers, also on horseback and bearing their white rods of office. Behind the heir rode the late Earl's Gentleman of the Horse, leading the riderless horse of estate, 'all covered and trapped with black velvet'. Next came eight other distinguished

---

[4] The gowns worn by the chaplains were probably not mourning but their official garments. They wore hoods 'according to their degrees', in this case, one being a Bachelor of Divinity and the other a Master of Arts.

[5] In the sixteenth century, the terms 'achievements' and 'hatchments' were interchangeable, referring to the coat of arms, helmet and crest, sword, gauntlets and spurs carried in the funeral procession. In modern heraldic usage a funeral hatchment is a painting of arms of the deceased on a black background, hung up over his doorway. A contemporary account of the funeral of James I uses both old and modern senses of 'hatchment'; see CA, I Series MS IV fols 32–45.

[6] The helmet and crest would each have been borne on the point of a lance; see Bod., Ashmole MS 857 fol. 196 and figure 1.

[7] BL, Egerton MS 2642 fol. 195v. For regulations governing how swords were to be borne in front of persons of varying rank on other ceremonial occasions, see Gerard Legh, *The Accedens of Armory* (London [?]: [n. pub.], 1562), p. 161.

mourners, headed by Lord Stourton, all of them with family links to the deceased. A single yeoman, bare-headed and on foot, preceded the two sons of the chief mourner, whose horses were led by two gentlemen. This completed the mounted section of the procession.

Two yeomen ushers, bearing white rods like their counterparts, conducted the five hundred yeomen, all in black coats, marching two abreast. Many of the servants of the gentlemen took part in the ceremony. They walked similarly in pairs and brought up the rear of the procession.

The basic structure of the Derby funeral procession was repeated in the funeral corteges of noble women, but with slight modifications. Take, for example, the funeral of Lady Katherine Berkeley (d. 1596). Her gender determined that the seventy poor people marching in her funeral convoy would be women rather than men. Similarly, all the principal mourners were women.[8] An Elizabethan ordinance stipulated that, 'a man being deade hee to have only men [principal] mourners at his Buriall. And at a woman's buriall to have only women mourners'.[9]

The funeral procession brought together a whole range of social groups: mourners related to the deceased in rank and family; officers and servants of the late Earl's household; his gentlemen retainers; yeomen; the poor and the church choir. The procession was thus a microcosm of the social unit of the kingdom, hierarchically organized according to status and degree. Overall the spatial organization of the funeral procession functioned as a statement of continued order and stability. The symbolic core of the procession and, significantly, its physical centre, was the coffin. Gradations of rank built up from the poor at the very beginning of the procession, through to the members of the nobility that immediately surrounded the coffin. The effect was a crescendo building up to a climax of dignity at the centre and then tailing off once the coffin and its immediate entourage had gone by.[10]

Before examining the implications of the hierarchical organization of the funeral procession, it is worth exploring the ways in which the messages of order and stability imparted by the spatial organization of the funeral procession were reinforced by its internally operating semiotics or visual codes.

At the simplest level, these messages were imparted through the sheer numbers of participants. The higher the status of the deceased, the greater the number of overall participants. Elizabeth I's funeral procession followed the same hierarchical organization as the Derby funeral but included participants from a broader range of social groups, as befitted the funeral of a monarch, head of the social body.[11] In addition to the poor women and the late Queen's

---

[8] Smith, *Lives of the Berkeleys*, II, 388–91; cited by Gittings, p. 174.
[9] BL, Egerton MS 2642 fol. 168.
[10] Cunnington and Lucas, p. 186.
[11] John Stow, *The Annales; or, General Chronicle of England begun first by Maister John Stow and after him continued [...] by Edmond Howes* (London: [n. pub.], 1615), p. 818; Francis

The Theatre of Death

household, from the highest officials down to the servants of the scullery, it incorporated representatives of the nobility, church and civic dignitaries, government officials and ambassadors, 1,600 of them in all.[12]

The inclusion of instrumentalists was also used to signal status in funeral processions. Trumpeters featured in the funerals of the higher nobility and royalty, with twelve trumpeters marching at Elizabeth's funeral. Trumpets were a symbol of the resurrection.[13] Fifes, and drums draped with black cloth, were a feature of military funerals and were included at the funeral of Sir Philip Sidney (1587). They did not appear in civilian funeral processions, including those of royalty.[14]

Status was also marked by the numbers within any one group of mourners. The number of assistant mourners, for example, varied according to the social position of the deceased. In a letter to Sir William Dethick (Garter 1570–1604, d. 1612) Elizabeth, widow of John, Lord Russell, son of the second Earl of Bedford, asked for particulars of the number of mourners due to her as a viscountess of birth.[15] In the case of assistant mourners, rank was more important than relationship with the defunct, underlining the primacy of display. Randle Holme (1627–99) lists 'the number of m[o]urners at funeralls according to the degree and estate of the defunct' whatever their personal relation to the deceased: 'It[em] Kinge to have m[o]urners – xv; It[em] Queene or a Prince – xiii'.[16] Dukes and marquesses had to have eleven principal mourners, earls and viscounts nine, barons seven, knights, bannerets or bachelors five, and esquires or gentlemen three. If there were insufficient mourners of the appropriate rank available, a little deception might be employed. At the funeral of Lady Katherine Berkeley women of lesser rank than required acted as mourners, but were dressed according to the higher status.[17] The tactic used on this occasion to ensure that the right number of mourners of the right rank were displayed draws attention to another important visual code of the funeral procession: dress.

The basic form of mourning dress for both men and women was the black, draped gown. The very shapes of mourning dress, with its long flowing trains

---

Sandford, *A Genealogical History of the Kings of England and Monarchs of Great Britain* (London: T. Newcombe, 1677), p. 497.

12 See Appendix I for a full list of participants at Elizabeth's funeral.
13 Percy A. Scholes, *The Puritans and Music in England and New England: A Contribution to the Cultural History of Two Nations* (New York: Russell & Russell, 1962), p. 218.
14 Camden (1630), p. 66.
15 College of Arms, Vincent MS 151 fol. 352.
16 BL, Harley MS 2129 fol. 27. For other examples of such rules see BL, Cotton MS Julius B. xii; Lancaster Herald, Nicholas Charles's 'Book of proceedyng at Funerals, 1613', in BL, Additional MS 14417; and other manuscripts cited by Gittings, p. 243.
17 R. W. Ingram, ed., *Records of Early Drama: Coventry* (London: Manchester University Press, 1981), Appendix VIII, p. 511. See also the funeral of Anne, Duchess of Somerset (1587), F. Tate, 'Of the Antiquity, Variety and Ceremonies of Funerals in England', in *A Collection of Curious Discourses by Eminent Antiquarians upon several Heads in our English Antiquities*, ed. T. Hearne, 2 vols (London; [n. pub.], 1771), I, p. 204.

and tippets, may be suggestive of weeping; the actual origins of mourning costume for both sexes lie, however, in the early years of the Christian Church, the styles being derived from the medieval robes of monks, widows and nuns.[18] Thus mourning dress possessed an unfashionable quality that signified withdrawal from society.

Although the thirty torch-bearers at the funeral of Richard II in St Paul's in 1400 wore white, black had generally been accepted as the colour of grief by the fourteenth century. Reds, browns and greys continued to be worn well into the sixteenth century but black mourning dress was dominant.[19] Edmund Bolton comments that, 'To mourne inn black is as a nationall a custome, as for the grave.'[20] The uniformity of black mourning gave the community a group identity and the procession a coherence. It also provided an effective foil to the brilliance of heraldic insignia and achievements.

The profusion of black was extended to the very streets and houses along the processional route. At the funeral of the Earl of Huntingdon (1560), for example, 'the strett [was] hangyd with blake and armes', transforming it into a theatre of death.[21]

English monarchs, however, like their French counterparts, did not mourn in black at the funerals of their subjects, but in purple. It was deemed inappropriate for a reigning sovereign to don the colour of mourning and death. Further, the colour of their robes provided another visual marker separating them from the masses in the funeral procession. Queen Elizabeth's inventory for 1600 included a set of 'Mourning Robes' comprising a mantle, surcoat and bodice of purple velvet trimmed with ermine and detailed in gold.[22]

The basic symbolic statement of mourning dress, withdrawal from the world, was overlain with a second code operating in the detail of individual costumes and which, in sharp contrast, was very much bound up with society.[23] The amount and quality of the fabric used to make mourning costumes was regulated by the College of Arms according to the wearer's rank and social position as well as his function in the funeral proceedings. The following list

---

[18] The association with weeping is made by Cunnington and Lucas, pp. 152–4.
[19] Lou Taylor, *Mourning Dress: A Costume and Social History* (London: George Allen and Unwin, 1988), pp. 66, 71, 252; 'The Death of Queen Jane [Seymour]', in John Goss, ed., *Ballads of Britain* (London: Bodley Head, 1937), p. 78. The cloth used at the funeral of Lady Isabel Berkeley (1516) was deliberately made to look old; see Ingram, Appendix VIII, p. 508. See also C. C. Rolfe, *The Ancient Use of Liturgical Colours* (Oxford: Parker Society, 1879), p. 226.
[20] Edmund Bolton, *The Elements of Armories* (London: [n. pub.], 1597), p. 131.
[21] Nichols (1848), p. 239. Many other examples of streets hung with black occur in Machyn's diary. The funerals concerned include those of civic dignitaries, knights and citizens; see pp. 2, 3, 8, 46, 59, 98, 106, 110, 117, 123, 169, 171, 181, 217, 240, 311.
[22] Cunnington and Lucas, p. 147. See also Bolton on purple, p. 141.
[23] On costume indexically denoting social position or profession, see Elam, p. 25.

gives the fabric and livery allowances for nobleman at the funeral of a king or noble prince:[24]

A Duke for his Crown, Slopp and Mantal	xvi yards of x^s the yard and livery for xviii Servants
An Earle for his Crowne, Capp and Mantall	xvi yards of viii^s the yard and livery for xii Servants
Every Baron	6 yards for his Gowne and Hood and Livery for viii Servants
A Knight	5 yards at vi^s viii^d the yard and livery for iiii Servants
Every Esquire	For the body as a Knight and livery for iii Servants

All other Esquires and Gentillmen at v^s the yarde and Livery for iii Servants and Gentillmen for One Servant

Every yeoman and page to have iiii yards and every Gentillmans servant to have iii yards.

Details in the design of the mourning costume further differentiated mourners' rank. The chief mourner's train, for example, distinguished him/her from his four associates (figure 2).[25] While noblemen wore gowns and hoods, the simplest form of mourning, the 'black cote', was worn by the yeoman conductors and the bearers, or underbearers, of the coffin and was a sign of their yeoman class.[26]

Headgear, the most visible item of funeral apparel, was especially useful for demarcating rank. First, the type of headgear worn was significant. Tippets and hoods were worn by those above the rank of esquire, tippets only by those of lower status.[27] The tippets themselves, which were a survival from fourteenth- and fifteenth-century liripipes, varied in size and design. Evidence exists of the exact dimensions of tippets worn by women of different rank. The queen and queen mother wore tippets 'a nayle and an inch' (3¼") wide, which were so long that they extended along the train, lying upon it. The tippets decreased in length by degrees until the baroness's tippet which was ¼ yard off the ground and 'scarce a nayle' (2") in width. Knight's wives and some of the gentlewomen of the Royal Household wore their tippets 'pinned upon their arme'. Servants of lower status and female commoners were completely debarred from wearing tippets.[28]

The hood, already a denoter of high rank, could be worn in different ways,

---

[24] Bod., Ashmole MS 857 fol. 188.
[25] Julian Litten, *The English Way of Death: The Common Funeral Since 1450* (London: Robert Hale, 1991), p. 175.
[26] Cunnington and Lucas, p. 184.
[27] BL, Harley MS 1354 fol. 4. See also Taylor, p. 81.
[28] CA, I Series MS III fol. 52 and BL, Harley MS 1776 fol. 8. See also Taylor, p. 75.

facilitating a second type of differentiation relating to the mourners' roles in the funeral procession. All those in the central section of the Derby funeral convoy, that is the bearer of the Great Banner, the heralds and pages, the usher seated on the chariot, the ten esquires, the chief and assistant mourners, the two ushers and the gentleman of the horse, together with the standard bearer, wore mourning hoods 'over the face'. Those with less significant roles, the eighty gentlemen, two secretaries, fifty knights and esquires, preacher, chief officers and sons of the chief mourner, were only entitled to wear their mourning hoods 'over the shoulder'.

The importance of the symbolic role of the hood is underlined by the note appended to the list of fabric allowances for noblemen given above, 'Noone to were hooddes under the degree of an Esquire of Household, but in time of neede'. As we have seen, when there was a shortage of people of sufficient rank others would be substituted so that none of the key roles would be omitted. The hoods, worn low, obscuring their faces as can be clearly observed in a British Library illustration of the funeral procession of a Garter Knight and Duchess, signified that their individual identities were subordinate to their symbolic functions.[29]

The hierarchical code of the funeral procession also operated through heraldic insignia: the banners and achievements, borne by esquires and heralds. These heraldic images and symbols functioned as visually encoded signals that told their own messages of noble status.

The achievements arrayed at the funeral of the Earl of Derby consisted of his coat of arms, sword, helmet and shield or target. To these might be added gauntlets, spurs, the insignia of knightly orders and coronets. At the funeral of a peer above the rank of Baron, and certainly at that of a king, even the complete armour of the deceased might appear, worn by a champion mounted on the horse of honour as, for example, at the funeral of Edward IV.[30]

> And then a lorde or a knight with a courser trapped of his armes, his herneys upon hym, his salet [helmet] or basenet on his head crowned, a shylde and a spere till he come to the place of his ent'ring.[31]

The inclusion of a horse of honour also indicated higher status. Still further up the scale, the procession might feature more riderless horses trapped in black – there were three such at the funeral of Elizabeth.

Women of royal and noble extraction sometimes had achievements carried at their funerals. A funeral manuscript depicting the 'Funeral of a Duchess',

---

[29] BL, Additional MS 35324 fols 1–6.
[30] Gittings, p. 174; Cunnington and Lucas, pp. 203, 207. The helm, shield and saddle used in Henry V's obsequies are preserved in the Undercroft Museum at Westminster Abbey; see *Westminster Abbey: The Chapter House, the Pyx Chamber and Treasury, the Undercroft Museum* ([London (?)]: English Heritage, [n. d.]), p. 28. Replicas of the Black Prince's funerary armour are on display in Canterbury Cathedral.
[31] 'An Extract relating to the Burial of King Edward IV', *Archaeologia*, 1 (1777), 348–355 (p. 349).

dating from the 1580s, shows heralds bearing a shield, coat-of-arms and coronet but no weapons.[32] A later Elizabethan ordinance states, however, that 'it is not convenient that a woman should have a Coate of Armes or Shielld Helme and creste, the which is not lawful today'.[33]

The primacy of the display function of the funeral achievements in the Renaissance period is underlined by the fact that they had no utility beyond representing the rank and nobility of the defunct. Up until the late sixteenth century a few families did relinquish genuine items of armour for use in funerals, and a few early tilt-helms and close-helms thus donated survive in churches, cathedral treasuries and museums. Rather like theatrical props, however, the majority of the armour utilized in funeral ceremonies was of a temporary nature, made of wood or perhaps metal, though never of substantial defensive quality.[34] Mourning swords, too, were specifically made for use in funeral ceremonies, being somewhat larger than the average arming sword. The coat of armour was made like the herald's tabard, embroidered or painted with the arms of the deceased on front and back, and on the short sleeves.[35]

The degree of workmanship invested in the achievements also varied according to the rank of the deceased; a helmet of 'steel gilt' for an earl's funeral cost £1, with a further £1 being charged for the crest, while a helmet for a knight cost 16s. and his crest 13s.[36]

The number and different types of flag included in any procession were similarly subject to a strict code of protocol determined by the rank of the deceased.[37] The banner, originally oblong in form, although as it evolved it became almost square, displayed the armorial coat of its owner spread entirely over the surface. Banners were permitted only at the funerals of peers and their ladies. The standard was oblong in form, its size being dependent on the status of its master: a duke's standard was seven and a half yards long, while a knight's was only four. Standards did not bear the arms of their owners. Rather they had the cross of St George in the chief (that is, next to the staff), and next the beast or crest with the owner's device or motto. They were split into two at the tip. Knights and their ladies could display standards but not banners. Pennons resembled the standard in form but were smaller and rounded at the end, instead of split. They were, however, entirely different in charges, bearing the arms of the deceased like the banner. Esquires and their ladies were allowed pennons but not standards.

The lowest type of heraldic ensign utilized at funerals was the escutcheon which also bore the arms of the defunct. While mere gentlemen could have no

---

32 BL, Additional MS 35324 fols 4–5.
33 BL, Egerton MS 2642 fol. 205.
34 Nigel Llewellyn, *The Art of Death: Visual Culture in the English Death Ritual c. 1500–c. 1800* (London: Robert Hale, 1991), p. 68.
35 Litten, pp. 176–7.
36 Bodleian Library, Top. Yorks MS d. 7 fols 23, 33.
37 Nichols (1848), pp. xxvi–xviii.

pennons, they could display as many escutcheons of arms as they wished. The funerals of the higher ranks were also provided with escutcheons, often amply, to the extent of four, six or eight dozen. The escutcheons that decorated the funeral palls, three along each broad side, one at each end and the ninth on the top at the central point of the coffin lid, were small canvas rectangles, roughly eight inches by six inches in size, and were prepared by the herald-painters.

The language of heraldry not only denoted rank but had also developed a mode for demonstrating both the interlinking of aristocratic lines through marriage alliances and, thereby, the network of power built up amongst the ruling families of the kingdom. The bannerols communicated these particular messages. In form, bannerols were similar to banners but made of increased width so that they could display impalements representing the alliances of the ancestors of the deceased. The six bannerols borne around the coffin of Derby were charged with the arms of distinguished families linked by blood with the Stanley family. The number of bannerols allowed was determined by the rank of the defunct. They were only permitted at the funerals of peers and their ladies: a knight was restricted to four, while a duke could have a dozen.[38]

Dukes and members of the royal family were also permitted a canopy, borne over or behind the funeral chariot. Although controlled by heraldic regulations, this sign of status was religious in origin, as will be discussed in connection with the funeral of Elizabeth I.

The heraldic symbols, gradations in dress and musical sections all further served to anticipate and mark out the central section of the funeral convoy. At the Derby funeral, one of the grandest, the build-up was signalled not only by increasing quality in the fabric and style of mourning dress and the grouping of heraldic insignia but also by the shift from mourners on foot at the beginning of the procession, to mourners on horseback at the core, and once again to mourners on foot at the rear. Internal codes thus reinforced the external appearance of the hierarchically organized funeral procession to give the desired overall impression of order and stability.

Participant and Observer Motivation[39]

The procession thus embodied status, hierarchy and the role of authority. It was at once a visual affirmation and confirmation of the social order. Both functions were recognized and articulated by contemporaries. A dedicatory poem included in John Ferne's *The Blazon of Gentrie* thus describes the heralds' role in ordering processions:

---

[38] Litten, p. 177.
[39] The motivations behind the executors' staging of the funeral will be discussed in the next section of this chapter which deals with the offering ritual.

> How status of men are martialed, and placed in degree,
> By sacred skill of heralds arte: that difference might remaine,
> Twixt King and Lord, twixt Lord and Knight, twixt Knight and simple Swain.[40]

More recently, Mervyn James described processions as a 'synchronic form of static hierarchical structure' and a 'visible means of relating individuals to the social structure'.[41] James similarly referred to the hierarchical ordering of processions as an embodiment of community at once supporting the hierarchy it images and encouraging the social integration of all participants.[42] By taking part in the procession each individual acknowledged and enacted his relative status in society.

Apart from respect for the deceased, various motives lay behind the decision to participate in a funeral procession, depending on the status of the person concerned. The poor received alms and also the black cloth of their mourning garment, a valuable item in itself. Those of higher rank were given an opportunity to demonstrate their position in society, reaffirming the hierarchy that gave them status. The honour conferred on participants functioned as a deterrent to disruptive behaviour. Thus, although precedence disputes were never far away from processional occasions, they rarely encroached on the actual performance of the ritual and the illusion of order was usually preserved.[43]

An audience was required to witness the picture of order and stability. Strickland rightly sees the presence and emotional participation of the audience as part of the whole performance.[44] Yet the reasons behind attending a funeral procession and the effect of the ritual experience on the spectators are difficult to assess. A fruitful area for probing contemporary ideas about how funeral ritual occasions operated on observers and what motivated their attendance is

---

40 John Ferne, *The Blazon of Gentrie* (London: Toby Cooke, 1586), p. iii; see also Segar (1602), p. 253.

41 James (1986), p. 30; Charles Phythian-Adams, 'Ceremony and the Citizen: the Communal Year at Coventry 1450–1550', in *Crisis and Order in English Towns 1500–1700: Essays in Urban History*, ed. by Peter Clark and Paul Slack (London: Routledge & Kegan Paul, 1972), p. 59; Ronald Strickland, 'Pageantry and Poetry as Discourse: The Production of Subjectivity in Sir Philip Sidney's Funeral', *English Literary History*, 57 (1990), 19–36 (p. 19).

42 James's remarks are made with reference to late medieval Corpus Christi processions. See his 'Ritual, Drama and the Social Body in the Late Medieval English Town', *Past and Present*, 98 (1983), 3–29 (pp. 5–10). See also Phythian-Adams, pp. 57–70; and Nathalie Zemon Davis, 'The Sacred and the Social Body in Sixteenth Century Lyon', *Past and Present*, 90 (1981), 40–70 (pp. 40–1, 54). On anthropological theories of the treatment of the body as an image of society, see Woodbridge, pp. 270–1.

43 Lewis, p. 12; Patrick Collinson, *The Birthpangs of Protestant England: Religious and Cultural Change in the Sixteenth and Seventeenth Centuries* (London: Macmillan, 1988), p. 142. On parish processional disputes, see Eamon Duffy, *The Stripping of the Altars: Traditional Religion in England c. 1400 – c. 1580* (London: Yale University Press, 1992), p. 126.

44 Strickland, p. 27.

heraldry, because of the existence of a large number of sixteenth- and early seventeenth-century texts in this field.

Some heraldic insignia would have been familiar to nearly all participants in and observers of funerals. Those, for example, of local or particularly eminent aristocrats would have been very well-known because of their multiple representations in everyday life. Edmund Bolton describes 'Armouries [...] occurring every-where, in Seales, in frontes of buildings, in utensils, in all things, Monarcks using them, mighty Peeres, and in briefe, all the noble tam maiorum, quam minorum gentium, from Caesar to the simplest Gentleman'.[45] Similarly some armorial charges and colours are likely to have had clear associations in the minds of the majority. Only kings, emperors and members of the blood royal could, for example, bear gold.[46] The royal coat of arms was seen at all funerals attended by members of the College of Arms because it was represented on the tabards of the heralds. Thus the loyalty of the ruling class to the Crown was underlined, as contemporaries were aware:

> The Officer of Arms weareth the King's coat of arms at the interment of a nobleman not only for the wel ordering of the funeral but also for the intent that it may be well beknown unto all men that the defunct died honourably, without any spot of dishonesty, the which might be dishonour to his blood, and the King's majesty's good and loyal subject.[47]

Similarly, observers were always reminded that the ultimate source of aristocratic power lay in the authority of the monarch, 'For all degrees of "Nobilite", are but so many "Beames" issueing foorth from "Regal Maiestie" '.[48] When a certain Thomas Wastcote, 'most presumptuously invested himselfe in ye Kinges Coat of Arms taking upon him to discharge ye Offices of an Herald' at a funeral in Exeter, the matter was viewed in a serious light and the case taken to the Earl Marshal's court.[49]

Yet while spectators would have recognized the insignia of royalty and well-known families, the subtleties of particular arrangements of ordinaries, not to mention the complexities of multiple quartering and the numerous 'marks, crescents and mollets' used to denote family relationships, would have

---

[45] Bolton, p. 2. See also James Dallaway, *Inquiries into the Origin and Progress of the Science of Heraldry in England* (London: B. & J. White, 1793), p. 101.

[46] Legh, p. 2. The art of covering banners and pennons with beaten gold and silver beaten into a very thin lamina and stuck on with resinous gum was developed by the thirteenth century, see Dallaway, p. 403.

[47] Bod., Ashmole MS 1116 fol. 51; Segar (1602), p. 254. The significance of state involvement in the funeral ritual is discussed further in chapter 2.

[48] John Guillim, *A Display of Heraldrie* (London: [n. pub.], 1610), Dedication to King James.

[49] Bod., Ashmole MS 836 fol. 609. The position of Earl Marshal was then held in commission by Worcester, Lennox and Arundel.

been inaccessible to most.[50] William Wyrley displayed a contemporary awareness of the problem, asking:

> How is it possible for a plain unlearned man [..] to discerne and know a sunder, six or eight (what speake I of six or eight) sometimes thirtie or fortie severall marks clustered all together on shield or banner, nay though he had as good skill as *Robert Glover* late Somerset that dead is, and the eies of an Egle, amongst such a confusion of things, yet should he never be able to decipher the errors that are daily committed [. . .] nor discerne or know one banner or standard from another, be the same ho'ever so large?[51]

At the end of the sixteenth century the writers of heraldic treatises began to argue for a simplification of coats of arms, which had become increasingly florid and detailed. Their stance implies a recognition of the fact that simple heraldic texts were accessible.[52] Yet this programme of reform was not to get really underway until the mid-seventeenth century. There was resistance to the movement from those who wished to preserve the 'Mysterious Art'.[53] Bolton refers to the 'secret' of arms, 'the mysteries in armorial numbers' and the 'Hieroglyphics of Nobility'.[54] Ferne, Wryley and Legh all feel the need to comment on their publication of heraldic treatises in the English tongue. Willing though they are to exploit the growing demand for such works, they seek to contain the potential demystification of their craft. Maclagan criticizes Ferne, author of the most popular Elizabethan manual, for 'subscribing to fanciful blazonings which employ the names of planets and precious stones for the tinctures instead of the normal terms'.[55] The concentration on obscure and fictitious matters may, however, have been deliberate. Ferne's spokesman for heralds, Paradinus, argues thus: 'for as in everye Science or Art, latet aliquid misterii, not fit to be made knowne to everye man, so hath the Science of theirs also, her misteries and secretes, inconvenient to be revealed'.[56] The function of heraldic symbols as a means of cultural definition depended, at least in part, on their being difficult to read.[57]

For the majority, heraldic semiotics worked on the immediate and direct level of size, number and, above all, colour, as is clear from the careful regulations imposed by the College of Arms. Those who could not 'decode' the complex

---

50 Guillim, p. 13; BL, Harley MS 2129 fol. 110; A. R. Wagner *Heralds and Ancestors* (London: [n. pub.], 1978), p. 28.
51 William Wyrley, *The True Use of Armorie* (London: Gabriell Cawood, 1592), p. 7.
52 Guillim, p. 13; Wyrley, p. 13.
53 Heraldry was described as such in a 1611 dedicatory poem to John Guillim's book by Thomas Guillim.
54 Bolton, 'To the Gentle Reader', pp. 170, 188. See also Legh, p. 112.
55 Michael Maclagan, 'Genealogy and Heraldry in the Sixteenth and Seventeenth Centuries', in *English Historical Scholarship in the Sixteenth and Seventeenth Centuries*, ed. by Levi Fox (Oxford: Oxford University Press, 1956), pp. 31–48 (pp. 42–3).
56 Ferne (1586), pp. 6–7; Legh, p. i; Wyrley, p. 41.
57 Steven Mullaney, *The Place of the Stage: License, Play and Power in Renaissance England* (London: University of Chicago Press, 1988), p. 19.

symbolism of the heraldic insignia displayed at a funeral, could, nevertheless, be impressed by their quantity and brilliance. The banners borne aloft drew the eye of the beholder, their bright colours rivalled only by the heralds' tabards and the funeral achievements, polished, resplendent and displayed to best advantage by the heralds who bore them aloft, fixed to staves.[58] The heraldic funeral procession was a rich visual feast, stimulating the ocular senses of the audience. Edmund Bolton, author of an early seventeenth-century treatise on heraldry, draws attention to the key role played by colour. 'For that as lines give them [coats of arms] shape or circumscription, so without colour [...] they neyther have life, nor distinction.' He goes on to analyse their effect on the individual: 'What innumerable affections are raised in the soule by colours, all admirers of beauty can tell, and I see not what the pride of life is the more ambitious in, or studious for, witnesse [...] ye pompe of cloathes, the ornament of building, and innumerable other: All which unto the blind worth nothing indeed, but to those who have the use of sight, a maine cause why they desire to live and bee.'[59]

The heraldic texts in the funeral procession thus operated on two levels. On the one hand banners and pennons delighted the eye, imparting affective and perhaps physiological pleasure to the beholder and increasing the attraction of the occasion. At the same time they told ideological messages of status, messages that were strong but unspecific, impressive but mysterious.[60] As the convoy passed by, each spectator witnessed a visual representation of social order without understanding how that order operated.

The duality of the way in which heraldic texts functioned in the elite funeral demonstrates the fusion of the emotional and the political achieved by ritual symbolism.[61] The brilliance of the heraldic colours and symbols evokes a direct emotional and physical response which is separate from any cerebral appreciation of the meanings of individual coats. In fact the 'meaning' seems to be necessarily obscure and mysterious to ensure the desired affective response. The very process of symbolization collapses meanings into images, inviting faith. At the same time, implicit within the heraldic code is a sense of ordering the universe, a sense which conveys itself to the observer irrespective of hidden

---

[58] Bod., Ashmole MS 857 fol. 196, and Thomas Lant, *The Funeral Procession of Sir Philip Sidney*, ed. by T. De Bry (London: [n. pub.], 1587): see figure 1.

[59] Bolton (1610), pp. 126, 130. Giovanni Botero similarly comments that people are to a large extent persuaded to live contentedly in the early modern city by 'alluring sights', *Of the Causes of the Greatness and Magnificence of Cities*, 2nd edn (London: H. Seile, 1635), p. 41. On the ritual mystery of the court masque, see Graham Parry, *The Golden Age restor'd: The Culture of the Stuart Court, 1603–42* (Manchester: Manchester University Press, 1981), pp. 44, 179.

[60] Nigel Llewellyn, 'Claims to Status through Visual Codes: Heraldry on post-Reformation Funeral Monuments', in *Chivalry in the Renaissance*, ed. by Sydney Anglo (Woodbridge: The Boydell Press, 1990), p. 145.

[61] This fusion could be seen as a model of Gluckman's process of 'sublimation'; see my Introduction.

specific meanings. Through the semiotics of heraldry, as through its overall spatial organization, the funeral procession again and again affirmed the continuation of order and stability in the face of the demise of a key member of society. It is in this fulfilment of the deep human need to be cushioned from the impact of death that the ultimate motivation behind spectator and participant attendance must lie. Elite funerals in Renaissance England did not constitute a simple manipulation of the populace on the part of the ruling class, as Marxist analysts with their unidirectional concept of *mystification* like to suggest. Rather heraldic funerals involved a two-way power relationship in which the organizers of the funeral were compelled to provide a performance sufficiently rich in symbolic content to enlist the co-operation of participants and observers. Paradoxically, such co-operation, whether proffered wittingly or not, was essential to the successful enactment of political power held by the elite. Yet, at the same time, the groups of participants and observers gained significant physiological pleasure and emotional reassurance from their actions. Ritual occasions bring benefits to both ruler and ruled.

The Form and Functions of the Heraldic Funeral Church Service

The Church Setting

At the heart of the church service, usually held the day after the funeral procession, was the central ritual performance of the heraldic funeral: the offering. Once again discussion will centre on the Derby funeral. Before turning to a detailed analysis of the offering ceremony, however, it is useful to consider how the church was transformed into an appropriate setting: a 'theatre' for death.

Inside the church black drapes were swathed about the pulpit and communion table and hung from the arches of the aisles, punctuated with escutcheons of the Earl's arms, some impaled with the arms of his three successive wives. A list of the hangings required in St Paul's for the burial 'of any Estate', while not providing a complete list of fabric quantities, gives a general indication of the amount of black cloth used and where it was placed:

> Black hanging the Quier –
> the blacke on the communion table being ordinary – 5 yardes
> the blacke in the upper quarter of that Quier
> the blacke in the Bishop's Sea[t]
> the blacke in the neyther Quier
> the blacke on the outfront of the rood loft[62]

---

[62] CA, Vincent MS 151 fol. 161. The expense accounts for the St Paul's funeral of Henry II (1559) include blacks to cover the chancel floor; see J. Strype, *Ecclesiastical memorials relating chiefly to religion and the reformation of it*, 3 vols (London: [n. pub.], 1721), I, 127.

The abundance of black acted as a foil to the bright heraldic colours of the coats of arms.

The black hangings also provided a backdrop for the magnificent hearse that was set up between the choir and the body of the church to receive Derby's coffin.[63] It stood thirty feet high, twelve feet long and nine feet wide, surrounded by a double rail. In the centre was a raised section upon which the coffin would stand (figures 3, 4 and 5). The whole was covered with black taffeta, silk and velvet, and adorned with numerous escutcheons. The canopy, or 'Majesty', was also of taffeta lined with buckram and embroidered on the underside with the Earl's arms in gold and silver.[64] Six great burial paste-escutcheons were fixed to the four corners, the top of the canopy and the valance, which was further adorned with small metal pencils or pensels, the diminutive of pennon.[65] Overall the hearse had a stage-like quality, making the coffin highly visible to the congregation and focusing their attention upon it.[66]

The size and design of the hearse were governed by heraldic regulations according to the rank of the deceased. The requirements for the hearse of an earl are given as follows:

> A hearse of tymber wth fyve principalls to be covered wth blacke clothe and the same to be furnished Accordinglie
> Item to have a Maiestie of taffetie[67]

A countess would similarly have a closed roof hearse with five principals but not all hearses had canopies, as manuscript drawings in the Ashmolean collection illustrate.[68]

The rails around the coffin and the church served a dual function: they both supported the black mourning fabric and marked out the spaces where the protagonists and the audience should locate themselves. They did not in any way obscure the audience's view of the coffin and mourners, being only about waist-height: the sides of the hearse were open.[69]

The arrangements at the Derby funeral illustrate the significance of the

---

[63] BL, Harley MS 2129 fol. 94.
[64] The seventeenth-century antiquary, James Dallaway, traces this custom back to the fourteenth century, see Dallaway, p. 101.
[65] Nichols (1848), p. xxviii.
[66] For an Elizabethan discussion of the origins of the hearse, see Tate, p. 219.
[67] Bod., Ashmole MS 836 fol. 43. See also CA, Vincent MS 151.
[68] Bod., Ashmole MS 836 fols 53, 149. Ibid. fols 146–63 have a number of contemporary diagrams and descriptions of hearses. See also BL, Harley MS 2129 fols 47–9, 54, 56–8; BL, Additional MS 14417 fol. 7.
[69] Compare the description of the temporary scaffold set up in the chapel at Whitehall for the wedding ceremony of Princess Elizabeth and the Elector Palatine (1613), which was 'rayled on both/ side; the rayles being covered with cloth of tissue, but open at the top, that the whole assembly might the better see all the ceremonies'; see John Nichols, ed., *The Progresses, Processions, and Magnificent Festivities of King James I*, 4 vols (London: J. B. Nichols, 1828), II, 544–6.

mourners' positions, particularly in and around the hearse. On arrival at the church, the coffin of the Earl of Derby was removed from the chariot by eight gentlemen and borne inside. The hundred poor men remained outside, lining the way into the church. The coffin was placed inside the hearse, on a three foot high table or platform. A black velvet pall was placed over it and the coat of arms, sword, target, helm and crest laid on top. Then the principal mourners all sat inside the rails around the hearse, on the black-draped stools provided for them, with the chief mourner at the head. A detail in the description of the funeral of Katherine Berkeley (d. 1596) states that all the mourners faced inward.[70] Before the chief mourner was placed a carpet and four cushions of black velvet to kneel and lean upon; the other mourners each had one cushion for the same purpose. At the feet of the defunct, outside the rail stood the two esquires holding the standard and the great banner and the other esquires bearing the bannerols. The three Kings of Arms stood outside the head of the hearse together with the four gentleman ushers. Lancaster, still wearing the arms of the defunct, stood between the standard and the great banner (figure 5).[71]

The Offering Ceremony and Ritual Succession
At the beginning of the service, Norroy King of Arms pronounced the names and titles of the deceased.[72] There followed a sermon from the Dean of Chester and the epistle and gospel read by the Vicar; yet these scriptural elements were but a prelude to the symbolic core of the church death ritual: the offering.

First Henry Earl of Derby, the principal mourner, was led up to the altar by the four heralds and offered a piece of gold to the celebrant on behalf of the deceased.[73] On either side of Garter stood a gentleman usher and an esquire to bear the chief mourner's train. The eight other principal mourners followed in order of degree, but did not offer at this stage. Then all returned to their places in the hearse.

After a short interval, the principal mourner rose a second time and went up to the altar to offer for himself. Now only Clarenceux and Lancaster escorted him to the altar. Once he had offered, he stood between the minister and Lancaster to receive the noble achievements of his father, the coat of arms, the sword, pommel borne forward, the target, helm and crest. These were offered by the other eight mourners, in pairs, each escorted by either Clarenceux or

---

[70] Ingram, Appendix VIII, p. 512.
[71] On the special seating constructed in Westminster Abbey for James's funeral, see Fritz, p. 64. See also BL, Stowe MS 152 fol. 136.
[72] As is generally the case in contemporary accounts of funerals, the form of the funeral service receives no comment. It is reasonable to assume, however, that the service followed that prescribed in the 1559 Prayer Book; see chapter 2, pp. 74–6. The style could also be pronounced after the offering; see Gittings, p. 178.
[73] Stone (1965) inaccurately has the chief mourner offer the coin to the heralds, p. 574.

Norroy.[74] Segar elucidates the meaning of the ritual, highlighting the significance of the chief mourner's role and the importance of the 'public' aspect of the ritual:

> And that his heire, if he have any, or next of whole blood, or some one for him (which commonly is the chief mourner) may publickly receive in the presence of all the mourners, the coate armour, Helme, Creast, and other Achievements of honour belonging to the defunct: whereof the King of Armes of the Province is to make record, with the defuncts match, issue and decease for the benefit of posterity.[75]

Thus the chief mourner ritually inherited the title of his father.

The 'creation' ceremony over, the new Earl returned to his stool in the hearse and remained there for the duration of the proceedings. At the funeral of the Earl of Salisbury (1462), to demonstrate further that the coat of arms of the deceased had been transferred to his heir, the Earl's herald stood before the hearse wearing it for the remainder of the mass until the burial.[77]

At Derby's funeral the eight mourners then offered again, this time 'for themselves', escorted once more by Clarenceux or Norroy, except the last pair, which was led up by a lower ranking herald, Bluemantle Pursuivant of Arms. Next the esquires offered the standard and great banner at the altar. Once they had offered they removed their hoods. Lancaster then escorted the chief officers of the defunct's household, white staves in hand, to make their offerings. Next, in pairs, the other mourners right down to the yeomen made their offerings of gold to the deceased. At the funeral of Lord Dacre (1563) the manuscript specifies that 'all others of the cyte and the country' offered, too.[78] The enactment of the succession was a highly public affair involving a wide range of people drawn from the local community.

The highly elaborate and intricate form of the proceedings described mark out the offering as the key episode of the heraldic funeral ritual. The offering ritual enacted the succession of the new Earl, thereby filling the gap in the ranks

---

[74] At particularly grand medieval and early Tudor funerals a horse of honour ridden by a champion wearing the armour of the deceased would also be offered. See the funerals of Thomas Howard, Duke of Norfolk (1524) in Francis Blomefield, *The History of [. . .] Thetford* (Fersfield: [n. pub.], 1739), Appendix VIII; Edward IV (1483) in *Archaeologia* 1 (1777), p. 354; Richard Neville, Earl of Salisbury (1462/3) in Sir A. Wagner, *Heralds of England: A History of the Office and College of Arms* (London: HMSO, 1967), p. 107; and Henry VII (1509) in BL, Harley MS 3504. Cunnington speculates that this part of the ritual had died out by the time of the Earl of Derby's funeral in 1572, p. 207. It is mentioned in a sixteenth-century ordinance for the funerals of kings (see BL, Egerton MS 2642 fol. 167b) but I have not come across any post–1524 instances of the practice.
[75] Segar (1602), IV, 254.
[77] Wagner (1967), p. 107.
[78] Bod., Ashmole MS 836 fol. 182. The gender of participants in the offering was regulated with women barred from offering at the funerals of men. See BL, Harley MS 1368 fol. 29.

of the aristocracy opened up by the death of his father.[79] At the funerals of noblewomen such as that of Elizabeth of York (1503) where achievements were absent, the principal mourners instead offered richly woven palls.[80] At funerals of women 'under the degree of Countess', however, only money was offered. Nevertheless, flags and banners were still received by the male heir, and thus the offering at a woman's funeral also demonstrated the transfer of aristocratic power.[81] Here was the motivation behind the executors' staging of the funeral ceremony.[82]

The solemnity of this ritual process of succession was signified in various ways. Of key importance were the spatial or, to borrow a term from the semiologist Kier Elam, proxemic codes.[83] The hearse was clearly a focal point in the ritual proceedings as was indicated by the centrality of its location in the church, usually in the choir, and the location of the chief participants, including the corpse of the defunct, in and around it. The main ritual movements were from the hearse to the altar and back. The periodic return of the mourners to their seats in the hearse separated the proceedings into distinct phases, or scenes. Some manuscript accounts tellingly mention a pause in the proceedings after the chief mourner has returned to the hearse.[84] The two locations, hearse and altar, were symbolically resonant, setting up a series of dialectics between secular and religious, static and dynamic, old and new. The hearse, with its multiple representations of the arms of the defunct, emphasized the worldly, the altar represented the divine. The hearse was the resting place of the dead earl; the altar, the mystical location for the creation of the new earl. An interesting contemporary diagram in a manuscript at the Bodleian shows a hearse, rather unusually placed in the nave rather than the chancel, but, nonetheless, carefully positioned in line with the choir door in the rood screen and the communion table beyond (figure 5).[85] The lines marked indicate the mourners' movements. Funeral ritual, unlike most medieval liturgical drama, progressed from the nave to the altar, perhaps imitating the process of the soul heavenwards.[86] The deliberate and careful positioning of the hearse thus created a secular focus

---

[79] Gittings, p. 179. My analysis goes further than Gittings by showing how the ritual succession was performed: how power was conferred through ceremonial.
[80] W. H. St John Hope, 'On the funeral Effigies of the Kings and Queens of England, with special reference to those in the Abbey Church of Westminster', *Archaeologia*, 40, part 2 (1907), 517–70 (p. 546).
[81] Ingram, Appendix VIII, p. 512; Gittings, p. 178.
[82] Only in rare cases where the defunct had no heir did the offering ritual not dramatize a succession; see for example BL, Harley MS 6064 fol. 97.
[83] Elam, pp. 56–69.
[84] BL, Harley MS 1368 fol. 29.
[85] Bod., Ashmole MS 836 fol. 212.
[86] In the topological symbolism of the medieval church, the east represented heaven and the west, earth; see John Wesley Harris, *Medieval Theatre in Context: an Introduction* (London: Routledge, 1992), pp. 38–9.

which stood, as if in homage, before the dominant religious focus of the building, the altar.[87]

Variations in costume, props, choreography and position, particularly in relation to the two key locations of hearse and altar, further contributed to the ritualization process and signalled changes in the roles adopted by the protagonists.

The number and heraldic rank of the escorts reflected on the role of the mourners at particular stages in the offering. The chief mourner was escorted by all four heralds when acting on behalf of the deceased, but by only two when offering for himself, indicating the lesser dignity of the role. At that moment he was only the heir; the title still pertained to the defunct and would not become his until he had symbolically received the achievements. Similarly, when the eight principal mourners offered the coat of arms, target, helm and crest, the special dignity of their role was underlined because they were escorted only by Kings of Arms. When offering on their own behalf, a lesser herald, Bluemantle Pursuivant, could take part as an attendant. (It may also have been the deliberate policy of the College of Arms to include as many heralds as possible, each of whom would then take a cut in the fees, heralds of lesser status being differentiated by role.)

In the account of the Derby funeral the presence or absence of train-bearers accompanying the chief mourner when he offered further accentuated his shift in role. When he offered for the first time, on behalf of the deceased and continued incumbent of the title, he was flanked by two Gentlemen-ushers and two esquires held his train. No attendants were mentioned when he offered on his own behalf, but when he returned to his seat, having received the achievements and with them the title, the two ushers and the two esquires were back in place. Similarly at the funeral of the Earl of Shrewsbury (1560) the chief mourner, 'making [a] reverence, gave a purse of gold for the offering. The which chief mourner had a cushion and a carpet laid by a gentleman usher, for him to kneel on.' When he made his second offering, this time in his own capacity, he approached the altar with 'neither train borne up, or cushion, or carpet to kneel on,' emphasizing his humility.[88] At the moment of his 'creation' the heir had to stand alone and unattended before the altar.

The symbolic import of the hood was indicated by the actions of the esquires who wore them over their heads when offering the standard and banner, putting them off when returning to their places. Similar behaviour is evident in the

---

[87] The relationship between the secular and the religious is discussed more fully in chapter 2. In post-Reformation England the altars in many churches were converted into communion tables and some were relocated at the steps of the choir rather than the east end of the chancel; see Harris, p. 4.

[88] Gittings, pp. 176–7. See also James I's funeral where the train of the chief mourner, Charles, was not carried for him when he offered for himself, CA, Nayler, pp. 55–6. See also Bod., Ashmole MS 818 fol. 24 and BL, Harley MS 2129 fol. 30; 6064 fol. 94.

account of the funeral of Anne of Cleves. When the chief mourner's two gentleman assistants were 'executing a charge' (i.e. a ceremonious duty) each wore his mourning hood over his head 'during the tyme of that chardge' but otherwise 'put it off or had it on his shoulder'.[89] The hood thus made an important contribution to the process of ritualization, suppressing the individual identities of the esquires. They acted merely as agents in the supremely important transfer of the title to the son and heir.

The focus of the proceedings was the public persona of the nobleman, signified by the heraldic titles and achievements. Once that public persona had been ritually transferred to the heir, attention was fixed on him and the body lost its significance, as the Derby funeral illustrates:

> And thus the offertory ended, the 100 poor men were placed to proceed homeward on foot, and after them were placed Esquires, and Gentlemen, on horseback; then the Garter Principal of Arms, then the Principal Mourner, with the other eight mourners, two by two, and then the Yeomen on foot, two by two.[90]

The chief mourner was now the centre of attention in this second procession, which took him, as the newly succeeded nobleman, back to the family seat, further emphasizing the continuity of the ruling class. At the Derby funeral the heir was not present at the interment of his father, giving him no opportunity to indulge in feelings of private grief at the graveside. His role was to display his public persona to the populace to demonstrate the continuity of the ranks of the aristocracy.

Although I have come across one or two examples of funerals where the mourners did not depart until after the interment, the majority of cases follow the Derby pattern suggesting that it was standard procedure for mourners not to witness the interment.[91] This was also the case at royal funerals as Lady Anne Clifford's account of Anne of Denmark's funeral (1619) makes clear: 'when all the company was gone and the Church door shut up, the Dean of *Westminster*, the Prebends, Sir *Edward Zouch* [. . .] came up a private way and buried the corpse at the east end of *Henry* the 7th Chapel about 7 o'clock at night'.[92] It was as if the moment of death was located not at the time of the physical demise of the body but at the symbolic transfer of nobility enacted in the offering ceremony.

At Derby's funeral, the interment of the coffin was conducted by the remaining three heralds with only about fifteen esquires, gentlemen, and yeomen,

---

89 Cunnington and Lucas, pp. 218–19. See also Taylor (1988), p. 88.
90 Collins, III, 62.
91 Further examples of mourners not witnessing interments can be found in Bod., Ashmole MS 857 fols 192–3; CA, I Series XI fol. 31; BL, Harley 6064 fol. 98. See also Gittings, pp. 178–9. For exceptions see BL, Harley MS 2129 fol. 31 and 6064 fol. 98.
92 V. Sackville-West, ed., *The Diary of Lady Anne Clifford* (London: Heinemann, 1923), p. 101.

together with the Treasurer, Comptroller and Steward of the late Earl in attendance. The private persona of the late nobleman received little recognition in the funeral ritual. The primary purpose of the heraldic funeral was social and concerned with the public persona of the dead nobleman, rather than the burial of his private body.[93] The church ceremony was about the transfer of the undying title, not taking leave of the dead.

The only personal impact of the Earl's death acknowledged at the interment was again one of changing social status, this time the status of the chief officers of the deceased's household. The latter, 'with weeping tears', broke their staves of office over their heads and threw them in after the coffin once it had been deposited in the open vault. The breaking of the staves ritually signalled the break-up of the old Earl's household. While their grief may have signified genuine attachment to the private person of their dead lord, in all likelihood it was coloured by anxiety as to their own future.[94] Derby's chief officers were, however, to be ritually reinstated, receiving both their offices and staves from the new Earl at the funeral banquet.

At the Derby funeral the six bannerols were then delivered up to the heralds, and placed, together with the other achievements, over and about the coffin in the grave; having played their part in the ritual transference of power, the actual objects were no longer required. Sometimes the banners and achievements would be buried with the coffin, while on other occasions they would be retrieved for display in the church.[95] The now-empty hearse was also often left standing in the church for some months.

The Funeral Feast
On returning to the ancestral home, the newly created heir would furnish the mourners with a feast, often extremely lavish. The accounts compiled by Sir Charles Montague detailing the expenses incurred for the funeral of the Bishop of Winchester (1618) include twenty pounds spent on the following breathtaking quantities of game: 'plovers, two dozen pigeons, quailes, two dozen, and four turkeys, ten dozen chickens, three dozen capons, twelve dozen snipe, four dozen duck and two dozen partridges'.[96] It is even harder to conjure up a mental image that does justice to the abundance of food served at the obsequies of the Earl of Shrewsbury (1560):

> At the Castle was prepared a great dinner, that is to say, there was served from the dressors (besides my lord's services for his own board, which were three messes of meat) cccxx. messes, to all manner of people who seemed honest; having to every mess, eight dishes; that is to say, two boyled messes, four roast,

---

[93] Gittings, pp. 167–8.
[94] Gittings, p. 179.
[95] Gittings, p. 179; for an example of a Bishop's mitre being placed in a coffin (1556), see Cunnington and Lucas, p. 166.
[96] Bodleian Library, North MSS c. 29 fol. 183.

and two baked, meats: whereof one was venison. For there was killed for the same feast, fifty does and twenty-nine red deere.[97]

The purpose of such feasting was to reinforce the community hierarchy enacted in the funeral ceremony. By receiving his food the guests accepted the heir's accession and acknowledged their obligation towards him.[98] It has been intriguingly suggested that the funeral repast was originally called an 'averil', a term derived from 'heir ale' or 'succession ale', but this etymology is not confirmed by the Oxford English Dictionary.[99]

It was usual to over-provide at the funeral repast. At the obsequies of Lady Katherine Berkeley (1596), when the company sat down, 'the excesse herein appeared, when with suche dishes as for most part passed untouched at former tables, more then one thousand poore people were plentifully fed the same afternoone'.[100] Similarly, after dinner at the funeral of the Earl of Shrewsbury, 'the reversion of all the said meate was given to the poore, with dole of two pence a piece; with bread and drink great plenty'. The distribution of funeral food and dole money constituted a valuable source of charitable giving, at the same time reaffirming the social hierarchy that divided rich and poor.

---

[97] F. Peck ed., *Desiderata Curiosa*, 2 vols (London: Thomas Evans, 1779), II, 255.
[98] Gittings, p. 180; Stone (1965), p. 575; Ingram, Appendix VIII, p. 313.
[99] Bertram Puckle, *Funeral Customs: Their Origins and Development* (London: T. Werner Laurie, 1926), p. 104.
[100] Ingram, pp. 512–13.

CHAPTER TWO

Funeral Ritual and the Reformation

> The xxiij day of Marche was bered at sant tellens ser John Sentlow knyght, with ij haroldes of armes, master Clarenshux and master Somerset, with standard and penon, and cott and elmet, target and sword, but nodur cross nor prest, nor clarkes, but a sermon and after a salme of Davyd; and ij dosen of skochyons of armes.[1]

In his account of this 1559 funeral, Henry Machyn registers something of the impact of the Reformation on funeral ritual. This chapter explores that impact and seeks to establish to what extent the Reformation changed the funeral ritual experience. An appreciation of the interaction of reformist attitudes and funeral practices is a necessary prerequisite to understanding the Elizabethan and Jacobean royal funerals discussed in later chapters.

Church Interiors and Ritual Accessibility

> Finally, whereas there was wont to be a great partition between the choir and the body of the church, now it is either very small or none at all, to say the truth, altogether needless, sith the minister saith his service commonly in the body of the church, in a little tabernacle of wainscot provided for the purpose.[2]

So William Harrison summarized the changes that were made to church interiors as a result of the Reformation.[3] These alterations to performance space would have profound implications for funeral ritual.

The partition Harrison refers to was the rood screen. The fate of rood screens was various, some being torn down but official sanction being given for their retention. Where screens were taken down, funeral hearses and offering ceremonies located in the choir would have been made more visible to the

---

[1] Nichols (1848), p. 191.
[2] William Harrison, *The Description of England*, ed. by Georges Edeles (Ithaca, NY: Cornell University Press, 1968), p. 36; originally published in 1577 with a new enlarged edition in 1587.
[3] On the central importance of churches as social spaces, see Margaret Aston, *England's Iconoclasts, I: Laws Against Images* (Oxford: Oxford University Press, 1989), p. 16; and J. J. Scarisbrick, *The Reformation and the English People* (Oxford: Blackwell, 1984), p. 44.

congregation, perhaps increasing the sense of community involvement but reducing the mystery that surrounded the once partially-visible proceedings.[4]

Harrison's 'tabernacle of wainscot' is the pulpit, examples of which reformers busily set about erecting in churches all over the country. Pulpits were usually located in the nave but the actual rubric of the Elizabethan Church was ambivalent enough to give the Bishops wide powers of interpretation in determining the minister's position for the offices.[5] Pulpit position contributed to the enhanced status of the sermon, including the funeral sermon, and reflects a Protestant bias towards text-based and congregation-focused worship. It is important to remember that at this time the pulpit functioned as the chief means of communication between government and people, as the impact of the printing press had hardly penetrated beyond the intelligentsia.[6]

A third alteration to the church performance space, not mentioned by Harrison, was the change in form, name and position of the altar. Under Edward VI, the altar began to be replaced by a communion table and in the 1552 *Prayer Book* the word 'altar' is replaced with 'table', 'Lord's table' or 'God's board'.[7] The communion table had the advantage of manoeuvrability, facilitating its relocation to the west end of the chancel or the nave itself, where it stood facing the people. The 1559 Injunction stated that the communion table should stand in the place where the altar had stood, i.e. at the east wall of the chancel, and was to be covered with a cloth but was to be moved into the middle of the chancel to facilitate participation by the congregation who now took communion in both kinds. It seems likely that the communion table would have been similarly moved to the more accessible position for the funeral offering service.

Eamon Duffy has convincingly argued in favour of the participatory nature of late medieval worship citing the widespread celebration of mass at nave and chantry altars. There is no evidence, however, that the funeral offering took place anywhere other than at the main altar in the chancel. Nevertheless, repositioning the altar/communion table from the eastern extremity of the church to the centre of the chancel would have increased the communal aspect of the ritual, especially where the rood screen had been removed.[8]

Communion tables were not always moved, however, and both official rule and official example facilitated a variety of interpretations.[9] The altar in the private Chapel Royal stood permanently at the east end of the chancel but in

---

4   W. J. Sheils, *The English Reformation 1530–1570* (London: Longman, 1989), p. 52; G. W. O. Addleshaw and F. Etchells, *The Architectural Setting of Anglican Worship* (London: Faber & Faber, 1948), pp. 16–17, 25, 30–40.
5   Addleshaw, pp. 23–4, 31–2; Scarisbrick, pp. 163–4.
6   See Sheils (1989), p. 69; Ingram, Appendix VIII, p. 512. On pre-Reformation pulpits and sermons, see Duffy, pp. 57–8, 79.
7   Addleshaw, pp. 25–35; Sheils (1989), p. 45.
8   Duffy, pp. 110–16, 129, 474.
9   Addleshaw, pp. 108, 117, 126; Aston, p. 292, Strype, I, 401; Wiffen, *House of Russel*, cited by A. P. Stanley, *Memorials of Westminster Abbey* (London: Murray, 1869), p. 458.

Westminster Abbey, the church of state public ceremony, the High Altar was replaced by an oak communion table and probably placed at the foot of the steps. At funerals held in Westminster Abbey, including royal funerals, the juxtaposition of hearse and altar and the offering ceremony enacted between them would both have become more visible to the congregation.[10]

Funeral Ritual and Iconomachy

> Thou shalt not make unto thee any graven image, or any likeness of *anything* that *is* in heaven above, or that *is* in the earth beneath, or that *is* in the water under the earth.[11]

Great stress was laid upon the second commandment by the leaders of the Reformation and many early expressions of reformist zeal were characterized by iconoclastic behaviour.[12] The desire to eradicate all images, painted and sculpted, from worship had a major impact on the appearance of church interiors. William Harrison summed up the changes as follows:

> As for our churches themselves, bells and times of Morning and Evening Prayer remain as in times past, saving that all images, shrines, tabernacles, rood lofts, and monuments of idolatry are removed, taken down, and defaced; only the stories in glass windows excepted.[13]

All images, as William Harrison says, were removed, excepting the stained-glass windows, spared because they were part of the church fabric. Particularly significant for funeral rituals was the whitewashing out of the rood cross, a carved image of the crucifixion set against a background representation of the Last Judgement and located on the tympanum above the rood screen.[14] A Royal Order to ecclesiastical commissioners of 10 October 1561 stated that 'some convenient crest' should replace the old rood cross. In effect that 'convenient crest' was to be the royal arms (figure 6).[15] Although in some instances the royal

---

[10] Stanley (1869), p. 406. See also figure 10.
[11] Exodus 20.4, *The Geneva Bible* (London: Robert Barker, 1605).
[12] 'An Homily against Peril of Idolatry and superfluous Decking of Churches' was the longest Elizabethan homily; see John Griffiths, ed., *The Two Books of Homilies* (Oxford: Oxford University Press, 1859), pp. 167–278. John Jewel, Bishop of Salisbury, compared the Tudor monarchs with the Byzantine emperors who had officially adopted a policy of iconoclasm. See John Ayre, ed., *The Works of John Jewel, Bishop of Salisbury*, 4 vols (Cambridge: Cambridge University Press, 1845–50), II (1847), pp. 644–68.
[13] Harrison, p. 35. For records of changes to church interiors, see Anthony Palmer, ed., *Tudor Churchwarden's Accounts* (Braughing: Hertfordshire Record Society, 1985).
[14] This occurred, for example, in the Guild Chapel at Stratford. The whitewashing of walls had also taken place under Edward VI; see Aston, p. 257; Duffy, p. 480. For whitewashing under Elizabeth in 1561, see Strype, I, 274.
[15] Aston, p. 313; Scarisbrick, p. 174; Duffy, p. 485; John Phillips, *The Reformation of Images: Destruction of Art in England, 1535–1660* (Berkeley: University of California Press, 1973), p. 119.

arms were already in place, the practice was now a government-led country-wide policy.[16]

The rood cross was a focus of much late medieval Catholic ritual.[17] The effect of replacing it with the royal arms was profound. It symbolized the Tudor conjunction of Church and State in the monarch achieved by the Acts of Supremacy, imaging Thomas Cromwell's concept of caesaropapism. Appropriation of the paschal symbolism of resurrection and eternal life is also implicit in the royal arms, image of the perpetual state or Body Politic that outlives the individual monarch. This is one reason perhaps why the royal arms, symbol of Tudor dynastic kingship, were chosen rather than an image of an individual monarch. In addition, the use of a stylised heraldic representation diffused the impact of replacing the Christian focus of worship with a royal image, forestalling charges of idolatry.[18] Heraldry was an acceptable form of representational art in iconophobic post-Reformation England.

The eradication of images from church interiors had its corollary in processional rituals including those staged for funerals. Pre-Reformation ordinances specify that four banners of saints should be borne about the corpse in the funeral procession: a Banner of Trinity (head right); a Banner of Our Lady (head left); one of St George (foot right); and one of a Saint having special significance to the defunct (foot left).[19] Banners, including presumably those that had been borne in funeral processions, were burned by reformist zealots.[20] The banners of the saints had been borne alongside the bannerols depicting the family coats of arms of the defunct. Their removal inevitably lent a more chivalric bias to the central section of the funeral convoy, the chariot bearing the coffin.

The Abolition of Purgatory and Prayers for the Dead

The concept of purgatory was a relatively late addition to medieval eschatology but came to occupy a large place in religious practices of the fourteenth and fifteenth centuries.

The medieval Church had developed the notion of a purgatorial state, midway between heaven and hell, in response to an increased emphasis on a final Day of Judgement which threatened to consign a large portion of mankind to eternal damnation. Purgatory was officially recognized as part of Christian

---

16 Addleshaw, p. 35; Aston, p. 247. Note that a picture of Henry VII and the royal arms featured in the *Great Bible*. See Collinson (1988), p. 9. On image removal, see Duffy, pp. 439–40.
17 See chapter 5.
18 Duffy, pp. 40, 157–8; Addleshaw, p. 101; Sheils (1989), p. 20; Collinson (1988), p. 118.
19 BL, Egerton MS 2642 fol. 168; Harley, MS 1776 fol. 81; Additional MS 45131 fols 41v–42 and Bod., Ashmole MS fol. 193. Mourners in the Unton portrait bear banners displaying the Unton family arms and the cross of St George (Neill (1985), p. 160).
20 John Weever, *Ancient Funerall Monuments* (London: Thomas Harper, 1631), pp. 50, 117.

Funeral Ritual and the Reformation

doctrine at a Church Council of 1274.[21] The idea was that the soul remained in an intermediary state until it had been purged of sin. Intercessionary prayers offered on behalf of the deceased could accelerate the process of purgation but the most effective means of reducing the purgatorial sentence was to employ a priest to say masses for the dead.[22] The practice of saying intercessionary masses and prayers took off and an extensive network of chantries, fraternities and guilds was soon founded. Wills abounded in bequests aimed at speeding the progress of the soul through purgatory.[23] Henry VII established the chapel at Westminster Abbey that would subsequently bear his name and specified that no less than ten thousand masses should be said for his soul immediately after his death.[24]

The liturgy of the medieval church surrounded elite death and burial with extended prayer, reflecting the influence of the doctrine of purgatory.[25] Latin psalms and litanies were said at the deathbed and after death a service of commendation was held. Psalms, antiphons and collects were said at intervals while the body was prepared for burial. The corpse was borne to church to the accompaniment of further psalmody and the church services were protracted: the Office for the Dead (Evensong, Matins and Lauds); the Requiem Mass; a short form of commendation together with censing and sprinkling of the body with holy water; and finally the Burial Service. After the death of Lady Isabel Berkeley (d. 1516) her 'special officer and servant', Thomas Try, 'caused David Sawter to bee said continually untill the day of her burying, for as soon as oon company had seid, on other company of prests bygan, and so she was watched with prayer continually fro Wensday untill Monday'.[26]

Prayers for the deceased infiltrated all areas of worship in a cult of the dead that persisted right up to the Edwardian reign. Funeral memorials were celebrated on the seventh and thirtieth days after burial and on the first anniversary, the week's, month's, and year's 'mind' or remembrance. On these occasions the deceased was symbolically present in the form of a draped hearse surrounded by candles. Annually, All Souls' Day provided a focal point for the Church's liturgy of supplication for the dead. Further, the Offertory in high Mass on

---

[21] Howard Colvin, *Architecture and the After-Life* (London: Yale University Press, 1991), p. 153.

[22] Duffy refers to Purgatory as perhaps '*the* defining doctrine of late medieval Catholicism', pp. 8, 301, 338–78. On indulgences see ibid., pp. 287–98. On purgatory, see Ariès, pp. 107, 148, 153–4, 261, 306, 462–7; and T. S. R. Boase, *Death in the Middle Ages: Mortality, Judgement and Remembrance* (London: Thames & Hudson, 1972), pp. 46–71.

[23] Haigh (1975), p. 68. On devotions to the 'Five Wounds', see Duffy, pp. 248–58.

[24] Colvin, pp. 172–4, 253.

[25] W. H. Frere and F. Proctor, eds, *A New History of the Book of Common Prayer* (London: [n. pub.], 1902); G. Rowell, *The Liturgy of Christian Burial: An Introductory Survey of the Historical Development of Christian Burial Rites* (London: Alcuin Club, 1977), pp. 57–72.

[26] Ingram, pp. 507–9.

Sundays was preceded by the bidding of the bedes which involved praying for the parish dead.[27]

The reformist attack on intercessionary practices was partly based on the belief that they were a means for the church to exploit the people. The main objection, however, was doctrinal. At the Lutheran Synod of Homberg in October 1526, it was recommended that all mention of Purgatory should be avoided since 'at the moment of death all men passed inexorably to Heaven or Hell'.[28] There was general agreement amongst leaders of the Reformation that Purgatory should be abolished. The first official Protestant policy in England was the 1547 dissolution of the institutions that had grown up around the concept, the chantries and fraternities, but the authorities were slower to reform the liturgy.[29]

The Burial Liturgy

A Calvinist Prayer Book, which omitted all prayers for the dead and the psalms, as well as the Office for the Dead and the Eucharist, was not issued until 1552. The Elizabethan Prayer Book adopted in 1559 is identical to the 1552 version with the exception of a few small textual variations.[30] The Crown chose to ignore the fact that in 1552 Protestant opinion on central theological and liturgical issues had been in a state of flux. It is to the 1552 Prayer Book, therefore, that we need to turn to establish the Elizabethan burial service.

At the actual interment, the text was altered so that it involved a mere committal of the body, excluding the 1549 Prayer Book commendation of the soul and a short litany asking God to deliver souls from hell. The fact that nothing more could be done on behalf of the deceased was underlined in the 1552 Prayer Book by the instruction to the minister to turn away from the corpse at the moment of committal and to address instead the remaining mourners that surrounded the grave.[31] The shift in tone and doctrinal emphasis from the 1549 to the 1552 Prayer Books can be most clearly demonstrated, however, by direct comparison of the final prayer.[32]

---

[27] Duffy, pp. 124–6, 220, 327–8, 368–76, 441.
[28] Aston, p. 12; Rowell, pp. 74–5; Keith Thomas, *Religion and the Decline of Magic: Studies in Popular Beliefs in Sixteenth-Century England* (London: Penguin Books, 1971), p. 702.
[29] Duffy, p. 454.
[30] On the programme for restoring the Edwardian religious order at the 1559 Parliament, see MacCaffrey, pp. 54–9, 299; and Norman L. Jones, *Faith by Statute: Parliament and the Settlement of Religion in 1559* (London: Royal Historical Society, 1982).
[31] Duffy, p. 475.
[32] Edward Cardwell, ed., *The Two Books of Common Prayer, [...] of Edward Sixth: Compared With Each Other* (Oxford: Oxford University Press, 1841), pp. 381–2. The 1549 version is on the left.

O Lord, with whom do live the spirits of them that be dead, and in whom the souls of them that be elected, after they be delivered from the burden of the flesh, be in joy and felicity; *Grant unto this thy servant, that the sins which he committed in this world be not imputed unto him; but that he, escaping the gates of hell, and pains of eternal darkness, may ever dwell in the region of light,* with Abraham, Isaac and Jacob, in the place where is no weeping and sorrow, nor heaviness; and when that dreadful day of the general resurrection shall come, *make him to rise also with the just and righteous, and receive this body again to glory,* then made pure and incorruptible. *Set him on the right hand of thy son Jesus Christ,* among thy holy and elect, that then he may hear with them these most sweet and comfortable words, Come to me, ye blessed of my Father, possess the kingdom which hath been prepared for you from the beginning of the world. *Grant this, we beseech thee, O merciful Father, through Jesus Christ our Mediator and Redeemer.* Amen.

Almighty God, with whom do live the spirits of them that depart hence in the Lord, and in whom the souls of them that be elected, after they be delivered from the burden of the flesh, be in joy and felicity; *We give thee hearty thanks, for that it hath pleased thee to deliver this N. our brother out of the miseries of this sinful world; beseeching thee, that it may please thee, of thy gracious goodness, shortly to accomplish the number of thine elect, and to haste thy kingdom;* that we, with this our brother, and all other departed in the true faith of thy holy name, may have our perfect consummations and bliss, both in body and soul, in thy eternal and everlasting glory. Amen.

The italics are mine and indicate the ways in which the text was modified to remove all hint of intercession on behalf of the soul of the deceased in the 1552 Prayer Book. In line with the doctrine of predestination the mourners rather thank God for already taking the soul of their elect brother to Him. The only remnant of intercession comes in the form of a petition that God will hasten the arrival of the kingdom of the elect or, in other words, the Second Coming.[33]

---

[33] Gittings, pp. 40–2; Rowell, p. 86.

The Theatre of Death

Priests, Incense, Candles and Torches: The Fabric of Intercession

While the ecclesiastical community retained a role in the post-Reformation funeral procession with the link between prayer and intercession broken, their numbers were greatly reduced. In the pre-Reformation procession of Lady Isabel Berkeley (d. 1516) there appeared 'the orders of freers wyght and gray, with their crosses' and 'prests to the number of oon C and more which went with their crosses next before the hersse'.[34] The Dissolution Acts of 1536 and 1539 inevitably meant that monks and friars disappeared from funeral processions. Beadsmen, such as those that had taken part in the funeral of the Duke of Norfolk (1524), met the same fate.[35] The poor were, however, retained despite the fact that their presence was originally associated with relieving the pains of purgatory. Their non-ecclesiastical status made the justification for their participation more easily transmuted into one of social benefaction.[36]

With the reduction in the numbers of the clergy went a diminution in their role. At Henry VIII's funeral the mini-procession which conveyed the coffin into the funeral chariot was dominated by bishops who preceded the coffin, 'two and two in order, saying their prayers'. When James I's coffin was transferred into the funeral chariot that would transport it from Theobalds to Denmark House, the ceremony was effected entirely by officers of the College of Arms.[37] The clergy's loss of status was underlined by modifications made to liturgical dress. Before the Reformation priests had worn special vestments for Requiem masses, such as the 'vestiment sengle du noir baudekyn' recorded in the church inventory for St Martin's, Ludgate at around 1400 (figure 7).[38] The 1552 Prayer Book determined that these should be replaced by plain surplices.[39] The magnificent dress of the heralds would now monopolize the attention of onlookers.

Before the Reformation it had been customary for the corpse to be censed on arrival at the west door of the church, as well as at intervals throughout the service: during the dirige, the magnificat, the benedictus, the burial and the

---

[34] Ingram, Appendix VIII, pp. 508–9.
[35] Gittings, p. 29. 'Innocents' are also mentioned in the Henry VII ordinance for funerals of noblemen but do not occur in later funerals; see BL, Cotton MSS, Julius B XII, fol. 6.
[36] Duffy, pp. 358–62, 505, 510.
[37] Gittings, pp. 224–5.
[38] See E. S. Dewick, 'On An Inventory of Church Goods Belonging to the Parish of St Martin, Ludgate', *St. Paul's Ecclesiological Society*, 5 (1905), 117–28 (p. 124).
[39] Sheils (1989), p. 45; Duffy, pp. 474, 484; Harrison, pp. 36–7; Thomas, p. 327. Martin Bucer's *A brief Discourse against the outward Apparel and ministering Garments of the Popish Church* (1565) offers some evidence for vestment retention but he objected to all forms of ecclesiastical dress and could have simply been referring to the surplice. See also Strype, II, 553–5; and, on the parliamentary bill against vestments, see MacCaffrey, pp. 311–12.

requiem, after the gospel.⁴⁰ With the religious reforms censing largely died out.⁴¹ The exclusion of olfactory stimulation reduced the sensual appeal of the funeral procession, limiting it to visual and aural modes of experience.

Candles had been an integral part of the pre-Reformation hearse. The original intention may have been to place one candle at each of the four corners of hearse, each candle bearing a shield of arms which represented one of the four quarters of the defunct's inherited nobility.⁴² Often, however, many more candles were employed and the catafalque was frequently described as 'a goodly hersse of wax'.⁴³ The French term for hearse, *chapelle ardente*, reflects the extent to which the candles had become a central feature of its physical structure (figure 8).

Candles were deemed to have an apotropaic power, that is they could charm away evil influence. In addition, they had a distinct intercessionary resonance in pre-Reformation worship. It was not unusual for the candles burnt by coffins to be moved to an altar or image after the funeral. Often testators specified that the candles should burn around the altar at the sacring time. Candles might also be placed around a tomb on the anniversary of death.⁴⁴ It is not surprising, therefore, that candles were the object of ritual reform. In 1547 an injunction on the use of candles was used to prevent them being lit around corpses when they were brought into church and the practice of adorning the hearse with candles seems to have completely disappeared under Elizabeth, at least in London.⁴⁵ Any mention of candles or wax is notably absent from Machyn's accounts of funerals after the Elizabethan accession.⁴⁶ In other regions, however, the use of candles seems to have persisted longer as Bishop Bentham of Coventry and Lichfield's 1565 injunction indicates:

---

40 CA I Series MS XIV, fols 75–7. BL, Egerton MSS, 2642 fol. 168; Rowell, p. 66; Sandford, p. 440.
41 Duffy asserts that many clergy in the 1560s and 1570s sprinkled corpses or placed crosses in their hands but gives no supporting evidence, p. 598. Incense appears to have been used at St Mary's, Cambridge from 1559 to 1575, possibly at funerals; see J. Charles Cox, *Churchwarden's Accounts From the Fourteenth Century to the Close of the Seventeenth Century* (London: Methuen, 1913), p. 184. As Jack Scarisbrick pointed out to me, this is strange as Cambridge was strongly Calvinist during this period and, if so, must have been in defiance of the rules.
42 Malcolm Vale, *War and Chivalry: Warfare and Aristocratic Culture in England, France and Burgundy at the End of the Middle Ages* (London: Duckworth, 1981), p. 90 citing BN, MS fr. 1280 fol. 131v: an anonymous chivalric treatise written for Louis de Bruges in 1481. Candles were also used during the pre-funeral vigil; see figure 8.
43 See Machyn's account of the funeral of the Duke of Norfolk (1554) in Framlingham Church, Nichols (1848), p. 70. For other examples, see ibid., pp. 81, 189.
44 Cox (1913), pp. 160–3; Puckle, p. 78; Duffy, pp. 96, 361. Candles similarly burned before the empty sepulchre, the symbol of Christ's tomb, in Easter week, ibid., p. 30.
45 Duffy, p. 462. The Ten Articles (1536) had allowed for the use of candles as symbols of the light of Christ rather than for apotropaic purposes, ibid., p. 394.
46 See for example the funeral of the Earl of Huntingdon (1560), Nichols (1848), p. 239 and the Countess of Bath (January 1561–2), ibid., p. 275.

> Away with your lights at the burial of the dead, and instead therof exhort them duly to receive the light of the Gospel, which is the true light [. . . Ensure] that you do not make the communion a Mass of Requiem for lucre and gain, persuading the people to pray for the dead, but rather call upon them daily to live godly in this life.[47]

The lighting of candles around the corpse was also constantly noted in episcopal visitations: clear evidence of their continued widespread use. Francis Tate's assertion, made in 1600, that 'the custom of burning candles be now growen into disuse, being thought superstitious' may not have been entirely true.[48]

The reformists' discomfort with candle-light extended to the use of torches, coarse forms of taper mixed with resin.[49] Pre-Reformation funeral processions had abounded in torchlight (figure 9). *The ordering of a Funerall for a noble person in Henry 7 time* includes: 'Item as many torches as the saide estate wax of yeres of age'.[50] The actual numbers used often vastly exceeded this limiting formula, however, making for a much more magnificent display. At the funeral of Lady Isabel Berkeley (1516) two hundred torches were borne by members of thirty-three 'crafts'.[51]

Early in her reign Elizabeth herself spoke out against the use of torches, publicly declaring it a superstitious practice by contemptuously dismissing the monks that met the royal procession with torches at the opening of parliament on 25 January 1559; 'Away with these torches, for we see very well', she declared. The Homily against idolatry was later to affirm the royal attitude, stating that it was 'ever a proverb of foolishness, to light a candle at noon-time'.[52]

The Funeral Offering Ritual and Intercessionary Practices

The funeral offering ritual is fraught with intercessionary resonance and one would have expected it to be a prime target for reform. Mervyn James has indeed suggested that the offering ritual was too controversial to be practised in the period immediately following the Elizabethan settlement and was not reintroduced until later in the reign. Further, he argues that on its reintroduction the

---

[47] Gittings, p. 44; Duffy, p. 572.
[48] Duffy, p. 577. Watch candles were still used; see Tate, I, 216.
[49] Cox (1913), p. 160.
[50] BL, Cotton MSS, Julius B XII, fols 5–6. See also BL, Additional MS 45131, fols 41v–42.
[51] Ingram, Appendix VIII, p. 508.
[52] Calendar of State Papers, Venice (CSPV): VII (1558–80), 22–3; *Sermons or Homilies appointed to be Read in Churches in the Time of Elizabeth* (London: Prayer-Book and Homily Society, 1817), pp. 157–247 (p. 211). See also Susan Brigden, *London and the Reformation* (Oxford: Clarendon Press, 1989), p. 396; and MacCaffrey, p. 51.

offering was practised in a secularized context that was chivalric or heroic rather than religious.[53]

James's comments come in the context of a comparative discussion of the funerals of Lord Dacre (15 December 1563) and Thomas, Lord Wharton (22 September 1568).[54] James's main interest is in the shifting social and political scene of Tudor England, apparent in the identity of the mourners. He contrasts the regional feudal household of a prominent Catholic family with the emergent gentry bureaucracy of the Elizabethan regime who had, he argues, no interest in preserving traditional funeral rites.[55] In the Dacre funeral procession, the usual three heralds were reduced to two and only the coat of arms was displayed, the helm sword and target being omitted. The achievements were offered during the church service but it is not apparent exactly when. Only one herald was present at the Wharton funeral and it is not clear if even the Baron's coat of arms was displayed in the procession. More significantly, no offering ceremony is mentioned in the account.

On the basis of this rather limited evidence James suggests that the traditional offering ceremony was difficult to reconcile with the Burial Service for the Dead in the 1559 Prayer Book because of its sensitive associations with the intercessionary funeral mass. James further speculates that the Dacre funeral retained only a vestige of the offering ritual, the simple laying of the achievements on the communion table. He goes on to argue that the Whartons, in contrast, abandoned the offering ceremony because they had no family tradition of heraldic funeral ritual to maintain.

I take issue with James's analysis in several ways, firstly disagreeing with his assertion that the offering ritual disappeared in the early years of Elizabeth's rule. Accounts of funerals with details of offering rituals survive for this period and throughout the reign: the Earl of Shrewsbury (1560); Lord Dacre (1563); the Earl of Derby (1572); the 'Instructions for the funeral of a Countess' (1576) which refer to the funeral of the Countess of Huntingdon; Lady Lumley (1578); John Allot (1591); Lady Katherine Berkeley (1596). The funeral offering continued to be practised into the Jacobean period. Examples include Henry Cock of Hertford (1610); and Gilbert, Earl of Salop, at Sheffield (1616). Clearer evidence that the Elizabethan government did not clamp down on funeral offerings comes from the fact that they were staged at the official London

---

[53] James (1986), pp. 176–87. Gittings recognizes that the offering was the central episode of elite funeral ritual but does not investigate it fully in the context of the Reformation, simply referring to its anachronistic survival in post-Reformation funerals, pp. 178–9.

[54] Bod., Ashmole MS 836 fols 181–2, 189–91.

[55] The great Lord Dacre, whose family had ruled the West March almost from the beginning of the Tudor period, is contrasted with Lord Wharton, first Baron, a man of 'modest gentry stock settled at Wharton in Westmorland' who, through service to the crown had risen to a peerage and extensive estates; see James, pp. 181–3. On Leonard Dacre's involvement in the Northern rebellion, see MacCaffrey, p. 126.

obsequies for the French Kings Henry II (1559) and Charles IX (1574).[56] They also occurred at the Sidney funeral in 1587 which was financed by Walsingham. These occasions effectively gave royal sanction to funeral offering rituals.

Where offering rituals are not mentioned in surviving records it does not necessarily follow that they were not enacted. Two separate manuscript accounts of Queen Anne of Denmark's funeral are extant. The College of Arms' version does not mention a funeral offering but the British Library manuscript version does.[57] Heralds, who kept most of the records, were primarily concerned with their fees together with identification of the main participants whom they needed to rank and order. Their objectives would normally be met in an account of the funeral procession and not require repetition in a description of the offering. The offering had a set form and did not need detailing on each occasion.

References to the achievements and materials for the construction of a hearse are more numerous than descriptions of offering rituals. The achievements could have been used exclusively in the procession but the construction of a hearse supports my contention that the practice of offering rituals was extensive. A hearse would seem to have been superfluous if no offering ceremony was to take place.

There is, however, some evidence to suggest that the funeral offering was indeed officially regarded as Catholic and inappropriate or illegal. In a pronouncement made in 1583 by Marmaduke Middleton, Bishop of St David's, in which he listed a large collection of popish abuses, offerings at funerals were included. Middleton was a red-hot Protestant with strong iconoclastic propensities. His colleague, Anthony Gilby, one of the most illiberal of the Protestant reformers, also labelled offerings at funerals a popish abuse.[58] The very fact that both Middleton and Gilby felt the need to comment indicates, however, that offerings were still common practice in the 1580s.

Not only did the offering ritual survive but it survived in its pre-Reformation form. The offering at the Dacre funeral is virtually the same as the pre-Reformation offering ritual form, an example of which is given in the account of the offering at the funeral of Richard Neville, Earl of Salisbury, and his son, Sir Thomas, at Bisham, on 15 February 1462/3. The only way in which the offering ritual appears to have been modified is that at the Salisbury funeral it was the bishop who received the achievements from the mourners and then presented them to the heir. At the Dacre funeral the chief mourner seems to have received them directly from the assistant mourners, the minister merely stands alongside. This appears to signal a reduced role for the clergy but,

---

56 On the English obsequies for Henry II, see CSPF (1588–9), 458–9, 471–7; 547–8.
57 CA, Nayler, pp. 1–24; BL, Harley MS 5176 fol. 325.
58 See Gittings, p. 44; F. O. White, *Lives of the Elizabethan Bishops of the Anglican Church* (London: Skeffington, 1898), pp. 253–9; and Anthony Gilby, *A pleasant dialogue* (London: [n. pub.], 1581), Appendix, p. 2.

significantly, in post-Reformation funerals where there was no legitimate heir present to receive the achievements, the minister continued to fulfil that role.[59] Where the dynastic message was precluded it was not deemed inappropriate for the clergy to step in and play a larger part.

If an heir did participate, the chief personnel of the funeral ritual in effect shifted towards the secular, yet the choreography of the funeral ritual remained the same. Even where the chief mourner received the hatchments directly, they were still offered at the altar or communion table, maintaining the religious focus of the proceedings. More surprisingly, the offering of the 'mass penny', money presented to the church on behalf of the defunct, originally to pay for masses, was retained. The clear intercessionary connotations of this practice were apparently no bar to its continued use under Elizabeth.[60]

The traditional thirty-day period during which the hearse remained standing in the church choir also persisted, despite its origins in the trental mass which traditionally signalled the end of the primary phase of intercessionary prayer in pre-Reformation obsequies.[61]

Part of the reason why the funeral offering ritual was not a prime target of reform may relate to the fact that its religious content was rooted in symbolic movement, or choreography, rather than iconography.[62] As I have demonstrated, it was the avoidance of idolatry that governed a large part of the reform of churches and church ceremony. All the images used in the offering ceremony are heraldic rather than religious, abstract symbols rather than anthropoid representations: veneration of the saints was peripheral to the cult of the dead. Intercessionary practices were usually subject to official censure, but especially so where, as in the case of torches and candles, they overlapped with the idolatrous. The symbolic movements of the offering ceremony were largely ignored. Choreography was more acceptable, or less dangerous, than iconography.

It is true that the symbolism and performance setting of the offering ritual was modified in various ways. With the disappearance of candles, coats of arms and escutcheons came to be the only adornments on the funeral hearse. The processional banners of the saints, formerly placed at the four corners for the church services, were no longer used.[63] Loss of these religious trappings sharpened the secular focus of the hearse. This shift in tone has, however, been exaggerated and the whole post-Reformation funeral service has been loosely described in terms of a process of 'secularization'. Gittings, for example, sees

---

[59] Wagner (1967), pp. 106–7; BL, Ashmole MS 836 fol. 182. See the funeral offering of Mary Queen of Scots, in chapter 4.
[60] Bod., Ashmole MS 857 fol. 192; Scarisbrick, p. 20.
[61] Harvey and Mortimer, p. 5.
[62] These symbolic movements could be termed kinetic art or the 'kinesic' codes of theatre; see Elam, pp. 49–50.
[63] BL, Ashmole MS 857 fol. 192.

the funeral ritual undergoing a continued process of secularization initiated by the Reformation and leading to the highly secular funeral occasions of the eighteenth century.[64] Such a description ignores the continuity of the core movements of the offering ritual. In addition, while the symbolism of the hearse and tympanum may have been 'secularized', they formed only part of the focal structure of the offering ritual. The other focus, the altar, remained spiritual and was arguably the more dominant since it was there that the succession was ritually enacted (figure 11).[65] The removal of chantries, statues, wall-paintings and nave altars reduced the multifocality which had characterized the medieval church. The blend of the religious and secular of the funeral service was, however, maintained and indeed tightened in the post-Reformation church. Apart from this symbolic heightening, the offering ceremony, the ritual centre of the heraldic medieval funeral, continued in its pre-Reformation form. Paradoxically, where rood screens were removed and/or communion tables moved it became more visible and thus a more familiar ritual form.

It might still be argued that the term 'secularization' could be applied to the hearse adornments and to the funeral procession, located, as it was, outside the church. It would be wrong to suggest, however, that the 'secular' was a new element of post-Reformation funeral ritual or, with Mervyn James, to set an Elizabethan 'chivalric' offering ceremony in opposition to the medieval religious version. The medieval funeral ceremony was itself chivalric in origin, and chivalry and religion are far from being antithetical.

Funerals, Chivalry and 'Secularization'

The heraldic funeral developed into an intricate and flourishing ritual in the fourteenth and fifteenth centuries, partly as a result of the rise of heralds as a professional group but also in response to the changing ritual requirements of the chivalric class.[66] As Maurice Keen has shown, 'blood' became the primary qualification for knighthood in the late thirteenth century. The logical consequence for ritual was a decline in the practice of the formal dubbing ceremony. Instead a ceremony was needed that would demonstrate the continuity of the nobility in blood lineage through the paternal line. I suggest that the heraldic funeral, with its central offering ceremony functioning as a ritualized succession, took over as the dominant rite of chivalry and of the elite. The heraldic

---

64 Gittings, pp. 56–7. Neill also writes rather misleadingly of an 'antiquarian feudalism' which characterized Renaissance royal funerals; see Neill (1985), p. 154.
65 See discussion in chapter 1. Vale agrees with this perception of continuity in funeral practice, pp. 90–3. For an offering ritual that took place at a 'communion borde' see the funeral of Thomas Howard, BL, Additional MS 14417 fol. 23b.
66 See Maurice Keen, *Chivalry* (New Haven: Yale University Press, 1984) to which I am much indebted in the following discussion; and Vale, pp. 92–3.

bannerols, with their record of family descent, underlined this role. The arms multiply displayed in both procession and church service were family insignia to which most men had become entitled as a result of heredity not because they had been dubbed as knights. The heraldic funeral was not a replacement ritual: dubbings to knighthood and knightly orders would continue to flourish well into the sixteenth century and beyond. The wider practice of heraldic funeral rituals meant, however, that they were to have greater significance.[67]

The social and secular aspects of the medieval heraldic funeral were always inseparable from the religious. Malcolm Vale has aptly called the funeral ceremony 'perhaps the quintessential late medieval expression of the fundamental and complementary relationship between sacred and profane'.[68] As in the wider world of chivalry, of which the funeral ritual was a part, 'martial, aristocratic and Christian elements were fused together'.[69] The heraldic funeral celebrated the social status of the deceased in this life as well as contributing to the fate of his soul in the next. The ecclesiastics and heralds who took part enjoyed a largely symbiotic relationship in the pre-Reformation funeral ritual, disturbed only by occasional wrangles over the division of funeral perquisites.[70]

The secular elements of the heraldic funeral, achievements, escutcheons of arms, heralds and funeral horses were crucial elements of the original medieval ritual form. Achievements, banners, heralds and war-horses are all present in the earliest surviving accounts of funeral rituals. In January 1269, for example, William de Beauchamp willed that a 'barbed horse [. . .] with warlike equipment' should precede his corpse in his funeral procession.[71] The only 'new' secular element of the Elizabethan funeral was royal, the royal arms which had replaced the rood cross on the tympanum. Positioned in a line of sight above the hearse they provided the congregation with a constantly-visible seal of state approval on all church services including the ritual proceedings of aristocratic succession. In churches where the communion table had been moved to the chancel steps, or where the rood screen had been dismantled, this symbol of state power would preside over the dual aspects of the offering ritual, religious and secular.

The royal arms had long since become a part of the funeral processions,

---

[67] Elizabethan chivalric rituals included, at an exalted level, the Garter processions; see Strong (1987), pp. 164–85. My argument does not constitute a denial of the 'revival' of chivalry as far as Elizabethan and Jacobean court display was concerned. On such court display, see Arthur B. Ferguson, *The Chivalric Revival in Renaissance England* (London: Associated University Presses, 1986); and Strong (1987), pp. 129–85.
[68] Vale, p. 91.
[69] Keen, pp. 2–3, 16–17, 53–7.
[70] Tate, I, 205. On heralds' rights to funeral perquisites, see BL, Harley MS 6064 fol. 109.
[71] M. H. Bloxham, *Fragmentaria Sepulchralia: A Glimpse of the Sepulchral and Early Monumental Remains of Great Britain* (Oxford: Oxford University Press, 1840–50), p. 132 cited by Vale, p. 89.

embroidered, as they were, on the tabards of the heralds (figure 1).[72] At funerals prior to their incorporation by Richard III, the King's heralds may have regularly worn the arms of the defunct. Such was the case at the funeral of the Earl of Salisbury in 1462/3. In the fifteenth century it had been quite common for individual members of the nobility to keep their own private officers of arms, heralds and pursuivants but this practice had declined by the sixteenth century.[73] At funerals in the early Tudor period it was the royal arms displayed on the tabards of the Kings at Arms that dominated. The practice at Derby's funeral, where only Lancaster herald wore the arms of the defunct and all the other Officers of Arms, who marched before the coffin, bore the royal coat, was by then well-established. The state was appropriating funeral ritual well before the Reformation.

Royal Appropriation and the Resilience of Funeral Ritual

The royal appropriation of the funeral ritual provides one of the reasons why its symbolic centre, the offering ceremony, was permitted to retain its pre-Reformation form despite bearing a marked intercessionary resonance. The ritual enactment of aristocratic succession, once placed within the context of a monarchical hierarchy, served the interests of the state.

The dominant presence of the royal arms in both procession and church services is not the only signal of royal interest in and approval of the heraldic funeral ceremony. Further evidence comes from the fact that on a number of occasions Queen Elizabeth and Lord Burghley interfered in the preparations of heraldic funerals, insisting on a level of pomp appropriate to the rank of the deceased. Where her own family was concerned the Queen even helped to foot the bill rather than allow a funeral to occur without the appropriate level of ceremonial. The sum of £1,047 6s. 1½d. was paid for the funeral of her cousin, Henry, Lord Hunsdon, in 1596, 'which was honourably solemnized according to the Queens Command, he dying Intestate'.[74]

On other occasions, pressure was put upon executors to comply with the requirements of the College of Arms which acted as royal agent. In her 1568 Visitation letter to Clarenceux, Elizabeth urged the herald to 'reform and controul such as at any Funerals should wear any Mourning Apparel, as Gowns, Hoods, Tippets, contrary to the Order limited in the time of King Henry VII in any other sort than to their States did appertain'.[75] Misappropriation of the

---

[72] Cunnington and Lucas, p. 207.
[73] Wagner (1978), p. 79; Maclagan, p. 37.
[74] BL, Harley MS 3881 fols 56, 59; BL, Lansdowne MS 82 fol. 123; BL, Harley MS 4774 fol. 128. Hunsdon was the son of Mary Boleyn and William Cary. The Queen also paid for the funerals of Lady Catherine Knollys (1569) (see Gittings, pp. 182–3, and Stone (1965), pp. 578–9), and William Parr (1571), brother of Catherine Parr, who is buried at St Mary's, Warwick.
[75] Strype, I, 558.

trappings of funeral pageantry seems to have been happening long before Elizabeth's reign. A manuscript from the papers of Thomas Wriothesley, Garter King of Arms from 1505–34, proclaims:

> That there ought noo personne to sette up at any interrement or at any other tyme any cottys of armes helmet crest target with otther the appartenances as banner or pennon or rayles about the hers without the knowledge and assent of the ffurst king of armes or the king of armes of the province or their mareschalles by cause of the dew ordering of every noble personne according to their estates and degrees upon payne of the pulling downe and losse of the saide thinge soo sette up and further to be punished by the king his connestable or mareschall or by their courte for the mysusing and exercising of the said office by the king and his predecesseurs and connestables to his king of armes and depputes commytted and graunted.[76]

The evidence suggests, however, that, despite the efforts of the Crown and its agents, such abuses became more widespread and frequent as the century progressed.

Elizabethan Crown intervention might also result in the relocation of a funeral ceremony. With increasing numbers of aristocrats gravitating towards the capital, the trend was for fewer heraldic funerals to be staged in the provinces. It was in the interests of the monarchy, however, to ensure that these regional displays of hierarchical order continued. When his father died in 1597, Henry, Lord Cobham, wanted to have a London funeral. Lord Burghley intervened, however, as this letter from Cobham to Burghley's son, Sir Robert Cecil illustrates:

> I could have wished your father would have allowed [...] my father's funeral to have been performed at London [...] for neither house nor the church is fit for the performing of it here. Your father's will amongst us must stand for law without any further dispute, otherwise this place is so unmeet for it, as whereas I had hoped to have had honour in burying of my father, I shall now receive shame.

Cobham bowed to the wishes of the state and performed his father's funeral in Kent.[77] Similarly, Sir Nicholas Bacon (d. 1578) recognized that the Queen had ultimate authority over the location of his burial, writing in his will, 'And as for my Body, I commit the same to be buried where the Queen's Majesty shall think most meet and convenient'.[78]

The continuity of aristocratic power enacted in the offering ritual and affirmation of society's hierarchical order in the funeral procession, both set in the context of the ultimate power of the monarchy, made heraldic funerals valuable instruments of state propaganda. The funeral procession would, in many areas, have been the only surviving parish procession. Parish processions

---

[76] BL, Additional MS 45, 131 fol. 196; cited by Strickland, p. 22.
[77] Historical Manuscripts Commission, *Salisbury MSS* Series 9, VII, 117.
[78] Strype, II, 547.

had figured large in late medieval Catholicism, preceding Sunday Mass and each major festival. In addition, guild processions had been held on feast days. While civic secular processions, such as mayoral inaugurations, continued, all religious processions were abolished in the 1547 Injunctions. The funeral procession, in many areas, was now unique in enacting social order and hierarchy.[79] While the size of the peerage remained constant, the Elizabethan period saw a vast increase in the number of armigerous families as gentry sought coats of arms, the 'visible and royally bestowed marks of distinction'.[80] Thus the numbers of families entitled to the heraldic funeral display of order and continuity grew.

The statements of social hierarchy made in the procession were reinforced inside the church, particularly through pewing, an alteration to church interiors that was accelerated by the Reformation, and brought social hierarchy into the church. Pews directed the worshippers' attention towards the Holy Table but, when congregational eyes strayed upwards, it was the depiction of the royal arms that would hold their gaze.[81]

The government's interest in funeral ritual reflects its general recognition of the social value of religious ritual and ceremony. Secretary of State, William Cecil, saw that the crux of religious controversy was not 'doctrine, but [...] rites and ceremonies'.[82] Archbishop Jewel (1522–71), whose *Apologia* (1562) was a key document in establishing the Anglican position, was convinced that the 'scenic apparatus' of worship was, as Aston puts it, 'more striking and more perceptible to most than specific or subtle alterations in the content of belief'.[83] Richard Hooker similarly writes of the 'visible signes' which are 'fittest to make a deep and lasting impression'.[84]

The ambiguity of the government position in relation to changes affecting ceremonial behaviour, already noted in the guidelines on the position of communion table and pulpit and on retention of the rood screen, is also apparent in official pronouncements on funeral ritual practice. The extreme Calvinist position which forbade prayers, singing and sermons was rejected.[85]

---

[79] Duffy, p. 451. Rogationtide boundary processions were retained in the 1559 Injunctions, ibid., p. 568. On the functions of processions, see discussion in chapter 1.

[80] MacCaffrey, pp. 356, 364.

[81] Addleshaw, p. 87; Scarisbrick, p. 164; Aston, p. 332; Collinson, p. 55. There is no evidence of general pewing until the fifteenth century. Previously there had been benches around the walls and piers for the aged and the infirm. The majority of the congregation would stand if not kneeling, Cox, (1913), p. 186.

[82] The comment was made in a letter to William Whittingham in 1562; see M. A. E. Green, ed., *Life of Mr William Whittingham, Dean of Durham* (Camden Miscellany 6, 1871), p. 16, cited by Aston, p. 12. Cecil would become Lord Treasurer in 1572; MacCaffrey, p. 169.

[83] Aston, p. 12. Jewel's phrase 'scenic apparatus' appears in a letter to Peter Matyr from early in Elizabeth's reign, 'Agitur nunc de sacro et scenico apparatu', Ayre, pp. 1209–11.

[84] See *The Works of Richard Hooker*, ed. by W. Speed Hill and others, 3 vols (London: Harvard University Press, 1977–90), I (1977), 274.

[85] Rowell, p. 82; Colvin, p. 296. The Calvinist position is reflected in John Knox's *Genevan*

Instead the government followed Luther who, believing that the masses were most moved by the 'surface displays' of ceremony, permitted funeral services with processions and singing.[86] The majority of Elizabethan funeral processions seem to have included singing men and boys from church or private chapel choirs.[87] Psalm-singing in English replaced the chanting of Latin prayers for the dead and organs were silenced, though few were taken down.[88] Despite superstitious associations with the driving out of evil and even the raising of the dead, bell-ringing, an important feature of the medieval funeral, was also retained.[89] The extensive ringing that had taken place at pre-Reformation funerals, such as that of Lady Isabel Berkeley (d. 1516) when a total of 156 peals was rung at various locations, was, however, stopped.[90] Yet the government recognized the social value of a bell being rung to mark the death of a member of the community and the Bishop's *Interpretations* (1561) allowed one short peal to be tolled before and after both death and burial. Thus an aural religious element was retained in the post-Reformation funeral.[91]

Yet, as the officially-permitted continuity of funeral ritual indicates, the Elizabethan government well understood that it was changes to the church ritual and furniture that were the most divisive and controversial, not changes to the liturgy. Traditionally, parishioners invested much both emotionally and financially in the ceremony and fabric of their churches and, sometimes, were prepared to defend them in such hostile reactions to reform as the Western Rising of 1549.[92] On that occasion the demands of the rebels included the restoration of processions and the cult of the dead.[93] The populace had been wholly unprepared for the radical changes imposed on religious life by Elizabeth's three royal predecessors. Liturgical change may have been less inflammatory, but the government still trod carefully, maintaining the ambiguity of its stance already demonstrated with respect to ritual. While, as we have seen, all prayers for the dead were removed from the Elizabeth Prayer Book and

---

Service Book (1556) and in the Scottish *Book of Discipline* (1560) which 'judged it best, that neither singing nor reading be at the burial'.

[86] Joroslav Pelikan, ed., *Luther's Works* (Saint Louis, Mo: Concordia, 1955–8), IX (1955), 7; cited by Aston, p. 13.

[87] Examples include the processions of Francis Talbot (1560); Margaret, Duchess of Norfolk (1563); the Earl of Derby (1572); Henry Sidney (1586); and Thomas Egerton (1599).

[88] One example is that of St Martin's, Leicester which was removed in 1562–3; see Cox (1913), p. 183; Aston, p. 335; Duffy, p. 465.

[89] Weever, p. 122; Thomas, pp. 34–6, 59–60, 85; Scarisbrick, pp. 44–5; Gilby, Appendix, p. 2.

[90] Ingram, Appendix VIII, p. 508.

[91] Bell-ringing was not acceptable to all, see Philip Henry, *Diaries and Letters 1631–96*, ed. by M. H. Lee (London: [n. pub.], 1882), p. 116.

[92] Sheils (1989), p. 41; Aston, p. 11. On struggles over ceremonies, see Duffy, p. 442.

[93] Duffy, pp. 131–2, 466; O'Day, pp. 187–8. On the demands of the rebels of the Northern Rebellion in 1569 for celebration of mass in Durham Cathedral, see MacCaffrey, pp. 128–33.

the 1560 Latin Primer, the 1559 Elizabethan Primer, or Book of Hours, paradoxically contained distinct intercessionary prayers, and praying for the dead was never expressly forbidden.[94]

In a letter to Archbishop Parker of Canterbury of January 1565, Elizabeth made it clear that she regarded religious uniformity as a mainstay of successful government and that 'varieties and novelties not only in opinions but in external ceremonies and rites' were a threat to the State.[95] Elizabeth's attitude towards prophesying and gatherings of district clergy for the purposes of education in preaching and doctrine further illustrates the point. She castigated Archbishop Grindal, who had dared defend the practice in contravention of her royal command to put a stop to it. On 7 May 1576 a royal letter was sent to all the bishops and judges on circuit stating her view that, 'It was like that religion, which of his own nature should be uniform would against his nature have proved milliform, yea, in continuance nulliform, especially in rites and ceremonies and sometimes also in matters of doctrine.'[96] Yet Elizabeth and her government were pragmatic: the catholicity of government-sanctioned ritual indicates a recognition that the goal of uniformity in religious practice, at least in relation to funeral ritual, was best served by retaining traditional forms.

The calculated ambivalence of government created a liminal space in which the core of the medieval funeral ritual was allowed to persist. Behind this policy was the view that in the 1560s and 1570s the 1559 religious settlement was taking root, with the majority of the clergy and populace accepting the reformed religion and any residual Catholicism slowly dying out.[97] If there was any danger, it was seen to emanate from the most ardent of the Protestant reformers, not from the remaining Catholics. Despite the evangelical zeal of believers, even by the beginning of Elizabeth's reign only a devoted minority had accepted the new Protestant faith. Paradoxically then, it was the religious practice of these Protestant zealots that attracted the censure of the Protestant ruler and her government. Non-conformity was equated with non-uniformity. Elizabeth would prove unyielding to all attempts to alter the 1559 religious settlement until the end of her reign.[98]

For their part, radical Protestants were quick to direct their hostility at the officially-approved but essentially catholic funeral ritual forms. How could the authorities defend and justify their position? Their method was propaganda.

---

[94] Duffy, pp. 209, 567; Strype, I, 82. Any change to liturgical form was strongly resisted throughout the reign; see MacCaffrey, p. 307.

[95] See *Documents Illustrative of English Church History*, ed. by H. Gee and W. J. Hardy (London, 1896), pp. 417–42; cited by MacCaffrey, p. 305. Lord Keeper Bacon may have urged the 'uniting of these people of the realm into a uniform order of Religion' at a speech to the Commons in Elizabeth's first Parliament; see ibid., p. 52.

[96] John Strype, *Life and Acts . . . of Edmund Grindal* (Oxford, 1821), 574–6; cited by MacCaffrey, p. 321. See also ibid., p. 51.

[97] MacCaffrey, p. 110.

[98] MacCaffrey, pp. 34, 45, 297, 303–26, 373.

Intriguingly, the continuity in funeral ritual forms and symbolism contrasts with a distinct alteration in the rhetoric that was employed to describe them. William Cecil's comments on the funeral of his wife (April 21 1589) illustrate the point: 'I do not celebrate this Funeral in this sort with any Intention thereby, as the corrupt Abuse hath been in the Church, to procure of God the Relief or the Amendment of the State of her Soul; who is dead in body only.' He declares himself confident that her soul already resides in heaven. (The very need to make this kind of explanation demonstrates the relative homogeneity of Catholic and Anglican funeral ceremonies.) Burghley goes on to identify the 'real' reasons behind the funeral ceremony:

> But yet I do otherwise most willingly celebrate this Funeral, as a Testimony of my hearty Love, which I did bear her, with whom I lived in the State of Matrimony 40 and two Years also, without any Unkindness, to move separation, or any Violation of Matrimony at any Time.
>
> Further, this that is here done for the Assembly of our Friends, is to testify to the World, what Estimation, Love and Reverence God bears to the Stock whereof she did come, both by her Father and Mother: As manifestly may be seen about her Hearse, by the sundry Coats of Noble Houses joyned in Blood with her. Which is not done for any vain Pomp of the World, but for Civil duty towards her Body; that is to be with Honour regarded, for the assured Hope of the Resurrection thereof at the last Day.[99]

Likewise the funeral sermon came to have a secular or civil focus, concentrating on a celebration of the life of the deceased, including his social status. In place of the religious doctrines of intercession came civil justifications for funeral ceremony, prompted by the need to deny that such ceremony reflected heretical beliefs in intercession for the souls of the dead.

The appeal to civil status was not an arbitrary choice in a desperate search for some means of justification; rather it reflected a central tenet of Elizabeth's political philosophy. According to Wallace MacCaffrey, she accepted wholeheartedly the presumption of supreme headship enshrined in the Henrician statutes. For her that title was and always had been inherent in the very nature of kingship. Thus, though obedient to her sister when she had been a subject, once crowned Queen Elizabeth inevitably resurrected the act of supremacy with its dual authority embracing both civil and religious, 'regnum' and 'ecclesia'. 'It was a corollary of this conception of the royal governance of the church that the sovereign should provide for a uniform mode of public worship which the subject would be required to attend. That compulsion would rest, not on any claim to doctrinal or dogmatic correctness, but simply on the command of the highest civil authority to perform a public duty.'[100] Elizabeth's secular view of the function of religion in society constituted a divorce between belief and

---

[99] Strype, III, 597. See also Richard Hooker's 'Of the Rites of Burial', in Speed Hill, II, 409–13; and on Cecil's religious convictions, including his horror of idolatry, see MacCaffrey, pp. 167–8.

[100] MacCaffrey, p. 50.

action that inevitably offended the consciences of rigorous-minded Protestants.[101]

The Protestants were right to fear the implications of the government's policy. Towards the end of Elizabeth's reign and under James, Puritan fears of a resurgence of popish and idolatrous ceremonies would be realised. Ritual practices that had initially met with official hostility, such as the bearing of torches, were to be re-adopted and given royal sanction. This was not, however, a government-led process. Many catholic funeral practices, especially outside London, were maintained throughout Elizabeth's reign in despite of official policy. In his *A Pleasant Dialogue* (1581), Gilby lists one hundred popish abuses which 'deforme the Englishe reformation', including the presence of beadsmen at funerals.[102]

Crosses had been borne in medieval funeral processions and a white cross adorned most funeral palls.[103] The Reformation attempted to do away with these images of the crucifixion and, as Machyn notes, at the funeral of Sir John Sentlow there was 'nodur cross nor prest, nor clarkes'. Yet, at the funeral of Francis Talbot, Earl of Shrewsbury (1560) a 'pall of cloth of gold, with a cross of white sattin' covered the corpse as it lay in the chapel at the manor of Sheffield where he had died. Talbot was a Catholic sympathizer and it is tempting to see the use of the cross as an indication of a surreptitious Catholic rite. The funeral took place, however, after the Acts of Royal Supremacy and Uniformity and the Royal Injunctions, all proclaimed in 1559, and before the Thirty-Nine Articles of 1563 when it is likely that the new ritual forms had not been formulated.[104] Yet other examples of a pall cross, at funerals at St Dunstan's in Canterbury for example, post-date the publication of the Thirty-Nine Articles (1563) when the status of the cross was no longer surrounded with confusion. In addition, episcopal visitations, which often focused on funeral ritual, expose the use of crosses as one of the most recalcitrant areas of continuing Catholic practice.[105]

There is clear evidence of abundant bell-ringing well into Elizabeth's reign, despite the 1563 restriction to single peals of only an hour in length. Many peals were rung, for example, at the funeral of Sir Nicholas Bacon (1578) and at each stage during the funeral journey of Sir Henry Sidney (1586) from Worcester to

---

[101] On Elizabeth's secular view of religion and her consequent insensitivity to the religious convictions of her fellow rulers and subjects, see MacCaffrey, pp. 7–8, 41–4, 48–59, 182–7, 212–15, 301. On the royal supremacy and Elizabeth's political and religious views, see also Jones, p. 9.

[102] Anthony Gilby, *A pleasant dialogue* (London: [n. pub.], 1581), Appendix, p. 2.

[103] Duffy, p. 467.

[104] Peck (1779), II, 253–5; Henry Gee and William John Hardy, eds, *Documents Illustrative of English Church History* (London: Macmillan, 1896). Other 'Catholic' funerals took place in 1558, including those of Mary Tudor (see Nichols (1848), p. 182) and Bishop Griffin of Rochester (see *Strype*, I, iii, 31).

[105] Duffy, pp. 577, 586.

Penshurst in Kent.[106] Gilby, for one, continued to voice attacks on the retention of bells but many funeral bills of account include charges for bell-ringing.[107] At Queen Elizabeth's funeral in 1603 a bell-ringer would feature in the procession. The tolling of bells to invite prayers for the deceased was of course vetoed, but even this practice seems to have continued and Grindal found it necessary to inveigh against bell-ringing on All Saints' Eve in 1571.[108]

The incidence of Catholic-style ritual forms may well have increased from the 1580s onwards as the Catholic community in England gained in political strength. The Government eventually embraced the aspects of medieval funeral ritual that had persisted alongside the core ritual forms that had always been accorded official legitimacy, as I shall demonstrate in chapter 7. The shift in state ceremonial may represent a repositioning on the part of the government in order to make its goal of uniformity in religious practice more achievable.

Medieval funeral ritual practices seem then to have been highly resistant to change. It is perhaps unsurprising, however, that the inertia attached to all ceremonial forms is found to be particularly pronounced in the case of funeral rituals. The emotional and psychological disturbance caused by a death in the community is profound. The value of the funeral ceremony's ritual re-statement of social stability and order ensured its survival despite opposition from reformers. It was in the ritual forms of the funeral and the cult of death that the community achieved its main solace.[109] Few would renounce the intercessionary benefits of funeral ritual. It was inevitably an area on which feelings were most conservative: no-one wanted to risk jeopardising the fate of his soul. *The Admonition to the Parliament* (1572) bears witness to the recalcitrance of the population in many regions when faced with funeral ritual reform:

> Bothe in Countrye and Citie, for the place of buryall, which way they muste lie, how they must be fetched to churche, the minister meeting them at churche stile with surplesse, wyth a companye of greedie clarkes, that a crosse white or blacke, must be set upon the deade corpes, that breade muste be given to the poore, and offrings in buryall time used, and cakes sent abrode to frendes, then by the authoritie of the boke. Small commaundement will serve for the accomplishing of such things. But great charge will hardly bring the least good

---

[106] Bod., Ashmole MS 836 fols 21–38; BL, Lansdowne MS 50 fols 191–4. See also Rowell, p. 91; W. P. Haugaard, *Elizabeth and the English Reformation: the Struggle for a Stable Settlement of Religion* (Cambridge: Cambridge University Press, 1968), pp. 167–8, 355.
[107] Aston, p. 335.
[108] Henry Chettle, 'The Order and Proceeding at the Funerall of [...] Elizabeth Queene of England [...] 28th April 1603', in *A Third Collection of Scarce and Valuable Tracts*, 3 vols (London: F. Gogan, 1751), I; Gittings, p. 44; Duffy, p. 548; Thomas, p. 722; Christopher Haigh, *English Reformations: Religion, Politics and Society under the Tudors* (Oxford: Clarendon Press, 1993), p. 251.
[109] Duffy, pp. 114, 213–20.

thing to passe, and therefore all is let alone, and the people as blind and ignorant as ever they were. God be mercyfull unto us.[110]

Much later, in his *Religio Medici* (1643), Sir Thomas Browne would list praying for the dead and the ringing of a bell amongst the heresies that he had been tempted to commit.[111]

It is important to remember also that the operative nature of ritual relies on its symbolic elements triggering a process of fusion, a bringing together of the emotional and the political. The continued use of the uncontroversial non-religious images, the heraldic achievements and banners, maintained a symbolic content in the funeral ritual. The persistent appeal of torches and bells can be explained in terms of an enrichment of the sensory appeal and symbolism of the ritual producing a concomitant enhancement of the operation of sublimation. Interesting in this context is the evidence that has been gathered by anthropologists for the neural and organic effects of percussion instruments, including bells and drums, and the high incidence of their use in death ritual.[112] The ambiguity of government policy on ceremony may reflect a recognition of the human need for a sublime ritual as a defence against the uncertainty and disturbance of death.[113]

Taken as a whole the evident resilience of ritual forms in the funeral context represents an important qualification of the generally-held view that the Reformation signalled a shift away from ritualism and symbolism.

---

[110] W. H. Frere and C. E. Douglas, *Puritan Manifestos: A Study of the Origin of the Puritan Revolt* (New York: Lenox Hill, 1907; repr. 1972), p. 28.

[111] Sir Thomas Browne, *The Major Works*, ed. by C. A. Patrides (Harmondsworth: Penguin Books, 1977), pp. 67–8.

[112] See Rodney Needham, 'Percussion and Transition', *Man*, n.s. 2, no. 4 (1967), 606–14.

[113] See Scarisbrick, p. 163; Collinson (1988), p. 99; Tessa Watt, *Cheap Print and Popular Piety 1550–1640* (Cambridge: Cambridge University Press, 1991), p. 136.

CHAPTER THREE

The Renaissance Royal Funeral and Succession Rituals: England and France

Succession and the Royal Offering Ritual in England

The function of the offering ritual in the heraldic funeral was to enact the succession of a noble family.[1] It is perhaps logical to assume a similar ritual would demonstrate the succession at royal funerals where the need for a display of continued social order would be that much greater. Certainly, as the obsequies of Henry VII demonstrate, an offering ceremony took place in the English royal funeral. During the church service, 'Three masses [were] solemnly sung by Bishops, at the last of which were offered the Banners, Courser, Coat of Arms, Sword, Target and Helmet, the nobility likewise offering their rich palls of cloth of Gold and Baudekyn'.[2] Here is the offering of the achievements that featured in the Derby funeral but it is not clear from the sources who offers the various items or to whom. Were the achievements offered directly to the new king in a form of 'creation' ceremony as they were to Derby's heir?

A surviving account of the funeral of Edward IV (1483) gives us a usefully detailed description of the royal offering ceremony. I suggest that we take this as a probable model for the offering ritual at the funeral of Henry VII. The offering took place while the Requiem Mass was being sung.

> [The] officers of armes wente to the vestyary, wher they receyved a riche embrowdred cote of armes, which Garter king of armes hyld wt as grete rev'ence as he cowde at the hede of the said herse till the offering tyme . aft' that the erle of Lincoln had offered the masse peny p'sented it to the Marquis of Dors' and to th' erle of Huntingdon, they to offre it; and the said Gart' receyved it ageyn of the archebishop, and hyld it stille at the high auter ende till the masse was done.[3]

The shield, sword, and crown were similarly offered and then the courser which was led up from the door of the church. After the achievements had been offered

---

[1] The offering ritual of the English heraldic funeral was also practised in this form at the funerals of French noblemen; see Vale, p. 92.
[2] College of Arms, Briscoe MS fol. 312; Bod., Ashmole MS 857 fol. 340.
[3] 'An Extract relating to the Burial of King Edward IV', p. 353.

to the altar they were returned to the heralds; the new king did not take part in the proceedings.

If this funeral occasion were to be considered in isolation, it might be supposed that the absence of Edward V from his father's funeral was related to his minority status or to strife over the Protectorship. Yet absence of the succeeding monarch at the funeral ceremony was traditional. None of the Tudor monarchs mourned at the funerals of their predecessors.[4]

The internal logic of the royal offering ritual was, however, compatible with the absence of the succeeding monarch. The achievements offered during the ritual pertained to the private titles of the deceased monarch, which would not be transferred to the new king. The symbolism that surrounds the offering was limited to commemoration of the dead King and commendation of his soul to God, thus the achievements were offered to the altar. The insignia of royalty, sword, orb and sceptre did not appear in this part of the royal ceremony. There was no enactment of the royal succession here.

The royal funeral did, however, play a crucial role in enacting the royal succession as will be seen in the subsequent chapters dealing with the funerals of Elizabeth and James. In order to prepare for these chapters, I here provide a brief survey of the succession rituals of royal funerals in Renaissance France, in particular the effigy ritual, to facilitate comparison with English practice and discussions of possible cross-fertilization. The royal funeral in France has usefully been the subject of detailed study in recent years, making a great deal of material readily available for comparative analysis.[5]

Succession Rituals in the French Royal Funeral: 1422–1574

The funeral of Charles VI in 1422 provides a useful starting point for an analysis of the succession rituals of French royal funerals. On this occasion the succession of the boy-king Henry VI of England was contested by the Dauphin Charles VII. The rivalry between the two claimants extended the usual gap between the death of one monarch and the coronation of the next, creating a ceremonial interregnum.[6] There were two ritual developments at the funeral of Charles VI that attempted to fill this ceremonial interregnum.

The first development involved the ritual declaration of the accession. It was at the funeral of Charles VI that the traditional call to pray for the soul of the

---

[4] The chief mourner at the funeral of Henry VIII was the Marquis of Dorset; at that of Edward VI, it was the Marquis of Winchester and at Elizabeth's, it was the Marchioness of Northampton. Edward IV assisted at the funeral of his father in 1495 but Richard of York had not been king.

[5] See Giesey (1960). My M.A. dissertation, 'The Theatre of Death: Politics, Ritual and Ideology in the Royal Funeral of Charles IX', builds on Giesey's work, looking at what happened to French royal funeral ritual during the upheaval of the Wars of Religion.

[6] Giesey (1960), pp. 132–5.

deceased king was first countered with the cry 'Vive le roi!' and the proclamation of the new king, Henry VI of England, in an effort to ritually forestall the claims of the Dauphin Charles. These pronouncements, that would later develop into the well-known formula, 'Le Roi est Mort! Vive le Roi!', provided an opportunity for a ritual demonstration and acknowledgement of the succession.

The succession ritual of the burial cries similarly took place at the interment in the funeral of Charles IX (1574).[7] Once the coffin was lowered into the vault, the heralds laid their coats of arms against the surrounding wooden railing and the captains of the guard laid their ensigns alongside. The King's achievements and the royal insignia, sceptre, crown and hand of justice were placed right inside the vault. The herald cried out three times, 'Le Roy est mort' and then, as the Banner of France was raised on high, he gave the counter cry, again thrice-repeated, 'Vive le Roy Henry troisième de ce nom a qui Dieu donne bonne vie'. At this, the ensigns and coats of arms were recovered from the barrier and held aloft. In contrast the royal insignia remained in the grave and were not seen publicly until the coronation of the next king.

The burial cries, however, merely repeated the proclamation which took place on the day of the previous monarch's decease. There remained a display problem as far as the person of the King was concerned. Up until 1380, the succeeding monarch had always participated in his father's obsequies. At each of the four successive royal funerals, however, the successor was absent for demonstrable reasons: minority status at the funerals of Charles V (1380) and Louis XI (1483); contested succession at that of Charles VI (1422); and estrangement from the father at the funeral of Charles VII (1461).[8] Apart from the anomalous situation in 1422, the succession in all these cases was legally effective from the day of the death of the previous monarch. Yet the non-appearance of the new king created a fictive interregnum in the realm of royal ceremonial. The armoury of ritual provided the perfect solution: the creation of a fictive king.

The fashioning of a life-like effigy of the defunct monarch was the second ritual development which occurred at the funeral of Charles VI, where the ceremonial interregnum was given greater urgency because it reflected a real political interregnum. The body of Charles VI could not have been preserved long enough for it to feature in the funeral procession which was delayed by the late arrival in Paris of the English Regent, the Duke of Bedford. Thus the effigy filled the ceremonial interregnum and demonstrated the perpetuity of kingship. It was displayed in the funeral procession and lay in a hearse during the church services until the interment when the death of the old king was finally publicly declared (figure 10).[9]

The French effigy ritual was to become a highly elaborate and magnificent

---

[7] See Appendix II for an account of the funeral of Charles IX (1574).
[8] Giesey (1960), pp. 41–6.
[9] Giesey (1960), p. 143. Display of the body in the funeral procession had been the French practice since the funeral of Philip IV in 1314, see Giesey p. 23.

form. At the funeral of Charles VIII (1498) the doleful convoy that brought the black-draped, encoffined body to the capital was transformed as it entered Paris, the richly dressed effigy then being placed on a brilliant cloth-of-gold pall, on top of the coffin. In the same instant the colourful heraldic ensigns borne in the procession were unfurled and trumpets sounded a note of triumph. All this strikingly pre-echoed the Royal Entry that the new king would make following his coronation rites.[10]

At the funeral of Francis I (1547) the role of the effigy was expanded. Traditionally the encoffined body was displayed in a bed of state for a month prior to the funeral. During the first part of the ceremony the effigy of Francis I usurped its place. For a period of eleven days the effigy lay in state on a richly decorated bed in the *salle d'honneur* while meals were served to it at the usual hours of dinner and supper with all the forms and ceremonies that had been observed during the king's lifetime.[11] In this ritual lying-in-state the fiction of the effigy perpetuating the dead monarch's sovereignty reached its zenith: the effigy being treated just as if it were the still living king.

The effigy ritual was to be inflated still further at the funeral of Charles IX (1574). Charles died in the midst of the French Wars of Religion at a time of Crown weakness when the need to demonstrate the continuity of monarchical authority was great.[12] On this occasion the effigy alone was displayed for the full four weeks of the lying-in-state ritual, thereby enacting the perpetuity of Majesty more emphatically than ever.

Modification of the ritual form at the funeral of Charles IX appears to have been deliberate. Admittedly, in his account of the Francis I funeral, Pierre Du Chastel, the humanist Bishop of Mâcon who was one of the organizers of the funeral, had glossed over the fact that the effigy had only been displayed for one week. If this had been the only source available to Catherine de Medici and her advisors when planning Charles IX's funeral, the expansion of the role of the effigy could be seen as an accidental misreading of precedent innocent of political intent. That is, to use Sally Moore's terms, a case of regularization rather

---

10 Giesey (1960), pp. 108–12. On the funeral ritual as a Triumph, see Segar (1602), p. 138.
11 For a full account of the effigy lying-in-state ritual at Charles IX's funeral, see Appendix II; and for discussion of the funeral, see Jennifer K. A. Woodward, 'Funeral rituals in the French Renaissance', *Renaissance Studies* 9 (1995), part 4, 385–94. Precedents exist for the ritual serving of a meal to the empty chair of the deceased; see Giesey (1960), p. 159. The ritual also recalls medieval German coronation ceremonies where noblemen served food to the newly-crowned king in 'a symbolic representation of their willingness to be regarded as the king's officers like the steward and his fellow officials'; Percy E. Schramm, *A History of the English Coronation*, trans. by Leopold G. Wickham Legg (Oxford: Clarendon Press, 1937), pp. 62–3, 70.
12 R. J. Knecht, *The French Wars of Religion 1559–1598* (Harlow: Longman, 1989), pp. 26, 38–9; J. H. M. Salmon, *Society in Crisis: France in the Sixteenth Century* (London: Ernest Benn, 1975), p. 154; Sarah Hanley, *The 'lit de Justice' of the Kings of France: Constitutional Ideology in Legend, Ritual and Discourse* (Princeton, New Jersey: Princeton University Press, 1983), pp. 154, 159, 161, 169–72.

than situational adjustment.[13] Yet the organizers undoubtedly also had available to them the recently published *Recueil Des Roys de France* (1567) by Jean Du Tillet, acknowledged expert on French court ceremonial who had witnessed the funeral of Francis I.[14] Here it was clearly stated that the effigy was to be served for only eight to ten days and then replaced by the corpse.

We seem, then, to be dealing with a calculated attempt to impress the factious nobility with a strong ritual statement of the perpetuity of royal authority. As Du Tillet is at pains to stress, the ritual serving of meals to the effigy was to involve not just the late King's household but all those who had been accustomed to speak or respond to his majesty during his lifetime and that this included 'tant princes, princesses, prelats, outre ceux de sa maison'.[15] The nobility thus had prescribed roles in the ritual and, if they wished to avoid overt rebellion, had little choice about their participation. The expanded effigy ritual allowed the Crown greater scope to demonstrate its power both to and over the nobility whose very presence implied support for the monarchy, like it or not. In the staging of the effigy ritual, the monarchy created power. Power can be a performative act.

The French monarchy understood the value and potential of funeral symbolism, and particularly effigy ritual symbolism, as a demonstration of power at a time of state vulnerability, the death of the sovereign.

The Royal Funeral Effigy in England and France: Ritual Cross-Fertilization

The effigy ritual was not, however, indigenous to France. Its first use in 1422 was in direct imitation of an English ritual practice probably originating in the fourteenth century.[16] In early English medieval royal funerals the corpse itself was exhibited. Edward the Confessor (d. January 1065–6) and William the Conqueror (d. 1087) were both carried to their graves unembalmed and covered on a bier. The corpse of Henry I, who died in France in 1135, was rudely embalmed to facilitate its transport back to England but it was still borne covered upon a bier. The funeral of Henry II (1189) was the first in which the body was openly displayed arrayed in the coronation ornaments, with the face

---

13 Moore (1978), pp. 48–53.
14 Jean Du Tillet's *Recueil Des Roys de France: Leurs Couronne et Maison* (Paris: Pierre Mettayer, 1567) was an historical treatise and analysis of the royal funeral ceremonial. Du Tillet was also Clerk of the Parlement of Paris; see Giesey (1960), p. 122.
15 Du Tillet, p. 243.
16 In the discussion that follows I am indebted to the work of W. H. St John Hope, 'On the funeral Effigies of Kings and Queens of England, with special reference to those in the Abbey Church of Westminster', *Archaeologia*, 40, part 2 (1907), 517–70; and also to *The Funeral Effigies of Westminster Abbey*, ed. by Anthony Harvey and Richard Mortimer (Woodbridge: The Boydell Press, 1994). In earlier French royal funerals, the embalmed body had been displayed atop the coffin in the funeral procession; see Giesey, pp. 19–28 and figure 9.

uncovered. There is evidence to suggest that Henry III was the first to be borne to his grave in a coffin with an image of wax outside but the first indisputable use of a royal effigy, made of wood, was at the funeral of Edward II (1327). The reasons for its introduction are unclear but probably relate to the three-month delay in organising the funeral. Edward died at Berkeley Castle on 21 September but was not buried in Gloucester Cathedral until 20 December. Medieval embalming techniques were insufficiently skilled to keep the body fresh for that length of time.[17] Whatever the impetus behind its introduction, the use of the effigy had a tradition-like effect. Edward III was buried within two weeks of his death and thus public display of his corpse was possible but nevertheless an effigy was made. Subsequently, barring one or two exceptions, an effigy customarily appeared in all English royal funerals.[18]

Just two months before the death of Charles VI in 1422 the young Henry V of England had died at the Chateau of the Bois de Vincennes. The technique of *mos teutonicus* was applied to the body, that is it was cut in pieces and boiled in wine or vinegar until the fat and flesh separated from the bones. Usually, when noblemen died abroad, only the bones were sent back to England while the soft tissues were deposited at the place of death. In Henry's case, however, both flesh and bones were sealed up in a leaden case with a huge quantity of spices and shipped back for eventual burial in Westminster Abbey.[19] In accordance with English tradition, an effigy was displayed atop the coffin, perhaps from St Denis and certainly from Rouen, in the convoy that transported his corpse back to England.[20] It was in direct imitation of this funeral that an effigy was made for Charles VI: a striking example of the cross-fertilization of ritual forms.

In the late medieval and early Tudor period, royal funeral occasions came to be seen as an opportunity for displaying the wealth and splendour of the ruling dynasty as, for example, at the magnificent obsequies staged for Elizabeth of York in 1502.[21] Effigies were borne in the processions of all Tudor monarchs and of James I but it has generally been held that the effigy ritual in England never developed the elaborate symbolism of its French counterpart.[22] In the light of the Reformation with its marked iconoclasm, it is perhaps surprising that the effigy ritual survived at all. Survive it did, however, and in the early seventeenth century, as I shall argue, its role in the royal funeral expanded to a degree that would rival the French models.

---

[17] On embalming techniques, see Litten, pp. 33–43.
[18] Hope, pp. 527, 541–2; Ernst Kantorowicz, *The King's Two Bodies: A Study in Medieval Political Theology* (Princeton: Princeton University Press, 1957), p. 420.
[19] H. F. Hutchinson, *Henry V* (London: Eyre and Spottiswoode, 1967), cited by Litten, p. 37.
[20] An English account of Henry V's funeral journey appears in Stow, p. 362.
[21] On this funeral, see Harvey and Mortimer, pp. 6, 45–8.
[22] Giesey (1960), p. 85; Kantorowicz, p. 421.

CHAPTER FOUR

The 1587 Funerals of Mary Queen of Scots

The 1587 funerals of Mary Queen of Scots are highly illustrative of Queen Elizabeth and her government's shared awareness of the need for and value of funeral ritual. They also demonstrate the role funeral ritual played in European diplomacy.

Mary Queen of Scots was executed on 8 February 1587. She had made her will ten years previously at Sheffield Manor. In this document, as was customary, Mary made certain requests regarding the disposal of her body. 'Je veulx et ordonne, que si je decedde en ceste prison, mon corps soit porté en France, et y conduict a mes despens, par tous les serviteurs et officiers de ma maison (francoys ou escosoys, qui en seront capables), estant pres de moy, lors de mon decez, pour estre inhumé, en l'Eglise Sainct-Denys, aupres du Corps du fue mon trescher et treshonoré seigneur et mary, le Roy de France, Françoys.'

She makes further requests about her funeral ceremony:

> Qu'aux funerailles qui se feront, en l'ad' ville, assistent tous mes serviteurs et officiers domestiques, qui s'y vouldront trouver revestuz en deuil, ch'n selon sa qualité; et oultre deux cens pauvres aussi vestuz de robbes de deuil, ch'n une torche allumée a la main. Les quattre mendians de Paris, les enfans de la Trinité, les bons hommes, Capussins, et aultres relligieux, ainsi que les executeurs de ces Testament adviseront, et verront bon estre. – Ausquels j'ordonne y faire celebrer le divin service, tant vigiles que messes, ainsi qu l'on a accoustumé de faire; et durant les jours de dictes ffunerailles, facent distribuer aux pauvres, la somme de mil livres'.[1]

Mary also requested the separate interment of her entrails and made provision for a dole to be distributed to the poor on the occasion. In a letter to the Duke of Guise, Mary further requested that he found an obit and 'do the necessary alms'.[2]

Mary was effectively requesting a full royal funeral in the Catholic French

---

[1] J. Nichols, ed., 'The History of [...] Fotheringay', in *Bibliotheca Topographica Britannica*, ed. by J. Nichols and others, 10 vols (London: the author, 1740–1800), IV (1740), pp. vii, 79–84.

[2] Nichols (1740), p. 83; W. Laing and D. Laing, eds, *Funerals of the Scottish Queen – Collections Relative to the funerals of Mary Queen of Scots* (Edinburgh: [n. pub.], 1822), pp. viii–ix.

The Theatre of Death

style, complete with mendicant friars, multiple masses and an interment at St Denis, the French royal necropolis just to the north of Paris where her second husband, François II, was buried.[3] Mary's motivation in requesting such a funeral may have been religious in part but her requests emphasise her links with the French Crown and may have been designed to encourage their support for her cause. Mary, it seems, recognised that an evocation of her funeral pageantry could bring powerful allies to her side while she yet lived.

Mary appointed as executors of her will the Duke of Guise, James Beaton, the Bishop of Glasgow, John Lesley, the Bishop of Ross, and M. de Ruysseau, her Chancellor.[4] In the event, these men had no role to play in the funeral ceremonies surrounding the interment of Mary's body in the country of her death. It was not the executors but Elizabeth and subsequently James who were responsible for the ceremonial events that marked the death of the Scottish Queen in England. Mary would receive not one but three funeral and memorial services in England over the next twenty-five years. Each, instead of catering for the wishes of the deceased, would reflect the particular political ends of its organisers and the cultural conditions of the historical moment. In this chapter I deal with Mary's 1587 funerals. In the interests of chronological and thematic continuity, discussion of the rituals organised by James after his accession to the English throne is postponed until chapter 7.

The Political Implications of Mary's Execution: Domestic and Foreign

Mary's execution placed both Elizabeth and James in politically ambiguous positions. A Latin epitaph pinned anonymously above the dead Queen's grave in Peterborough Cathedral illustrates the point.

> Mary Queen of Scots, daughter of a King, widow of the King of France, Cousin and next heir of the Queen of England [. . .] by barbarous and tyrannical cruelty, the ornament of our age and truly Royal light, is extinguished. By the same unrighteous judgement, both Mary Queen of Scots, with natural death, and all surviving Kings, (now made common persons) are punished with civil death. A strange and unusual kind of monument this is wherein the living are included with the dead; for, with the sacred ashes of this blessed Mary, know the Majesty of all the Kings and princes, lieth here, violated and prostrate.[5]

The anonymous epitaph did not remain in place long. Its import was far too

---

[3] See Appendix II for extracts from the funeral of Charles IX (d. 1574) as an example of a French royal funeral.
[4] James Beaton (1517–1603) was the last Roman Catholic Archbishop of Glasgow (1552–71). He went to France on the death of the Queen regent and continued to live in Paris, where he acted as Scottish ambassador at the French court, until his death in 1603; see *DNB*. On Ross, Mary's agent since 1569, see MacCaffrey, pp. 117, 136.
[5] Laing, pp. 51–2; Nichols (1740), p. 58. On the Latin poem by Adam Blackwood pinned on the door of Notre-Dame, Paris on 13 March, the day of Mary's official Requiem Mass,

sensitive for it went to the heart of the difficulties experienced by Elizabeth. By condemning a fellow monarch to death Elizabeth made her own sovereignty vulnerable. Fear of this logical consequence had lain behind much of Elizabeth's reluctance to have her cousin executed despite the personal danger involved in allowing her to live.[6]

The implications of regicide were similarly near to James's heart although in his case they were bound up in a tight ideological framework: the Law of Divine Right. 'What law of God', James declared, 'can permit that justice shall strike upon them whom he has appointed supreme dispensators of the same under him, whom he hath called gods.'[7] It might seem reasonable to assume that James's attitude to this particular royal death would be further complicated by filial ties. It is impossible, however, to determine James's private attitude to the execution of his mother. As Maurice Lee puts it, James digested the news, 'with or without satisfaction, depending on whose account you believe'.[8] Nevertheless, since James was separated from his mother at the age of ten, it is unlikely that public and political considerations received much opposition from personal feelings of affection.

On a political level, Mary's death had advantages for James. It rendered his status as King of Scotland entirely unequivocal. The legitimacy of her deposition had always been a painful issue.[9] Further, it removed her as a potential rival to the fulfilment of James's great ambition: the succession to the English throne. Ambiguity in James's correspondence with Archibald Douglas, his ambassador in London, suggests that while publicly James was seen to be doing all he could to save his mother, privately he was actively encouraging the English to precipitate her end.

Even in death, however, Mary could be a threat to James's hope of the English succession. A 1584 Act of Parliament, based on the Bond of Association for the protection of Queen Elizabeth's person, included a clause that would keep from the throne anyone who (even without their own knowledge) had been intended by the conspirators to be Elizabeth's successor. When Mary was convicted of plotting against Elizabeth's life, James worried that his enemies would use the clause to bar his own succession.[10] James thus had strong motives for urging

---

see M. Greengrass, 'Mary, Dowager Queen of France', in *Mary Stewart: Queen in Three Kingdoms*, ed. by Michael Lynch (Oxford: Blackwell, 1988), pp. 174–94 (p. 186).

[6] Calendar of State Papers, Foreign Series (CSPF), XXI (1586–88) part I, 189, 203. On the hardening of Elizabeth's attitude, see MacCaffrey, pp. 139, 343.

[7] Letter of 16 January 1587; see G. P. V. Akrigg, ed., *The Letters of James VI and I* (London: University of California Press, 1984), pp. 81–3 (p. 82).

[8] Maurice Lee, *Great Britain's Solomon: James VI and I in His Three Kingdoms* (Urbana: University of Illinois Press, 1990), p. 33. See also Akrigg (1984), p. 86; D. Harris Willson, *King James VI and I* (London: Cape, 1950), p. 78; and MacCaffrey, p. 104.

[9] Lee (1990), pp. 32–3.

[10] Akrigg (1984), pp. 77–8; Willson, p. 139; Paul Johnson, *Elizabeth I: A Study in Power and*

his mother's innocence. Her perfidy would inevitably cast a shadow upon his own honour.

The need to defend Mary's honour in order to safeguard James's succession claims coincided with the need to satisfy the unequivocal and barely concealed outrage of his people, some of whom were threatening war with England.[11] James had to play a careful game: the show of support for his mother necessary to placate domestic opinion must not antagonize the English. He did not want to jeopardize the succession. Before Mary's death James had sent repeated tactical embassies to plead for her life. When it was certain that she would die he sent two ambiguous statements of protest, saying enough to protect his honour and interest but leaving unsaid any threat of revenge.[12]

Elizabeth, like James, strove to minimize the negative political repercussions of Mary's death. At first Elizabeth chose to emphasize the impossibility of taking any other course of action given the plots against her royal person in which Mary had been implicated.[13] This policy did not, however, quell popular unrest in Scotland. The Master of Gray advised that 'the Queen of England in effect should let the King see, by some honest proof, that the cruel accident fell out far contrary to her meaning'.[14] There followed a protracted charade in which Elizabeth pretended fury with her Council and took to her bed in an exaggerated display of grief. Her performance was, however, neither convincing nor sufficient and ultimately a scapegoat had to be found.[15] Elizabeth argued that she had given a warrant to her servant, Davison, in order to satisfy the demands of her subjects but had never intended to use it, and 'he was so rash as to have overstepped his commission'.[16] Davison's denials were useless. He was sent to the Tower and fined £10,000, a victim to state policy.[17]

Thus Elizabeth and James endeavoured to demonstrate their innocence to audiences at home and abroad. Despite the ambiguity surrounding events, some feared the execution would provoke a strong reaction from her overseas supporters, particularly the French, who had sent ambassadors to plead for Mary's life before her Fotheringay trial. In the eyes of many Mary had been seen as a potentially threatening source of increasing French power in the English

---

Intellect (London: Weidenfield & Nicolson, 1974), pp. 280–1; MacCaffrey, pp. 139–44, 344–5.

[11] Calendar of State Papers, Scotland (CSPSc), I (1509–1603), 542; PRO SP52/42/18; Willson, p. 74.
[12] MacCaffrey, p. 436.
[13] Salisbury MSS, III, 218; MacCaffrey, pp. 351–2.
[14] Salisbury MSS, III, 225–6, 230.
[15] CSPF, XXI (1586–8) part I, 242, 266, 276; PRO SP78/17; CSPV, VIII (1581–91), 255.
[16] This excuse also met with a degree of scepticism; see CSPV, VIII (1581–91), 255.
[17] The money was quietly given to James as a sweetener to make him accept the fact of his mother's death. He would always be vulnerable to accusations of venality; see CSPF, XXI (1586–8) part I, 320; PRO SP78/17/90; Calendar of State Papers, Domestic Series (CSPD), II (1581–90), 398; Salisbury, XIII, 404.

realm, particularly in the early years of Elizabeth's reign.[18] From the 1570s onwards Mary also figured at the centre of growing concerns about Spanish intentions in England, although the Spaniards never openly supported the Scottish Queen. Such worries were not curtailed by her demise, since the event could be regarded as the removal of an impediment to Spanish invasion.[19] Indeed, James had written to Henry III, Catherine de Medici and the Duke of Guise asking for aid in avenging his mother's death and, in April, Philip II took soundings of the Papal position in order to discover whether a joint attack with France, in support of James, on England were possible. If James did genuinely entertain the idea of a Spanish invasion of England via Scotland, he decided the risks were too great and that his goals might be achieved peaceably. Perhaps he did not receive the necessary guarantees of support. Just before the execution Stafford reported to Burghley that the Queen's supporters in Paris believed James would declare war if his mother were killed but added 'He will never begin it, I think, if he be not assured of a better back than his own'.[20] Thus James's militaristic overtures became in effect a show to appease his outraged Scottish nobles.[21]

Cecil, for whom the underlying dynamic of European politics since the late 1560s had been the re-establishment of universal papal power by the Catholic princes, may have suspected an armed response.[22] Walsingham, who had long supported the elimination of Mary, was confident, however, that while Mary's overseas supporters might storm with words they would not act, 'the papists being now out of hope to advance their religion by the taking of her away: because as well the King of Scotland as all others that pretend right of succession are protestants; and they have no reason nor I think any meaning to hazard themselves in the quarrel of the dead'.[23]

The Ceremonial Response to Mary's Death: France, Spain and Scotland

In the long run, Walsingham was proved right: the international response to Mary's death was confined to the ceremonial arena. Support for the dead Catholic Queen was demonstrated through the security of ritual rather than a war fraught with risk.

Although there was much loud condemnation in Paris at the news and all the French court was reported to deplore the execution, both because Mary was

---

[18] MacCaffrey, pp. 47, 350.
[19] Charles Howard McIlwain, ed., *The Political Works of James I* (Harvard: Harvard University Press, 1918; repr. New York: Russell & Russell, 1965), p. xxviii; MacCaffrey, pp. 66, 175, 185–7, 218–31, 241, 327–42, 343–54.
[20] CSPF, vol. 21, p. 220.
[21] Willson, pp. 79–80; CSPV, VIII (1581–91), 264; MacCaffrey, p. 439.
[22] MacCaffrey, p. 166.
[23] CSPF, XXI (1586–8), 242; CSPV, VIII (1581–91), 256; MacCaffrey, pp. 169, 350.

The Theatre of Death

a Queen of France and because of its detrimental effect on the hopes of Catholics in England, condemnation was limited to the spheres of diplomatic protocol and ceremony.[24] First, shortly after the execution, Stafford, whose mission was to explain that it had all happened 'without her Majesty's intent and meaning', was refused an audience.[25]

There followed official ceremonies to mark Mary's death, although there is no evidence that Mary received the elaborate funeral in France that she had requested. Bernardino de Mendoza, the Spanish ambassador in France, reported on 7 March that the King, Queen and all the nobles at the French court had publicly appeared in mourning. Royal finances had, however, been stretched by the civil war and the ladies-in-waiting were told to dress in ordinary black serge because the King could not afford to provide them with the customary mourning attire.

The French obsequies did not, however, constitute a unified response; rather they were hijacked by the Guise as a means of scoring political points. Mendoza also reports that the French were to hold obsequies for the dead Queen at Notre Dame and that the King would be present. Later, he records that the funeral service was held at the French court. The Duke of Guise, one of Mary's executors, is identified as the motivating force behind the event.[26] His behaviour appears at first glance to be a natural extension of the patronal role played towards Mary, whose mother was a member of the House of Guise, during her lifetime.[27] Greengrass, however, noting the central role of the Guise in Mary's French obsequies, argues that the execution provided him with an opportunity to orchestrate a demonstration of overt Catholic solidarity that was separate from and, by implication, critical of the King.[28] He goes on to claim that Mary became an image for revolution in France, an image which played a key part in the propaganda that led to Henry III's exclusion from Paris fourteen months after her death. The Guise also showed concern for a wider audience. All the foreign ambassadors were invited to attend in mourning and reports of the funeral were intended to circulate.[29]

Also in March 1587 a memorial service was held in Rheims. This, too, was attended by the Duke of Guise, while the Bishop of Glasgow, James Beaton, another of the executors, was also present. Apparently the hope of being created the Cardinal of Scotland was uppermost in his mind, rather than any reverence

---

[24] PRO SP12/199/20.
[25] CSPF, XXI (1586–8) part I, 227; CSPV, VIII (1581–91), 249–55. See also Greengrass, pp. 184–8.
[26] Calendar of State Papers, Spain: Relating to English Affairs (CSPS), IV (1587–1603), 34.
[27] On the Guise's involvement in Mary's plots, see MacCaffrey, p. 341.
[28] Greengrass, p. 185.
[29] CSPV, VIII (1581–91), 255–6; Samuel Jebb, *The History of the Life and Reign of Mary Queen of Scots* ([n. p.]: [n. pub.], 1725), p. 354.

for the deceased or sense of duty in carrying out the obligations placed upon him by the late Queen.[30]

In April the Venetian ambassador in Spain reported that Philip II had been in some doubt as to whether he should order funeral services for the Scottish Queen. There was no genuine sorrow at her death. Her status had been equivocal in Spain and her death a fortunate release from all pressure for supporting her claims to the English throne.[31] Indeed, Philip could now assert his own claims, if not for himself then for his daughter.[32] Safely dead, Mary could now be ceremonially commemorated but only if she qualified as a Catholic martyr. The Spanish celebration of obsequies for Mary was seen primarily in a religious context. Once the Pope had privately pronounced her a martyr, Philip went into mourning and a funeral was held which he attended in person.[33]

In Scotland too, James stifled his subjects' thirst for revenge with the black cloth of mourning. The Scottish court was in full mourning for Mary Queen of Scots for a whole year. At first Bothwell refused to put on mourning until he had avenged Mary's death but the King reproved him. For James the show of mourning was sufficient.[34]

There is evidence that some Scots contemplated requesting custody of Mary's body in anticipation of a Scottish funeral. Robert Melvill refused a request to find out whether or not it was James's desire to have 'the defunct soul transported in this country [Scotland]' saying, 'I cannot take it upon me to meddle therein, knowing how heavy and displeasant it shall be to move the same unto his Majesty.' There is no evidence that James personally wished to have a Scottish funeral for his mother. In June, however, he did inquire as to whether his mother's body had been buried or not.[35]

---

[30] CSPF, XXI (1586–8) part I, 535. The Guise also celebrated the funeral in Lorraine. See CSPF, XXI (1586–8) part IV, 345.
[31] Willson, p. 80.
[32] John Lynch, *Spain 1516–1598: From Nation State to World Empire* (Oxford: Blackwell, 1991), pp. 380–1, 447–8. Philip's claims were improved, at least in papal eyes, because of the protestantism of Mary's son, James VI.
[33] Mary's obsequies were also celebrated by the Pope, CSPV, VIII (1581–91), 268; CSPS, IV (1587–1603), 54–7, 200. See also Greengrass, pp. 186–7 on Mary's image as a Catholic martyr in France.
[34] Mary's third husband had been the 4th Earl of Bothwell (d. 1578). On James's ritual protests, see CSPSc, I (1509–1603), 543, 545; MacCaffrey, p. 436 and Willson, pp. 74, 79.
[35] CSPSc, I (1509–1603), 344; Salisbury, XIII, 261.

The Peterborough Funeral: 1 August 1587 [36]

The disposal of the dead Queen's body was left to Elizabeth and her advisors. An undated letter from M. De L'Aubespine, the French ambassador, to Queen Elizabeth states that immediately after the execution the body was wrapped in black cloth, carried to the late Queen's chamber and there opened and embalmed.[37] Similarly, according to a letter from Sir Amias Paulet to Sir Francis Walsingham, dated Fotheringay Castle, 25 July 1586 [sic], the body was embalmed and enclosed in lead under the direction of a physician from Stamford, on Walsingham's orders. Then, under the care of Andrews the Sheriff, it remained in the castle awaiting funeral arrangements.[38]

Walsingham's account of the deliberations surrounding the execution and burial of Mary Queen of Scots implies that early plans involved a hasty private disposal of the corpse at Fotheringay. He notes, 'The body [is] to be buried in the night in the parish church in such *uppermost* place as by the two Earls [Kent and Shrewsbury] shall be thought fit.'[39] In the end, however, although Mary's interment would take place at night, she was to be given a public funeral at the expense of the state.

It is not clear when the decision to stage a state funeral for Mary Queen of Scots was taken by Elizabeth and her councillors. I have discovered no evidence relating to deliberations made over the funeral arrangements. Delays of a month

---

[36] The account of the funeral is reconstructed mainly from the following sources: (i) *The Scottish Queens Buriall at Peterborough, upon Tuesday beeing Lammas Day 1587* (London, 1589) printed for Edward Venge and reproduced in Edward Arber, *An English Garner* (London: Constable, 1897), VIII, 341–50; Laing, pp. 1–8; and Nichols (1740), pp. 60–2 (referred to as Venge); (ii) *The Order for the Buriall for Marie Queen of Scotts att Peterborough Observed the First of August on Tuesdaye 1587*, based on the accounts in Bod., Ashmole MS 836 fol. 273 and BL, Harley MS 1354 fol. 46 drawn up by William Dethick, Garter King at Arms, reproduced in Laing, pp. 9–16 (referred to as Dethick); (iii) BL, Harley MS 1440, also drawn up by Dethick and reproduced in Laing, pp. 37–41; (iv) Gunton, *A History of the Cathedral Church of Peterborough* (London, 1686), p. 77, supposedly based on an account by Dr Fletcher, Dean of Peterborough Cathedral at the time of the funeral, and reproduced in Laing, pp. 45–52 and Nichols (1740), pp. 50–6; (v) Bod., Ashmole MS 857 fols 315–17. An account of the funeral is also given in CSPD (1581–90), PRO SP12/203/2. The sheer amount of evidence that survives relating to the funeral of Mary Queen of Scots, in comparison with that of Elizabeth, is indicative of its notoriety.

[37] CSPV, VIII (1581–91), 256.

[38] Laing, p. x. According to one legend the Queen's head was buried separately. Two of the late Queen's Ladies of the Bed-Chamber, Barbara Mowbray and Elizabeth Curle, were permitted to retire abroad following the execution of their mistress, taking with them the head which they had interred near a pillar opposite the Chapel of the Holy Sacrament in the Church of St Andrew in Antwerp. The tale has, however, no foundation in fact; see ibid., pp. 76–8.

[39] Salisbury MSS, III, 216–18. The italics indicate that Burghley interlined the word 'uppermost' in his own hand and refer to the location of the church interment.

or so between death and burial, to allow the College of Arms to make the necessary preparations, were usual amongst the aristocracy. The seven-month delay in the case of Mary may have been due to worries over the form of any prospective funeral ritual. It would be hard to avoid controversy given the religious opinions held by Mary's household and overseas supporters. Alternatively, and this is perhaps more likely, the delay may have been a strategy calculated to allow time for memories of her execution to fade.

In this context it is worth recalling that just eight days after Mary's execution, a magnificent funeral commanding national attention was held in London. On 16 February 1587 Sir Philip Sidney's obsequies were staged and, according to the description included in Thomas Lant's pictorial record of the occasion, the London funeral attracted crowds of onlookers:

> He was carried from the Minorities (wch is without Aldgate) along the cheefe streets of the cytye unto the Cathedreall church of St Paules the which streets all along were so thronged with people that the mourners had scarcely rome to pass; the houses likewise weare as full as they might be.[40]

It seems as if the splendour of Sidney's funeral was deliberately inflated. Intriguingly, the chief mourner (Robert Sidney) had six assistants, the number prescribed for barons, rather than the four allowed for knights.[41] Also the Great Banner was carried although it was usually reserved for use at the funerals of peers and their ladies. Further, in clear contravention of the heraldic principle 'that no man of greater title than the defunct should be permitted to mourne' at heraldic funerals, the Earls of Leicester, Huntingdon and Essex, and Lords Willoughby and North were present, enhancing the magnificence of the occasion.[42] Such deviations from normal procedure at this funeral seem to signal that it was being deliberately transmuted into a national affair.[43]

The series of engravings produced by Thomas Lant (c. 1554–1600), a member of Sidney's household who was taken on by Walsingham after Sidney's death, further inflated the occasion since they followed a tradition developed in the Habsburg Dutch provinces to commemorate imperial deaths (figure 1).[44]

---

[40] Lant, p. 30. For the funeral see Bod., Ashmole MS 818 fol. 40; John Nichols, ed., *The Progresses and Public Processions of Queen Elizabeth*, 3 vols (London: the author, 1823), II, 483–94. On Lant's series of engravings, see Sander Bos, Marianne Lange-Meyers and Jeanine Six, 'Sidney's Funeral Portrayed', in *Sir Philip Sidney: 1586 and the Creation of a Legend* (Leiden: Leiden University Press, 1986), pp. 37–67.

[41] See chapter 1. Robert Sidney (1563–1626) was Philip's brother and his heir.

[42] Segar (1602), p. 251 cited by Strickland, p. 31. Strickland explores the ways in which the aristocratic propaganda of the funeral was undermined by Sidney's ambiguous social status, p. 25. The Lord Mayor of London was also in the procession.

[43] Bos, p. 51.

[44] Perhaps the most famous example is the series which depicts the funeral ceremonies held for Charles V in Brussels (1558); see Bos, pp. 46–7. Thomas Lant was appointed Portcullis Pursivant in the College of Arms in 1588; see ibid., p. 39 n. 1.

They represent the first systematic pictorial account of an English heraldic funeral and were intended for publication.

It has been suggested that Protestant propaganda was a motive behind the staging of such a grand funeral for Sir Philip Sidney.[45] Strickland has identified Protestant partisanship in Lant's book and in a broadside funeral elegy by John Phillip. Bos, Lange-Meyer and Six note that the funeral occurred at a time when Elizabeth was involved in negotiations with Dutch delegates over the future of English support for the Dutch cause. The magnificent funeral of Sidney, who had died as a result of wounds inflicted at the battle of Zutphen, would naturally draw attention to the Dutch campaign. Yet at least a part of the motivation behind this Protestant propaganda strategy may have been to distract attention away from the death of the Catholic Mary Queen of Scots and subvert or contain any propensity towards making her demise a focus for rebellion.[46] Such reasoning would certainly help to explain the delay in staging the Sidney funeral. Although Sidney had died overseas his body was quickly transported back to England and arrived in London on 5 November 1586, over three months before the funeral.

The extended delay has also been explained with reference to the difficulties that Sir Francis Walsingham, Sidney's father-in-law, experienced raising money to pay for an appropriately elaborate funeral. Yet Walsingham's financial involvement once again suggests that Sidney's funeral had become a highly political event. It was unusual for the costs of a funeral not to be borne by the deceased's estate but the family fortune had been used up in paying for the funeral of his father, Sir Henry Sidney, the year before.[47] Elizabeth herself had paid for the obsequies of some of her royal relatives to ensure a fitting level of pageantry.[48] It, would, however, have been highly inappropriate for Elizabeth to foot the bill for Sidney's funeral because, although he was a hero, he was not of noble blood. She may, nonetheless, have pressurized Walsingham into paying.[49]

If Sidney's funeral was indeed a piece of political propaganda on the part of the state, its effect may have been undermined by his ambiguous status as an

---

[45] Strickland, p. 29; Bos, p. 51.

[46] Bos, Lange-Meyer and Six note that the atmosphere at court was very tense after the death of Mary Queen of Scots. Walsingham absented himself for a period and may also have deliberately not attended Sidney's funeral in person, pp. 39, 51. James VI also demonstrated an interest in the death and funerals of Sidney, composing a sonnet on the occasion which was included in Cambridge's *Cantabrigiensis Lachrymae*. See Jan Van Dorsten, Dominic Baker-Smith and Arthur F. Kinney, eds, *Philip Sidney: 1586 and the Creation of a Legend* (Leiden: Leiden University Press, 1986), pp. 92–3 and Appendix I.

[47] Lawrence Stone, 'The Anatomy of the Elizabethan Aristocracy', *The Economic History Review*, 28 (1948), 12–13.

[48] See chapter 2.

[49] Strickland, pp. 19, 27–8, 34 n. 1. See also Bos, pp. 49–50.

aristocrat.⁵⁰ Sidney was a grandson of the Duke of Northumberland and nephew to the Earls of Leicester and Warwick, but was himself no more than a commoner. Further, not only was this the most extravagant funeral ever accorded a man of such lowly state, but the power of the display spilled out beyond the usually strictly controlled regulations laid out by the College of Arms. So many are the mourners that Lant cannot depict them all:

> Of the mourners, every Gent had a man, every knight 2, some Noblemen 12, some more, some less as also sundry English Capt of the low countrie, with divers other Gent that came voluntary and are not in this woorke expressed, So that the whole number were about 700 persons.

The unofficial mourners included representatives from the States of Holland, the Lord Mayor and aldermen of London, members of the Grocers' company and a large band of armed citizens. As Strickland puts it, 'in showering funeral honors on Sidney the emerging middle class competed with Walsingham and the aristocracy for a share in the symbolism of Sidney's "heroic" death and for a share of the propaganda power inhering in his funeral'.⁵¹

With the diversionary tactics of the Sidney funeral, it is possible that originally there were no plans to stage an elaborate funeral for the Scottish Queen. Such a funeral would, however, be staged, though not until a full five months after Mary's death.

Various factors may have influenced the decision in favour of marking the occasion with ceremony. The reader may recall that it was common practice for the obsequies of foreign monarchs to be celebrated in London. There may have been a natural propensity for this tradition to exert a drive towards conformity, but in addition pressure for Elizabeth to hold an English funeral may have come from abroad. Pope Sixtus V wrote a poem on the death of Mary Queen of Scots in which he deplored the fact that she had not been given a funeral.⁵² Although when the funeral was finally performed, no foreign ambassadors would be invited to attend, reports of the ceremony went overseas, placating Mary's sympathizers.⁵³

For whatever reasons Elizabeth and her government accepted that staging a funeral was advisable but took care that the occasion matched their own political purposes. When the funeral finally occurred on 1 August 1587, it was performed at Peterborough, far away from London, the symbolic centre of the English monarchy, thereby satisfying international expectation while exciting a minimum level of public attention at home.

Precedent may have helped determine the Peterborough location. It was

---

⁵⁰ The following paragraph draws on Ronald Strickland's interpretation of the Sidney funeral and its elegiac and pictorial records as a discourse which subverts the dominant aristocratic ideology of the heraldic funeral; see Strickland, pp. 19–36.
⁵¹ Strickland is at pains to underline that this is a discursive effect rather than 'a conscious attempt at ideological subversion on the part of the merchant class'; see Strickland, p. 33.
⁵² Nichols (1740), p. 57.
⁵³ CSPS, IV (1587–1603), 135.

decided that Mary should be interred on the right side of the Choir near to the grave of Queen Catherine of Aragon (d. 1536). There was distinct irony in this since Catherine had also died as a Queen out of favour or, to take the opposite point of view, 'no less a martyr in her life than the queen of Scotland in her death'.[54]

Peterborough was no doubt mainly chosen for its proximity to Fotheringay Castle, a distance of only eleven miles. There would be no extended funeral journey to display Mary's body to the populace. Nevertheless, it was not a humble cart but a chariot draped with black velvet and adorned with escutcheons and penons of the arms of Scotland that bore the body of Mary by torchlight during the night of Sunday 30 July from Fotheringay to Peterborough. Pre-Reformation funerals, as we have seen, abounded in torches but they had come to have associations with popery that would have been unwelcome in the context of Mary's funeral journey, especially, perhaps, given the strong Catholic presence in the diocese of Peterborough.[55] The advantages of accomplishing the task under cover of darkness were thus compromised by the necessity of using torches.[56]

While the location was deliberately remote, Elizabeth sent her officers and heralds to make sure that Mary's funeral was of royal stature. Officers of Elizabeth's household were despatched to Peterborough in advance of the heralds to make the necessary preparations.[57]

The funeral chariot was escorted from Fotheringay by William Dethick, Garter King at Arms, together with five other heralds and forty horse. Arriving at the cathedral door at 2.00 a.m., it was met by Bishop Howland of Peterborough, the Dean, the Master of the Wardrobe, and Melville, Master of the late Queen's household.[58] The coffin, with a Scottish escort, was immediately taken into the church and interred by torchlight. The open vault was then capped off leaving only a small aperture into which the staves could be broken during the ceremony on the following day.[59]

In Gunton, the reason given for the hasty disposal of the body was its extreme heaviness resulting from the weight of the lead, 'the Gentlemen could not have endured to have carried it, with leisure, in the solemn proceeding: and besides, (it) was feared that the solder might rip; and (it) being very hot weather, might be found some annoyance'.[60] This may have been the case; embalming

---

[54] Arber, p. 342; Bod., Ashmole MS 857 fol. 315; CSPS, IV, 158.

[55] Sheils (1979), pp. 20, 34, 105, 112–18. The strong Catholic presence in east Northamptonshire does not, however, invalidate the argument that Mary's funeral was easier to control and contain at the Peterborough location.

[56] Bod., Ashmole MS 857 fol. 315. This is the only funeral account I have come across during the reign of Elizabeth in which torches are mentioned.

[57] Bod., Ashmole MS 857 fol. 315.

[58] Nichols (1740), p. 54. 'Melville' or 'Melvin' – the spelling was not at this point fixed.

[59] Laing, p. 2.

[60] It weighed 900 lbs; see Laing, p. 47, and PRO SP12/203/2.

techniques were far from fail-safe in the sixteenth century and it is possible there was a genuine threat of noxious odours.[61] Whether true or not, the excuse would deflect any accusations of indignity should rumours of the hasty burial circulate. It is unlikely, however, that such charges would be made since, as we have seen, the interment was not regarded as an integral part of the public funeral proceedings.[62] Nevertheless, one account writer takes pains to preclude any criticism resulting from the lack of religious accompaniment to the nocturnal interment. He emphasizes that the Bishop had been 'redie to have executed theron, but it was by all that weare present as well Scottish as others thought good and agreed that it should be done all the daye and tyme of solemnitye, uppon Monday in the afternoon'.[63] The state funeral ceremony was staged the day after the interment, using an empty coffin since the body was already in its vault.[64]

The Funeral Procession

At eight o'clock in the morning the chief mourner, Bridget Russel, Countess of Bedford, was brought into the Presence Chamber of the Bishop's Palace which had been hung with black drapes. The Countess was positioned beneath a cloth of estate of purple velvet and proceeded to give the staves of office to the Treasurer, the Chamberlain, the Comptroller and the Steward. This accomplished, she went into the great hall where the coffin stood. The heralds then marshalled the mourners and the procession began.[65]

According to the Dethick accounts, the procession followed the usual order of an heraldic funeral commencing with two conductors bearing black staves.[66] Dethick, then Garter King at Arms, naturally took part in the funeral procession, marching directly in front of the chief mourner, the Countess of Bedford. He would also have played a key role in the organization of the occasion.

In total the participants numbered three hundred, a small gathering in comparison with other elite funerals of the period – there had been seven hundred at Sidney's funeral.[67] Many of the nobles and gentry in attendance were not there because of any personal link with the dead Queen but by royal command. They included Lady Talbot, Lady Mary Savill, daughter of George Talbot, 6th Earl of Shrewsbury, and her husband, Sir George Savill, who bore the standard in the procession, Lady Cecil and her husband Thomas Cecil, eldest son of Lord Burghley, and James Harington. Letters had been sent out in early

---

[61] Gittings, p. 167.
[62] See chapter 1.
[63] Bod., Ashmole MS 857 fol. 316; Arber, p. 343.
[64] PRO SP12/203/2; Laing, p. 28. See discussion in chapter 10.
[65] Laing, pp. 34–5; Arber, p. 344. For other examples of the heralds marshalling mourners, see Ingram, Appendix VIII, p. 510; Guillim, p. 251; Gittings, p. 173.
[66] Laing, pp. 9–16, an account which seems to be extracted from BL, Harley MS 1354, apparently drawn up by William Dethick.
[67] Lant, p. 30.

July to those selected by the Privy Council to attend the funeral. Presumably this was to ensure that there would be an appropriate level of display at the funeral and that a demonstration of political consensus would occur.[68] Quite evidently, as far as the State was concerned, Mary's funeral was an occasion concerned with public display rather than private grief.

The total cost of the proceedings seems to have been a mere £321 14s. 6d.[69] This was a very cheap elite funeral by the standards of the period. Edward, 3rd Earl of Rutland was buried in the same year at a cost of £2,297, while even the more modest funeral of Henry Sidney in 1586 had cost £1,571. The allowances for blacks appear to have been on the whole somewhat less than the usual amounts, although the statistics I am using for comparison refer to the allowances for male mourners.[70] More significant perhaps is the fact that the number of attendants allocated to each aristocrat was consistently less. An Earl, for example, normally had twelve attendants but was to have only eight at Mary's funeral.

Yet the achievements borne at the funeral represented the full set appropriate to a queen: a helm and crest, a target and a coat of arms. The helm and crest was borne by William Segar, then Portcullis Pursuivant; the target by Rouge Dragon; the sword by York and the coat of arms by Somerset.[71] Clarenceux followed with a Gentleman at Arms and then came the coffin, a crown of gold resting on its velvet canopy.[72]

The bannerolls proudly proclaimed Mary's multiple royal connections. Five of the eight bannerolls borne in the procession represented the arms of kings of Scotland, including the arms of James IV, impaled with those of Henry VII of England, and James V impaled with the arms of the Guise. There were also the arms of the Scottish Queen's husbands, Francis II and Lord Darnley, both impaled with Mary's own.[73]

Thus, although the funeral was relatively inexpensive and the mourners coerced into attendance, the trappings appropriate to the funeral of a queen all appeared in the procession. The display itself and reports of the funeral, both verbal and printed, would underline Elizabeth's respect for Mary's royal status,

---

68 Acts of the Privy Council (1587–88), p. 152; CSPV, VIII (1581–91), 256. Similarly, nobles and gentry in the locality had been commanded to attend the execution. Many of the mourners had also been at Mary's trial or, in the case of the ladies, were related to men that had been there; see Nichols (1740), pp. 54–6.
69 Laing, p. 56.
70 Bod., Ashmole MS 857 fol. 188; BL, Harley MS 1354 fol. 45 in Laing, p. 43; and chapter 1.
71 Laing, p. 63. The Elizabethan ordinance mentioned in chapter 1 might post-date this funeral.
72 Nichols (1740), p. 61.
73 Laing, p. 65.

demonstrating to both domestic and European audiences her innocence in respect of her cousin's death.[74]

By determining who should act as mourners in the funeral proceedings, the Privy Council made the occasion less vulnerable to appropriation by its enemies. They could not, however, exert authority over the members of Mary's household who took part in the funeral. It was from this quarter that the one element of dissent reported in the funeral procession sprang. Mary's French Jesuit priest, Du Preau, was deliberately provocative, wearing a gold crucifix about his neck although he was told the 'people disliked it'.[75] The impact of his blatant Catholic partisanship was, however, minimized by the regional location of the funeral.

The Church Service

The service itself, although more secluded from the public eye than the procession, was potentially a source of greater conflict because of the clash of religious allegiances amongst the mourners.

The trappings of the church service, as in the procession, were appropriate to the dead Queen's status. The whole of the choir and the body of the church were hung with black baize and escutcheons of the Queen's arms as was customary at elite funerals. In the nave two breadths of black cloth were hung between five and seven yards from the ground.[76] Similarly, a hearse with pillars supporting a valance was set up in the body of the church, above the first step of the choir. Escutcheons of the arms of Scotland, bearing the motto 'In my defence God me defend', were attached to the pillars and one hundred penons adorned the canopy. The hearse was of a size and design suitable to Mary's rank.[77]

The prebends and the choir met the procession at the church door, greeting them with songs and anthems and then leading the way to the chancel. As the procession entered the church, the poor women divided themselves, taking up positions on either side where they stood throughout the ceremony. Two knights with banners stood at the east end of the hearse outside the pale; eight squires with bannerols, four on each side, similarly stood outside the pale. The remainder of the mourners were escorted to the hearse by a herald and positioned on either side, the women nearest the altar.[78]

It was, of course, a Protestant service. Psalm-singing and organ music were included but, as we have seen, neither had been outlawed by the Reformation and indeed psalm-singing had become a significant Protestant practice.[79] The

---

[74] Sandford, p. 505.
[75] Arber, p. 345.
[76] Bod., Ashmole MS 857 fol. 315; BL, Harley MS 1440 fol. 13.
[77] BL, Harley MS 1440 fol. 13; Laing, pp. 2, 47, 59; Arber, pp. 343, 347.
[78] Arber, p. 345.
[79] See chapter 2.

Bishop of Lincoln preached on the thirty-ninth psalm, 'Lord let me know myne order; and the number of my days, that I may be satisfied howe long I have to live' and included citation of a saying of Luther's that 'Many (a) one liveth a Papist; and dieth a Protestant'. While there was no direct attempt to assert that there had been a death-bed conversion, Mary's Protestant salvation was not precluded.[80]

All the Scottish except Melville absented themselves from the sermon. According to some accounts they refused to witness any of the ceremony as well.[81] It was no doubt in anticipation of this kind of divisive behaviour that the funeral was deliberately staged away from great public scrutiny.

There was no royal succession to be enacted at this funeral ceremony and in the absence of burial cries, the offering ritual, with its commemoration of the dead Queen, formed the ritual centre of the proceedings. It is perhaps significant, then, that in the English published account of the proceedings (London: Venge, 1589) all the mourners, including the Scottish and French, witness the offering ceremony, giving an impression of unity and order.[82]

After the offering, the mourners departed. In the Venge account, the writer remarks that as the Scottish ladies approached the chancel door, they parted on both sides and as the English ladies passed they kissed them all. The account thus emphasises unity between Scots and English mourners. Finally the Dean supervised the closing burial ritual. He read the words of the burial service and then the staves were broken and cast into the vault. The company headed for the Bishop's palace for the funeral dinner and the 'concourse was of many thousands'. After the feast the company dispersed and dole was dispersed to the poor.[83]

The Dethick and Venge accounts make no mention of an effigy of Mary. It is the 'body' that was borne by the six gentlemen in cloaks with a black velvet canopy fringed with gold carried behind by four knights.[84] The only piece of evidence that could be associated with the construction of an effigy involves a death mask at Lennoxglove belonging to the Hamilton family which has always been referred to as the death mask of Mary Queen of Scots.[85] The attribution is, however, suspect. William Maitland (1525–73) spent time at Lennoxglove, then known as Lethington, when he was Secretary of State to Mary following her return from France in 1561. The mask came to be associated with him, hence the retrospective connection with Mary Queen of Scots.[86] In any case, even if a death mask was taken, it does not necessarily follow that an effigy was

---

80 Bod., Ashmole MS 857 fol. 316; Arber, p. 348.
81 Laing, p. 4; Bod., Ashmole MS 857 fol. 316.
82 Laing, p. 4.
83 PRO SP12/203/2; Bod., Ashmole MS 857 fol. 319; Arber, p. 349; Nichols (1740), p. 62.
84 Laing, p. 13.
85 Death masks were usually used in effigy construction; see chapter 5.
86 The identification is suggested in letters to Howgrave-Graham from Mrs B. Johnston, Holyrood House, 14 October 1955; and E. M. McGory, at the Headquarters of the Scottish

constructed. To have given Mary an effigy would have been tantamount to acknowledging her claim to the English throne.[87]

Alternative Versions of the Peterborough Funeral
A series of alternative versions of the funeral of Mary Queen of Scots were produced which differ from the account above compiled from Dethick and Venge.

The earliest was written in French and entitled *Les Magnifiques Obseques de la Royne d'Ecosse. 8me Aoust 1587*. There are two editions of this tract, one printed by Jean Naffield in Edinburgh, 1589 but the other, by the same printer, dated 1587. Thus it predates the English account published by Venge in 1589. It may be that this tract was published with a Scottish and/or French Catholic public in mind. The writer was certainly used to Catholic funerals and notes the distinctively Protestant elements of the ceremony while associating himself with their Catholic counterparts. He comments on the fact that the Dean and 'Chanoines' who received the corpse at the door of the cathedral were dressed in surplices; on the absence of candles on the hearse, 'au milieu du Choeur, estoit elevé un dome, à la façon de nos chapelles ardentes, sans cierges'; and on the Protestant style of the funeral service 'en lange Anglois'.[88]

The writer also mentions that the late Queen's household departed before the service, 'ne voulans assister à leurs prieres'. Interestingly, in direct opposition to the Venge account, they do not return for the offering, 'Les Herauts à quelque temps de là, & apres le Sermon (...) les fut inviter dans le cloistre où ils estoient de venir à l'offrande, cequils refuserent de faire, disans, qu'ils n'offroient point à un autel qu'ils n'approuvoient pas'. The household only returned for the breaking of the staves that concluded the ceremony. Another French account goes further stating that when Mary's servants were finally prevailed upon to return from the cloisters to perform the stave-breaking ceremony, they found that the ritual had already been enacted.[89] A Catholic would want to emphasize that the Catholic mourners took no part in the Protestant church ceremony. The French version follows one English version, that contained in the Bodleian manuscript Ashmole 857, but differs from Venge's published English account. Were either or both of these account writers twisting events to suit their readership or simply describing what they felt must have happened, moulding history to suit expectations?

The French account differs from Venge in several other respects. First, the

---

Ministry of Works, 8 November 1955. Both are held at the Westminster-Abbey Library, Box: Royal Funeral Effigies.
[87] Similarly it is unlikely that an effigy was constructed for the politically controversial Catherine of Aragon despite Thomas Wriothesley's instructions that one should be prepared; see Harvey and Mortimer, p. 6.
[88] Laing, pp. 27, 30.
[89] Richard Gough, *Sepulchral Monuments in Great Britain* ([London (?)]: [n. pub.], 1786), p. 165 cited by Laing, p. 78.

Scottish mourners are segregated for the funeral feast at the Bishop's palace. They eat in a chamber apart where they 'meslerent force larmes avec leur boire et leur manger', suggesting, perhaps, a refusal to play a part in the English propaganda exercise.[90]

A second departure takes us back to the beginning of the funeral proceedings. On arriving at the castle to receive the encoffined body, Garter goes up to 'la chambre où estoit le corps, lequel il fist mettre dans le chariot, avec un grand respect et un profond silence'.[91] Is this account trying to suggest that Mary's body had been lying-in-state in a manner appropriate to a royal funeral during the long delay before her funeral, thereby placing the funeral within a context of greater magnificence?

The most striking discrepancy however, is that the 'body' of the Dethick account becomes 'la représentation' in the French account. This can be translated as 'effigy'. The inclusion of an effigy, a key element, as we have seen, of royal funeral processions in both England and France, would represent a radical reinscription of the proceedings.

The term 'représentation' appears again in the funeral service description: 'Sous ce dome fut mise la représentation de sa Maiesté, sut une biere couverte de velours noir, & sur un oreiller de velours cramoisi estoit posee une Couronne'.[92] Here, however, use of the term seems confusing. If there is an effigy, why is the crown not upon its head? And where is the cushion upon which the crown lies? On the effigy? Next to it?

The key to understanding the texts lies in the duality of meaning inherent in the sixteenth-century French word 'représentation'.[93] While it certainly could mean 'une figure moulée et peinte qui, dans les obsèques représentent le défunct', it could also simply refer to a simulated coffin covered with a pall and bearing a coat of arms or a crown.[94] Often the term 'représentation' did refer to an effigy but not necessarily; its meaning was fluid. In the case of Mary Queen of Scots, the Venge account states that a golden crown rested upon the coffin.[95] We also know that the coffin was empty, the body having been buried the evening before, suggesting another reason why the term 'représentation' was used. We should conclude, then, that in all probability, Mary's 'représentation' was a crown resting on a pall on top of the coffin.

The double meaning of 'représentation', while saving the account writer

---

[90] Laing, p. 30.
[91] Laing, p. 27.
[92] Laing, p. 30.
[93] Émile Littré, *Dictionnaire de la Langue Française*, 7 vols (Paris: Gallimard, 1964), VI (1964).
[94] Giesey (1960) gives several examples of the latter use of the term 'représentation' including a memorial service performed by Louis XI at Avesnes in 1461 when he heard of Charles VII's death. The hearse contained a 'représentation' upon which rested a very rich drapery of cloth of gold. Evidently here an effigy was not used; see Giesey pp. 85–91.
[95] PRO SP12/203/2; Laing, p. 4.

from the charge of deliberate fabrication, nevertheless permits a fluidity of meaning and interpretation on the part of the account reader. While an effigy might not have been meant it could have been understood.

A second French account, included in a tract entitled *La Mort de la Royne d'Ecosse, Dovariere de France* which was published in France in 1589, takes the form of a description of the funeral convoy.[96] This version also uses the term 'représentation'. Further, since any description of the church service is omitted, there is no mention of the 'représentation' with its crown lying in the hearse to clarify the way the term was being used. With this clue to the non-effigy meaning of the term absent, the presence of the 'représentation' in the convoy remains unspecific but suggestive.

The French versions of the funeral, with their allusions to lying-in-state and to the use of an effigy, may be trying to make the occasion more royal than it actually was, perhaps as a propaganda exercise to satisfy those who felt Mary Queen of Scots deserved a full state funeral. At the same time the record of the absence of the Scottish mourners from the offering ceremony could have been directed at the Catholic reader who would have been shocked if they had attended a Protestant service. It seems that we may be dealing with a deliberately ameliorated account of the funeral for a Catholic public.[97]

If none of the written accounts of Mary's funeral make a direct claim for the use of an effigy, a pictorial version does. The British Library manuscript collection includes an interesting black and white Indian ink drawing of the funeral procession of Mary Queen of Scots which depicts the funeral chariot complete with a crowned effigy of the dead queen wearing robes of state (figure 16).[98] A fringed canopy is borne above the effigy but its hands are empty: the sceptre and orb usually borne by royal funeral effigies are absent. The drawing, bound with various other depictions of royal and noble funerals, has been dated as products of the early seventeenth century, suggesting that it was drawn retrospectively. This representation may have been based on the ambiguous descriptions in the French accounts of the funeral or, and this is probably more likely, it could have been part of a process of deliberately rewriting and ameliorating the funeral of Mary Queen of Scots as the reign of her son drew near.[99]

William Dethick, now Garter herald and writing in 1599, revises the costing of what had in fact been a relatively cheap funeral, to bring it in line with the expected expenditure at a royal funeral. The £321 14s. 6d. actually spent

---

[96] Laing, p. 18.
[97] For evidence of Catholics dwelling at length on the virtues of Catholic burials and unfavourable comments on Protestant obsequies, see D. Person, *Varieties: A Surveigh of rare and excellent matters* (London: T. Alchorn, 1635), p. 164; Gittings, p. 51.
[98] BL, Additional MS 35324 fols 14–17.
[99] There remains the possibility that it was guess-work on the part of an artist not present on the occasion. However, since such drawings were almost exclusively produced by heralds familiar with funeral ritual regulations, accidental inclusion of an effigy seems unlikely.

becomes greatly inflated: 'The Countesses of Rutland and Bedford representing the royall estate with the assembly of noblemen, countesses, baronesses, and ladies attending expressly, from and by her majesty's pleasure, and at her highness's expenses to the amount of 4000 librar. in the provision of all which, and the ceremonies pertaining to the same, on account of my office, I myself had principall direction'. This was a considerable sum, exceeding the £3,500 spent on the funeral of Robert Dudley, Earl of Leicester (1588), one of the most expensive contemporary heraldic funerals.[100] Dethick, too, seems to have been revising matters in the light of the imminent accession of James VI to the English throne.

The funerals of Mary Queen of Scots at home and abroad, together with their textual and visual record, were reinscribed according to the religious and political affiliations of the organisers, writers and artists. Contingency was paramount.

In staging the Peterborough obsequies, Elizabeth herself demonstrated that she recognized the social significance and propaganda potential of funeral. James was to emulate his predecessor in paying close attention to the theatre of death. Before looking at the post-accession rituals that he staged for his natural mother, it is useful to look at James's first experience of English royal funeral ritual: the funeral of Elizabeth I.

---

[100] Tate, I, 204; Gittings, p. 180.

CHAPTER FIVE

The Royal Funeral of Elizabeth I (1603)

Building on the general analysis of heraldic funerals undertaken in chapters 1 and 2, discussion in this chapter focuses on the use of the funeral effigy, a feature that, in Elizabethan England, was unique to royal funerals. The effigy ritual is explored in its political, cultural and post-Reformation context. Unfortunately there is no extant account of the church services at Elizabeth's funeral, including the offering ritual. Analysis is, therefore, necessarily confined to the funeral procession and lying-in-state ritual.

Elizabeth's Funeral and the Jacobean Succession

The Effigy and the Funeral Procession

Queen Elizabeth's funeral procession, held on 28 April 1603, was recorded in two series of drawings depicting the mourners walking towards Westminster Abbey.[1] The focal point of the funeral procession, as the drawings show, was not Elizabeth's physical remains but the life-like effigy of the dead Queen (figure 15). Henry Chettle describes it as 'The lively Picture of her Highnesse whole body, crowned in her Parliament Robes, lying on the corpse balmed and leaded, covered with velvet, borne on a chariot, drawn by four horses, trapt in Black Velvet'. Six bannerols were carried on each side of the chariot by barons. Three Earl's assistants followed them on each side. Then came two groups of gentlemen pensioners, their axes pointing downwards, and following them a group of footmen. Four noblemen bore a canopy over the chariot. The Earl of Worcester followed leading the 'Palfrie of Honour'.[2]

The pre-eminence of the effigy relative to the corpse was underlined by the

---

[1] The two sets of drawings extant are: (i) BL, Additional MS 5408 – black and white depiction on a roll by William Camden; (ii) BL, Additional MS 35324 fols 26–39 – colour drawings in Indian ink, anonymous. These are the first pictorial records of the funeral procession of an English sovereign, see Fritz, p. 64.

[2] This account is based on Henry Chettle, 'The Order and Proceeding at the Funerall of the Right High and Mighty Princesse Elizabeth Queene of England, France and Ireland from the Palace of Westminster, called Whitehall: to the Cathedrall Church of Westminster. 28th April 1603', in *A Third Collection of Scarce and Valuable Tracts*, 3 vols (London:

way each was dressed. Before the use of effigies, kings were all buried in royal apparel.³ Edward II, however, was buried in the linen coif, sleeveless shirt, tunic and gloves that he had worn at his anointing. The remaining coronation garments and ornaments were apparently used to adorn the effigy. The corpses of all subsequent monarchs were merely embalmed and wrapped in cerecloth.⁴

Display was the primary function of the effigy as is made clear by the construction methods used. The face was usually modelled using a death mask, the making of which was the responsibility of tallow-chandlers. The process involved taking a negative mould from the dead face up to a line well forward of the ears but including the main features. A wig of human hair would later hide the imperfect ears. On the effigies of Edward III and Henry VII the ears were omitted altogether.⁵ Verisimilitude mattered only in what would be seen.

What purpose lay behind the display of the effigy of the dead Queen? John Stow, writing not long after the event, described the effect of the effigy upon onlookers as follows: when 'they beheld her statue and picture lying upon the coffin set forth in Royall Robes, [. . .] there was such a generall sighing and groning, and weeping, and the like hath not beene seene or knowne in the memorie of man'.⁶ Such widespread grief seems idealized, however, particularly in the light of a contemporary record of the remarks made by the spectators who were busy analysing Elizabeth's reign with a predictable blend of positive and negative comment.⁷ It is not surprising that there was no national consensus of support. The political success and popularity which Elizabeth had enjoyed in the 1580s had severely waned in her last decade and she died leaving a legacy of government debt together with an unsolved war in the Netherlands. The country scarcely mourned her. All attention was focused on the arrival of the new King who, it was fondly hoped, would revitalize the policies of government as well as providing a new charismatic leader and male hero.⁸

F Gogan, 1751) I, 51–4; and CA, Vincent MS 151 fol. 521. See also Stow, p. 815; BL, Additional MS 5408; 35324; Bod., Ashmole MS 818 fol. 20.

3   St Edward, Henry II, Richard I and Edward I are examples; see Hope, pp. 518–31.
4   The same development occurred in France where the bodies of Charles VIII (d. 1498) and all succeeding kings were buried naked; see Giesey (1960), pp. 108–12.
5   R. P. Howgrave-Graham, 'Royal Portraits in Effigy: Some New Discoveries in Westminster Abbey', *Journal of the Royal Society of Arts* (29 May 1953), 465–74 (pp. 159–60); he cites John Harvey, fellow of the Society of Antiquaries.
6   Stow, p. 815. Stow's *Annales* were originally published in 1592 and re-issued in 1605. Stow died in 1605 and if this was his account it was written not long after the actual events. The 1615 edition which I have looked at was completed and considerably altered by one Edmond Howes. See also Thomas Dekker, *The Wonderful Year* ([London (?)]: [n. pub.], 1603), p. 3.
7   John Clapham, *Elizabeth of England: certain observations concerning the life and reign of Queen Elizabeth* ed. by E. P. Read and C. Read (Philadelphia: University of Pennsylvania Press, 1951), p. 113.
8   Christopher Haigh *Elizabeth I* (London: Longman, 1988), p. 165; MacCaffrey, pp. 243, 443–4. On Elizabeth's unpopularity amongst common people, see ibid., pp. 160–1. On

In her final years, Elizabeth's political difficulties threatened to mar her official public images: the Virgin Queen; or Gloriana, Spenser's 'most royall Queene or Empresse'.[9] At the same time, Elizabeth as Cynthia, Diana or Belphoebe, Spenser's personification of the private virtues of his Queen, also suffered from the ever-widening disparity between the projected image of an eternally youthful virgin queen and the reality of old age. Courtiers were not beyond engaging in mockery.[10] Even Elizabeth's godson John Harington produced pen-caricatures of the Queen as a silly old woman.

Elizabeth's defence was to don the trappings of her Gloriana image. John Clapham comments, 'In her latter time, when she showed herself in public, she was always magnificent in apparel, supposing haply thereby, that the eyes of people, being dazzled by the glittering aspect of those accidental ornaments would not so easily discern the marks of age and decay of natural beauty.'[11]

Artists had greater power and could rejuvenate the ageing features that Elizabeth could not disguise. The *Ditchley*-type portrait, which dominates the years following the Armada, embodies a relatively realistic approach to the ageing Queen, which may have been due to the Flemish influence and the atelier of De Critz/Gheeraerts. However, later portraits of the Queen adopt a mask of youth: she becomes, for example, Belphoebe, 'most vertuous and beautiful Lady', in *The Rainbow* (c. 1600–3). The *Coronation Portrait of Elizabeth I* (National Portrait Gallery), painted either shortly before or just after the Queen's death (c. 1600–10), places the mask of youth on the public Gloriana image. Interestingly, the portrait may have functioned as a funerary image. It depicts the Queen in her coronation regalia, orb and sceptre in hand, her long hair flowing down her shoulders in a sign of virginity.[12] In 1596 the Privy Council ordered all public officers to aid the Queen's Serjeant Painter in seeking

---

James's initial popularity, see N. E. M. McClure, ed., *The Letters of John Chamberlain*, 2 vols (Philadelphia: The American Philosophical Society, 1939), I, 189–90; Lee (1990), p. 106.

[9] For references to Gloriana in Edmund Spenser's *The Faerie Queene* see Prologue, 2, 4; I. i.3, vii.46, ix.13–6, x.58–9, xi.7, xii.18–41; II. ii.40–3, ix.4–7 in J. C. Smith and E. De Selincourt, eds, *Spenser: Poetical Works* (Oxford: Oxford University Press, 1912). See also Jeffrey Fruen, ' "True Glorious Type": The Place of Gloriana in *The Faerie Queene*', *Spenser Studies: A Renaissance Annual*, 7 (1986), pp. 147–73.

[10] Haigh (1988), pp. 164–6.

[11] Clapham, p. 86. The Queen's wardrobe was reputed to have brought £60,000 when it was auctioned off after her death; see Malcolm Smuts, *Court Culture and the Origins of the Royalist Tradition in Early Stuart England* (Philadelphia: University of Pennsylvania Press, 1987), p. 141.

[12] Roy Strong, *Portraits of Queen Elizabeth I* (Oxford: Clarendon Press, 1963), p. 22; John N. King, 'Queen Elizabeth I: Representations of the Virgin Queen', *Renaissance Quarterly*, 43 (1990), 30–74 (pp. 42–3); Elizabeth W. Pomeroy, *Reading the Portraits of Queen Elizabeth I* (Hamden, Conn.: Archon Books, 1989), pp. 9–12. The original painting (c. 1559) has been lost.

out all unseemly portraits of her, that they might be destroyed. Disguising the Queen's age in portraits had become an official policy.[13]

Death completed the split between image and reality: Gloriana, the imperial ruler was reduced to a corpse. Yet the funeral effigy provided a means of preserving at least one of the fictional images of Elizabeth. It is debatable whether or not the Belphoebe face of youth was aimed at in the effigy production. Elizabeth's original funeral effigy does not survive but, as I shall argue later, it is likely that a death mask was used in its production and, thus, that wrinkles and other features of ageing would have been reproduced on the effigy's face.[14] Nevertheless, it seems that the figure was made to appear vibrant. In the written accounts, Clapham comments that the Queen's image was 'all very exquisitely framed to resemble life'. Similarly the Venetian ambassador states that the effigy was carved in wood and coloured 'so faithfully that she seems alive'.[15] These reports need, however, to be considered with care. References to verisimilitude are a constant of funeral accounts from at least the late fourteenth century and correspond to an emergent interest in portraiture.[16] For the funeral of Edward III (1377), for example, a certain Stephen Hadley was paid £22 4s. 11d. 'pro factura unius ymaginis ad similitudinem Regis'.[17] Yet verisimilitude obviously meant something rather different to the fourteenth-century craftsmen who modelled the head of Anne of Bohemia (d. 1394) than it did to the Renaissance masters who worked on the image of Henry VII (figure 12 and 13).[18] The art historian Eric Mercer concludes that textual references to similitude are similarly unreliable in the field of tomb sculpture and that evidence must be gleaned from the tomb effigies themselves.[19] The tomb effigy of Elizabeth depicts an ageing woman, a distinguished ruler but not a figure of eternal youth. In sharp contrast is the iconographic evidence of the procession drawings. In the British Library roll the effigy has flaming red hair and eyes wide open, strongly suggesting that it was coloured and wore a wig. If this is an accurate record, in part, at least, an attempt was made to reproduce the Belphoebe 'maske of youth' of the *Coronation* portrait.[20]

---

[13] See Strong (1963), p. 5 citing *Acts*, ed. by J. R. Dasent, xxvi, 69.
[14] See my discussion later in this chapter.
[15] Clapham, p. 112; CSPV, X (1603–7), 212.
[16] Harvey and Mortimer, p. 34.
[17] Hope, p. 532. See also Thomas of Walsingham's description of the effigies of Henry V (d. 1422), cited by Hope, pp. 535–6, and Henry VIII, ibid., p. 540.
[18] Ernst Benkard, *Undying Faces: A Collection of Death Masks*, trans. by Margaret M. Green (Hogarth Press: London, 1929), p. 29. Howgrave-Graham concludes that within the stylistic canons of the period, the sculptors working on the effigy head of Anne of Bohemia made an attempt to reproduce the actual appearance of the young woman; see Harvey and Mortimer, pp. 37, 42. For further comment on Henry VII's effigy, see my section on effigy design later in this chapter.
[19] See Eric Mercer, *English Art 1553–1625* (Oxford: Oxford University Press, 1962), pp. 238–9.
[20] BL, Additional MS 5408. The open eyes of funeral effigies may have originally been

That the Elizabeth effigy perpetuated the Gloriana myth is much more certain. It wore the trappings of rule and majesty as the charges for the funeral confirm:

> Item for x yarde of crimson sattin to make a
> Robe for the representacon at xvj^s the yard   viij^{li}
>
> Item for xj yard of white fustian to lyne the
> same Robe at xviii^s the yard   xvj^s iij^d [21]

The crimson robes worn by Elizabeth's effigy were traditional, although the decision to line them with white may have been a symbolic reference to her status as Virgin Queen. It is not exactly clear which set of robes was used for the effigy in the procession. A complete set of both Coronation and Parliamentary robes appear in the inventory of the Wardrobe at 1600 and both were still present when a check was carried out in 1604. The Parliamentary robes, a purple mantle, and robes of crimson velvet, adorned with miniver and ermine, were perhaps the more likely choice, since they had also been worn by the effigies of Henry V, Henry VII and Henry VIII.[22] In either case costume signalled royal stature. Upon the effigy's head was the imperial crown and in its hands the orb and sceptre, symbols of sovereignty. All these features indicate that the effigy was intended to perpetuate the Majesty of the Crown, a suggestion that Ernst Kantorowicz made in the context of French royal funeral effigy rituals.[23] The happy conjunction between the style required to fulfil the function of displaying royal immortality and the Gloriana image of Elizabeth made the effigy symbolism particularly resonant on this occasion.

The effect of the dead Queen's magisterial and idealized, yet life-like effigy on observers was the spontaneous expression of grief recorded by Stow. Clapham emphasizes the causal relationship between effigy and emotion: 'At the sight thereof, divers of the beholders fell a weeping.' The image of the dead queen functioned as a means of generating an expression of community feeling, or 'communitas' to borrow the term used by Victor Turner. In spite of the ambivalence felt by her subjects at the close of Elizabeth's reign, the performance of the funeral procession seems to have succeeded in creating an impression of political consensus or *collective effervescence*, to borrow Durkheim's term.[24] Yet, one must be wary of taking such descriptions of national grief at face value. The record of sorrow in Clapham and Stow may simply be conventional or a careful

---

intended as a visual paradigm of Job 19. 26–7: 'Yet in my flesh shall I see God: Whom I shall see for myself, and mine eyes shall behold, and not another'; see Harvey and Mortimer, p. 4.

[21] P. R. O. Lord Chamberlain's Records, Series I. Vol. 554; cited by Hope, p. 553.

[22] Queen consort effigies also wore red robes; see Hope, pp. 535–6, 541, 551; and CA, Briscoe MS II fol. 313.

[23] Kantorowicz, pp. 423, 446.

[24] The same may well be true of Dekker's statement that 'Never did the English Nation behold so much black worne as there was at her funerall'; see Dekker (1603), p. 3.

re-writing of the occasion for posterity. I am not arguing that there were none who genuinely mourned the Queen but simply that the homogeneity of the emotional response may have been deliberately contrived in order to fabricate a national 'grief' for the ageing and unpopular Queen.

The form of the funeral procession itself served to underline the desired social values of consensus and continuity. The effigy of the dead Queen appeared within a hierarchically-ordered convoy. It comprised representatives of a range of social groups, including the whole of the late Queen's household and 'besides the greatest part of the nobilitie, all the connsaile'.[25] As the transcription of the funeral procession of Elizabeth given in Appendix I illustrates, apart from the inclusion of the effigy the structure was basically the same as that of a nobleman, differences being largely in terms of scale, as described in chapter 1. All members of the royal household, right down to the workers from the scullery and stable, were included.[26] 12,000 yards of black fabric were apportioned to the mourners but it was thought they would be insufficient for the 1,600 participants.

All were organized according to their relative status, mirroring society. The Lord Mayor of London, representing the City, occupied, for example, a position close to the effigy. Proximity to the royal representation, which itself occupied a central position in the procession, directly equated with status. Whereas in the funerals of the nobility the procession embodied the local community, in the royal funeral the form became an embodiment of the state. The royal funeral procession constituted a visual paradigm of social order, centring around the effigy as society was centred around the monarch.[27]

The heraldic language of the royal funeral provided a means of expressing authority on a national scale. At Elizabeth's funeral there appeared the royal standards of the Dragon (Wales), Greyhound (Tudor) and Lion (England, later Scotland).[28] The French ambassador and the agents for Venice and the Estates marched in the procession, underlining the significance of royal funerals for international diplomacy.

Other symbolic features similarly marked the royal status of the defunct. Three groups of four trumpeters, an instrument with strong royal associations, and three horses, in addition to the usual Horse of Honour, were included in the procession. Each horse was trapped to the ground in black and bore black feathers on its crest and rump together with a shafferon on its crown.[29] Achievements were borne at Elizabeth's funeral despite the fact that an

---

[25] Details of the participants are given in PRO SP14/1/21. The chief mourners comprised two Marquesses, sixteen Countesses and thirty Baronesses 'with all their traine'.

[26] Salisbury, XV, 56; Sandford, p. 497.

[27] See chapter 1. On anthropological theories that treat the body as an image of society, see Woodbridge, pp. 270–1.

[28] J. P. Brooke-Little (Norroy and Ulster King of Arms), *Royal Heraldry: Beasts and Badges of Britain* (Derby: Pilgrim Press, 1987), pp. 3, 9. See also Bod., Ashmole MS 818 fol. 1.

[29] BL, Additional MS 5408.

The Royal Funeral of Elizabeth I

ordinance of the time dictated that 'it is not convenient that a woman should have a Coate of Armes of Shielld Helme and creste, the which is not lawful today'.[30] Elizabeth, the Virgin Queen who had relinquished her femininity and wed herself to the State, might have a helm, crest, sword and coat of arms at her funeral. Spurs and gauntlets, perhaps the most masculine items, were, however, omitted.

Succession Theories and Display of the Royal Person
The ritual demonstration of order effected by the funeral procession had obvious value for King James as he took the reigns of his new kingdom. Certainly James and his English councillors attached value to the occasion. Estimates of the total cost of the proceedings vary from £11,305 to £20,000 but even the lower sum was enormous at a time when the cost of the most extravagant noble funerals did not exceed £3,000.[31] Yet the effigy directed the collective emotional response back towards the dead Queen. What purpose could this serve for the new monarch? The politico-legal theory of the king's two bodies, which Kantorowicz used to elucidate the symbolism of the effigy ritual in the French royal funeral, provides a useful context in which to begin exploring answers to this question.

Despite its French application, it was in England, not France, that the theory was developed and expounded by jurists, most famously by the lawyer Edmund Plowden in relation to the Duchy of Lancaster case in 1564. It went on to play an important role in Elizabethan succession politics.[32] Plowden distinguished between the king's body natural and the body politic, mystically incorporating all the subjects of the realm of which the king was the head. The former was subject to error, decay and ultimately death, the latter was unerring and immortal.

For our purposes Plowden's most important application of the theory is his explanation of what happens when a monarch dies. Normally the body politic is contained within the body natural but at death a disjunction occurs as the body politic is vested in the natural body of the successor:

> As to this Body the King never dies, and his natural Death is not called in our Law [...] the Death of the King, but the Demise of the King, not signifying by

---

[30] BL, Egerton MS 2642 fol. 205.
[31] Gittings (p. 226) has £11, 305 1s. but does not cite her source. Roger Lockyer, *The Early Stuarts: A Political History of England 1603–1642* (London: Longman, 1989), p. 82 gives £20,000, a figure derived from D. H. Willson, ed., *The Parliamentary Diary of Robert Bowyer 1606–1607* (Minneapolis, 1931), Appendix A, p. 372. Lockyer's figure may be a later estimate based on a broader definition of the funeral proceedings, including, for example, extra costs such as construction of the tomb in Westminster Abbey, £765.
[32] See Marie Axton, *The Queen's Two Bodies: Drama and the Elizabethan Succession* (London: Royal Historical Society, 1977), p. 11; Kantorowicz, p. 447; J. R. Hale, *Renaissance Europe 1480–1520* (London: Fontana, 1971), p. 307.

the Word [Demise] that the body politic of the King is dead, but that there is a Separation of the two Bodies, and that the Body politic is transferred and conveyed over from the Body natural now dead, or now removed from the Dignity royal, to another Body natural.[33]

It is easy to see how the Plowden theory could be applied to the royal funeral ritual with the two bodies of the monarch, the body natural and the body politic, being represented by the corpse and the effigy respectively. In this interpretation the effigy preserves the body politic or Majesty of the King during the ceremonial interregnum between the death of one king and the public display of his successor, thus demonstrating the perpetuity of kingship.[34] There is, as far as I am aware, no contemporary application of the theory to the royal funeral; however, the herald recording the offering ceremony at the funeral of Sir Geoffrey Ellwas, Alderman of London (14 May 1616) remarks, 'Be it remembered that the two pennons of his Company are not to be offered at all because the Companyes dye not.'[35] Ellwas's words provide interesting evidence that funeral symbolism was indeed understood in terms of the theory of the king's two bodies.

Certainly, the theory of the king's two bodies was in vogue at the time of the succession and its exponents expected to find favour with James. A presentation copy of Plowden's succession treatise, which had been written in support of Mary Queen of Scots' claims to the English throne and published in 1569, was prepared for the new King.[36]

James, predictably, had always been interested in succession theories and expressed his ideas in his *Trew Law of Free Monarchies*. This was first published in 1598 and then published again, with *Basilikon Doron*, as James's message to his new English subjects on his succession. However, James's exposition of the succession process differs from that of Plowden in significant ways. He does not make the theoretical distinction between the body natural and the body politic, referring only to the personalities of the new and old kings.[37] Thus, kingship is inseparable from the person of the King.[38] He also does not envisage the process of transference in the rather cumbersome way described in Plowden. Instead James argues that the throne was never vacant, 'for at the very moment of the

---

[33] Edmund Plowden, *Commentaries or Reports* (London, 1816), p. 212a, cited by Kantorowicz, p. 13. See also Giesey (1960), pp. 177–8; Axton, pp. 27–8.
[34] See my discussion in chapter 3.
[35] BL, Harley MS 1368 fol. 29.
[36] Axton, pp. 19–20.
[37] Bacon similarly characterized the king's person and the Crown as inseparable in the 'Post-Nati' debate in Parliament. See J. Spedding and D. D. Heath, eds, *The Works of Francis Bacon*, 7 vols (London: [n. pub.], 1892), VII, 665–7 and Kantorowicz, p. 365.
[38] Tudor political thinkers, like Plowden, had attached divinity to the office rather than the person, a necessary distinction given the circumstances under which the Tudor dynasty acceded to the throne.

expiring of the king reigning, the nearest lawful heir entereth in his place'. Thus James emphasizes that royal succession happens instantaneously.

James's succession theory is reminiscent of Jean Bodin, the French advocate of absolute monarchy. Bodin had written, 'Car il est certain que le Roy ne meurt jamais, comme l'on dit, ainsi si tost que l'un est decedé, le plus proche masle de son estoc est saisi du Royaume et en possession d'iceluy au paravant qu'il soit couronné'.[39] While Bodin's use of the phrase 'comme l'on dit' suggests that the maxim was well-known by the time that he was writing in c. 1576, his particular expression of the succession process is close to the language used by James in the *True Law*, suggesting the latter may have been directly indebted to Bodin's work. Bodin's *Les Six Livres de la République* was not to be published in English translation until 1606 but it had appeared in French in 1576 and 1583. Bodin was well known in England. In 1579 the poet Gabriel Harvey claimed that at Cambridge 'You can not stepp into a schollars studye but (ten to on[e]) you shall litely finde open ether Bodin de Republica or Le Royes Exposition uppon Aristotles Politiques.'[40]

Whatever the source of James's theories of instantaneous succession they were formally acknowledged by the representatives of his new subjects in the opening of Parliament in 1603. James himself alluded to the concept in his address, thanking them for receiving him so joyously into this 'Seate (which God by my birthright and lineall descent had in the fulnesse of time provided for me)'. Parliament responded 'That immediately upon the Dissolution and Decease of Elizabeth late Queen of England, the imperial Crown of the Realm of England, and of all the Kingdoms, Dominions and Rights belonging to the same, did by inherent birthright, and lawful and undoubted succession, descend and come in your most excellent Majesty, as being lineally, justly and lawfully, next and sole heir of the Blood Royal of their Realm.'[41]

James's political theories were in harmony with legal reality. From the thirteenth century the new king's reign had been dated from the day of his predecessor's demise. Further, James's legal position was ritually affirmed in the public ceremonies of proclamation which took place on the very morning of Elizabeth's death. The ritual nature of the proclamation is signalled by its repetition in key London locations: Whitehall Gates, Temple Bar and Cheapside. According to Stow, princes, peers, prelates and knights were in attendance in

---

[39] Kantorowicz, p. 409, n. 319 citing Bodin, *Les Six Livres de la République*, I, 8, 160.

[40] J. P. Sommerville, *Politics and Ideology in England, 1603–1640* (London: Longman, 1986), p. 39 citing Edward J. L. Scott, ed., *Letter-Booke of Gabriel Harvey A.D. 1573–1580* ([London (?)]: Camden Society, 1884), p. 79. See also J. H. M. Salmon, *The French Religious Wars in English Political Thought* (Oxford: Clarendon Press, 1959), p. 6 and Appendix B, pp. 181–3. On the English tradition of absolutist thought, independent of Bodin, see Sommerville, p. 38.

[41] McIlwain, pp. xxxvii, 269. See also Edward Forset, *A comparative discourse of the bodies natural and politique. Wherein [. . .] is set forth the true forme of a commonweale, with the dutie of subjects, and the right of the soveraigne* (London: [n. pub.], 1606), p. 33.

Cheapside, 'besides the huge number of common persons, all which with great reverence gave attention unto the Proclamation being read by M. Secretary Cecill'.[42] In the next few days proclamations would follow in the provinces.[43]

James's staging of Elizabeth's funeral ceremony, complete with effigy ritual, is an acknowledgement, however, that legal accession and ritual proclamation were not enough. He seems to have recognized that a ceremonial interregnum remained as far as display of the royal person was concerned. The apparent incompatibility of James's succession theories and Plowden's theory of the king's two bodies was less important than the strongly felt need to smooth the period of transition and avoid a ceremonial interregnum. Thus the fiction of the effigy was enacted.

Why could James not fill the ceremonial interregnum in person? The simple explanation seems to be that at the time of his proclamation as King, James was far away in Edinburgh. In fact he did not even receive confirmation of Elizabeth's death until Robert Carey, son of Lord Hunsdon, arrived in Edinburgh five days later.[44] There would be no public ceremonial display of his person and no affirmation of his position in London until his coronation on 26 July 1603. Display of Elizabeth's effigy in the funeral procession, by perpetuating the public ruler image of the dead Queen, filled the ceremonial gap, demonstrating a continuity of rulership until the arrival of the new King.[45]

The distinction between ritual proclamation and ritual display was felt by contemporaries. In his sermon preached at Paul's Cross on the Sunday after Elizabeth's death, John Hayward highlighted the perceived difference between the declaration of the new king and his physical presence: 'His name hetherto onely proclaimed in our streetes, hath stilled the ragings of the people, danting the enemies of true religion, and causing the enemies of peace, that thought now to look out, to hide their heads. What shall we not hope that the presence of his person will doe, when the sound of his name hath done so much already?'[46] This preoccupation with the physical presence of the King fits in with David Starkey's assertions that Tudor and Stuart kingship, while it retained the

---

[42] Stow, p. 816. See also Salisbury, XV, 25–6; CSPV, IX (1592–1603), 540; John Bruce, ed., *The Diary of John Manningham* (London: Camden Society, 1868), p. 147; Sackville-West, p. 4; Dekker (1603), pp. 9–10.

[43] Clapham, pp. 106, 107. For earlier, less elaborate proclamation ceremonies, see Stow, p. 634 and Nichols (1848), p. 178 (Elizabeth); Stow, p. 612 and Duffy, p. 527 (Mary); and Stow, pp. 471–2 (Henry VII).

[44] Willson, p. 159.

[45] There has been a suggestion that obsequies for Elizabeth were celebrated at each of the London churches using a *corpus fictum*; see R. E. C. Waters, *Parish Registers in England* (London: F. J. Roberts, 1887), p. 47. It is unlikely, however, that this refers to multiple effigies of Elizabeth and is much more likely to refer to empty coffins perhaps bearing replica royal symbols to represent the dead Queen; see chapter 4.

[46] John Hayward, *Gods Universal right proclaimed: A sermon preached at St. Paules Crosse, 27 March 1603* (London: [n. pub.], 1603), p. 140. See also Millar Maclure, *The Paul's Cross Sermons, 1534–1642* (Toronto: University of Toronto Press, 1958), pp. 225–6.

theocratic bias of medieval kingship, 'centred [itself] round the sanctity of the royal body [. . .] rather than around the heavily Christian symbolism of the coronation'.[47] The significance of the coronation was no longer rooted in the anointing of the monarch, but in the display of his royal person to the populace.

James and Elizabeth's Royal Funeral: the Exploitation of Tradition
James's absence did not mean that he took no interest in the detailed planning of the funeral of his predecessor. Many of his early decisions reflect a desire to maintain a high degree of continuity in both government and royal household at his succession.[48] Part of this process was to ensure appropriate obsequies for his predecessor: 'The Quenes funerall is appointeed the 28th of this present month with as much solemnitie as hath been used to any former prince, and that by the kings owne direction.'[49] The details were in the hands of Robert Cecil and the remainder of the late Queen's Council, kept in place by a warrant requested of the Scottish King during Elizabeth's final illness. Cecil, who had a keen interest in antiquarian scholarship and libraries and was a friend of Sir Robert Cotton, may have relished his task. James kept abreast of the arrangements and willingly accommodated himself to the requirements of royal funeral ritual. He wrote to Cecil on 11 April 1603 enquiring about progress made in the arrangements: 'we look to hear by you also how all things stand for the funeral and the coronation'.[50]

James's recognition of the general utility of traditional customs in governing his people is clear from his comments in *Basilikon Doron* (1598) where he declared himself in favour of 'May games, public spectacle and exercise of arms' since they kept the people happy.[51] James would also be persuaded to continue touching for the King's Evil despite his Calvinist misgivings. Brought up as an Anglican, Charles I would not share his father's scruples. Belief in the royal miracle became part of the Caroline *religion royale*.[52]

---

[47] David Starkey, 'Representations Through Intimacy: A Study in the Symbolism of Monarchy and Court Office in Early Modern England', in *Symbols and Sentiments*, ed. by Ioan Lewis (London: Academic, 1977), pp. 187–224 (p. 221).

[48] Salisbury, XV, 345–6; Willson, p. 175. The Councillors that James inherited were Archbishop Whitgift; Egerton, Lord Keeper; Sackville, Lord Treasurer; Nottingham, Lord Admiral; the Earls of Shrewsbury and Worcester; and Robert Cecil, the central figure of government. See Neil Cuddy, 'The Revival of the Entourage: the Bedchamber of James I, 1603–1625', in *The English Court from the Wars of the Roses to the Civil War*, ed. by David Starkey and others (London: Longman, 1987), p. 176.

[49] PRO SP14/1/21.

[50] McClure, I, 193. After 1608 Robert Cotton became increasingly identified with Cecil's rival, Northampton; see Kevin Sharpe, *Sir Robert Cotton* (Oxford: Oxford University Press, 1979), p. 119.

[51] James I, *Basilikon Doron* (Edinburgh: Robert Waldegrave, 1599: repr. Menston: Scolar Press, 1969), p. 63; McIlwain, p. 27.

[52] See Marc Bloch, *The Royal Touch: Sacred Monarchy and Scrofula in England and France*, trans. by J. E. Anderson (London: Routledge and Kegan Paul, 1973), pp. 191–2.

The funeral ceremony was, as we have seen, useful in filling the ceremonial vacuum occasioned by the absence of a monarch in the capital while James was still journeying south and did so in a manner that would engage the expectations and emotions of the people. The rationale behind the performance of Elizabeth's funeral ceremony and, crucially, of its effigy ritual was, however, more complex than this. An examination of the correspondence which took place between James and his advisors reveals that in London, the ritual centre of royal power, display of the dead Queen's effigy took ceremonial precedence over the display of the new King. Even after his arrival James had to wait outside the capital until the funeral proceedings were over before making his entry. Thomas Howard, Lord Admiral, and Cecil wrote to Henry Howard on 14 April 1603 to advise on the timing of the King's progress towards London. They argued that it was 'impossible for the ladies to wait on the Queen [Anne], at Berwick, till after the late Queen's funeral'. The King, therefore, should not come to London until after Easter and then await the arrival of his wife between twelve and twenty miles from London before they entered the capital together.[53] Similarly, Robert Cecil advised the Council that the King needed to slow down his journey south because: 'the State could not attend both the performance of that duty [the funeral] to our late Sovereign, and of this other of his Majesty's reception'.[54]

The obsequies of dead monarchs were traditionally staged before the royal entry of their successors, a custom that no was doubt partly due to the practical considerations highlighted by the above correspondence. The same officials and dignitaries were required for the two ceremonies and could not play their part in both at the same time.[55] There was also, however, a shared assumption that the new King could not be displayed in London until the old Queen was buried.

We have seen how a tradition regarding the absence of the succeeding monarch may have arisen in France but there is no evidence to explain why the same tradition evolved in England. Yet certainly no Tudor monarch mourned at the funeral of his or her predecessor.[56] Disparities of age and gender between new and old monarchs, which contravened heraldic regulations, may have been contributory factors on these occasions, as they may have been in determining James's non-inclusion in the funeral proceedings.[57] What is clear is that it was not deemed acceptable for James to display his royal person in London before Elizabeth's funeral. The ceremonial logic of the effigy ritual filling the interregnum in royal public display was actively maintained.

The need to avoid eclipsing the display of Elizabeth's effigy in the funeral

---

53 PRO SP14/1/23; CSPD, VIII (1603–10), p. 3.
54 Salisbury, XV, 40, 53; D. R. Woolf, 'Two Elizabeths? James I and the Late Queen's Famous Memory', *Canadian Journal of History*, 20 (1985), 167–91 (p. 173).
55 In the event James's royal entry would be delayed until March 1604 because of plague in the capital; Clapham, p. 116.
56 For the French tradition and on chief mourners at Tudor funerals, see chapter 3.
57 See chapter 1 and Loach, p. 61.

procession also impinged upon James during his journey south. The new King was eager to display his person in full majesty to his new subjects. He planned a royal entry into the second city, York, and ordered jewels, regalia, coaches and heralds to be sent up from London.[58] The Council had not wanted to send these appurtenances further north than Burghley, Northamptonshire, but James insisted and also called for some of the Councillors, including Cecil, to journey up and meet him at York. The York entry was staged on 16 April. James progressed on foot to the minster, refusing to use a coach: 'I will have no coach for the people are desirous to see a King, and so they shall, for they shall as well see his body as his face.'[59] James clearly understood the fascination his subjects had with viewing the royal body. As Edward Forset expressed it, 'so when the person of a Prince is looked upon (whereon we doe so seldom gaze enough) our inward cogitations [are] filled with a reverence of the regall maiestie seated in the flesh (otherwise as infirme and full of imperfections as other is)'.[60]

Nevertheless, James acknowledged that the display of his own royal person had to be a secondary consideration. He wrote to Henry Howard on 12 April with reference to the planned York entry, saying, 'We mean to enter in a manner more public; and therefore like it well that some of our servants and officers have authority to meet us, not being any of those principals, which may diminish part of the honour and dignity which belongs to our dearest sister as long as her body is above ground.'

James went on to give reasons for curbing the display of his royal person, declaring that he was not only her successor, 'but so near of blood as we will not stand so much upon the ceremony of our own joy, but would have all things observed which may testify it well that they [Elizabeth's household] remain still entire as they were at her death'.[61] James here points to the primary reason behind his desire to see Elizabeth's funeral performed with full effigy ritual in accordance with tradition. Fulfilment of his duties to the dead Queen demonstrated his family or lineal association with her and thus the rightness of his succession. Primogeniture was at the root of James's claim to the English throne. As Maurice Lee puts it, 'whatever English common law or Henry VIII's will or the English parliament might say, James, at the moment of Elizabeth's death, would become King of England by hereditary right'.[62] In encouraging the staging of the funeral, James may have been partly constrained by public expectation but this coincided with his own political need to enact a 'traditional'

---

58 Willson, p. 162.
59 Nichols (1828), I, 78.
60 Forset, p. 32.
61 Salisbury, XV, 44.
62 Lee (1990), p. 65. See also the wording of the proclamation which gave details of James's descent from Margaret, daughter of Henry VII, emphasizing his lineal secession from Tudor stock and note the hereditary basis of James's succession claims in both the *Trew Law* and *Basilikon Doron*; see Lee (1990), p. 61; Nichols (1828), I, 27; Willson, p. 141.

funeral ritual.[63] It enabled him to mobilize bias in favour of his right to the English throne: imagined power, through ritual, can create power.

Ironically the tradition that James was exploiting necessitated his own absence from the proceedings, making him vulnerable to criticism from some quarters. Scaramelli, the Venetian ambassador provocatively interpreted James's behaviour as indicative of a deep antipathy for his predecessor: 'he wishes to see her [Elizabeth] neither alive nor dead, for he can never expel from his memory the fact that his mother was put to death at the hands of the public executioner'.[64] James's willingness to accommodate himself to the requirements of a traditional royal funeral makes nonsense of Scaramelli's malicious remarks.

The Vulnerability of the Royal Funeral: Threats to the Ritual Demonstration of Order

Despite James's right of lineal succession, he was not the only contender for the English throne and his status as an alien made his own candidature equivocal. His first cousin, Arabella Stuart, similarly traced her descent through the line of Margaret Tudor, but she had been born and brought up in England. The will of Henry VIII also presented difficulties. It passed over Margaret Tudor and stipulated that, should Henry's children die without issue, the succession should pass to the line of Mary, his younger sister, who had married Charles Brandon, Duke of Suffolk. The current representative of that line was virtually excluded on the grounds of the dubious legality of his parents' marriage and his personal unfitness for rule. However another Suffolk claimant, the Lord Beauchamp, was rumoured to be gathering forces just after the Queen's death. There was also a foreign contender, the Spanish Infanta, whose claims were eloquently set out by the English Jesuit Robert Parsons in his *Conference about the Next Succession to the Crown of England* (1594), a pamphlet which denied the principle of hereditary right.[65]

Although historians have been traditionally dismissive of these other claimants, contemporaries could not have foreseen how smoothly the succession would be effected. Elizabeth had consistently refused to name a successor or, in later years, to confirm James's status as heir to the throne and very few were aware of the secret correspondence between the Scottish King and Robert Cecil,

---

[63] The only way in which Elizabeth's funeral broke with tradition was in the costume of the female mourners who wore fashionable farthingales in place of the customary medieval-style garments.

[64] CSPV, X (1603–7), 9. Woolf (p. 173) says this testimony must be taken with a pinch of salt and not as evidence, as Trevor-Roper has argued, that the King had a strong antipathy to the Queen. See Hugh Trevor-Roper, *Queen Elizabeth's First Historian: William Camden and the Beginnings of English 'Civil' History* (London: Jonathan Cape, 1971), p. 10.

[65] Willson, pp. 138–40; McClure, I, p, 190. See also my chapter 4.

who was to mastermind the transfer of power.⁶⁶ John Harington certainly seems to have anticipated a contested succession and wrote a tract defending James's claim to the throne, presumably with the intention of getting it published should the accession have been disputed.⁶⁷ Harington's worries reflected a general fear that something might happen to jeopardize James's position and that consequently the country could be plunged into civil disorder and possibly even war, perhaps with foreign intervention. Anxieties of this kind had punctuated the reign and become a habit of mind. Certainly, had Elizabeth died without issue in the early years of her reign, the rival claims of the various candidates for the succession would have made civil war very likely.⁶⁸

The Venetian ambassador reported 'London is all in arms for fear of the Catholics.'⁶⁹ On 12 March 1603, Chief Justice Popham wrote to Robert Cecil, 'Of all other places, the confines of London would be well looked unto, for the most dissolute and dangerous people of England are there, and upon the least occasion will repair thither.' These fears may not have had much ground in real danger but, as historians agree, stability or the lack of it was a central issue in Renaissance London and that 'the *perception* of crisis in the capital was common'.⁷⁰ Precautionary measures were instigated by the Privy Council mainly under the auspices of Cecil. A watch was appointed in London during the time of Elizabeth's last illness. Catholic priests, 'likely to raise sedition' were sent to France, while other Catholics were taken into custody and 'all wandering and suspected persons arrested in all parts of the realm'. The Council sent warnings to strategic fortresses and war-ships were at the ready to guard the sea-coast against 'any outward attempts'.⁷¹

The ritual demonstration of order in the funeral ceremony would be welcome and play its part in the successful process of transferring power to the new King. There is some evidence of opposition to the Council's plans to use the funeral ritual to help smooth the succession process. The Privy Councillors met privately at the Lord Admiral's house to arrange conveyance of the body from Richmond to Westminster. Clapham reports that 'the barons of the realm, to whom it belonged as peers to direct affairs for the present, consult ordinarily with the Council of Estates, and now and then some of them, finding their own

---

66 Willson, pp. 153–5; Sir Ralph Winwood, *Memorials of Affairs of State*, ed. by Edmund Sawyer, 3 vols (London: [n. pub.], 1725), I, 324; MacCaffrey, pp. 94–100, 139–43, 292, 401, 434–41. Robert Cecil's father William had long entertained the desire for England and Scotland to become one monarchy and thus attain 'perpetual peace'; see ibid. p. 63.
67 Lee (1990), pp. 65, 95–6; Willson, p. 140; Clapham, p. 101; John Harington, *A tract on the succession to the crown, AD 1602*, ed. by C. R. Markham (London: Roxburghe Club, 1880).
68 MacCaffrey, p. 71.
69 Ian Dunlop, *The Palaces and Progresses of Elizabeth I* (London: Jonathan Cape, 1962), p. 193.
70 Knowles, pp. 159–60.
71 Letters were sent to noblemen in the provinces instructing them to maintain order; Salisbury, XII, p. 671; Clapham, p. 104; CSPV, IX (1592–1603), 63.

strength and not willing to lose the least advantage of the prerogative, would for slight causes contend with the ancient Councillors, whose power they knew was determined by the Queen's death'. Some of the lords took exception to the Privy Council meeting, 'alleging that they ought not to propound and conclude anything in Council without their privity and consent'.[72] This attempt to take political advantage of the ceremonial interregnum seems, however, to have had no wider repercussions.

There were, nevertheless, other threats to the ritual display of order and homage that was the intended product of the royal funeral ceremony. The interests of two protagonists conflicted with those of the organizers, isolating them from the propensity towards co-operation desired from participants in ritual display and rendering them a potentially serious source of disruption.[73]

Lady Arabella Stuart had been intended as chief mourner, a key symbolic role which heraldic regulations determined should be taken by the woman nearest in blood to the deceased.[74] Lady Arabella's candidacy rested with her 'royal blood'. Clapham reports, however, that, 'the Lady Arabella refused, saying that since her access to the Queen in her lifetime might not be permitted, she would not after her death, be brought upon the stage for a public spectacle'.[75] In the event, the Marchioness of Northampton took the role.

There was also a difficulty over the involvement of Scaramelli, the Venetian ambassador. He was sent court blacks but refused to attend the funeral because he would not be involved in a heretic service. In contrast the French ambassador did attend although it had not been the practice for the incumbent of this position to be present at English services since the Catholic conversion of Henry IV.

In the event these two issues were kept firmly within what Ernst Goffman would call the 'back regions'.[76] Both the funeral procession and the Jacobean succession were enacted smoothly. The former was not simply a reflection of the latter but an instrumental determinant.

It was only in the pictorial and verbal record of the funeral that two minor hints of discord mar the impression of order and decorum. The British Library funeral roll contains a small, stunted figure, representing Sir Robert Cecil, cut out and pasted over a larger, whited out figure. The discontinuity in the procession of regular, stylized figures effected by this depiction of the Chancellor's physical deficiencies may have been a deliberate slur against the unpopular

---

[72] Clapham, p. 107.
[73] On participant co-operation, see chapter 1.
[74] PRO SP14/1/21.
[75] Clapham, p. 114.
[76] McClure, I, 193. Arabella Stuart's estrangement from Elizabeth is indicated in the Salisbury papers where she is reported to be eager for news of the Queen's death, Salisbury, XII, p. 693. Erving Goffman, *The Presentation of Self in Everyday Life* (New York: Penguin Press, 1959), pp. 109–10, 114.

politician and strikes a note of disharmony into the visual record of the proceedings.[77]

The verbal threat to the image of order was directed at the Queen herself and concerned rumours that spread in relation to the embalming of her body. The contemporary historian John Manningham reports that Elizabeth had expressed the wish for her body not to be opened for this purpose, but Elizabeth Southwell, a minor courtier, relates that Cecil nonetheless ordered the process to be carried out. Clapham states that 'the Queen's body was left in a manner for a day or two after her death and meane persons [embalmers] had access to it'.[78] A story began to circulate that Elizabeth's body was so poorly embalmed that during the funeral the coffin exploded due to the pressure of the build up of gases produced by the body's decomposition. Yet the rumour has no basis in fact. Examination of the vault in 1868 revealed that while the wooden coffin was damaged, the corpse was still securely enclosed in its leaden shell.[79] Even a total fabrication can, however, damage the impression of a ceremony in the minds of those who can only experience it second-hand.

The Royal Funeral Effigy and the Reformation

Funeral Effigies, Tomb Effigies and Elizabethan Iconophobia

The political value of the royal funeral, with its effigy ritual, has been clearly established but there remains the question of how the effigy ritual, with its overtly idolatrous overtones, was accepted and justified in the context of post-Reformation England. The Reformation had a strong iconophobic bent with the second commandment, 'Thou shalt not make unto thee any graven image, or any likenesse', holding a central place in the reformist psyche.[80] In the sixteenth century the word 'image' referred primarily to a sculpted figure or model and thus effigies were a particularly sensitive medium of representation.[81] The Elizabethan *Homily against peril of idolatry*, the longest of the thirty-three homilies designed to homogenize pulpit dissemination, condemns the sculptor outright:

> Cursed be he that maketh a carued image, or a cast or moulten image, which is abomination before the Lord, the worke of the artificers hande, and setteth it up in a secret corner.[82]

---

[77] See figure 17.
[78] Clapham, p. 110. McClure has, the body was 'wrapt up in searclothes and other preservatives' but not opened, I, 190.
[79] Litten, p. 42.
[80] Exodus 20. 4, *The Geneva Bible*. See my discussion of iconophobia in chapter 2.
[81] Aston, p. 17; Llewellyn, *Royal Body* (1990), p. 219; Watt, p. 132.
[82] 'An Homily Against Peril of Idolatry and superfluous Decking of Churches', in *Sermons or Homilies*, p. 162.

Parishioners could have been left in little doubt as to the sinfulness of sculpted images.

It appears that iconophobia put a stop to the use of effigies in episcopal funeral processions. In pre-Reformation England, effigies had been made for the obsequies of bishops. An effigy seems to have been used, for example, at the London funeral of Steven Gardiner, Bishop of Winchester, on 24 February 1555/6.[83] There is no evidence for a post-Reformation continuation of the practice.[84]

In her lifetime Elizabeth had been heralded as she 'by whose hands the Lord hath quite expelled idolatry'.[85] How was it that in death she could become the subject of an idolatrous effigy? Royal effigies occupied a more equivocal space than episcopal effigies: their subjects were kings not bishops but their mode of representation could equally well be described as idolatrous. I have not come across any direct evidence of attitudes to the royal effigy ritual in relation to the Reformation. In order to explore the issue, therefore, it is useful to look at a closely related area of funeral representation: tomb monuments. The tomb effigies of Henry II and John were created using the actual body as a model but later tomb effigies were often carved from the intermediary funeral effigy.[86]

There is a wealth of contemporary material providing evidence both for the government defence of tomb effigies, and the antagonistic and destructive attitudes that they engendered in the minds of at least some reformers. The discussion as a whole is illustrative of the Elizabethan awareness of the ways in which images helped to create and wield power.

Iconoclasm and the Official Protection of Tombs
In the early days of the Edwardian Reformation much iconoclastic behaviour was directed against tombs.[87] Edwardian and, later, Elizabethan governments, however, consistently issued proclamations designed to protect funerary architecture. The 1547 orders on image-breaking contained the proviso that the commemorative function of imagery was permitted. It is specifically idolatry that was outlawed. A 1550 statute aimed to protect the tombs of royalty and noblemen but the acts of vandalism continued.[88] Under Edward VI, the tombs

---

[83] See Nichols (1848), p. 101. The effigy is not, however, mentioned in another account of the funeral; see CA, I Series MS XI fol. 121b.
[84] On bishops' effigies in fifteenth-century funerals, see BL, Harley MS 6064 fol. 80; CA, I Series MS III fol. 52b; Kantorowicz, p. 434; Cunnington and Lucas, p. 168; Loach, p. 60.
[85] The words are from John Stubbs's pamphlet decrying the Elizabeth-Anjou match in 1579; see MacCaffrey, p. 204.
[86] Hope, pp. 523, 526; Llewellyn, *Royal Body* (1990), p. 224.
[87] Stow gives repeated examples of the destruction of tombs in London churches from Edward VI's reign; see Aston, pp. 256, 315 n. 75.
[88] *Statutes of the Realm*, iv/1. 111; 3–4 cited by Aston, p. 269.

of the dukes of York at Fotheringay were destroyed together with the tombs of the earls and dukes of Lancaster at Leicester.[89]

Elizabeth endeavoured to reinforce tomb protection in a proclamation of 19 September 1560 which ran:

> The queen's majesty, understanding that by the means of sundry people, partly ignorant, partly malicious, or covetous, there hath been of late years spoiled and broken certain ancient monuments, some of metal, some of stone, which were erected and sett up as well in churches as in other publique places within this realm only to show a memory to the posteritie of the persons there buried, or had ben benefactors to the buildings or donations of the same churches or publique places and not to norishe any kind of superstition [...People should] forbear the breaking or defacing of any parcel of any monument, or tomb, or grave, or other inscription and memory of any person deceased in any manner or place, or to break any image of kings, princes or noble estates of this realm, or of any other that have been in times past erected and set up for the only memory of them to their posterity in common churches and not for any religious honour.[90]

Preservation of the memory and dignity of the nobility was a primary motive for the protection of tombs. John Weever stresses these functions of the tomb when he bewails the destruction of monuments, 'by which inhumane, deformidable act, the honourable memory of many vertuous and noble persons deceased, is extinguished, and the true understanding of divers Families in these Realmes [...] is so darkened, as the true course of their inheritance is thereby partly interrupted'.[91] Henry Peacham goes further and voices the opinion that contemplation of the achievements of ancestors functions as 'a spurre in brave and good Spirits'.[92] Contemporaries understood the value of tombs and their effigies in social or 'civil' terms. They contributed towards the preservation of order and, conversely, their violation was a threat to order. Given their value in helping to effect a smooth succession, funeral effigies could similarly have been justified on civil grounds.

Civil justifications for the use of effigies may also have gained weight from the Roman example, particularly as antiquarian activity increased towards the end of the sixteenth century. An anonymous pamphlet was published in February 1599 entitled *Of the Antiquitie of Ceremonies used at Funerals in England*. It included a description of the funeral of Sylla, a celebrated Roman of noble family, which featured 6,000 biers bearing effigies of his ancestors and

---

[89] Colvin, p. 255. Catherine of Aragon's tomb at Peterborough was also defaced; see Wyrley, p. 37.
[90] Paul L. Hughes and James F. Larkin, *Tudor Royal Proclamations*, 4 vols (London: Yale University Press, 1964–9), II (1969), 146–8. See also Bolton, p. 90; Ferne, p. 25.
[91] Weever, pp. 52–3. See also Bod., Ashmole MS 836 fol. 16; Mercer, pp. 221–2; Llewellyn, *Royal Body* (1990), p. 222.
[92] Henry Peacham, *The Compleat Gentleman*, 2nd edn (London: [n. pub.], 1634), p. 14. See also Wyrley, p. 30.

honours.[93] Roman precedent certainly came to be used as an argument in favour of the erection of tombs in, for example Richard Brathwait's *Remains after Death: [...] including divers memorable observances* (1618).

Despite the growing secular context for sepulchral monuments, there remained a residual superstitious belief that the defacement of a tomb effigy constituted an attack on the person represented as if he were still alive. The feeling that there was something murderous about tomb destruction is closely paralleled by the attempts that appear to have been made on Elizabeth's life by defacing her portrait.[94]

It was perhaps in recognition of these lingering superstitions that not all accepted the official justification for images. Even within the episcopacy only Edmund Guest (1518–77), Bishop of Salisbury, seems to have intervened actively to protect monuments. His colleagues were more interested in wiping out all traces of idolatry. Nicholas Ridley (1500?–1555), Bishop of London, had to be restrained in his reform of St Paul's: the Council issued a special order to protect the tomb of John of Gaunt.[95] That some iconoclastic attacks on tombs continued is evident from Weever's complaints in his *Tombs and Monuments* published in 1631.[96] Nevertheless, after 1560 the official Anglican position was to make a clear distinction between a legal effigy, which represented its subject as a mark of civil honour, and a 'scandalous image which was an art object replicating nature and rivalling the creativity of God'.[97]

Tomb and Funeral Effigy Design: Functionalism vs. Naturalism
The primacy of the civil and functional aspects of Elizabethan tomb effigies affected their design. The stiff and relatively primitive style of many tomb effigies of the second half of the sixteenth century was a product of the post-Reformation attitude towards representations of the human body, particularly representations in a religious setting.[98] In such contexts naturalism was not a legitimate goal.[99] The third quarter of the sixteenth century may have been particularly sensitive to sculpted human representations. This period produced few tombs which included the carved family figures that had replaced medieval weepers (figure 18). Thomson speculates, for example, that the absence of

---

[93] Tate, I, 207.
[94] Ferne, pp. 83, 269; Gent, pp. 76–7. See also Thomas, p. 612.
[95] Aston, pp. 270, 320–8.
[96] Weever, p. 54.
[97] Llewellyn, *Royal Body* (1990), p. 223.
[98] Mercer, pp. 226–7.
[99] Llewellyn, *Royal Body* (1990), p. 223. This is, of course, a generalization. The government concept of tombs as family properties over-rode its desire for religious conformity and tombs with religious scenes continued to be produced into the Elizabethan period; see Mercer, p. 220.

statuary on the Denton tomb at Hillesdon was based on a notion of reform propriety.[100]

Instead heraldry dominated Elizabethan tombs. One manifestation of this is the numerous coats of arms which were sometimes incorporated into depictions of family trees.[101] Heraldry was not only, however, an alternative to the depiction of the human form (I am thinking, for example, of the royal arms replacing the rood cross), it also had a subtle influence on how that form was portrayed. In her essay 'Lady Elizabeth Pope: the Heraldic Body', Ellen Chirelstien convincingly argues that the style of Elizabethan portrait painting reflects the non-illusionistic ordering of heraldic coats of arms. Similarly the stiff tomb effigies of the Elizabethan period aimed at symbolic rather than naturalistic representation.[102]

The heraldic mode of symbols and emblems was imitated in portraiture. Paintings were to be 'read'. In the main readers and sitters both came from the ruling elite, portraiture contributing to their sense of group coherence, identity and security. The overlap in technique corresponds to a shared interest in marking the status and family position in society: portraits and tomb effigies, like coats of arms, were statements of social standing and the antiquity of lineage.[103] Heraldry provided a suitably anti-naturalistic mode of visual expression. It was the acceptable face of art in a deeply iconophobic society.[104]

Although the evidence is limited, it seems that the form of the post-Reformation funeral effigy displayed the same kind of non-naturalistic style noted in tomb effigies.

Of the post-Reformation and pre-Stuart funeral effigies, only Mary Tudor's survives. On this occasion the crude medieval method of carving the body in wood was used but the effigy had arms jointed at the shoulder with hinged elbows and legs jointed at the knees for convenience in dressing (figure 14). As far as the head is concerned naturalism certainly does not seem to have been a top priority. It was carved in wood and, while recognisably a portrait of Mary, has been described as a 'poor piece of work' but sufficient to fulfil the functions of funeral effigy, being 'well enough to pass at a distance'.[105] The low quality of

---

[100] Thomson, p. 191.

[101] Nigel Llewellyn, 'Claims to Status' (1990), pp. 145–55; Ariès, pp. 245–58, 288–93, 747; Stone (1979), pp. 135, 225–6. Bosola satirizes worldy tombs in John Webster's play *The Duchess of Malfi*, IV. ii. 156–61.

[102] Mercer (p. 251) has noted the close parallels between sculpture and portrait-painting in the period.

[103] Gent, p. 47; Karl Joseph Höltgen, 'The English Reformation and Some Jacobean Writers on Art', in *Functions of Literature: Essays presented to Erwin Wolff on his Sixtieth Birthday*, ed. by Ulrich Broich, Theo Stemmler and Gerd Stratman (Tübingen: Max Neimeyer Verlag, 1984), p. 123.

[104] Lucy Gent and Nigel Llewellyn, eds, *Renaissance Bodies: The Human Figure in English Culture, c. 1540–1660* (London: Reaktion Books, 1990), p. 20.

[105] Howgrave-Graham (1953), pp. 160, 168; Harvey and Mortimer, pp. 55–8; *Westminster Abbey*, pp. 19–20.

workmanship employed meant that the plaster head was awkwardly positioned on the wooden torso. The lack of care lavished on Mary's effigy suggests that in 1558 the funeral organizers may have been uncomfortable with the idolatrous implications of constructing a life-like funeral effigy. This funeral was, however, staged in the turbulent days before Elizabeth's religious policy was clear. The whole form of the obsequies was Catholic indicating that the funeral liturgy and ceremonial had not yet come under official scrutiny.[106]

Nevertheless, in marked contrast to the Mary effigy, the design of the pre-Reformation funeral effigies of her grandparents, Katherine de Valois and, in particular, Henry VII, reached a high point in naturalism (figure 18). Katherine de Valois's effigy shows clearer signs of derivation from a death mask than do other carved heads. The effigy's features are depicted with subtlety and realism and bear a strong likeness to surviving portraits of the Queen.[107] Henry's effigy signalled a significant shift in taste from the earlier medieval effigies, like that of Edward III, which were carved out of a single block of wood.[108] Instead it consisted of a wooden frame, padded with hay and covered with canvas, upon which the figure was modelled in plaster. The head was finely modelled and painted with the skull being left bare for a wig and the hands fashioned to hold an orb and sceptre. The effigy was highly Italianate in conception.[109] For the face a death mask was used: the features directly reflect the use of the corpse and the outer edge of the original mask can be traced on the effigy head. The head is very close to the terracotta portrait in the Victoria and Albert Museum which was also based on a cast of Henry's face but with the tell-tale signs of death smoothed away. I disagree with Nigel Llewellyn who says that the makers showed no interest in the late King's personality: for me the features speak the King.[110] Henry VII's tomb effigy, carved by Pietro Torrigiani, is also an example of realistic portraiture.[111]

There was not to be another funeral effigy until Elizabeth's own obsequies. Unfortunately, Elizabeth's original effigy does not survive. It had been generally thought that, apart from the wooden legs, the figure was entirely remade in 1760.[112] However, recent research has revealed that the torso is also a survivor

---

[106] Nichols (1848), pp. 182–4; Strype, II, 665; Bod., Ashmole MS 857 fol. 340.

[107] Harvey and Mortimer, pp. 41, 48. Roy Strong, *Tudor and Jacobean Portraits*, 2 vols (London: HMSO, 1969), I, 97–8.

[108] On the death mask used for the effigy of Edward III, see Harvey and Mortimer, p. 32.

[109] Late fifteenth-century Italian votive figures were constructed using closely comparable techniques; see Harvey and Mortimer, p. 52.

[110] Llewellyn, *Royal Body* (1990), p. 229 n. 40. The body of Henry VII's funeral effigy was destroyed by flood water at the Abbey during the last war. It does not appear that Henry VIII's effigy survived the sixteenth century and thus we have no direct evidence of its construction and appearance.

[111] Stow, p. 487; Neill (1985), p. 181. There is a contemporary woodcut of Henry's effigy; see Harvey and Mortimer, p. 51.

[112] Hope, pp. 517–70; L. E. Tanner and J. L. Nevinson, 'On Some Later Funeral Effigies in

of the 1603 model.[113] Some believe that a wooden head, which recently turned up at the London Museum, is that which was carved by Maximilian Colt and painted by John de Critz for the funeral effigy. For a time this head belonged to an equestrian figure of Elizabeth on show in various tableaux at the Tower during the eighteenth and nineteenth centuries. The veracity of this claim is, however, impossible to establish.[114] For an idea of how the funeral effigy of Elizabeth looked, we must turn to her tomb effigy, drawings of the procession and written accounts made by eye-witnesses.

Although the evidence is limited, there are hints that naturalistic principles were rehabilitated for the royal effigy of Elizabeth. If we accept the link between the design of the tomb and the funeral effigy, then we can assume that the latter shared the realism of the features displayed by the tomb effigy. It is probable that a death mask was used for both.[115] Such an assumption would give us a funeral effigy much closer to the realistic portrayal achieved in Henry VII's effigy than the rough effigy head of Mary Tudor that would 'pass at a distance'. Fortunately, we possess one description of the funeral effigy head made by a visitor to Westminster Abbey in 1725.[116] His testimony supports the theory that the makers of Elizabeth's effigy aimed at realism. He describes it as 'cutt in wood, a little wrinkly her face, though the truest countenance of her face'.[117]

There are some indications that the design of Elizabeth's effigy may have gone further towards naturalistic representation than that of her grandfather. Recent detailed research on the effigy of Henry VII has revealed that although the King was portrayed with eyes open, the colours used to paint his features were intended to represent the pale face of death.[118] In striking contrast, as we have seen, the effigy of Queen Elizabeth was carved in wood, coloured 'so faithfully that she seems alive' and was depicted in the funeral procession drawings with flaming red hair, blue eyes, rouge and reddened lips – she was certainly not coloured to appear dead.[119]

The descriptions of funeral effigies in Stow also indicate that naturalism in representation was a primary concern. The account of Henry V's funeral effigy is a case in point. Stow described how upon the coffin was placed:

Westminster Abbey', *Archaeologia*, 85 (1935), 169–202 (pp. 188–9); *Westminster Abbey*, p. 20.

[113] *The Times*, early June 1995. Colt constructed the effigy 'with a paire of straight bodies'; see my discussion in chapter 10.
[114] Olivia Bland, *The Royal Way of Death* (London: Constable, 1986), pp. 27–8.
[115] See Howgrave-Graham, pp. 465–74. For the earlier view that only Henry VII's effigy involved use of a death mask, see Benkard, pp. 28–9.
[116] The effigy was to be displayed in the Abbey after the funeral; see chapter 7.
[117] BL, Additional MS 23069, cited by Tanner and Nevinson, p. 189.
[118] Josephine A. Darrah, 'The Funeral Effigy of Henry VII at Westminster Abbey' (unpublished report to the Dean & Chapter of Westminster Abbey, 1986, WA, Box: Royal Funeral Effigies). The eyes were, however, open; see Benkard, p. 29, and also Harvey and Mortimer, p. 53.
[119] CSPV, X (1603–7), 22; BL, Additional MS 35324 fol. 38.

> A figure made of boiled hides or leather, representing his person, as nigh to the semblance of him as could be devised, painted curiously to the similitude of a living creature: upon whose head was set an Imperiall diadem of golde and precious stones [...] and besides that, when the bodie should pass through any good towne, a Canapie of marvellous great value was borne over the chariot, by men of great worshippe.[120]

Stow's *Chronicles* came out in ever-expanding editions from 1565 to 1580 with reprints to 1633 and may have exerted an influence over popular attitudes in the late sixteenth century.

If these suggestions of a shift back towards the naturalism evident in the Henry VII effigy are correct, they would certainly equate with the increased naturalism and growing interest in portraiture in tomb sculpture of the late sixteenth and early seventeenth centuries.[121]

The move towards naturalism was part of a general change in attitudes towards the arts that occurred towards the end of the sixteenth century. After the temporary hiatus imposed by the Reformation, the influence of Italian art theory began, once again, to be felt. Richard Haydocke (c. 1570–1642) has been identified as its main disseminator in Elizabethan and Jacobean England.[122] His *Tracte of Curious Paintinge, Carvinge and Buildinge* (1598) is a part-translation of Lomazzo's *Trattato dell'Arte* but adapts and accommodates it to the Protestant ethos.

A direct translation of Lomazzo's section on proportion, which Vitruvius calls 'Eurythmy', would read:

> The further importance of this beauty and majesty of the body is seen more clearly in the *divine cult* than in anything else, for it is a marvellous thing how piety, religion and reverence for God and the saints are increased in our minds by the majesty and beauty of scared images, caused by the presence in them of Eurythmy.

Modifications occur in the Haydocke version:

> But if we shall enter into further consideration of this beauty, it will appear most evidently, in things appertaining to *Civile discipline*. For it is strange to consider, what effects of piety, reverence and religion, are stirred up in mens mindes, by meanes of this sutable comelinesse of apte proportion.[123]

The function of art as a *culto divino* in Lomazzo becomes a 'civile discipline' in Haydocke and he suggests that the function of art lies in the maintenance of

---

[120] Stow, p. 362. For another account see Hope, pp. 535–6.
[121] Mercer, pp. 234, 238–43. On the increased emotionalism, freedom of pose and revived religious images of early seventeenth-century tomb sculpture, see chapters 6 and 9; and figure 19.
[122] Höltgen, p. 120.
[123] M. Jenkins, 'The State Portrait, Its Origins and Evolution', *Monographs on Archaeology and Fine Arts*, 3 (1947) cited by Strong (1963), pp. 35–6; Phillips, pp. 119–20; Strong (1987), p. 16.

public order and the establishment of a hierarchy of state. Haydocke's argument mirrors the functional justification of tombs discussed above.

Royal Appropriation of Religious Images and Symbolism
The civil justification of utilizing images was, like Cecil's 'Civil duty' used to justify the funeral of his wife, largely a question of rhetoric. Representational forms might have temporarily been modified towards non-naturalistic heraldic styles but ultimately they were still images. As Haydocke makes clear, the effects on the mind of the observer of 'civil' images are almost identical to the effects of observing 'sacred' images. The same processes of sublimation lay behind each. The switch in terminology was, in some ways, an equivocation but by defining acceptable modes for the use of images, differentiating them from the old Catholic religious images, the ruling elite was able to exploit the power of iconography.[124]

As far as the funeral effigy is concerned, similar processes are at work as is evident from parallels between its use and the pre-Reformation Christocentric rituals of Easter Sepulchre: *Adoratio crucis, Depositio crucis, Elevatio crucis* and *Quem quaeritis*, which dated from the fifth century. In these ceremonies a cross, sometimes with an image of Christ upon it, was adored by worshippers who crept across the floor to it and kissed it. The cross was then symbolically buried by placing it on a permanent or portable 'Easter sepulchre' (often an altar tomb in the north wall of the chancel).[125] On Easter Sunday, following Matins, the cross was raised from the sepulchre in token of the resurrection and carried in a procession to the altar. En route the cross was held up before the congregation to be adored.[126] The link that contemporaries perceived between these rites and funeral obsequies is made clear by the fact that often wealthy parishioners would erect a tomb for themselves which would also serve as the sepulchre, the tomb of Christ.[127] At the beginning of the fourteenth century, these rites were influenced by the institution of the Corpus Christi festival, observed in England from 1318. With the increased emphasis on the Host as the real body of Christ, the practice of reservation and recovery perhaps inevitably became associated with the Easter symbolism of the burial and resurrection of Christ. Sometimes the Host was buried instead of or as well as the cross. In 1496 John Pymper of Nettlestead, Kent, willed the following with regard to his burial:

---

[124] Llewellyn, *Royal Body* (1990), pp. 219, 223; Smuts, p. 140.
[125] The Easter sepulchre might be one of three types: (i) a temporary structure made of wood; (ii) a specialised structure of masonry; or (iii) a chest or canopied tomb with a flat upper slab on which to place the wooden framework. See Francis Bond, *The Chancel of English Churches* (London: Oxford University Press, 1916), p. 231.
[126] In 1559 Thomas Naogeorgos published a Latin verse at Basel, *Regnum Papisticum*, a satirical work, derisive of the Catholic rites of the Easter sepulchre. The poem was 'Englyshed' by Barnabe Googe in 1570; see Bond, p. 227.
[127] Suffolk examples include John Hopton's tomb at Blythborough and the Clopton tomb at Long Melford (Duffy, pp. 32–3, 43). See also Bond, pp. 234–6.

> Whereas the Sepulchre of our Lord is wont to stand at the feast of Easter, and to be laid there in a tomb of tone, made under such form that the Blessed Sacrament and the Holy Cross may be laid upon the stone of the said tomb in manner of Sepulchre at the feast abovesaid.[128]

Similarly, at Durham a cross was laid in the sepulchre:

> With another representation or image of our Saviour Christ in whose breast they enclosed with great reverence the most Holy and blessed sacrament of the Altar, censing and praying to it upon their knee a great space; setting tapers lighted before it [. . . it was] buried till Easter Day in the morning it was taken forth.[129]

The involvement of a funeral effigy denoting royal immortality in royal obsequies inevitably echoed these religious rites.[130]

Perhaps more pointed, however, are the religious connotations of the canopy borne over the funeral effigy in the procession. The canopy was of the same design as those borne over the Host in Corpus Christi and Palm Sunday processions.[131] The Corpus Christi symbolism of the immortal presence of Christ in the Host paralleled the continued presence of the King's Majesty in the funeral effigy.[132] Use of the canopy may have recalled Corpus Christi symbolism in the minds of some of the older spectators at Elizabeth's funeral since these ceremonies persisted in some locations until the late 1580s. At York the last performance of the Corpus Christi play cycles was staged in 1568, at Chester performances continued until 1575 and the final performance at

---

[128] Bond, p. 234. At Rolveden in Kent in 1513 John Asten similarly left six pounds 'to the making at my proper cost an honest sepulchre for the Blessed Body of our Lord to be laid in at Easter in the church'; ibid., p. 221.

[129] Bond, p. 225.

[130] Bond, pp. 229–30; Neil C. Brooks, 'The Sepulchre of Christ in Art and Liturgy', *University of Illinois Studies in Language and Literature*, 7 (1921), 7–51; E. K. Chambers, *The Medieval Stage*, 2 vols (Oxford: Clarendon Press, 1903), II, 138, 160, 329; E. K. Chambers, *The Elizabethan Stage*, 4 vols (Oxford: Clarendon Press, 1923; repr. 1961), II, 11–36, 310–11; Karl Young, 'The Dramatic Associations of the Easter Sepulchre', *University of Wisconsin Studies in Language and Literature*, 10 (1920), 5–130 (pp. 102–3); Duffy, pp. 23, 29–30, 109, 421, 461. Very similar processions took place on Palm Sunday; see Ariès, p. 65.

[131] Dewick, p. 120; Duffy, pp. 24–38, 44, 137, 493; Harris (1992), pp. 71–80; Nichols (1848), p. 107. In Paris, up until the sixteenth century, the very same canopy was used in royal and in Corpus Christi processions. Lawrence M. Bryant, *The King and the City in the Parisian Royal Entry Ceremony: Politics, Ritual and Art in the Renaissance* (Geneva: Librarie Droz, 1986), p. 103.

[132] Comparisons between the carrying of the body of the king at French royal funerals and the Corpus Christi procession were made by a number of fifteenth-century chroniclers; Giesey (1960), p. 103 n. 101, p. 107 n. 12. On canopies, see also Bernard Guenée and Françoise Lehoux, *Les Entrées Royales Françaises de 1328 à 1515* (Paris: Centre Nationale de la Recherche Scientifique, 1968), pp. 7–18; Bryant, pp. 101–3.

Kendal was as late as 1586.[133] Even without direct experience, however, the sacred resonance of the canopy would have touched many Englishmen. For many it carried associations with Catholicism. The cache of 'monuments of popery' found in a town house by the churchwardens of Scaldwell in 1581 included a sacramental canopy.[134]

Royal ritual thus appropriated religious symbolism in order to confer charisma upon the effigy of the monarch. The liminality of ritual and the ambiguous nature of symbols functioned as a barrier to critical attack.[135] The sacral associations of canopies and effigies were not articulated but nevertheless remained beneath the surface civil justifications of funeral ritual. They attracted and influenced the spectator, impressing upon him the divine sanction of kingship.[136] Religious symbolism thus contributed to the process of sublimation which gained the spectator's acquiesence to the display of royal power. Here we see the beginnings of a *religion royale* built on the understanding that power lies in what is enacted rather than in what is comprehended.

English Awareness of the French Effigy Lying-in-State Ritual
There is a substantial amount of evidence to suggest that the English authorities were well aware of the French ritual effigy lying-in-state ritual, described in chapter 3.

Foreign ambassadors were usually allocated places in the funeral processions of French monarchs. Sir Nicholas Throckmorton, English ambassador to France, had been in Paris at the time of the death and funerals of Henry II (1559). He took part in the funeral procession that bore the encoffined body and the effigy from Tournelles to Notre Dame. Further, he reported back to the Elizabeth that the funeral oration and everything connected with the interment would shortly be available in print. While there is no evidence to suggest Throckmorton attended the effigy lying-in-state ritual, his interest and involvement in the remainder of the funeral proceedings makes it highly likely that he was aware of its performance.[137] The English publication of an account of the funeral also suggests that there was a market for such material in England, even if only at court.

William Cecil, whose son would be closely involved in the organization of Elizabeth's funeral, certainly knew of the arrangements, too. He reported to

---

[133] Duffy, pp. 137, 580–2, 566; Glynne Wickham, *Early English Stages 1300–1600*, 3 vols (London: Routledge & Kegan Paul, 1959–81), II, part 1 (1963), 69–71.
[134] Duffy, p. 587.
[135] See the discussion in my introduction.
[136] The religious celebrations for St Hugh's Day were similarly appropriated for the Queen's Accession Day festivities (Duffy, p. 590). A similar canopy was borne over Elizabeth in the *Procession Picture* c. 1600; and as she rode into London on a chariot throne on 24 November 1588 as part of the Armada victory thanksgiving celebrations. See MacCaffrey, p. 241.
[137] CSPF, I (1558–9), 472–7.

Sadler that the funeral and proclamation of the new king had been accomplished in the 'accustomed style'.[138]

In 1584 Sir Edward Stafford attended the funeral of Alençon, heir to the French throne and erstwhile potential marriage-partner for Elizabeth. Stafford reported on the ceremony to Francis Walsingham and his account includes a description 'of the great ceremonies and magnificency of his effigies lying in an abbey at St Jaques suburbs, and the great honour that was there done to it Friday and Saturday, after their ceremonious manner, by all the world, especially by the Princes and Princesses of France'.[139] Walsingham, like William Cecil, would die before his Queen but could easily have passed on his knowledge of the French funeral ritual to other members of the Council.

The English also had access to the classical sources describing the funerals of Roman emperors that Giesey has identified as providing a model for the expansion of the French effigy ritual at the funeral of Charles IX (1574).[140] The most significant of these was Herodian's account of the funeral of Septimus Severus in 211 AD, a French translation of which was published in 1541. Not long after an English translation of the same account was published in *The Historie of Herodian, a Greeke Author, Treating of the Romayne Emperors* (1550 [?]).[141]

Antiquarians like Sir William Segar also may have been aware of the French royal funeral form. In his *Honor, Military and Civill* (1602) Segar argues that a forty-day period should elapse between death and burial at the funerals of 'Princes and persons of honour', following the model of the Old Testament funeral given in honour of Jacob.[142] Under the Tudors, English practice had varied ranging from two weeks for Henry VIII to a month for Edward VI.[143] It is possible that in urging a forty-day period for royal funerals, Segar is alluding to the French funeral rite in which, from 1547, the lying-in-state ritual was conflated with the forty-day mourning period, or *quarantaine*.

The English authorities must, then, have been aware of the French effigy lying-in-state ritual in 1603 but it was not to be emulated at the funeral of Elizabeth I.

---

[138] CSPF, I (1558–9), 493.
[139] Salisbury III, 39.
[140] Giesey (1960), pp. 145–54.
[141] Nicholas Smith, *The History of Herodian, a Greeke Author, Treating of the Romayne Emperors* (London: [n. pub.], [1550 (?)]), IV, lxvi–ii; Giesey (1960), p. 147, n. 5. See also Tate, I, 217 for a 1599 account of the funeral of Sylla.
[142] Genesis 50.3. The Jacob example was not new: Ambrose used it to defend his adoption of the quarantaine for the funeral of Theodosius I in 395 which was probably in reality a piece of political expediency, in deference to the custom of the Eastern churches of celebrating the 3rd, 9th and 40th days after death, Giesey (1960), pp. 160–2.
[143] Hope, pp. 541–2.

1. Sir Philip Sidney's spurs and gauntlets borne at his funeral by officers at arms (though pursuivants, they wear their tabards herald-wise). From T. Lant, *Sequitur Celebritas* (1587), by permission of The British Library, shelfmark C20f12.

2. Chief mourner with two escorts (1578), Additional MS 35324 fol. 21, by permission of The British Library.

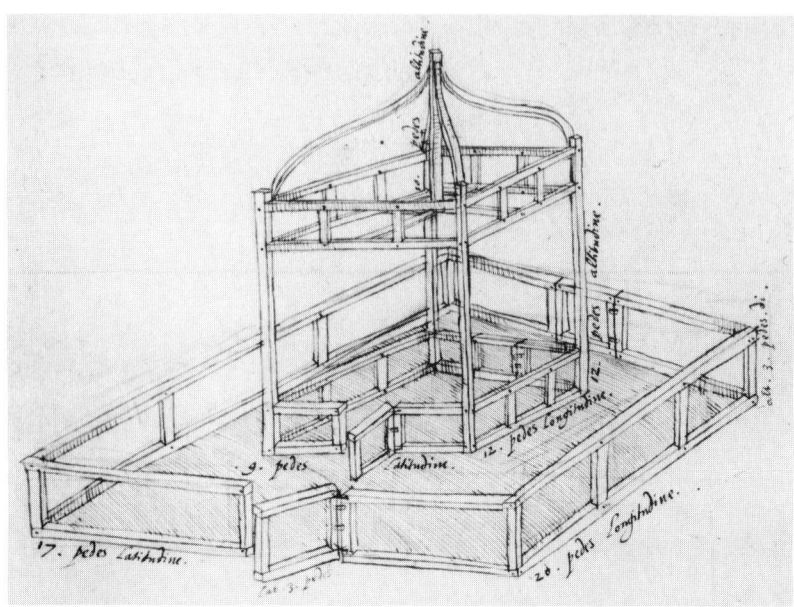

3. Structure of the hearse for the funeral of William Paulet, Marquis of Winchester (1572), MS Ashmole 836, fol. 212, the Bodleian Library, Oxford.

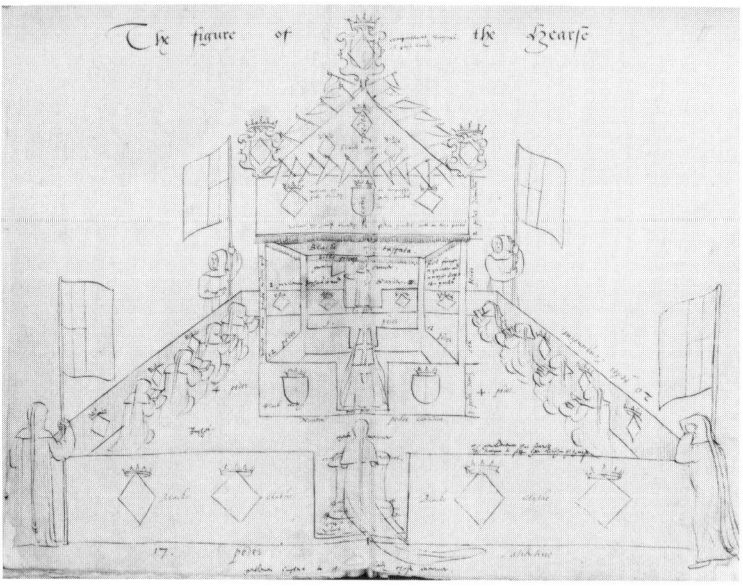

4. 'The figure of the hearse' for the funeral of a Countess (c. 1576), Harley MS 6064 fols 96v–97, by permission of The British Library.

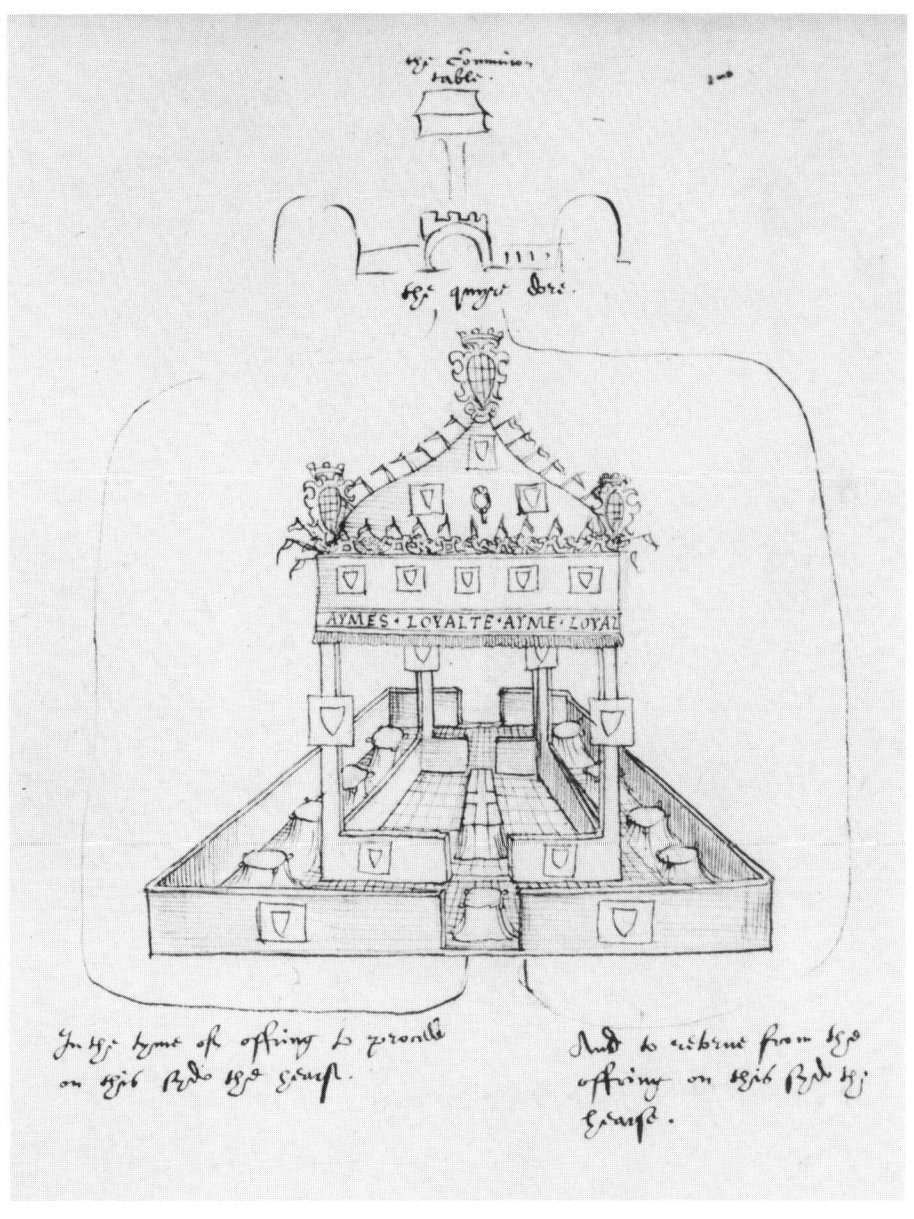

5. Hearse design for the funeral of William Paulet, Marquis of Winchester (1572), MS Ashmole 836, fol. 212, the Bodleian Library, Oxford. It is annotated to indicate that the mourners will proceed down the left side of the hearse to the offering and return on the right.

6. Elizabeth I's arms painted over the medieval Last Judgement in St Margaret's Church, Tivetshall, Norfolk, RCHME, © Crown copyright.

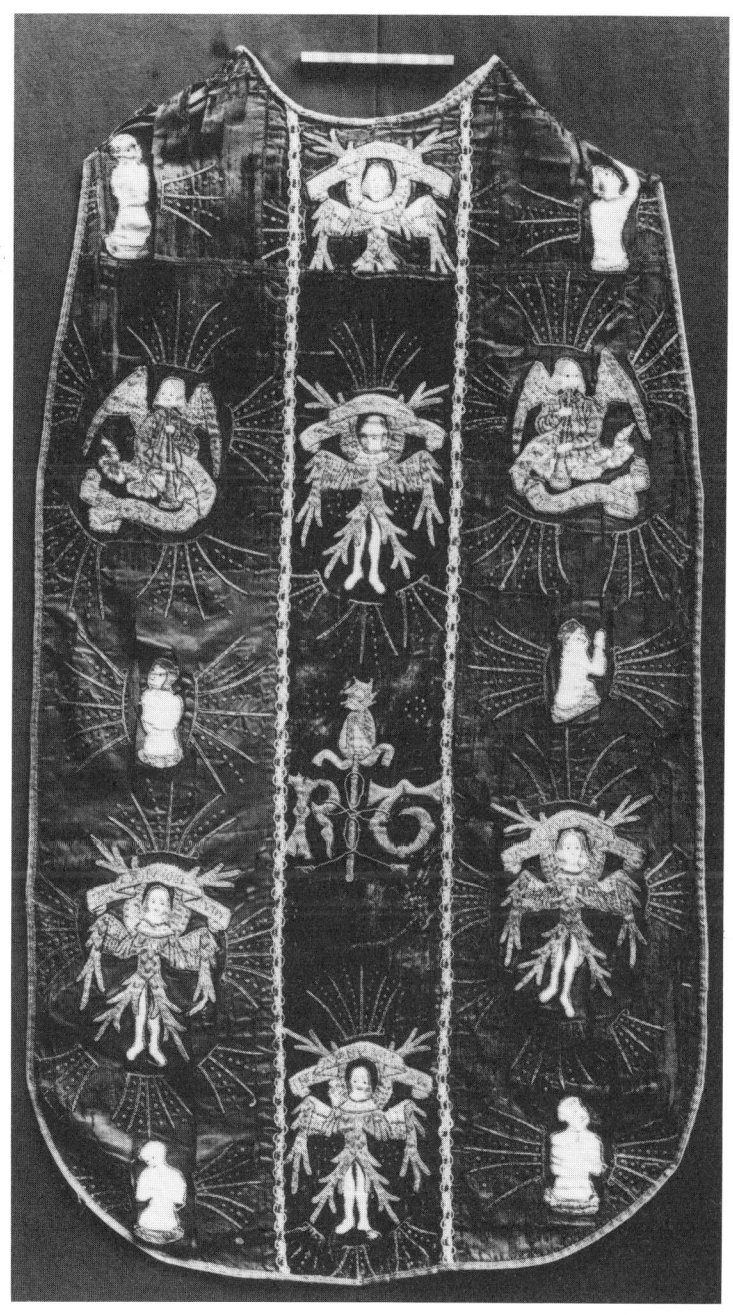

7. Back of chasuble for Requiem Mass, velvet embroidered in silks and metal thread, Victoria & Albert Picture Library.

8. The chapelle ardente enclosing the effigy of Anne of Brittany, in 1514, at the Notre-Dame, Paris, fr. 5094 fol. 40v, Bibliothèque Nationale de France, Paris.

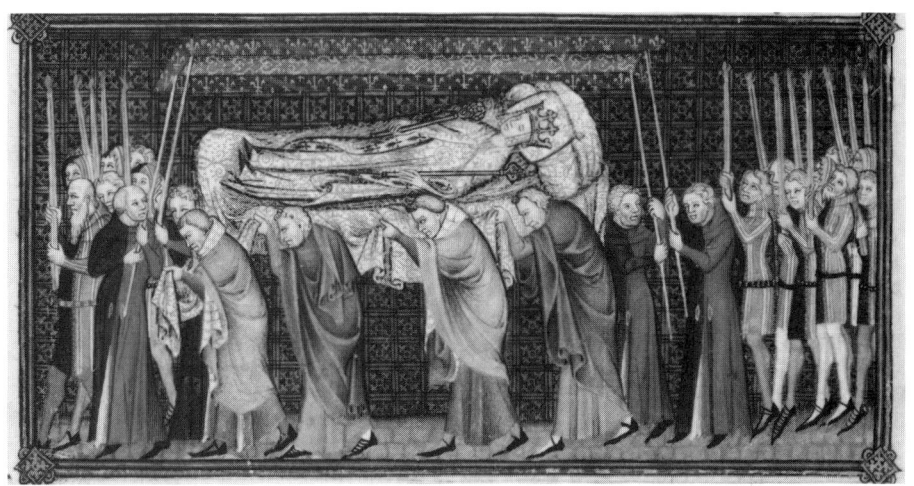

9. The embalmed body borne in the funeral procession of Jeanne de Bourbon (d. 1378), fr. 2813 fol. 480v, Bibliothèque Nationale de France, Paris.

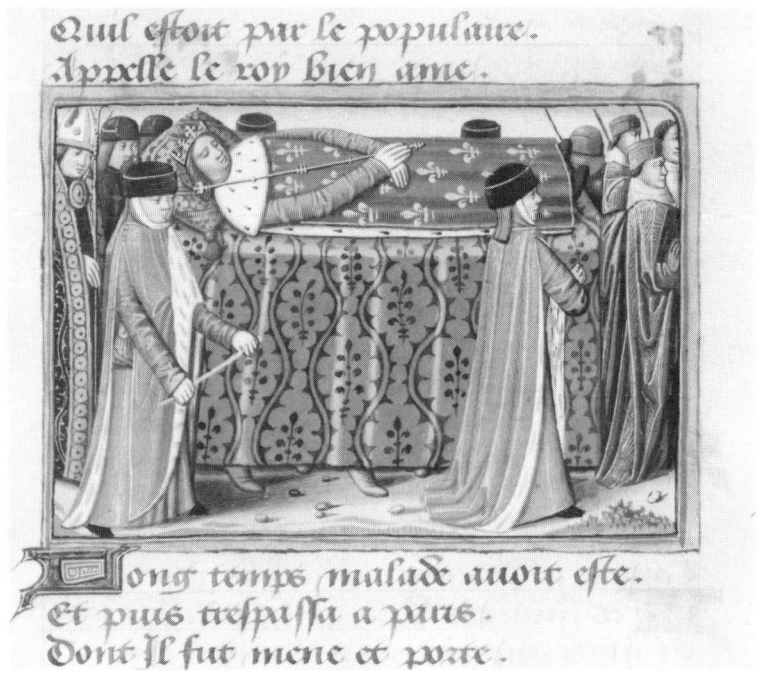

10. Funeral procession of Charles VI (1422), fr. 5054 fol. 27v, Bibliothèque Nationale de France, Paris.

11. The funeral hearse and the high altar at the obsequies of Abbot Islip, Westminster Abbey, from the Obituary Roll of John Islip. By Courtesy of the Dean and Chapter of Westminster.

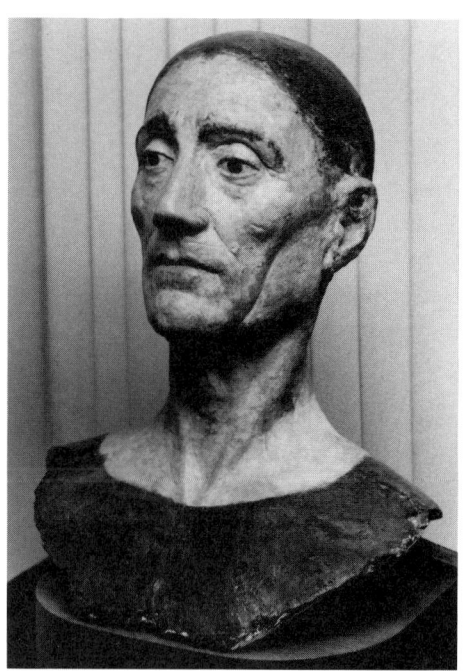

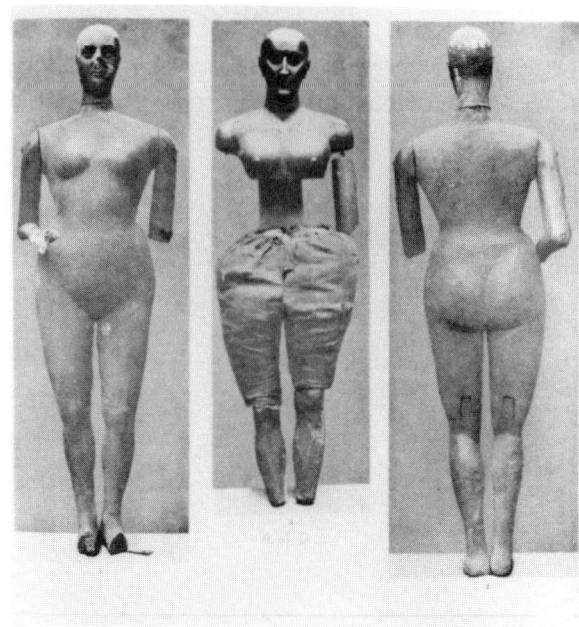

12. Head of effigy of Anne of Bohemia (d. 1394), Undercroft Museum, Westminster Abbey. By Courtesy of the Dean and Chapter of Westminster.

13. The reconstituted effigy head of Henry VII (d.1509), Undercroft Museum, Westminster Abbey. By Courtesy of the Dean and Chapter of Westminster.

14. The funeral effigies of Queen Mary I (d.1558) (left and right) and Queen Anne of Denmark (d.1619) (centre), from W. H. St John Hope, 'On the funeral effigies of the Kings and Queens of England', *Archaeologia*, 40 part 2 (1907), pl. LXIV. By Courtesy of the Dean and Chapter of Westminster.

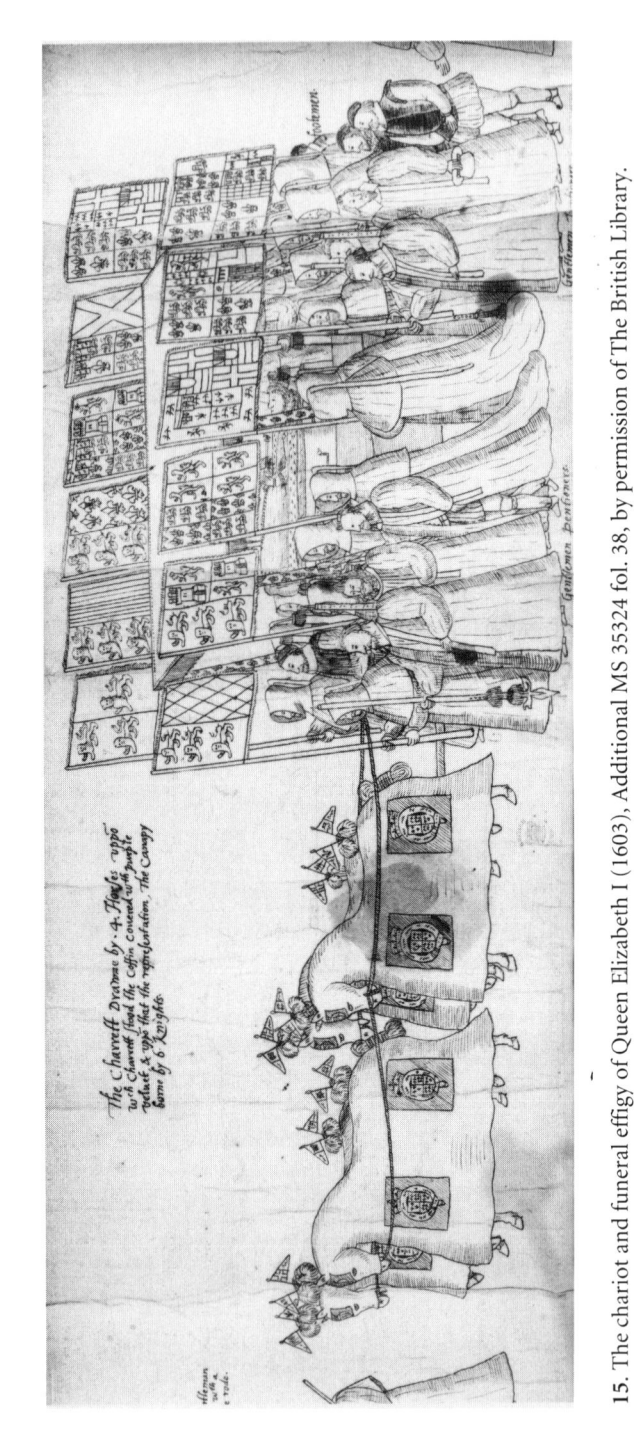

15. The chariot and funeral effigy of Queen Elizabeth I (1603), Additional MS 35324 fol. 38, by permission of The British Library.

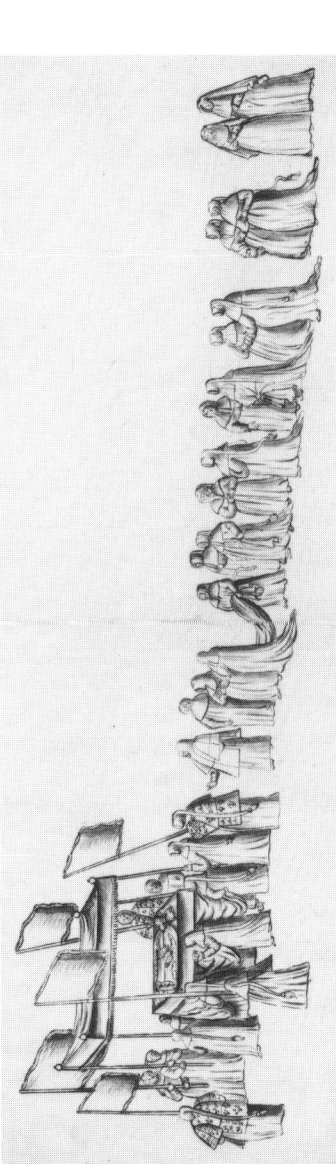

16. Effigy of Mary Queen of Scots (1587), Additional MS 35324 fol. 16, by permission of The British Library.

17. Sir Robert Cecil in the funeral procession of Elizabeth I (1603), Additional 35324 fol. 35, by permission of The British Library. The small, stunted figure, pasted over a larger, whited out figure, seems to represent a deliberate slur against the unpopular Chancellor and strikes a note of disharmony in the visual record of Elizabeth's funeral procession.

18. Monument to Raphe and Elizabeth Wyseman, alabaster and imported 'marbles', after 1594. St Mary and All Saints, Rivenhall, Essex, RCHME, © Crown copyright.

19. Detail of the monument for the Catholic Sir Thomas Hawkins, Boughton-under-Blean, Kent, RCHME, © Crown copyright. The weeping daughters of the defunct express family loss. Sculptor, Epiphanius Evesham.

20. The tomb of Mary Queen of Scots, Westminster Abbey, from Sandford's *Genealogical History*, by permission of The British Library, shelfmark LR301ee5.

21. Hearse of James I with funeral effigy (1625), from Sandford's *Genealogical History*, by permission of The British Library, shelfmark LR301ee5.

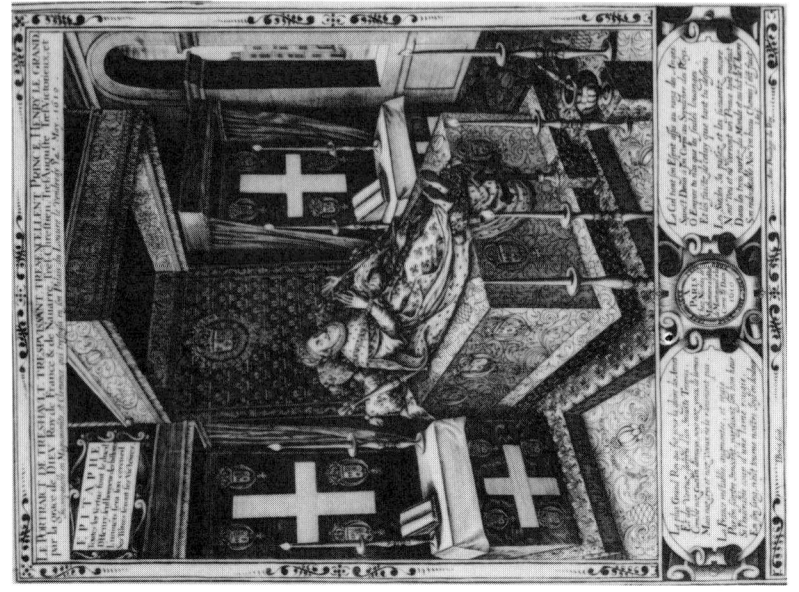

23. Effigy of Henry IV on the bed of state (1610), Cabinet des Estampes, Hennin XVII fol. 23, Bibliothèque Nationale de France, Paris.

22. Hearse and funeral effigy of Prince Henry Stuart (1612), from Sandford's *Genealogical History*, by permission of The British Library, shelfmark LR301ee5.

The Royal Funeral of Elizabeth I

Idolatry and Elizabeth's Lying-in-State Ritual

As I have demonstrated the religious associations of the funeral effigy and canopy in the procession were distanced. This was not the case with the French lying-in-state ritual with its open act of homage to the funeral effigy. Such a ritual would have been difficult to stage in England in view of Protestant interpretations of the second commandment which stated: 'Thou shall not bow down thy self to them [images], nor serve them: for I the LORD thy God *am* a jealous God.'[144]

Nevertheless the Elizabethan authorities took an ambiguous position as far as paying homage to representations of the sovereign was concerned. As Strong has pointed out, the Anglicans denounced the use of religious images as popish superstition while maintaining the sacred nature of royal portraiture. Homage could be paid to a ruler's sceptre, seal or sword 'without sin'. Thomas Bilson, in his *The True Difference betweene Christian Subiection and Unchristian Rebellion* (1585), argues that homage to royal coats of arms or images which Princes set up 'is accepted as rendred to their owne persons, when they can not otherwise be present in the place to receive it'.[145] Bilson was aware of the ambiguity of the Anglican position, however, and defined the type of homage that was appropriate to royal images with care. 'The images of Princes may not wel be despised or abused, least it be taken as a signe of a malicious hart against the Prince, but bowing the knee or lifting up the hand to the image of a Prince is flat and inevitable idolatrie.' The Anglican position would inevitably exclude any emulation of the ritual serving of the effigy enacted in the French royal funeral.

At Elizabeth's funeral there is no mention of an effigy in the pre-procession rites but a lying-in-state ritual was staged. More than a month passed between the death of Elizabeth at Richmond and her funeral at Westminster Abbey on 28 April 1603. In the interim her body was taken by night in a black-draped barge from Richmond to Whitehall, attended by a great company of ladies. Privy Councillors were also present on the royal barge, while pensioners and officers of the royal household followed on other barges. At Westminster the coffin lay in state on a black velvet bed in a chamber all hung with mourning.[146]

While at Whitehall, as Lady Anne Clifford, a thirteen-year-old at the time of the funeral, confirms, the encoffined body 'continued a good whil standinge in the Drawinge-chamber, wher it was watched all night by severall Lords and Ladies: with my mother sitting up with it two or three nights: but my Lady

---

[144] Exodus 20. 5, *The Geneva Bible*. On the debate over idolatry in reformed religion, see Watt, p. 132; Aston, pp. 379–82, 391, 393.
[145] Bilson, pp. 547–80 (p. 561) cited by Strong (1963), pp. 39–40 and Phillips, p. 120. John Bale similarly argues that reverence may be done to the seal; see H. Christmas, ed., *The Selected Works of John Bale* (Cambridge: Parker Society, 1849), pp. 94–9.
[146] Clapham, pp. 110–11.

would not give me leave to watch by reason I was heald too yonge'.[147] Scaramelli provides the most detailed commentary on the lying-in-state ritual, saying that the Council waited on the dead Queen with the same ceremony and expenditure, 'down to household and table service'.[148]

The continuation of the Queen's household comes close to the French model, but Scaramelli underlines the fact that it was not the effigy but the corpse that was thus honoured. He ridicules the homage paid to the dead Queen, 'as though she were not wrapped in many a fold of cere-cloth, and hid in such a heap of lead, of coffin, of pall, but walking as she used to do at this season, about the alleys of her gardens'.[149]

The lying-in-state of the coffin was itself a traditional ritual originating in the Middle Ages. Initially, display of the embalmed body occurred in specifically religious locations. Edward I (d. 1307) was the first to lie in state for an extended period, perhaps facilitated by improvements in embalming procedure. After his death his corpse was conveyed to the abbey church of Waltham, where it remained from 4th August to the latter end of October.[150]

It is with the first Tudor monarch, Henry VII, that we have evidence of the lying-in-state ritual being formalized into various stages and including periods of display in secular locations. Henry died at Richmond on 21 April 1509. The Council and friars attended the King's body until a hearse had been set up in the chapel and the great chamber and chapel had been hung with black.[151]

> After that all thinge necessary for the enterement & funerall pomp of ye late kinge were sumptuously prepared and doded / ye corps of ye said defunct was brought owt of his chamber / where he deceased into his grete chamber where he rested iij days / & every day had dirige & was solempnely song / wt a prelate mytred / & so other iij days in the hall & other iij days in ye chapell wt lyke service & morners gyving their attendaunce / and in every place, was a herce garnessed wt banners scochines & pencelles.[152]

It is clear here that the lying-in-state of the body was originally associated with intercessionary prayers for the soul of the dead king.

During the whole time that the body was at Richmond, 'ther was contynually kept a Right sumptuous household [with] lords and [other] officiers as they did

---

[147] Sackville-West, pp. 4–5.
[148] Given the involvement of the court ladies in the lying-in-state ritual, it is unsurprising that they were not available to attend on Queen Anne until after the funeral; CSPD, VIII, 3.
[149] CSPV, X (1603–7), 22.
[150] Hope, pp. 522, 528. Henry IV has been described lying-in-state at Westminster, but with no evidence given, ibid., p. 535. On Edward IV, see *Archeaologia*, I (edn. 1777), pp. 348–9. See also W. J. White, 'Changing Burial Practice in Late Medieval England', *The Ricardian*, vol. 4 no. 63 (1978), 23–30 (p. 28).
[151] BL, Additional MS 4531 fol. 53.
[152] CA, I Series MS XI fol. 82b.

in the kings lyvyng'.[153] With Henry VII, then, we also have clear evidence of the continuation of the King's household at the death of the monarch.

The interesting medieval ritual practice of serving meals to the empty chair of the monarch may have acted as precedents for the serving of the coffin. This practice survived at least until 1599 when Thomas Platter witnessed it at Nonsuch Palace. On this occasion, 'the long table had been fully laid and served and the same obeisance and honours performed as the queen herself had sat there'. The Queen, who was in residence, ate privately in her apartment.[154] In late sixteenth-century England homage to an empty chair was acceptable but homage to an image was not. Development of the English royal funeral effigy ritual would have to wait twenty-two years until the death of Elizabeth's successor, James I.[155]

---

[153] BL, Additional MS 45131 fol. 53.
[154] Thomas Platter, *Travels in England* (1599), ed. by C. Williams (London: [n. pub.], 1937), pp. 194–5. See also Giesey (1960), p. 159.
[155] See my discussion in chapter 10.

CHAPTER SIX

Religion and Culture under the Early Stuarts

The shift in attitude towards the arts at the end of the sixteenth and beginning of the seventeenth centuries, noted at the end of the last chapter, had a profound impact on funeral ritual. This chapter enlarges on the cultural developments which took place in James's reign and focuses on the interaction between the arts and changing religious policy. The discussion is necessarily brief and concentrates on establishing those cultural changes which have the greatest implications for funeral rituals. A grasp of these cultural conditions is a necessary preliminary to understanding the Stuart funerals which will be analysed in subsequent chapters.

Cultural Developments under James and Charles

The end of the war with Spain, a country with a dominant influence in Europe, meant that the continental influences that had begun to be felt towards the end of Elizabeth's reign were able to flourish. European travel became easier and Italy, Flanders and Spain were opened up to a relatively large number of aristocratic tourists. This facilitated the collection of continental art works and allowed continental, especially Italian, ideas about the status of art to filter into England. In addition, embassies were re-established in Brussels, Madrid, Venice and Florence after a gap of nearly four decades. Among their other functions, embassies provided a convenient agency for art collectors. When Carleton, for example, went to Venice as ambassador in December 1610 he undertook to acquire paintings for Prince Henry.

Gradually, the new attitudes towards art and its collection became established. Limited art collection had taken place under Elizabeth. Leicester had acquired several Italian paintings as early as the 1580s and William Cecil had agents collecting specimens of statuary for him from Venice and probably elsewhere. In the early years of James's reign, the Earl of Shrewsbury and Queen Anne were both collecting paintings. It was only after 1610, however, that a small coterie of courtiers began collecting art on a larger scale. By the late 1610s leading courtiers were expected to profess an interest in the arts. In this period Buckingham retained his own architect and art expert, Balthazar Gerbier, who collected art treasures on his behalf in Europe over the next five years. When

Rubens came to England in 1629 he admired the magnificence of English art collections.¹

Perhaps the leading figure promoting cultural change was James's eldest son, Prince Henry Stuart. James established an independent household for Prince Henry at Oatlands on their arrival in England. The Prince's court soon grew in size. In 1607 Sir Thomas Chaloner, the Prince's Chamberlain, called it a 'great court' and a few years later Foscarini described it as an 'academy of young nobles'.²

Financial independence gave the Prince the freedom to pursue his own interests. Cornwallis reports that the Prince 'greatly delighted in all kinds of rare inventions and arts [. . .] in limming and painting, carving, in all sorts of excellent and rare Pictures, which he had brought unto him from all countries'.³ Of particular significance for the rehabilitation of effigial images was Henry's request for a collection of fifteen bronze statues from Tuscany. They were to be part of a gift from Cosimo II in connection with the marriage negotiations of 1611. These statues were probably the first Italian sculpture to reach England since the break with Rome. Art for its own sake was beginning to penetrate into Jacobean England and the impetus was coming from the monarchy.⁴

Henry's court was also a centre for art patronage. This is a large subject and I wish just to point out one or two of the more significant implications for the development of sculpture and classical architecture.

Nobles attracted to the vibrant court of Prince Henry included Northampton, Pembroke, Arundel and Lennox.⁵ The Earl of Arundel, Thomas Howard (1585–1646), played a particularly prominent role in initiating cultural change. He sent agents all over Europe, even dispatching one to the Ottoman Empire to hunt for Greek antiquities, and assembled England's first collection of ancient statues, now in the Ashmolean museum.⁶ Peacham acknowledges in his *Compleat Gentleman* that Arundel was responsible for introducing a taste for classical statuary into England.⁷ Arundel, who would be a member of the commission organizing James's funeral, had a strong interest in funeral symbolism and architecture. In his will, written in 1617, Arundel requested the

---

1   DNB; Parry (1981), pp. 115, 126; Mercer, p. 248; Smuts, pp. 119–20.
2   Parry (1981), p. 67; Smuts, p. 119; CSPV, XII (1610–13), 464; G. P. V. Akrigg, *Jacobean Pageant or The Court of King James I* (London: Hamish Hamilton, 1962), p. 132.
3   Sir Charles Cornwallis, *The Life and Death of Our Late Most Incomparable and Heroique Prince, Henry, Prince of Wales: A Prince (for Valour and Vertue) fit to be Imitated in Succeeding Times* (London: [n. pub.], 1641), pp. 100–101; Nichols (1828), II, 489;
4   Roy Strong, *Henry, Prince of Wales: England's Lost Renaissance* (London: Thames & Hudson, 1986), pp. 195–6; Mercer, pp. 10–11.
5   Parry (1981), p. 69; Strong (1986), pp. 26–44.
6   See David Howarth, *Lord Arundel and his Circle* (London: Yale University Press, 1985), p. 63; Smuts, p. 119. Daniel Mytens' portrait of Arundel shows him seated at the entrance to his statue gallery. The painting hangs in Arundel Castle, Sussex, England.
7   Mercer, pp. 247–8, 255; Parry (1981), p. 113; Sharpe (1979), p. 102.

removal of his father's body from the Tower and his grandmother's body from Framlingham, both to be relocated at Arundel Castle. He further specified: 'I desire that the Tombs may be made plain without painting or gilding but either in good Marble or Brass and that my most approved good friend Mr Inigo Jones may order the designs of them', thereby demonstrating his preference for neo-classical styles. In 1625 the coffin of Philip Howard, Earl of Arundel, was reinterred in the Fitzalan Chapel at Arundel Castle but Arundel's grandmother, Lady Mary Fitzalan, remained at Framlingham and the tombs were never built.[8]

In 1610 Inigo Jones was appointed by Prince Henry as his Surveyor of Works. It is difficult to associate Jones with any work for the Prince, who died just two years later, but his position was instrumental in forging a relationship with Arundel with whom he travelled in Germany and Italy in 1613–14. The Earl's passion for classical statuary dates from this period.[9] Jones did not leave England again after 1614 but his experience, which included the Roman antique, the mannerism of Florence and Bologna, Palladio and Scamozzi, was sufficient to give impetus to the development of classical architecture in England.[10] In the 1610s Jones and a few other court architects began to develop comprehensive classical styles, rejecting the ornateness of earlier architecture in favour of a more sober and dignified form. Jones was to be Surveyor to James I (1615–25).[11]

It was in the realm of monumental architecture that most examples of Italianate influence occurred. Early on Jones designed a tomb for the wife of Sir Rowland Cotton (d. 1608) which still stands in the church of St Chad, Norton-in-Hales, Shropshire, probably working from a symbolic programme drawn up by the Hebrew scholar, Hugh Broughton (1544–1611). The sarcophagus is unlike anything else in England of that period being of a classical type with harpies at the corners.[12] Nicholas Stone also began to look to classical models in his tomb design. He and his master Isaac James were responsible for designing a tomb commissioned by Arundel for Northampton (d. 1614). The figures of the four cardinal virtues that stand at the corners of this tomb's canopy represent perhaps the earliest English response to the Arundel marbles. Tomb sculpture was beginning to demonstrate increased naturalism and an enhanced emotional content (figure 19).[13]

---

8 Howarth, p. 105.
9 John Harris and Gordon Higgott, *Inigo Jones: Complete Architectural Drawings* (London: Royal Academy of Arts, 1989), pp. 15–16; Howarth, p. 97. It was Jones who designed the gallery at Arundel House in which the Earl's statues were displayed.
10 Jones was not, however, the first to look towards classical architecture as the arches of the 1604 Royal Entry illustrate.
11 Harris and Higgott, pp. 16, 62–3; Smuts, pp. 98–9, 104–6.
12 Interestingly a variant of this tomb appeared as Merlin's tomb at the opening of the *Barriers*. See Strong (1986), pp. 135–6, 149; Harris and Higgot, pp. 42–3.
13 Howarth, p. 35; Stone (1979), p. 225; Mercer, pp. 237–51; Margaret Whinney, *Sculpture*

Prince Charles was to inherit the art collections of his brother and Prince Henry's example helped to form his aesthetic taste. His trip to Madrid in 1623 gave him direct experience of a sophisticated European court where he saw the greatest royal art collection in Europe. The visit fuelled a desire to compete against his foreign rivals, Philip IV and Louis XIII, in the realm of royal display.[14] One example of Charles's art-collecting ambitions is his acquisition of a collection of antique statues from the Duke of Mantua to be housed in a gallery completed at St James's Palace in 1630.[15]

Charles was surrounded by people with direct experience of continental court culture. Henrietta Maria came from the cultured French court and brought Parisian artistic values with her. Nearly all the leaders of Charles's court had visited the continent. Among those who were members of the Privy Council in the late 1620s were Sir Francis Cottington who had lived at the English embassy in Madrid for more than a decade, the Earls of Holland and Carlisle who had substantial diplomatic experience, and Arundel.[16]

Malcolm Smuts has traced the personal way in which Charles shaped court culture, partly through the patronage of leading figures such as Daniel Mytens and Inigo Jones. Gradually there developed a more cohesive and unified court culture than had ever existed under James. It is important to remember, however, that the cultural innovations of James's reign did not instantly displace the court culture of the late sixteenth century. In the early 1620s there remained an eclectic cultural atmosphere in which, as Smuts puts it, 'prodigy house architecture, neo-chivalric pageantry, and verse and costume portraiture in the tradition of Hilliard survived side by side with newer forms, creating a cultural mosaic of bewildering diversity'.[17]

Religion and Art

For many Englishmen the increasing influence of Italian and antique culture was bound up with a growing tendency to regard art and religion as separate realms of human experience. The publication of a growing number of works on matters relating to continental art and travel promoted a relaxation of

---

in Britain 1530 to 1830, revised by John Physick (London: Penguin Books, 1964; repr. 1988), p. 63; Llewellyn (1991), p. 122. On Van Dyck and the development of naturalistic representations of the human form under Charles, see Parry (1981), pp. 219–20.

[14] On the court of Philip IV, see John H. Elliott, 'Philip IV of Spain: Prisoner of Ceremony', in *The Courts of Europe: Politics, Patronage and Royalty, 1400–1800*, ed. by A. G. Dickens (London: Thames & Hudson, 1977), pp. 169–89.

[15] Smuts, p. 120; Harris and Higgott, p. 140.

[16] Smuts, p. 185.

[17] Smuts, pp. 120, 132, 183.

attitude towards Catholic countries and a segregation of matters artistic from matters religious.[18]

Some, however, endeavoured to recover art for Protestants, building on Richard Haydocke's civil justifications for art in his translations of Lomazzo, as described elsewhere.[19] Sir Robert Dallington (1561–1637), Gentleman of the Privy Chamber at Prince Henry's court, produced two travel guidebooks: *The View of France* (1604) and *A Survey of Tuscany* (1605). His writings reflect a key aspect of the aesthetic culture of Henry Stuart's court: the combination of the culture of Medician Florence and Henrician Paris with a strong adherence to Protestantism. Henry Peacham similarly made an important contribution to the Protestant justification of art in his *The Arte of Drawing* (1606), arguing the case for a Biblical justification of art while still rejecting any use of images to represent the Trinity.

During James's reign a significant number of men with Protestant allegiances became deeply involved in the world of art. Henry Wotton returned from more than a decade of service at the Embassy in Venice to write the first book on architecture by an Englishman since 1553, *The Elements of Architecture* (London, 1624).[20] Sir Dudley Carleton, who served as a diplomat in both Brussels and Venice, put together a large collection of statues that he exchanged for paintings from the personal collection of Rubens in 1620. Both men were Calvinists who might have been expected to repudiate such 'images'.[21]

Wotton had a very keen perception of the functional value of art for the state. Commenting on the functions of the statuary that 'strewed' the highways of ancient Athens and Rome, he says they were, 'not a bare transitory Entertainment of the Eye, or onely a gentle deception of Time, to the Travailer: But had also a secret and strong Influence, even unto the advancement of the Monarchie, by continuall representation of vertuous examples; so as in that point ART becomes a piece of state'.[22]

For some, however, the relationship between religion and art remained problematic and for significant numbers the court of Charles I functioned as a paradigm of the inevitable and dangerous link between the two. It is not difficult to see why many Calvinists perceived a connection between royal taste and a suspect religious proclivity. Charles and Henrietta commissioned work from the sculptor Bernini, perhaps the greatest sculptor of his time but effectively under the patronage of the Papacy. Such commissions gave rise to resentment.

---

[18] See John Stoye, *English Travellers Abroad, 1604–1667, their Influence in English Society and Politics* (London: Cape, 1952); Höltgen, p. 133.

[19] See chapter 5. Inigo Jones annotated Lomazzo c. 1614; see Harrison and Higgott, p. 54.

[20] Henry Wotton, *The Elements of Architecture* (London: [n. pub.], 1624); Höltgen, pp. 128, 133; Parry (1981), pp. xi, 81; Smuts, p. 118; Stoye, pp. 133–74.

[21] Smuts, pp. 118, 186. See also Tyacke, p. 89.

[22] Wotton, p. 106.

How could the King tolerate Catholicism for the sake of *objêts d'art*?[23] William Prynne argued that works of art were being used by the Vatican as bait to lure Charles into Catholicism and there is some evidence that the Papacy allowed Bernini to accept his commission for those very reasons. As Strong has demonstrated, under Charles I the arts as cultivated at court were to be fatally linked with concessions to Catholicism and with England turning its back on its Protestant allies in Europe.[24]

Jacobean Religious Policy and the Rise of Arminianism

On his accession James embraced the Church of England largely because it suited his concept of kingship. The English Bishops were Erastian, accepting the supremacy of the State in ecclesiastical affairs, and James approved of the ritual of the English church, probably because it exalted the monarch and enhanced his divine status. He declared himself uncontentious in matters of ritual and held that participation in religious ceremony was a matter of choice. Confrontation soon came, however, as the Calvinist contingent at the Hampton Court Conference in 1604 was dominated by an extreme group that rejected ritual.[25] James was unsympathetic and reacted in an antagonistic manner, declaring that he would have one religion in 'substance and ceremony'. In his post-conference policy, James sought to impose conformity on the Church of England, taking a tough line with dissident Calvinists. A crucial element of his strategy was the creation of the one Authorised Version of the Bible (1611) for uniform use.[26]

This policy of enforcing conformity in the Church rapidly led to Calvinist disillusionment with their new King and gave the lie to earlier hopes that he would favour their cause. James soon relaxed his position and required only occasional conformity from clergymen who subscribed to the legality of the Prayer Book and the bishops. However, the Calvinists found further fuel for their disappointment with the King because he was similarly tolerant of Catholics. They criticized him severely for apparent leniency towards papists.[27] Prior to his accession, James had pragmatically cultivated all religious groups, including the English Catholics, believing that their support would enhance his hold on the succession. It seems that the Catholics did not expect James's conversion but did anticipate that he would grant them toleration in religion, in line with the assurances he had given those who had visited his court in Scotland.[28]

---

[23] Arundel and Buckingham were both collecting the sort of Italian and Flemish artists who were committedly Catholic; Lockyer, p. 297.
[24] Parry (1981), pp. 223–4; Strong (1986), p. 219.
[25] A stand was made against the ritual use of the cross in baptism.
[26] Wilson, pp. 203–6, 217; Parry (1981), p. 326.
[27] Parry (1981), p. 230; Tyacke, p. 185; Lockyer, p. 288.
[28] See James's pre-accession correspondence with the Earl of Northampton in which he had

There were some 40,000 Catholics in England when James came to the throne. Leniency was displayed towards them from the beginning of the reign and soon their numbers began to increase.[29] After the Gunpowder Plot crisis James sharpened the focus of his domestic policy towards Catholics, making a clear distinction between lay Catholics, who would profess loyalty to the Crown, and priests, especially Jesuits. Harsher measures were adopted against the latter but the earlier indulgent attitude was maintained towards Catholic laymen who would take the Oath of Allegiance (1606). Political allegiance brought relative freedom in religion and many took advantage of James's tolerant attitude towards religious ceremony.[30] Thus James endeavoured to separate religion and government.

For many, however, such a division was inconceivable. For them the perception of laxity was compounded by the presence of Catholics and their sympathizers amongst prominent members of the court. The Queen herself had refused to take part in Anglican communion at her coronation, a very public statement, and her Catholicism was always a source of embarrassment and annoyance to the King. The Privy Council included men like the Catholic Henry Howard, Earl of Northampton, and Henry Percy, Earl of Northumberland, who was sympathetic to Catholic recusants. Both were actively hostile towards Calvinism.[31] Even Robert Cecil leaned towards Catholicism, emphasizing the sacraments in his will (1612). From 1603, the inner core of James's Privy Council, at the very least sympathized with Catholicism.[32]

James's court was often the subject of hostile comparison with that of his eldest son, Prince Henry, whose court had a strong Protestant bias. Prayers were said twice a day in Henry's household and attendance at sermons was obligatory. Daniel Price was to say of Prince Henry that 'he hated *Poperie* with a perfect hate' in a sermon preached in 1613 on the anniversary of the Prince's death. Henry had a great antipathy towards the crypto-Catholic Howards. Thomas Howard, the Earl of Arundel, was, of course, an exception. He displayed no overt Catholic sympathies and took part in court tilts, thereby aligning himself with the Protestant chivalric ideal propagated by Prince Henry and his supporters. (Arundel entered the Church of England on 25 December 1625.) Roy Strong

---

written, 'As for the Catholics; I will neither persecute any that will be quiet and give but an outward obedience to the law, neither will I spare to advance any of them that will by good service worthily deserve it.' See Willson, p. 148–9; McIlwain, p. xlix; Akrigg (1984), p. 207; Lockyer, p. 281.

[29] Willson, pp. 219–22; Lockyer, pp. 281–3. See also Stow, *Preface*.

[30] McIlwain, p. liii; Willson, pp. 197–200, 228, 242, 269; Lockyer, pp. 282–3; McClure, II, 490–525. The oath confirmed the subordination of matters religious to matters of state, placing the rights of the King above those of the Pope. In the field of international politics James took a strong stand against Catholicism and published many writings, in part to defend the oath.

[31] Willson, pp. 178, 221, 156.

[32] William Cecil had also been anti-Calvinist; Tyacke, p. 38; Willson, pp. 176–8.

has even speculated that had Prince Henry survived there would have been no suspicion that Italianate artistic culture was a vehicle for 'covert Catholicism or indeed incipient Laudian Anglicanism'.[33]

Ironically, James's own religious beliefs were in line with orthodox Calvinism as far as matters of predestination were concerned and for most of James's reign Calvinism enjoyed greater royal favour than under Elizabeth. Calvinists, such as George Abbot (1562–1633), Archbishop of Canterbury from 1611 to 1627, and James Montagu (1568?–1618), Bishop of Winchester from 1616 to 1618 and James's personal chaplain, dominated Church government until late in the reign.[34] Both men exerted a strong Calvinist influence on James's theological position but also supported the divine right of kings.[35]

One result of the Calvinist grip on the Church was a pressure on the emergent Arminian opposition to define itself.[36] While relations with Spain had been poor, it had been easy to see England as an homogenous religious entity: the elect nation of Protestants. In the 1590s, however, as the international situation relaxed, Calvinism became more vulnerable to internal splits. Arminianism began to exert an influence in England under Bishop John Overall, Regius Professor of Divinity at Cambridge in 1595, but the spread of Arminian ideas was held in check by Whitgift's approval of the Calvinist Lambeth Articles in the same year. William Laud (1573–1645) did not come out against Calvinism until 1615 in a Shrove Sunday sermon at Oxford.[37]

The controversial heart of Laud's theological position was, in line with Arminianism, to elevate the role of the sacraments and the grace which they conferred, effectively supplanting the grace of predestination. Alongside his Arminian doctrine, Laud actively promoted the re-ceremonialization of the Church, aiming at what he called 'the Beauty of Holiness' through a revival of liturgical practices inherited from the medieval church. Sommerville sees the emphasis on ceremonies at the expense of preaching as an arbitrary result of Arminian sacramentalism. Tyacke brings the two plausibly together, however, focusing on church furniture. In the 1630s, during the ascendancy of Arminianism, altars and fonts came to dominate church interiors, illustrating the way in which sacramental grace was replacing the grace of predestination.[38]

The ambiguity of Elizabethan policies on church interiors and ritual had left the way open for the re-ceremonialization of the Church of England.[39] Most of

---

[33] Strong (1986), pp. 17, 52–4; Parry (1981), p. 115.
[34] Abbot technically remained Archbishop until his death in 1633 but his powers were curtailed in 1627.
[35] Tyacke, pp. 21, 25, 28, 41; Sommerville, p. 208.
[36] Arminianism derived its name from the Dutch theologian Jacobus Arminius.
[37] Tyacke, pp. 4–7, 35–6, 49, 62–7, 70. On Laud's debt to Richard Hooker, see Parry (1981), p. 246. Laud became Bishop of St David's in 1621, Bishop of Bath and Wells in 1626 and Archbishop of Canterbury in 1633.
[38] Sommerville, p. 22; Tyacke, pp. 7, 176.
[39] See my chapter 2.

the alterations to church interiors would come in the 1630s. The 1610s and 1620s were a period of struggle and under the Calvinist Archbishop Abbot, there were frequent confrontations over ceremonies and clerical vestments, as well as ecclesiastical government. Richard Neile (1562–1640), Archbishop of York, and Laud began, however, to make significant changes, moving communion tables back to the altar position and introducing decorative sacramental props like the communion chalice at St John's College, Oxford.[40]

As the St John's chalice illustrates, the process of re-ceremonialization involved a re-legitimization of the religious image. There are other Jacobean examples of art being reintroduced into church settings. In 1621 Lord Maynard built a private chapel in his family home, Easton Lodge, in which the painted glass featured a picture of Christ's crucifixion. Spiritual symbolism began to reappear in more public locations, such as on tombs in parish churches, as well. The tomb of Edmund West at Marsworth, Bucks (c. 1618), sculpted by Epiphanius Evesham, is full of religious images including a Risen Christ.[41] By the end of James's reign the changing attitude to art and the Laudian programme of liturgical enrichment had proceeded to the point where John Cleland could remark on 'the speaking power of pictures' (1626).[42] For many, however, religious images remained taboo. Thomas Warmstry, one of the clerks for the Worcester diocese, reviewed the changes of the 1630s and attacked the new 'altars' and 'images', complaining that the 'preaching of the word is discouraged' and 'pictures brought in'.[43]

Counter-Reformation attitudes helped to promote the re-legitimization of the religious image in England. Puritans assiduously avoided images, their meditations, diaries and sermons rarely including any visual detail. The Catholic Church, however, actively encouraged the development of the visual imagination as an aid to piety. Laud similarly argued that sensual experience played an essential role in shaping the soul to receive grace.[44]

James maintained his anti-Arminian position until towards the end of his reign, making a stand, for example, against the Dutch Arminians at the Synod of Dort in 1618.[45] There was, however, a radical shift in James's religious position from mid-1622. Political considerations were the root cause. The outbreak of the Thirty Years War in 1618 and the pursuit of a Spanish marriage for Charles pushed James away from the Calvinists who largely adopted an

---

[40] Tyacke, pp. 71, 116–18, 199, 208. The chalice dates from 1615 when Laud was President. Richard Neile had been Robert Cecil's chaplain and went on to become the 'organizing genius of English Arminianism'; see Tyacke, p. 12; Smuts, p. 220.

[41] Mercer, pp. 9, 244–6. See also Colvin, p. 257; Parry (1981), p. 250.

[42] Collinson (1988), p. 120. For a discussion of the poetry of George Herbert and the pre-Laudian revival of ceremony and ritual, see Parry (1981), pp. 243–5.

[43] Warmstry *Convocation Speech*, pp. 2, 5–6, 10, 13–15, cited by Tyacke, p. 242.

[44] Smuts, pp. 229, 234; H. Outram Evenett, *The Spirit of the Counter-Reformation* (Cambridge: Cambridge University Press, 1968), p. 48.

[45] Tyacke, pp. 45, 89, 146.

anti-Spanish policy. He became more sympathetic to Neile and Lancelot Andrewes, Bishop of Winchester (1555–1626), and more concessions were made to Catholics.[46]

The ascent of the Arminians was signalled in various ways. Andrewes was promoted to Winchester in 1618 and Bishop Montaigne to London in 1621. Similarly, William Lucy preached an Arminian sermon at Cambridge in 1622 and by 1623 both universities had shifted markedly towards Arminianism.[47]

Charles, Arminianism and the Development of a Ceremonial Religion Royale

Charles demonstrated an affinity with the Arminians well before his accession. Two Arminian chaplains accompanied him on his marriage-negotiation trip to Spain in 1623. One was Matthew Wren who reported to Andrewes, Neile and Laud that the King's judgement was 'very right'.[48] Once Charles was King, the Arminian influence fast took hold of the centre of power. Laud was chosen by Charles to preach at the opening of Parliament in 1625 and 1626 and to draw up the coronation service in February 1626. With the Arminian ascendancy came the Calvinists' fall. The Calvinist element was virtually excluded from the committees appointed over the next few months and Abbot was sequestered from his ecclesiastical jurisdiction in 1627.[49]

Arminianism suited the Stuart vision of kingship and therein lay its success. There was a symbiotic relationship between Charles's support of Laud's ecclesiastical innovations and Laud's active defence of divine right kingship. Arminian theology was in harmony with the idea that the royal prerogative was derived from eternal principles and its exponents dismissed as blasphemous attempts to argue that kings arose from historical causes.[50] The overall result was the formation of what might be termed a religion of monarchy: 'in the 1620s and 1630s the court's Arminian theology and sensual approach to religious mysteries began to color the political theology of loyalist clergy, who treated the king, in a very literal way, as the living image of God on earth'.[51] In 1609 James himself had declared before Parliament that, 'Kings are justly called Gods for they exercise a manner of resemblance of Divine power upon earth: if you will

---

[46] Lockyer, pp. 290–6: Sommerville, p. 218; Tyacke, pp. 103–4.
[47] Tyacke, pp. 46–7, 75–6, 103, 114, 124–5, 151, 177, 225. Tyacke also comments on the publication of the anti-Calvinist writings of Richard Montagu, who published *A New Gagg for an Old Goose* in 1624, and William Prynne.
[48] Lockyer, p. 307.
[49] Lockyer, p. 311; Tyacke, pp. 8, 166–7. See also W. Scott and J. Bliss, eds, *The Works of the Most Reverend Father in God William Laud*, 7 vols (Oxford: [n. pub.], 1847–60), VI, 245–6.
[50] Sommerville, pp. 45, 193; Smuts, pp. 231–3.
[51] Smuts, p. 230; Parry (1981), p. 26.

consider the attributes to God, you shall see how they agree in the person of a King.'[52]

Royal authority was described by contemporaries as a tangible projection of God's majesty. Matthew Wren, royal chaplain, preached: 'If any man say I fear God and feareth not the *King*, he is a liar [...] It is impossible for him that feareth not the King, whom he hath seen, to fear God, whom he hath not seen [...] Because the Image of God [...] is upon Kings.'[53] Such rhetoric helped to blur the distinction between sacred and profane, expanding the liminal space in which royal ceremonial operated and facilitating the development of a *religion royale*. Under Charles the power of the king and the visual splendour which surrounded him were mutually dependent, as will be demonstrated in my discussion of James's funeral ceremony.

Catholicism was also set to benefit from the change in reign. Initially some Catholics feared that there would be a clamp down on their religious freedoms in conjunction with the aggressive policy towards Spain that Charles and Buckingham pursued at the beginning of the reign. After the collapse of the Cadiz expedition, the attitude towards Spain relaxed. In any case, despite his initial rift with Spain, Charles had appointed some Catholics and crypto-Catholics to power, fuelling Calvinist suspicions of a Catholic conspiracy theory and the widespread fear that an increased toleration of Catholics would follow his accession.[54] Francis Cottington, for example, was now secretary to Prince Charles and would later become Chancellor of the Exchequer. He was widely assumed to be sympathetic towards Catholicism.[55] Charles's French Queen also provided a centre of Catholic activity at court. Her household included a Catholic ecclesiastical hierarchy presided over by a bishop. By the mid-1630s Catholicism was to become fashionable at court and Charles became the first monarch since Mary Tudor to welcome a papal envoy to his court.[56]

Charles's own attitudes facilitated Catholic influence. He shared his father's hopes for the reunion of Christian churches. In the 1630s the court clergy would argue quite openly for eventual reconciliation with Catholicism and introduced Catholic devotional practices into the Chapel Royal. This led to fears that the King himself would convert, following the earlier French example of Henry IV.

In this context Calvinist discomfort with the toleration of Catholic ritual and art is easier to understand. Throughout the period considered, early Stuart religious policies gave out signals that would have been confusing to many, particularly those who did not accept the separation of religion and politics.

---

52 McIlwain, p. 307.
53 M. Wren, *A Sermon Preached Before His Majesty* (Cambridge, 1627), p. 25, cited by Smuts, p. 235. Similarly, see Isaac Bargrave's 1627 sermon, cited by ibid., p. 235.
54 Lockyer, pp. 25–6.
55 Conrad Russell, *The Crisis of Parliaments: English History 1509–1660* (Oxford: Oxford University Press, 1971; repr. 1984), pp. 310–11; Lockyer, pp. 289–90.
56 Lockyer, pp. 297–8; Smuts, pp. 2, 8, 226–7.

CHAPTER SEVEN

Playing with Death: The Exploitation and Subversion of Funeral Ritual (1603–1625)

The programme of propaganda that James used to promote his royal image after his accession to the English throne included a calculated exploitation of the tomb effigies of the two dead Queens whose funerals have already been discussed: Elizabeth I and Mary Queen of Scots. The funeral effigy of Elizabeth was also utilized in support of the new Stuart King, while the erection of a Westminster tomb for Mary led James into staging a second funeral for his mother. James's manipulation of the royal theatre of death is discussed here in terms of the changing religious and cultural conditions of his reign. James's funereal innovations may have contributed to more widespread alterations in funeral ritual practice and the role of the royal example in relation to the subversion of the traditional heraldic funeral is assessed.

Elizabeth's Funeral Effigy

Once Elizabeth's obsequies were over her funeral effigy remained lying in its hearse in Westminster Abbey for a month.[1] Subsequently it is reasonable to assume that the effigy joined others surviving from earlier royal funerals, all of which were kept at Westminster Abbey. We have evidence suggesting that this occurred at the funeral of Elizabeth of York. Once the offering and the sermon were over, 'the Ladyes departed / after whos departyng the Image w^t the crowne & the riche robes were had to a secret place by St. Edwarde Shryne', and then the body was interred.[2] Similarly, at the funeral of Henry VIII, the effigy was taken into the vestry by six knights before the coffin was lowered into its vault.[3]

It is not known exactly when the Westminster effigies first went on display to the public. It has been suggested that the jointing of Mary Tudor's effigy is indicative of an intention to stand the figure upright and exhibit it.[4] The fact that the effigies were depicted with eyes open would facilitate this secondary

---

[1] CSPV, X (1603–7), 22.
[2] CA, I Series MS XI fol. 31.
[3] CA, Briscoe MS II fol. 314; Hope, p. 541. Henry VIII's effigy does not survive.
[4] Harvey and Mortimer, p. 55.

function of the funeral effigy and the practice of display would certainly help to explain the survival of effigies for so long after the funeral ceremonies in which they featured. However, there is no clear evidence for effigial display until the seventeenth century.

In 1561 it was recorded that the chief verger had oversight of 'the pictures of kings and queens within all the said church remaynyng', but there is no hint of display.[5] The first Keeper of the Monuments was appointed in 1593 when the Abbey was under the auspices of Dean Gabriel Goodman between 1561 and 1601. Visiting the Abbey in 1599, Thomas Platter, a continental traveller, testifies to the way in which the royal monuments there had already become a tourist attraction. He described the Henry VII chapel where he 'witnessed some most magnificent and stately tombs of the kings and queens of England, finer than ever I beheld'. Platter refers only to the tombs, however, and makes no mention of any funeral effigies.[6]

Just a few years later, in 1606, Elizabeth's effigy was certainly being exhibited. On 4 August of that year Prince Henry took King Christian IV of Denmark, who was making a state visit to England, to the Abbey, as is recorded in the Treasurer's Accounts for 1606. These accounts also state that an advance of £50 was sent to the Dean for dressing the effigies, including that of Elizabeth I. Stow confirms that the image of Queene Elizabeth was 'newly beautified, amended and adorned with royal vestures' for the occasion.[7] The Westminster Abbey records include a charge of £5 3s 9d for 'the making of the presse of wainscot in which the statues do stand'.[8] The effigies may well have been displayed in the Upper Islip chapel, a location which would have facilitated their survival during the Commonwealth regime.[9]

When Prince Henry Stuart's effigy went on display in 1612 it was placed 'amongst the Representations of the Kings and Queenes his famous predecessors, where it remaineth for ever to be seene'.[10] By this time the Abbey tombs and effigies were a veritable tourist attraction. The Keeper acted as a guide for the cost of one penny, the same price as entrance to the public playhouse.[11] Public awareness of the Abbey displays and the system for visiting them is demonstrated in Middleton's *A Chaste Maid in Cheapside* (1613, Lady Elizabeth's Swan). When Tim lacks a weapon (to 'watch' his sister), he cries:

---

5   WA, Lease Book IV, fol 33; cited by Hope, p. 52.
6   Platter, p. 178; Stanley (1869), p. xxxix.
7   Hope, pp. 566–7; Stow, p. 886.
8   WA, MS 33659, fol 6v.
9   Harvey and Mortimer, p. 21.
10 Nichols (1828), II, 503. The term 'representations' in this context refers to funeral effigies; see the discussion in my chapter 4. Prince Henry's effigy was in fact wilfully outraged and robbed of its rich robes only three years after being placed in the Abbey chapel; see CSPD, IX (1611–18), 361.
11 Platter, pp. 166–7; Andrew Gurr, *The Shakespearean Stage 1574–1642*, 3rd edn (Cambridge: Cambridge University Press, 1992), p. 215.

Playing with Death

> Take you no care for that, if need be I can send for conquering metal [...] 'tis but at Westminster: I am acquainted with him that keeps the monuments, I can borrow Harry the fifth's sword... (IV.iii.57–62)[12]

In the 1630s Weever was to remark, 'What concourse of people come daily, to view the lively Statues and stately Monuments in Westminster Abbey wherein the sacred ashes of so many of the Lords anointed, beside other great Potentates are entombed'.[13] Perhaps the strangest exhibit noted by Weever was the body of Katherine de Valois. She had been buried in front of the high altar of the Lady Chapel in Westminster Abbey in 1483 but in 1502 her body was taken up because Henry VII intended to have her reinterred in the new chapel. Unfortunately he died himself the day after the chapel was consecrated and his Queen's body was left exposed, 'in a chest or coffin with a loose cover to be seen and handled by any who will much desire it'.[14] However ghoulish the prospect of 'handling' the long-dead queen might seem today, such thoughts did not deter Samuel Pepys when he visited the Abbey on 23 February 1668–9 where, by 'particular favour' he was shown her embalmed corpse: 'I had the upper part of her body in my hands, and I did kiss her mouth, reflecting upon that I did kiss a Queene, and this was my birthday, thirty-six years old, that I did kiss a Queene.'

It is probable that the display of the effigies, begun in the early years of his reign, was initiated by James in a deliberate transposition of the usual function of the funeral effigy.[15]

Elizabeth's Tomb Effigy

The funeral effigy was not the only image of Elizabeth to be on display in Westminster Abbey in 1606. In 1605 James ordered a tomb for Elizabeth to be constructed in the Henry VII Chapel.[16] It, too, would be completed in the year of Christian IV's state visit.

James's action does not appear unusual until it is contextualized. The last projected royal tomb, that of Elizabeth's father at Windsor, was never completed.[17] It is likely to have been abandoned for a combination of reasons

---

[12] David L. Frost surmises that Tim really means the sword of Edward III as Henry V's had been stolen. See the note to the text in his *The Selected Plays of Thomas Middleton* (Cambridge: Cambridge University Press, 1978).
[13] Weever, p. 41.
[14] Weever, p. 30.
[15] James's action constitutes an example of Sally Moore's situational adjustment; see my introduction. It appears that the French effigies were also put on display after the funerals. When an eighteenth-century traveller, Johann Jocab Volkmann (1732–1803), visited St Denis he saw 'the succession of French Kings, life-size, modelled in wax, robed in red, and sitting on chairs with sceptres and crowns'; see Benkard, p. 24.
[16] Woolf, p. 176.
[17] Llewellyn, *Royal Body* (1990), pp. 224–5, 231, 233–8.

grounded in cost and inappropriateness of design. The probable original plan for a tomb for Henry VIII by Baccio Bandinelli incorporated no less than 134 statues together with forty-four panels of bronze relief and several effigies. Its incompatibility with the Reformation is underlined by the proposed inclusion of a representation of God the Father with the souls of the deceased.[18] Work on the tomb was still in progress in the mid-1560s but it appears that unease about the decorations was delaying its completion, as a report made for Lord Burghley on 'speciall thinge[s] wantinge' for the tomb suggests. In 1599, when Thomas Platter visited Windsor, he commented on the state of the tomb: 'The pillars made of brass are all very graceful, and eight angels likewise of brass overlaid with gilt. In the centre is a stone of black marble, it is one of the very finest tombs that I have seen; if only it were finished and complete!'[19] That was never to be, however, and the half-finished tomb would be destroyed in 1645.

No tomb was built for Edward VI or Mary Tudor. Elizabeth's only tomb-building venture was the provision of new monuments for her Yorkist ancestors at Fotheringay in 1573. The originals had been mutilated by iconoclasts.[20] In ordering Elizabeth's tomb, James was reviving a tradition that had been in abeyance since the Reformation. There was no political mileage to be gained from completing Henry VIII's tomb. Rather James would turn his attention to providing a tomb for his immediate predecessor.

The tomb was sculpted by Maximilian Colt, Master Sculptor to the Crown. Colt was a Huguenot from Arras who had come to England as a political refugee in the mid-1590s and subsequently built up a considerable reputation as a member of the Anglo-Netherlandish Southwark School.[21] The framework is a free-standing canopied structure with ten Corinthian pillars of black marble, showing the influence of classicism. Inside lies a recumbent figure, in full-length white marble.[22] Although the features are reproduced with great realism, suggesting that a death-mask was used, the stiff attitude of the figure is traditional. There is no sign yet of the innovative postures and emotion-speaking features

---

[18] Sandford, p. 464. Representations of God were top of the reformers' prohibition list; see Michael O'Connell, 'The Idolatrous Eye: Iconoclasm, Anti-Theatricalism and the Image of the Elizabethan Theater', *English Literary History*, 52 (1985), 279–310 (p. 287).

[19] Platter, p. 209; Llewellyn, *Royal Body* (1990), p. 235. A description of the tomb is preserved in John Speed, *Historie of Britaine* (London: [n. pub.], 1623).

[20] Mercer, p. 220; Llewellyn, *Royal Body* (1990), p. 227.

[21] Whinney, p. 62.

[22] Sandford, p. 492. Vast architectural tombs of this type had begun to appear in the second half of the sixteenth century, for example the tomb of John Lewiston (d. 1584) at Sherborne Abbey. By the end of the sixteenth century they were particularly associated with the Southwark school (Mercer, pp. 223–4). The use of coloured marbles dates from the last quarter of the sixteenth century; ibid., p. 231.

of tomb sculpture later in the reign.²³ The impact of this marble image on contemporaries was augmented by colouring executed by Nicholas Hilliard and gilding by John de Critz. This transient decor has long since disappeared, however, together with the crown on the monument, and other accessories.²⁴

The purpose behind the construction of a tomb for Elizabeth was, as Cecil put it, to provide a 'material focus for' public loyalty to Elizabeth.²⁵ Although the monument would cost the Crown and the City a considerable sum, Cecil felt that it was a good investment as he indicated in a letter to Sir Thomas Lake: 'For [. . .] it does his Majesty honour that the people see some little thing in doing [sic] for [Elizabeth]'. Presumably, the same impulse lay behind the refurbishment and display of Elizabeth's funeral effigy. As patron of the effigy projects, James associated himself with Elizabeth and endeavoured to appropriate loyalty to her memory for himself.²⁶ The Westminster Abbey funerary images of Elizabeth extended James's policy of demonstrating his familial duty to his predecessor and thus underscored the legitimacy of his lineal descent. In a sense, Elizabeth was commemorated as James's political mother. This was a state-led propaganda exercise, a deliberate mobilization of bias in favour of the new Scottish King. Cecil was motivated by a desire to bask in the reflected glory due to Elizabeth's chief minister.²⁷

James's theatre of death with its funeral and tomb effigies, each dressed in royal robes and bearing symbols of sovereignty, bears witness to his recognition of the propaganda potential of the Gloriana image of Elizabeth as imperial ruler. Similarly, William Camden's *The Historie of the Most Renowned Princess Elizabeth* was written at James's behest between 1608 and 1617 'for the propagation of the Queenes honour'.²⁸ Ironically, however, James's patronage would lead to the propagation of a new image of Elizabeth. Camden presented Elizabeth as a model of constitutional propriety, financial probity and Protestant energy. Implicit in the work was criticism of Jacobean extravagance, political corruption and policies of peace. Camden's work demonstrates the vulnerability of James's attempt to exploit the images of Elizabeth beyond her funeral. His image of Elizabeth, together with a revival of Spenser's Gloriana, was to be developed as a rhetorical weapon with which to attack James.²⁹

James did not even have a monopoly on the appropriation of the funeral images of Elizabeth. The erection of Elizabeth's tomb in Westminster was part of a reciprocal process of image-fashioning in which subjects as well as ruler

---

23 There are also no secondary statues on this tomb or that of Mary Stuart, perhaps a residual result of the iconophobia that prevented the completion of Henry VIII's tomb.
24 Parry (1981), p. 254; Johnson (1974), p. 441; Strong (1963), pp. 153–4.
25 Mullaney, p. 13; Llewellyn, *Royal Body* (1990), pp. 225–6.
26 Nichols (1828), I, 505; Woolf, p. 176.
27 King (1990), pp. 34–5, 69–71.
28 Camden (1630). Cecil had a hand in this project as well as the tombs; see King (1990), p. 35. Camden's *Historie* was published in Latin in 1615, and in English in 1625.
29 Sharpe (1979), pp. 89–95.

could indulge. Pictures of Elizabeth's tomb were set up in many churches and thirty-two parish churches in London erected adulatory memorials:

> Chaste Patroness of true Religion,
> In Court a Saint, in Field an Amazon
> Glorious in life, deplored in death,
> Such was unparallel'd ELIZABETH.[30]

The iconographic revival was part of a wider reclamation and manipulation of Elizabeth's political image, in which, often, adulation of Elizabeth equated with criticism of James.[31] The Protestant pro-war faction at court held up Elizabeth as the ideal monarch who had practised austerity, put religion first and followed an active Protestant foreign policy, all of which contrasted with the extravagance and perceived pro-Spanish policies of James.[32] There was a strong affinity between this early seventeenth-century image of Elizabeth and the Elizabeth of the late 1580s, a Queen at the height of her popularity in the reflected glory of the Armada victory. She was once again Gloriana, the empress of imperial reform. The disparity between this image and the historical Elizabeth, particularly of the last years of her reign, was not important. Elizabeth-Gloriana was re-fashioned as a foil to the Stuart King. The political integrity of the Virgin Queen was the polar opposite of the corrupt King whose behaviour and policies were equally flawed.[33] As Goodman was to write looking back on the early part of the reign:

> After a few years, when we had experience of the Scottish government, then – in disparagement of the Scots and in the detestation of them – the queen did seem to revive. Then was her memory much magnified – such commemoration of her, the picture of her tomb painted in many churches; and, in effect, more solemnity and joy in memory of her coronation than was for the coming in of King James.[34]

Mary Stuart's Tomb Effigy

Elizabeth's was not the only tomb that James erected in Westminster Abbey. There was also to be a tomb for Mary Queen of Scots. The Salisbury papers include an item, dated to 1603, suggesting that Robert Cecil proposed the

---

[30] Copies of Elizabeth's epitaph were found in Suffolk churches; see Robert Reyce, *The Breviary of Suffolke, 1618*, ed. by Lord Francis Hervey (London, 1912), pp. 203–4, cited by Llewellyn, *Royal Body* (1990), p. 129. See also Stow (1633), p. 823; Smuts, p. 29.

[31] See chapter 7.

[32] Haigh (1988), pp. 167–9; Smuts, p. 29.

[33] King (1990), p. 67.

[34] Dr Godfrey Goodman, *The Court of King James The First*, ed. by John S. Brewer, 2 vols (London: Richard Bentley, 1839), I, 97–8. See also Thomas Fuller, *The Church History of Britain: from the Birth of Jesus Christ untill the year 1648*, ed. by J. S. Brewer (Oxford: Oxford University Press, 1845), X, 4.

project to the King early in the reign. It reads, 'The pattern for the tomb of the Queen of Scots I have already finished, the which you and I will show to the King. The charge thereof is estimated £2,000.'[35] Once again, Cecil acted as the King's agent with regard to the tomb, briefing Cornelius Cure, the Crown's Master Mason, and ordering designs to be made.

The tomb design was a free-standing tester with two groups of four columns connected by a large coffered arch which supported the superstructure. The recumbent effigy of the dead Queen was set high up and depicted her in state robes (figure 20).[36]

Some have linked the project to James's plans for the Union of England and Scotland, as expounded in his 'A Speech to both Houses of Parliament, Delivered in the Great Chamber at White-Hall', 31 March 1607.[37] Privately, James may have seen the project as a means of absolving any residual guilt he felt for the role he played in his mother's death.[38] Her execution may have played on his mind. In 1607, during an audience with Sir John Harington, James mentioned his mother's execution in the midst of a discourse on witchcraft. To the embarrassment of the former, James said that her death had been foretold by soothsayers in Scotland who had seen a bloody head dancing before them in the air.[39] Whatever the extent of any personal reasons James might have had, they were overlain with political expediency.

Motivations for James building a tomb for his natural mother centred around the enhancement of his own image. As we have seen, prior to his accession James had felt it necessary to defend Mary's reputation in order to strengthen his claim to the English throne.[40] Once he was King, however, the urgency of James's need to defend Mary diminished. There is no evidence, for example, that Dekker suffered royal disapproval for his *The Whore of Babylon* (1606) with its allusions to Mary Queen of Scots. Similarly, while in 1596 James had stormed against certain passages in Spenser's *Faerie Queene* that slandered his mother, demanding that Elizabeth have the author tried and punished, the

---

[35] Salisbury XV, 347. Often the date given for initiation of the project is 1607 but Llewellyn argues that it must have been planned well before then; see Llewellyn, *Royal Body* (1990), p. 228. Woolf (p. 176) argues that the project was initiated in 1605.

[36] HMC Hatfield Papers, XV (London, 1930), p. 347 cited by Llewellyn, *Royal Body* (1990), p. 228. See also Sandford, p. 506; Roy Strong, *Tudor and Jacobean Portraits*, 2 vols (London: HMSO, 1969), I, 222; II, pl. 438.

[37] See Glynne Wickham, 'Romance and Emblem: A Study in the Dramatic Structure of *The Winter's Tale*', in *The Elizabethan Theatre III*, ed. by D. Galloway (London: Macmillan, 1973), pp. 82–99 (pp. 93–6); Michael Neill, 'Monuments and ruins as symbols in *The Duchess of Malfi*', *Themes in Drama*, 4 (1981), p. 77. For the speech to Parliament, see McIlwain, pp. 290–305; and, on the Union, see Lockyer, pp. 158–68; and Lee (1990), pp. 105, 113–22.

[38] Goldberg, pp. 14, 84.

[39] Willson, p. 288.

[40] See chapter 4.

poem was republished in 1604 without a hint of royal annoyance.[41] Yet, while he might no longer wish to castigate others, James evidently still felt he could profit from propaganda which encouraged a positive image of his mother and the veneration of her memory, promoted in part through the Westminster tomb project.[42]

The involvement of Robert Cecil, whose father had not opposed the execution of the Scottish Queen, is indicative of the project's political dimension. The Earl of Northampton, who had been of assistance to Mary Queen of Scots during her imprisonment, characterized Cecil's behaviour as political expediency.[43] Lennox may also have encouraged James's strategy of resurrecting the memory of his mother. In a letter to Robert Carr, James praised Lennox for helping him 'to rake up from the bottomless pit the tragedy of my poor mother'.[44]

Mary's tomb was to be the first in a series of tombs in the Henry VII Chapel that would effectively appropriate it as a royal necropolis for the Stuart dynasty.[45] While work was in progress on Elizabeth's tomb, James lost two daughters and Colt was further commissioned to provide monuments to commemorate them.[46] James would himself be laid to rest in the vault beneath the monument of Elizabeth of York and Henry VII, founder of the chapel. The Chapel would also house the remains of Arabella Stuart, Queen Anne of Denmark and Elizabeth of Bohemia. James also tellingly erected a monument to his grandmother, Margaret Lennox, niece to Henry VIII's eldest sister. Her tomb underlined the lineal connection between Elizabeth and James.[47] Among the figures of her children that knelt around the tomb is Henry Darnley with a crown upon his head.[48]

The idea of public sculpture to celebrate the monarchy was new in early seventeenth-century England.[49] James's programme of tomb-building, with its display of royal effigies, may have been influenced by the Medici tombs constructed in Florence. He had blood links with Tuscany and Duke Ferdinand through Ferdinand's wife and the House of Lorraine. Dallington's travel book,

---

41 CSPSc, I (1509–1603), 723–4, 747; Goldberg, p. xii. *The Faerie Queene* was republished in 1611, 1612, 1613 and 1617.
42 On Mary's poor reputation, with regard to the Darnley murder, see MacCaffrey, pp. 103–4, 110; and the Ridolfi plot, ibid., pp. 119–25. James had written an account of Mary's 1587 funeral to Henry Howard, Earl of Northampton, who like his elder brother, the Duke of Norfolk, had had mysterious dealings with Mary Queen of Scots; see Willson, pp. 156, 287.
43 PRO SP14/71/16; CSPD, IX (1611–18), 151. On the rivalry between Cecil and Northampton, see Sharpe (1979), p. 119.
44 Akrigg (1984), pp. 342–5.
45 Llewellyn, *Royal Body* (1990), pp. 231–2.
46 Joan D. Tanner, 'Tombs of the Royal Babies in Westminster Abbey', *Journal of the British Archaeological Association*, 16 (1953), 25–41.
47 Elizabeth paid for Margaret Lennox's obsequies in 1578; Camden (1630), p. 90.
48 Stanley (1869), p. 178.
49 Strong (1986), p. 197.

A Survey of the Great Dukes State of Tuscany, inn the yeare of Our Lord 1596, had drawn attention to the Medici world and the statues of the Medici that adorned the *piazze* of Florence. In addition, two of James's Privy Council, Shrewsbury and Lord Burghley, had both been to Florence.[50]

The Mary Stuart monument is of the same style as Elizabeth's but there are discernible differences in size, with Mary's the larger of the two. Similarly, the cost of Mary's tomb was the greater, probably in excess of the £2,000 estimated by Cecil in 1603.[51] Only £765 was spent on Elizabeth's.[52] James venerated both political and natural mothers but judiciously gave slight ascendance to the latter.[53] An early indication of the relative status of the two Queens under James is indicated in Scaramelli's report that after Elizabeth's funeral, portraits of the dead Queen were taken down and hidden, replaced in many cases by images of Mary Queen of Scots.[54] Whether this constituted spontaneous gestures on the part of subjects anxious to please their new King or was a government-driven initiative is, however, unclear. Perhaps it was merely a fabrication on the part of the gossipmongering Venetian ambassador.

Mary Stuart's tomb came to be revered by devout Scots as the shrine of a canonised saint and was associated with a series of miracles.[55] This development illustrates just how narrow the line was between the posthumous cults of Elizabeth and Mary and the cults of the saints in the Catholic church. While the former might have political motivations, they inevitably carried with them religious connotations. The tomb and funeral effigies of Elizabeth and Mary that went on show in London in 1606–7 re-legitimized the secular veneration of images and were dangerously close to sending signals of royal approval for Catholic rites.[56]

---

[50] Robert Dallington, *A Survey of the Great Dukes State of Tuscany, 1596* (London: Edward Blount, 1605), p. 9; Strong (1986), pp. 30–1. Another source may have been the tomb of William the Silent at Delft.

[51] The sculptor, Cornelius Cure, received £825 10s. for Mary's tomb while James Mauncey, of the Southwark School, was paid £265 for the painting and gilding; Mercer, p. 231.

[52] Tanner (1953), p. 40.

[53] The balance may have been redressed, however, by the fact that Elizabeth's tomb was located in the north aisle and Mary's in the south. In medieval church topography, north signified good and south bad; see Harris (1992), p. 38.

[54] See CSPV, X (1603–7), p. 10. Similarly portraits of Louis XIV were removed following his death in a quite systematic process of 'delouisification'; see Burke (1992), p. 122.

[55] Stanley (1869), pp. 154–5 citing Demster, ed., *Hist. Eccl. Ant. Scot.* (Bannatyne Club, 1829). On Mary's transformation into a Catholic martyr in France, see CSPF, XXI (1586–8) part I, 316, 678; Lynch (1988), pp. 1–2; Greengrass, pp. 187–8.

[56] It seems to me that these issues are explored in the stage-play *The Second Maiden's Tragedy* (1611–12, Blackfriars).

A Second Funeral for Mary Queen of Scots

Soon after his coronation on 26 July 1603 James felt it politic to stage a memorial service at the site of Mary's interment in Peterborough Cathedral. On 14 August 1603 Sir William Dethick, Garter, travelled to Peterborough with a rich embroidered velvet pall bearing the arms of Mary Queen of Scots. It 'was by him solemnly carried and laid upon and over the corpse of the said late Queene, assisted by many knights, and gentlemenne, and much people at the time of the Divine service'.[57] A sermon was delivered by the Bishop of Peterborough in the morning. Then the company received a magnificent dinner and in the afternoon the Dean preached a second sermon 'relative to the late Queen'.

The service was not, however, to satisfy James's desire to honour his mother's memory. Nor was the construction of the Westminster Abbey tomb, but it was the completion of the monument that suggested to James the idea of moving Mary's body to London. On 11 October 1612 the corpse of Mary Queen of Scots was transferred from Peterborough Cathedral to Westminster Abbey.[58]

Second burials were a rare but not an unknown occurrence in the period. Margaret, Duchess of Norfolk had been interred in Norwich on 27 January 1563 but was afterwards moved to Framlingham.[59] An earlier but royal example involves Edward IV who had the corpse of his father, Richard, Duke of York (d. 1460), transferred to Fotheringay, presumably with the intention of establishing a focus for the York dynasty.[60]

James's letter to the Dean of Peterborough ordering the transfer of the body of his mother to London stresses the motive of filial duty:

> For that wee think it app'aynes to the Justice wee owe to our deerest mother that like honour should be done to hair bodye and like Monument be extant to her as to others (...) first as our progenitors have been used to be done, and our selves hae alreadie pfourmed to our deare Sister the late Queene Elizabeth wee have commanded a Memoriall of hir to be made in our Churche of Westminster, the place where the Kings and Queenes of this realme are usually interred. And for that we think it inconvenyont that the Monument and hir bodie should be in severall places, wee have ordered that hir saide bodye remayning nowe interred in that our Cathedrall Churche of Peterborough shalbe removed to Westminster to her said monument'.[61]

As we have seen, with Elizabeth's death and the succession secured James still

---

[57] BL, Harley MS 293 fol. 211.
[58] Stanley incorrectly has 1606 for the year of the transfer of the body; see (1869), p. xl.
[59] Bod., Ashmole MS 836 fol. 185. See also chapter 6 for Arundel's wish to move his father and grandmother's bodies to Arundel Castle.
[60] Tate, I, 203. Richard III had the body of Henry VI (d. 1471) moved from Chertsey Abbey, where it had become the focus of pilgrimage, to the St George Chapel, Windsor, where presumably public access would have been very limited. See White (1978), p. 27; and W. J. White, 'The Death and Burial of Henry VI', *The Ricardian*, vol. 6 no. 78 (1982), 70–80 and vol. 6 no. 79 (1982), 106–17.
[61] Letter to the Dean and Chapter of Peterborough Cathedral, dated 28/9/1612; see Bod.,

felt the need to reinscribe his relationship with his real mother, lineage being a key mode for the authorization of absolute rule. The tomb had begun that process; a second funeral to inter her remains within that tomb would complete it.

Mary's hearse was to remain the property of Peterborough Cathedral.[62] James's letter specifies that the pall, which was still on the hearse following the 1603 funeral ceremony, should serve as the Church's fee for its part in the second funeral.[63] The achievements would remain hanging in the cathedral church until 1643 and when Dugdale visited it in 1641 he made a drawing of them.[64]

Richard Neile, Bishop of Coventry and Lichfield and Dean of Westminster, as well as Clerk of the Closet to James, was made responsible for the transfer of the body. No detailed account of the procession which escorted the body has survived but it appears to have been effected with some magnificence. The Archbishop of Canterbury, the Lord Privy Seal, the Earl of Worcester and other noblemen together with the Bishop of Rochester and the Dean of Westminster met the corpse at Clerkenwell at 6.00 pm and conveyed it to the Chapel Royal in Westminster Abbey.[65]

The evening timing of the procession could be interpreted as a deliberate attempt to promote the occasion as a private and personal gesture on the part of the King towards his late mother. The account cited below suggests that the original intention had been to avoid crowds in the streets but, on the other hand, many people could be expected to be freed from their work-time activities at this hour and on the look out for spectacle. A further possibility is that the College of Arms made no provision for second funerals (there is no mention of heralds in any accounts of the ritual) but presumably special arrangements could have been made if required. Certainly, it was not a surreptitious nocturnal procession like that which had conveyed Mary's body to Fotheringay twenty-five years previously. Northampton confirms that as the body neared London various Lords prepared to meet it and, once the funeral procession arrived in town, many were waiting to see it.

> Though the King's mother's body was brought late to town to avoid a concourse, yet many in the streets and windows wattched her entry with honour into the place whence she had been expelled with tyranny. She is buried with honour, as dead rose-leaves are preserved, whence the liquor that makes the kingdom sweet has been distilled.[66]

Ashmole MS 836 fol. 277; Akrigg (1984), pp. 326–7; Llewellyn, *Royal Body* (1990), pp. 227–8.
[62] Bod., Ashmole MS 857 fols 320–1.
[63] Akrigg (1984), p. 327.
[64] A facsimile of the helm, crest and coat of arms is reproduced in Laing, p. 53.
[65] Stow, p. 913; Sandford, p. 535.
[66] PRO SP14/71/8, 16. CSPD, XI (1611–18), 152; Willson, p. 56; J. W. Williamson, *The Myth of the Conqueror: Prince Henry Stuart: A Study of Seventeenth Century Personation* (New York: A.M.S. Press, 1978), p. 9.

James was ritually and publicly reaffirming the role of filial devotion that he had adopted towards his mother after her execution. At the same time, by having Mary reinterred in the Henry VII Chapel of Westminster Abbey, the royal sepulchre established by the Tudor dynasty, he was underlining the legitimacy of the Stuart succession.[67] James clearly felt that there was a strong relationship between ceremonial and power.

At the time of Mary's second funeral in 1612 dynastic themes had a particular contemporary resonance. It was just a few months before the already scheduled marriage of Princess Elizabeth and the Elector Palatine. Lineage had an important role to play at this time of dynastic union. The honour James accorded to his progenitor would reflect upon his progeny. At this juncture plans were also still being made for the marriage of Prince Henry Stuart to a Catholic princess. A rumour that James had been pressed not to move his mother because it would bring ill luck is reported by Aubrey but smacks of a retrospective construction placed on events. Prince Henry Stuart, heir to the throne, was dead following a sudden infection less than a month later.[68]

James's policy of rehabilitating his mother's memory persisted beyond the completion of the tomb project and was to form part of his intention in encouraging William Camden to resume his *Annales* of Elizabeth's reign. He wanted Camden to defend Mary against the accusations of the French historian, de Thou. Camden praised Mary as 'A Lady fix'd and constant in her Religion, of singular piety towards God, invincible magnanimity of mind, wisdom above her sex, and admirable beauty, and to be rank'd in the list of those Princesses, who have exchang'd their grandeur for misery and calamity'. Camden was even to praise the Guise for their ceremonial commemoration of Mary's death: 'Her funerall [was] most pompously solemnised at Paris by procurement of the Guises who to their great commendations performed all good offices of kindnesse to their kinswoman both alive and dead.'[69]

Night-Burials and the Re-Legitimization of Torchlight

We have seen how the use of torches in funeral processions was outlawed at the time of the accession of Elizabeth I, although it was used for the exceptional nocturnal procession of Mary Queen of Scots's 1587 Peterborough funeral. On the very different occasion of Mary's 1612 funeral procession in London, the night-time staging meant that once again the procession had to be conducted 'with plentie of torch-lights'. This funeral was, however, being deliberately promoted as a royal propaganda exercise. The liminality with which the

---

[67] Another queen, Catherine of Aragon, once an embarrassment, was rehabilitated in Shakespeare's *Henry VIII* (1613) just a year after Mary was transferred to London.
[68] Nichols (1740), p. 86.
[69] Willson, pp. 298, 358; Camden (1630), p. 110; Sharpe (1979), pp. 89–95.

Elizabethan government had surrounded funeral ritual practice permitted James to manipulate tradition and re-legitimize the use of torch-light in funeral processions.[70] In some eyes, however, such funeral accoutrements would still appear popish. Wilson, arch-satirist of James's court, was to characterize Mary's funeral as a veiled Catholic rite:

> She had a translucent passage in the night, through the City of London, by multitudes of Torches: The Tapers placed by the Tomb and the Altar, in the Cathedrall, smoking with them like an Offertoire, with all the Ceremonies, and Voices, their Quires and Copes could express, attended by many Prelates and Nobles who payd this last Tribute to her memory.[71]

Over the next few years nocturnal funerals became increasingly common. In a letter to Alice Carleton of 16 February 1615, John Chamberlain makes it clear that nocturnal funerals were a phenomenon that took off in the mid-1610s. 'Lady Cheeke', he reported, 'died on Saterday, and was buried by night with above thirty coaches and much torch-light attending her, which is of late come much into fashion.'[72] A later letter of April 1623 demonstrates that it was not only the procession that took place at night. Sir Thomas Lowe (Lord Mayor of London 1604–5) 'was buried privatly on Tewsday night though there were a great deale of companie'. Similarly, Sir Christopher Hatton was buried by night at Westminster Abbey on 11 September 1619.[73] It is not possible to say for certain that Mary Stuart's second funeral set the fashion for nocturnal burials, but it did give them royal sanction.

Contemporaries cite two possible sources for nocturnal funerals. Chamberlain suspects Catholics were behind the new fashion and comments, 'I rather thincke yt was brought up by papists which serve theyre turne by yt many wayes.'[74] He was not alone in this suspicion. A list of objections to the practice of night burial found in the Harleian collection makes the same connection. Funeral torches, it is claimed, will lead some to 'draw neare unto poppery and heathenisme'.[75]

The association of torches with Catholicism was, however, diluted by an alternative, retrospectively identified 'source' increasingly pushed into public awareness by the writings of antiquarians and heralds. Sir William Segar (Garter 1607-33) used Roman precedent as part of the justification of elaborate heraldic funerals, while, in a treatise on the antiquity of ceremonies, Ley commented on the Roman style of funerals in Britain, referring to them, in rather suspect Latin,

---

[70] See chapters 2 and 4.
[71] Arthur Wilson, *The History of Great Britain Being the Life and Reign of King James the First, Relating to what passed from his first Accession to the Crown, till his Death* (London: Richard Lownds, 1653), p. 56.
[72] McClure, I, 578.
[73] McClure, II, 262, 492.
[74] McClure, II, 578.
[75] BL, Harley MS 1301 fol. 12.

as *funalibus* because they were solemn and by torchlight.[76] The growing fashion for night burials may have been facilitated by the provision of this non-Catholic 'source'.

Heralds may have unwittingly helped to promote the fashion for night burials through the descriptions of classical burial practices in their writings. Books like Weever's *Ancient Funerall Monuments* (1631) and Sir Thomas Browne's *Urne Buriall* (1658) would stimulate continued interest in ancient mortuary ritual.[77] Ironically, night burials permitted executors to avoid heraldic regulations and thus heraldic fees. Here is perhaps the chief reason behind the popularity of nocturnal funerals with executors: economy. By the time Weever comes to write on the subject in 1631, he identified cost-saving as the reason behind the popularity of both Roman and contemporary nocturnal funerals.[78] In his letter to Alice Carleton, Chamberlain confirms that nocturnal funerals were thought to aim at the avoidance of 'trouble and charge'.[79] The evidence of litigious activity supports his conclusions. Norroy herald requested warrants to proceed against several executors in Staffordshire who had staged nocturnal funerals and thereby avoided the payment of fees due to the College of Arms. In April 1620, for example, Sir Alexander Barlow 'was buried att Manchester church by torchlight, whose executors cannot yet resolve whether to have a funerall or noe by reson sume of them [are] as yet in the South parts neere London and not come downe'. Another case involved the burial of Sir Edmund Trafford 'by torchlight' with a 'funerall sermon by candlelight'.[80] Nocturnal funerals also enabled executors to save on the cost of commissioning a sermon and the traditional distribution of alms to the poor.

However, not all nocturnal funerals were staged with the aim of cost-cutting. In 1623 the Countess of Warwick 'was convoyed out of Holborn to be buried in Essex by more than two hundred horse all with torches and above threescore coaches, among whom were both the Duchesses [Richmond and Buckingham]'.[81] This was hardly a recipe for economy but may suggest another

---

[76] Segar (1602), p. 251; Tate, I, 210. Interesting in this context is the use of the term 'Antick Shield' in the manuscript account of the funeral of William, Earl of Glencairn, Lord High Chancellor of Scotland: Bod., Ashmole MS 857 fol. 198. See also Wagner (1978), p. 43 on the tendency for heraldic painters to dress figures in Roman armour in their pedigree rolls.

[77] Browne, pp. 261–315.

[78] Weever, pp. 12–17.

[79] BL, Harley MS 1301 fol. 12. Stone suggests that the desire to economize was the primary factor in the switch to nocturnal burials; see Stone (1965), p. 194. Gittings offers a far more sophisticated argument to which the discussion that follows is indebted. See Gittings, pp. 175, 195–7.

[80] For details of other circumventions of heraldic control by painter stainers, sculptors, etc., see Bod., Ashmole MS 836 fol. 551. Ironically, Walsingham (d. 1590) incurred such great expense in staging Sidney's funeral that he had to be buried at night to save money (Strickland, p. 30).

[81] McClure, II, 531.

contributory factor influencing the fashion for nocturnal funerals: the growing use of coaches. Processions involving such large numbers of coaches would have been much easier to stage during the night when the streets were empty of normal daytime traffic.

Nocturnal rites seem, in part, to have become a place to be seen. Chamberlain, describing the interment of Sir Thomas Lowe in April 1623, writes, 'He was buried privately on Tewsday night though there were a great deale of companie, and Sir John Bennet with much ado got leave to be there.'[82] Executors were perhaps exploiting the theatricality bestowed upon nocturnal funerals by their torchlit settings. Onlookers may also have been drawn by the spectacle and powerful sensual appeal afforded by the multiplicity of candlelight. Here was a ritual performance that could activate the process of sublimation.

Another reason for avoiding heraldic funerals related to an increasing discomfort with the prospect of embalming, a necessary process because the elaborate funerals took weeks to organize. Women in particular were becoming more and more unhappy with embalming. The will of Mary, Countess of Northumberland, provides an early example of the emotional origins of this view. She expressed the desire 'not in any wise to let me be opened after I am dead. I have not loved to be very bold before women, much more would I be loath to come into the hands of any living man, be he physician or surgeon.' The modesty of this testamentary directive, as Gittings points out, 'has strong undertones of sexuality about it' and is suggestive of the eroticism that is such a fascinating feature of the changing attitudes towards death emerging at the beginning of the seventeenth century. In the directions for her funeral the Duchess of Richmond willed: 'Let them wind me up again in those sheets [...] wherein my Lord and I first slept that night when we were married.'[83]

Whatever the reasons behind their growing popularity, night burials were subversive in two ways. On the one hand they broke the College of Arms's monopoly over the staging of aristocratic funerals, undermining their function as a form of social control, and on the other, they sent out confusing signals regarding the official position on religious ritual. Both effects were compounded by the accompanying rise in the incidence of other alternative burial forms, fuelled in part by James's tolerance of matters religious, including ritual.

---

[82] McClure, II, 492.
[83] Gittings, pp. 190–4. Weever complains about those who garnish their tombs 'with pictures of naked men and women', p. 249. On eroticism and death, see Ariès, pp. 369–81, 392–5, 404.

The Non-Homogeneity of Jacobean Funeral Ritual

As long as they took the Oath of Allegiance (1606), Catholics were accorded relative freedom in their religious practices.[84] In death, Henry Howard, Lord Privy Seal and first Earl of Northampton (d. 1614), pushed that freedom to its logical end: his executors were to give him a full Catholic-style funeral.

Northampton's body was transported to Dover Castle where it was to be buried in the chapel. A bell was tolled for one or two days prior to the funeral in loud contravention of the early Elizabethan pronouncements against bell-ringing. What followed was, however, even more stridently Catholic. Chamberlain reported that 'Northampton had extreme unction, and his body lay covered while yt was here with a velvet pall that had a white crosse clean thorough yt, with two burning tapers upon his coffin day and night, where six of his gentlemen watcht continually by turnes with torches borne by other servants and in that order he was caried all alonge thorough Kent in all the ynnes where he reste.' The tone of Chamberlain's account, which mentions 'much descanting' and 'rumour', illustrates that Northampton's funeral took on scandalous proportions. The mention of 'extreme unction' indicates how the other aspects of the ritual, including the use of hearse lights, would have been seen by many as distinctly popish.[85]

Henry Howard was a notorious Catholic, but one who had manoeuvred himself into favour with James at the accession, swiftly rising to the position of Lord Privy Seal in 1608.[86] Howard's political power, and perhaps his position as one of the commissioners for the post of Earl Marshall, probably provided the executors with sufficient confidence to perform Howard's Catholic-style funeral.[87] The fact that the funeral was allowed to take place demonstrates that James, however assiduous he might have been in manipulating the funerals and posthumous images of Elizabeth and Mary, was careless about controlling the funeral rituals of his subjects.[88] His indifference may in part have stemmed from his Scottish origins. While Lyon, King of Arms held jurisdiction over Scotland on behalf of the English College of Arms, many Scots seem to have found it easy to circumvent heraldic regulations and they appear to have played an active role

---

[84] See my chapter 6.
[85] McClure, I, 540–2.
[86] On Northampton, see Linda Levy Peck, *Northampton: Patronage and Policy at the Court of James I* (London: Allen & Unwin, 1982) and Linda Levy Peck, 'The Mentality of a Jacobean Grandee', in *The Mental World of the Jacobean Court*, ed. by Linda Levy Peck (Cambridge: Cambridge University Press, 1991), pp. 148–68. On Northampton's unpopularity, see Dutton, p. 199.
[87] On Howard's patronage of the heralds, see Guillim, p. 275.
[88] In 1611 James did, however, make complaints about the numbers of people attending mass in the chapels of Catholic ambassadors; Willson, pp. 197–200, 269.

in popularizing nocturnal funerals.[89] On 20 April 1616, for example, Chamberlain witnessed the funeral of Sir John Grimes or Graemes, a Scottish courtier and favourite of George Villiers, who 'was solemnly buried in the night at Westminster with better than 200 torches, the Duke of Lennox, the Lord Fenton, the Lord of Roxborough and all the grand Scottish men accompanieng him'.[90]

There is no evidence of James intervening to ensure an appropriate level of ceremony at the funerals of any of his subjects. This contrasts markedly with the policy of his predecessor as described in chapter 2. By 1618, however, James seems to have realised, at least in part, the important role played by funerals in the maintenance of the social framework.[91] In that year a commission of enquiry, headed by the Earl Marshal, was set up and a number of measures recommended by the heralds were adopted.[92] Yet, while James clamped down on the abuses of painter-stainers and other artisans who were encroaching on the College of Arms' monopoly on the provision of funeral accoutrements, he did not legislate against nocturnal funerals, thereby setting no limits on consumer choice with regard to funeral rites.[93] He was interested mainly in the need to maintain social records of the aristocracy but was prepared to extend support to the College of Arms on the issue of fees.[94] The wording of the 1618 decree makes this clear:

> From henceforth all Noblemen, Baronets, Knights, Esquires and Gentlemen of eminent Place, Office, Birth, Quantitie, that shall be either silently buried in the Night time by torch-light, or otherwise, by Day or Nighttime without the attendance of an Officer of Armes, shall nevertheless immediately after the death and buriall of every such Defunct, returne a true Certificate of the Matches, Issues and times of Decease with their Armes which of right they bore for which they shall pay the said Officer of Armes such Fees as we have and doe hereby set downe.[95]

While these regulations resulted in the prosecution of some illegal painters, they

---

[89] Arthur C. Foxe-Davis, *A Complete Guide to Heraldry* (New York: Bonanza Books, 1978), p. 29.
[90] McClure, I, 623. Inevitably, given their strong Calvinist tradition, many Scots regarded even the English funeral service as popish, as is illustrated by the refusal of one of their ecclesiastics to receive communion during the funeral service of an English guardsman in Edinburgh in 1617; see McClure, II, 66. On the same occasion the Dean of St Paul's was forced to retract after asking the congregation to recommend the soul of the defunct to God and Laud was censured for wearing a surplice at the interment.
[91] Gittings, p. 199; Wagner (1967), pp. 110, 238–9.
[92] It is perhaps significant that the position of Earl Marshal was held in commission between 1602, after the execution of the Earl of Essex, Earl Marshall 1597–1601, and 1621 when Arundel was appointed. See Dallaway, Appendix 52.
[93] On the concomitant decline of the College of Arms, see Fritz, pp. 75–7; Wagner (1967), p. 237; and Litten, pp. 189–94.
[94] Dallaway's statistics for the attendance of heralds at funerals between 1597 and 1605 reveal a peak in 1600; see Dallaway, p. 259.
[95] 'Orders issued by the College of Arms regarding the abuses at funerals', Bod., Ashmole MS 845 fol. 124.

had little effect on the general trend towards eclecticism in funeral practice. By 1631 John Weever comments that the fashion for nocturnal funerals had spread markedly:

> Funerals in any expensive way here with us, are now accounted but as a fruitlesse vanitie, insomuch that almost all the ceremoniall rites of obsequies heretofore used, are altogether laid aside; for we see daily that Noblemen and Gentlemen of eminent ranke, office and qualitie, are either silently buried in the night-time with a Torch, a two-penie linke and a lanterne, or parsimoniously interred in the daytime.[96]

Around 1635 Charles I announced a prohibition on all nocturnal funerals but it seems that the proclamation was largely ignored. Soon afterwards the Earl Marshal, Arundel, wrote to the Lord Mayor with reference to the death of Alderman Sir Richard Deane. It had come to Arundel's attention that Deane was to be buried nocturnally and he wrote vetoing the plan and ordering an appropriate funeral to be held.[97] Such moves were, however, by now too late. Ironically, in 1685 Charles II would be buried at night by torchlight.[98]

From the mid-1610s there was, then, no homogeneous funeral rite for the aristocracy. Nocturnal funerals sent out confusing signals of the validity of religious symbolism and individual choice which impinged upon the traditional heraldic funeral with its state demonstration of orthodoxy and order. In addition Catholic-style funerals were occasionally staged. At the other end of the spectrum, the bare ritual of Puritan interments only added to the confusion of forms. In 1607, William Bird was reported in Essex 'for buring the dead being a meare laye mann [. . .] he hath buried manye deed bodys in the parish of Coggeshall but hathe not redd the forme of buriall sett forthe in the book of Common Prayer neither was ther anye minister present'.[99] Although discussion of these scant ritual proceedings is beyond the scope of this book, they cannot be forgotten in any assessment of the place occupied by the funeral in the cultural milieu of the early seventeenth century. Puritan funerals constituted a real threat partly because they denied hierarchical order altogether but also, perhaps, because they stripped away the rich sensual symbolism of the heraldic funerals, denying the effects of sublimation. As Person commented in 1635, the 'pompous solemnities' of the Catholic funeral produced a 'kinde of pious compassion in the beholders, [and] so it begetteth a manner of content', but the 'silent and dumbe' obsequies of the Puritans 'doth not so take the spectators'.[100] Puritan anti-ritual did not promote homogeny in behaviour, nor did it order and contain; instead it was socially divisive and encouraged dissent.

---

96 Weever, pp. 17–18.
97 Waters, pp. 50–1; Gittings, p. 200; Puckle, p. 198.
98 CA, Briscoe MS I fols 1–6; Fritz, p. 67.
99 Act Books, Archdeacon of Colchester, D/ACA, no. 27, p. 124, cited by Stuart Barton Babbage, *Puritanism and Richard Bancroft* (London: SPCK, 1962), pp. 78–94, 155.
100 Person, p. 164.

The non-homogeneity of funeral ritual is indicative of the strains on social cohesion at this time of increasing religious divisions. The function of the funeral ritual, which was to heal the breach in the community caused by the death of one of its members, could not continue in a community which practised diverse and separate rites.[101]

---

[101] See Benjamin Carier, *A Missive to his Majesty of Great Britain King James*, ed. by N. Strange (Paris: [n. pub.], 1649) for the strong and divisive feelings aroused by differing funeral rites, cited by Gittings, p. 51. See also Collinson (1988), p. 143.

CHAPTER EIGHT

The Funeral of Prince Henry Stuart (1612)

The Prince of Wales, Henry Stuart died suddenly and unexpectedly at the age of eighteen on 11 November 1612. At the beginning of October he was showing signs of a fever but continued to lead a full public life until he was forced to take to his bed on 25 October. Less than two weeks later he was dead.[1]

Prince Henry was interred in the vault of his grandmother, Mary Queen of Scots, in the Henry VII Chapel. Thus James continued his policy of emphasizing the link between the Stuarts and the Tudor dynasty and legitimizing the succession.[2]

Henry was, however, never to receive a tomb, a fact which has led Graham Parry to charge James with neglecting the Prince's memory. The discussion in this chapter questions this view in two ways. First, analysis of the funeral reveals that the scale and magnificence of the affair broke all precedents and constituted a great tribute to the Prince's memory. The ephemerality of funeral display does not, as Huizinga thought, diminish its significance.[3] Certainly the evidence of cost is suggestive of the importance which James and his councillors accorded to the funeral ceremony. One year after the event, £16,000 was still owed for the expenses of the sumptuous obsequies.[4] Secondly, the personal and political motives behind the elaborate funeral that was staged for Prince Henry are probed, further contradicting any charges of neglect. Finally I argue that the post-obsequy display of the funeral effigy of Prince Henry precluded the need for a funeral monument.

---

[1] For a detailed account of the illness, see Strong (1986), p. 220.
[2] Akrigg (1962), p. 139; Parry (1981), p. 87; Sandford, p. 530.
[3] J. Huizinga, *The Waning of the Middle Ages: A Study of the Forms of Life, Thought and Art in France and the Netherlands in the Fourteenth and Fifteenth Centuries* (London: Edward Arnold, 1924), p. 45.
[4] Akrigg (1962), p. 139. This contrasts with the £13, 000 spent on the celebrations for the wedding of Henry's sister, the Princess Elizabeth, to Frederick, the Elector Palatine; Parry (1981), p. 255.

The Magnificence of the Prince's Funeral

The arrangements for the funeral were set in motion with alacrity. Three days after the Prince's death the Privy Council met at St James's palace to give orders for the funeral.[5] (One member of the Council who was not involved in the deliberations was Arundel. He was abroad at the time of Prince Henry's death and funeral.) On 23 November the whole court went into mourning, with the ambassadors following suit the next day.[6]

Meanwhile, the Prince's encoffined body lay in state at St James's Palace for a month. It lay first in the Bedchamber which was hung with mourning drapes, 'on a place above an ell in height'. Here the body was served with the 'same service and order of meals as when he was alive', just as Elizabeth's body had been. He was attended by seventy gentlemen of his household, ten at a time.[7] As far as I know, this is the first instance of a ritualized lying-in-state ceremony involving the continued service of the household being extended to the body of anyone other than a monarch.[8]

The Prince's encoffined body was also accorded the elaborate process of gradual transfer from chamber to chamber in preparation for the funeral procession. The coffin rested in the Privy Chamber for one night, then in the Presence Chamber for one day, then in the Great Chamber for fifteen minutes before being removed to the chapel and placed in a hearse to await the day of the funeral. All four rooms were hung with blacks. Prayers were said in whichever chamber held the remains every day, both morning and evening.[9]

The funeral procession, which took place on 7 December 1612, further marked Prince Henry's funeral out as a highly unusual event. The cortege, which comprised approximately two thousand participants, was comparable in size with that of Henry IV of France. (Elizabeth's procession had only had 1,600 mourners.) According to Cornwallis, it took four hours to marshal the participants in Henry Stuart's procession.[10] The funeral of Henry IV, Prince Henry's godfather, had taken place only two years previously and was likely to have been in the forefront of the minds of both organizers and observers. The Venetian ambassador made an explicit parallel between the deaths of the two Henries, lamenting that he could do nothing but follow Henry Stuart's bier with 'useless

---

[5] Cornwallis, p. 82. Cornwallis had been Treasurer in the Prince's household and took part in the funeral proceedings.
[6] Howarth, p. 35; CSPV, XII (1610–13), 450.
[7] Cornwallis states that forty gentlemen were in attendance, p. 83; Akrigg (1962), p. 136.
[8] See chapter 5 for a discussion of the origins of the royal lying-in-state ritual.
[9] Cornwallis, p. 85; *The Funerals of the High and Mighty Prince Henry* (London, 1613) in Nichols (1828), II, 493–512 (p. 493).
[10] Foscarini provides the estimate that there were 2,000 people involved in the procession, CSPV, XII (1610–13), 468; Nichols (1828), II, 499; Cornwallis, p. 85; Sandford, p. 497.

tears'.[11] It may be that the recent example of Henry IV's funeral influenced the decision to have an effigy of the dead Prince constructed for the obsequies.

The effigy was the most striking element of the procession. Hope has demonstrated that the funeral of Henry, Prince of Wales was the only pre-Restoration instance of a funeral effigy being made for anyone other than a king or queen. Chronicles of the time and the detailed records kept at the Herald's College describing the funerals of the children of Henry VIII reveal that there was no effigy for the Lady Elizabeth (d. 1495), nor for Edmond (d.1499), nor for Prince Arthur (d. 1502), nor for Prince Henry (d.1510). Hope does note one exception, the funeral of Mary, the Duchess of Suffolk, Henry VIII's sister, who was buried in Bury St Edmunds (d. 1533). The use of a funeral effigy on this occasion can be explained, however, by her status as Queen Consort of Louis XII of France.[12] Another exception, missed by Hope, was the funeral of Richard Plantagenet, father of Edward IV (d. 1460). One can only guess that Edward IV wished to enhance the status of his father as part of his bid for the throne.[13] Effigies were also made for bishops before the Reformation.[14] These occasions would, however, have been long forgotten by 1612. More recent is the funeral of Anne, Duchess of Somerset (d. 1587) for which William Dethick says 'there was a portaieture of the same duchesse made in robes of her estate, with a caronicall [coronet] to a duchess, and the same representation borne under a canopie'.[15] There is, however, as far as I am aware, no other evidence to corroborate Dethick's claims and it may be that he was embroidering the facts. Dethick, who in any case was writing his account of the funeral in 1599 long after it had taken place, is not always a reliable witness.[16]

The use of the effigy in the early seventeenth century was essentially, then, the mark of the funeral of a deceased monarch. It was highly exceptional that an effigy should have been made for Prince Henry. Nevertheless, made it was, 'in so short warning, as like him as could be', and on the Sunday before the funeral it was brought to St James's palace.[17] This is a clear case of the adjustment or adaptation of ritual forms to suit the present needs of a situation.

During the procession the effigy, dressed in the Prince's creation robes, was laid upon the coffin and carried on an open chariot.[18] The latter was constructed for the occasion by one John Bankes who received twenty pounds for 'a newe chariotte of Tymber worke and Ironwoorke with wheeles carriadges etc and for altering the same after it was made divers tymes accordinge to the harrallde

---

[11] CSPV, XII (1610–13), 448.
[12] Hope, pp. 548–55.
[13] BL, Egerton MS 2642 fol. 176.
[14] See chapter 5.
[15] Tate, I, 204. On the fluidity of the term 'représentation' in sixteenth-century French, see my discussion in chapter 4.
[16] See chapter 4.
[17] Cornwallis, p. 85.
[18] Nichols (1828), II, 494; Akrigg (1962), p. 137.

direttions'.[19] On arrival at Westminster Abbey the bier, which supported both body and effigy, was borne shoulder-high into the heart of the church and placed on a specially constructed catafalque (figure 21). The body and effigy lay in state during the two-hour funeral oration, delivered by the Archbishop of Canterbury, and for a further three days of services for the dead. Both remained in the catafalque 'to be seene of all' for nine more days until 19 December when the coffin was interred.[20]

The hearse itself was highly innovative. There is no evidence for attributing the design to Inigo Jones despite his role as the Prince's Surveyor of Works, in which capacity he walked in the funeral procession. Whichever architect was responsible applied classical ideas to the traditional hearse design.[21] The base of the structure was neo-classical in design, with six columns rising up to a canopy. The latter was traditionally shaped, rising to a point in the centre, and was heavily decorated with the arms, plumes and motto of the Prince of Wales.[22] Foscarini, the Venetian ambassador, described the form of the canopy as a 'pyramid' hinting at a growing eclecticism in the response to architecture and indicating the assimilation of Egyptian symbolism into Renaissance culture.[23] The hearse certainly attracted comment and Cornwallis makes much of it in his account.[24] It is worth noting, however, the odd juxtaposition of neo-classical hearse and medieval-Tudor funeral effigy. The designer may well have derived inspiration from the Colt tombs for Elizabeth and Mary in Westminster Abbey which similarly combined a neo-classical framework with medieval coloured effigies.[25] For some contemporaries, however, such a combination produced a jarring effect on the aesthetic sensibilities. In his *Elements of Architecture* (1624) Wotton refers to 'the *Fashion* of *colouring* even *Regall statues*, which I must take leave to call an *English Barbarisme*'.[26]

Replication of funeral ceremonies at the Universities and at Bristol further aggrandized Prince Henry's funeral to the level of a sovereign king. 'A solemne obsequie for him at Oxford with a sermon and a funerall oration after yt at St. Maries and the like in the afternoone at Christ Church both which places were hanged and furnished with blacks, and they have set out a booke of Latin elegies and funerall verses'. Cambridge similarly celebrated an obsequy for the

---

[19] PRO E351/3145 fol 50r; cited by Harvey and Mortimer, p. 60.
[20] CSPV, XII (1610–13), 469; Akrigg (1962), p. 139.
[21] John Peacock, 'Inigo Jones's Catafalque for James I', *Architectural History*, 25 (1982), 1–5 (p. 2). See figure 22.
[22] This is the first use of feathers on a hearse that I am aware of.
[23] CSPV, XII (1610–13), 468. The Romans themselves absorbed the Egyptian style into their funeral culture: the mausoleum of Augustus was built in a pyramid-shape as if he had been another pharaoh; see Burke (1992), p. 197.
[24] Cornwallis, p. 87.
[25] Harvey and Mortimer, p. 61.
[26] Wotton, p. 89. On the classicism of the Princes's entertainments, see Parry (1981), p. 75.

prince.²⁷ At Bristol 'the Mayor, with his Brethren and the Common Councell, and all the Companies going before them in their gowns, did so solemnize Prince Henry's Funeral, going from the Tolzey, every one in order, to Redcliffe Church to hear a Sermon, maintaining thereby their love to the Prince and their sorrow for his death; and the Magistrates put themselves in mourning attire'.²⁸ It is not clear why Bristol should have staged a funeral for the Prince. There were, as far as I am aware, no specific links between the Prince and that city. It is possible that such civic memorials were held elsewhere in the provinces but I found have no evidence in support of this supposition.

Motives behind the Magnificence of the Funeral: the Management of Public Grief and Political Loss

Henry Stuart's funeral was, then, a deliberately inflated affair. Members of his Privy Council dealt with the detailed planning of the event and it has been suggested that the decision to use an effigy may have been influenced by the fact that the basic arrangements were made by the Lord Chamberlain rather than the Earl Marshall.²⁹ It was James, however, who was ultimately behind all major decisions affecting the funeral of his son. What prompted him to give Henry such an elaborate funeral?

One motivation was the need to smooth over the potential disruption caused by the dissolution of Prince Henry's household. We have seen how extensive and sophisticated this establishment had become and its closure would create a large gap in the patronage system, leaving many people without the means to sustain themselves. At the time of his death Prince Henry's household incorporated 315 Gentlemen of the Chamber and 102 Gentlemen of the Household.³⁰

James did distribute 50,000 crowns amongst the members of the dead Prince's household but such financial help could be of little long-term assistance. Individual grants were made but actual payment was often delayed. Many looked to the establishment of a comparable household for Prince Charles, 'wherein each would be admitted to his old post', as the Venetian ambassador reported on 30 November.³¹ In the meantime the funeral facilitated deferment of the dissolution of the household, giving its members time to adjust to their new situation. As Foscarini commented, the household officially broke up when

---

27 McClure, I, 396; Cornwallis, pp. 90–2.
28 Samuel Seyer, *Memoirs historical and topographical of Bristol*, 2 vols (Bristol: [n. pub.], 1821–23), II, 264, cited by Nichols, II, 503 n. 1.
29 Harvey and Mortimer, p. 9. By the end of the seventeenth century, royal funeral, baptisms, christenings and weddings were all under the direction of the Lord Chamberlain's Office and had been largely removed from the control of the Earl Marshal's Office; Fritz, pp. 74, 78.
30 CSPV, XII (1610–13), 450.
31 CSPV, XII (1610–13), 453.

the staves were broken at the end of the funeral ceremony about a month after the Prince's death.[32] The funeral also provided an emotional outlet for those who had been identified with Prince Henry. Through the magnificence of the funeral James gave implicit sanction for his son's memory to be honoured.

Beyond the benefits to the late Prince's household, the funeral provided a focus for the grief of the nation. Cornwallis describes the 'innumerable multitude of all sorts of all ages and degrees of men, women and children [...] some holding their heads, not being able to endure so sorrowful a sight, all mourning [...] some weeping, crying, howling, wringing of their hands, passionately bewailing so great a losse'. Similarly, Foscarini reports that the trumpeters in the procession 'by the sound of their funeral march, most beautifully played, they drew tears from the eyes of all who heard'.[33] In the days before his death, the whole country had been praying for Henry's recovery. After the event almost fifty different volumes of memorial writing were produced for him: elegies; epicedia; epitaphs; emblems; impresa; devices; meditations and sermons. The sorrow felt at the death contrasts with the deliberate and calculated 'fabrication' of grief evident at the death of Elizabeth, the ageing Queen who received no comparable literary pouring forth of lament.[34] The contrast in situations is marked, however, as Henry had been the young, aspiring heir to the throne. Perhaps, as Williamson puts it, 'it was the sudden loss of a living national myth for which men cried out' rather than the loss of Prince Henry as an individual.[35] Henry did have a substitute, Prince Charles, whose role as heir would be underlined in the offering service where he appears to have received his late brother's funeral hatchments, in accordance with heraldic tradition.[36] Charles was, however, physically weak and had not yet become a public figure.[37] He could not yet assuage the grief felt for his lost brother. The public position Prince

---

[32] CSPV, XII (1610–13), 450, 469; Cornwallis agrees that the Prince's household resigned at the breaking of the staves, p. 92. Parry (1981), however, comments that the formal dissolution of the Prince's household was at the end of the year, on which occasion Dr Hall preached a farewell sermon to 'the Family of Prince Henry', p. 87. See also Historical Manuscripts Commission, *Downshire* MSS, III, 436.

[33] Cornwallis, p. 86; CSPV, XII (1610–13), 468. See also Sir John Throckmorton's comments in *Downshire* MSS, III, 436.

[34] See chapter 5. On the literary outpouring that followed the death of Sir Philip Sidney and, in particular, on the contrast between the Latin elegies of the elite composed by the universities and the English commentary provided in Lant's pictorial record of the funerals, see Strickland, p. 27.

[35] Williamson, pp. 171–3, 155.

[36] Although there is no explicit reference to Charles receiving his brother's achievements in the published account, he was led up to the altar by Garter just before the achievements were offered. See Nichols (1828), II, 500.

[37] Prince Charles would not be created Prince of Wales until 1616. Subsequently physical weakness seems to have delayed his involvement in court festivities until New Year 1618; see Graham Parry, 'The Politics of the Jacobean Masque', in *Theatre and Government Under the Early Stuarts*, ed. by J. R. Mulryne and Margaret Shewring (Cambridge: Cambridge University Press, 1993), pp. 87–117 (pp. 109–10).

Henry had commanded points to the more complex emotions which lay behind the excessive sorrow displayed at his funeral.

Henry had gained a reputation as a champion of Protestant and national interests, promoted in the context of a neo-chivalric revival.[38] In 1610, as his investiture approached, Prince Henry played his part in persuading James to ally himself with the French in the battle over Cleves (1610) and looked forward to active involvement in a glorious campaign against the Habsburgs and the papacy. Henry's ultimate dream was of a crusade against the Turks.[39]

Even before Henry IV's death, Prince Henry had come to be seen as the true leader of European Protestantism. The French King had disillusioned many, including French Huguenots living in England, with his politic conversion to Catholicism. By 1612, with Henry IV dead, Henry Stuart had set up a network of agents abroad and appears to have been on the verge of heading his own Protestant campaign. On his death-bed Prince Henry had given orders for a number of private papers to be burnt perhaps as a measure to protect those who may have been incriminated by his grand schemes. Certainly his militaristic plans were the subject of intense speculation. After his death the Venetian ambassador reminisced that 'his whole talk was of arms and war'.[40]

The international appeal of Prince Henry's Protestant ambitions, suggested already by his popularity with the French Huguenots, is further illustrated by the number of German Princes that grouped themselves around him.[41] Among these was the Count Palatine who was to marry Prince Henry's sister. The Palatine had been primed to take a leading role alongside the Prince in the European Protestant crusade envisaged, for example, by William Fennor in his poem, 'A description of the Palsgraues Countrey' which was declaimed before the royal family a short time before Henry fell ill. Fennor spoke of:

> Five Princes in this iron age survive,
>   which makes it seeme the silver worlde againe:
> To match them hardly shall we finde out five
>   yet weell forbeare to speake of *France* or *Spaine*,
> Five heires, five youths, five kinsmen, and five Princes,
>   Of one Religion, though in five Provinces [...]
> Each of these are their Countries joyfull hope,
>   friends to the Gospell, foes to th'Divell and Pope.[42]

Strong has identified the five as the Prince of Hesse, the Prince of Brunswick, the Prince of Brandenburg, the Count Palatine and Prince Henry. The English

---

[38] Williamson, pp. 29–42; Strong (1986), pp. 68–9; Smuts, pp. 29, 82.
[39] Strong (1986), p. 73; Williamson, pp. 109–41; Parry (1981), pp. 93, 96.
[40] CSPV, XII (1610–13), 450; Strong (1986), pp. 56, 74; Williamson, p. 151.
[41] CSPV, XI (1607–10), 469. Some of the Protestant Princes of Germany would also have preferred Prince Henry as leader because they had no wish to 'aggrandize France'.
[42] William Fennor, *Fennors Descriptions, or A True Relation of Certaine and divers speeches spoken before the King and Queenes most excellent Maiestie, the Prince his highnesse, and the Lady Elizabeths Grace* (London, 1616); cited by Strong, p. 176.

The Funeral of Prince Henry Stuart

Prince was related through his mother Anne of Denmark to a number of German Protestant Princes including the Dukes of Brunswick and of Hesse. From the 1590s there had been a steady stream of visits by German princelings to the English court. Prince Henry was particularly close to Frederic Ulric (1591–1634), son of the Duke of Brunswick, with whom he corresponded from 1604 and who visited England in 1610, staying with Henry at St James's Palace. Otto, Prince of Hesse, visited during the summer of 1611, making an unsuccessful bid for the hand of the Princess Elizabeth. His retinue included Henry, Count of Nassau, who was to influence Henry in his opposition to the Savoy Catholic marriage proposed for him by James.[43]

The mutual ambitions of these men were, at least temporarily, neutralized by the Prince's death. Frederick, Count Palatine's sphere of political activity was abruptly curtailed and he was constrained to the passive role of following Henry's effigy and coffin in the funeral convoy. He walked directly after the chief mourner, coming between Prince Charles and his twelve assistant mourners. Thus the Count was accorded a status which might be classified as 'second chief mourner', a role unique in royal funeral processions. He was attended by his own group of eleven attendants, who followed the assistant mourners. These men included Count Lewis de Nassau and Count Wigenstein.[44]

Similarly, members of the Prince's household who had shared his military ambitions could now only register their neo-chivalric role in the context of the funeral. Robert Devereux, third Earl of Essex (1591–1646), for example, walked as assistant to the chief mourner in the Prince's funeral procession and offered the gauntlets in the church service.

All these men experienced an exaggerated sense of loss, partly because for them Prince Henry had no heir but also because his death had been untimely and unheroic. Even more than the death of Philip Sidney, Henry's demise was difficult to present in an heroic light.

Elegies and sermons written for Henry abound with personations offered in an attempt to place and understand the Prince's sudden death: he is seen as Abner, Josiah, Alexander, Marcellus and the Black Prince. Henry II of France is offered as one who was 'slaine in like sort'; yet even his death, fatally wounded as he was while taking part in martial sports, was more heroic than Prince Henry's.[45] Shakespeare and Fletcher are arguably exploring the implications of

---

[43] Strong (1986), pp. 77–9; 83. Nassau was to take part in the Prince's funeral procession with a large retinue; see Nichols (1828), II, 494.

[44] The Prince's death was also lamented in Paris. Yet, while the Catholic Louis XIII put the French court into mourning, he hesitated over sending an official to condole with James. No French ambassador appeared in the funeral procession, see Winwood, III, 410. Ambassadors were sent to offer the condolences of the Duke of Guise and the Prince of Conti; see McClure, I, 402.

[45] Sir William Alexander, *An Elegie on the Death of Prince Henrie* (Edinburgh: Andro Hart, 1612). On the elegies, see Nichols (1828), II, 504–12; Dennis Kay, *Melodious Tears: The English Funeral from Spenser to Milton* (Oxford: Clarendon Press, 1990), pp. 124–203;

Prince Henry's death in *The Two Noble Kinsmen*, first performed in 1613 or early 1614, where the demise of Arcite thrown from his horse demonstrates how perilous chivalric values are in the face of time and chance.[46] David Bergeron persuasively argues that his death similarly supplied the emotional impulse behind Webster's *The Duchess of Malfi* (1614).[47]

Many of Henry's elegists sought to transpose Prince Henry's death into the realms of chivalric honour and glory. The neo-Spenserian 'The Olympian Catastrophe', written by Sir Arthur Gorges (1557–1625), seems, for example, to be an attempt to create a chivalric context for Prince Henry's inglorious death.[48] Gorges, who was aggressively anti-Catholic, lamented the loss of Prince Henry, the anticipated leader of the Protestant crusade that he yearned to take part in. In the poem, he delights in recreating an image of Prince Henry who appears resplendent in full armour and excels against all challengers in the martial feats held in the Olympian fields. Yet the fact of Henry's inglorious death remains difficult to deal with. The Prince is suddenly snatched away by Fate who weakly argues that thus Prince Henry will gain a richer crown in heaven and will not live long enough to sin. He will be no Hannibal, Marcellus, Scipio or Nero. Yet Gorges still insists on choosing the personation of a noble warrior who died in battle as his image for his Prince: 'New Troy, her Prince, James wayles his Hector heire'. In death Prince Henry was, however, no Hector.

Appeal to the heroic genre was also evident in the funeral procession where, through the inclusion of martial percussion, Prince Henry's death was translated into that of a military hero. Drums, suitably covered with black cloth, accompanied the mourners, as they had done at the funeral of Sir Philip Sidney.[49]

John W. Draper, *The Funeral Elegy and the Rise of Romanticism* (New York: New York University, 1929; repr. New York: Octagon Books, 1967), pp. 28–30; Parry (1981), p. 88; Williamson, pp. 171–92.

[46] William Shakespeare and John Fletcher, *The Two Noble Kinsmen*, ed. by Eugene M. Waith (Oxford: Clarendon Press, 1989); J. R. Mulryne, ' "Here's Unfortunate Revels": War and Chivalry in Plays and Shows at the Time of Prince Henry Stuart', in J. R. Mulryne and Margaret Shewring, eds, *War, Literature and the Arts in Sixteenth-Century Europe* (Basingstoke: Macmillan Press, 1989), p. 184.

[47] David M. Bergeron, 'The Wax Figures in *The Duchess of Malfi*', *Studies in English Literature*, 18 (1978), 331–9 (p. 333). See also Neill (1981), pp. 76–7.

[48] 'The Olympian Catastrophe' was in fact a re-working of a poem begun in honour of the Prince in 1610. Gorges, a cousin of Ralegh, was a Gentleman of the Prince's Privy Chamber from 1611; see Strong (1986), p. 41.

[49] Nichols (1828), I, 494.

Posthumous Glory: James, Henry and a Conflict Resolved

The disparity between the kind of funeral which Prince Henry might have been expected to receive and the elaborate one that he was given is further thrown into relief by evidence suggesting that there was considerable antagonism between James and his son during the latter's lifetime.

Some testimonies need to be taken with a pinch of salt because of the probable bias of their exponents. For example, Godfrey Goodman (1583–1655), Bishop of Gloucester, wrote of Prince Henry, 'truly I think he was a little self-willed, which caused the less mourning for him'.[50] Goodman was, however, a High Anglican of Romanish tendencies and his *History of the Court of King James* was written retrospectively. His opinion does gain weight from Arthur Wilson's account of the reign of James I but it must not be forgotten that Wilson was strongly prejudiced against the Stuarts. Describing James's attitude towards his son at the time of the *Barriers* (1610), Wilson wrote:[51]

> For as yet the King could discover nothing in him but the harmless and wanton innocence that commonly accompanies youth, being of a light nature and soon blown away. But how far the Kings fears (like thick clouds) might afterwards blind the eye of his Reason, when he saw him (as he thought) too high mounted in the peoples love, and of an alluring spirit, to decline his paternall affection to him, and bring him to the lowest condition he fell in, may be the subject of my fears but not of my pen.

Yet Wilson, too, was writing long after the event and had particular reasons for disparaging James.

Contemporary evidence is available, however, to support Wilson's assertion that James tried to contain the public display of his son while he was alive.[52] Reporting on the celebrations of Henry's investiture as Prince of Wales, the Venetian ambassador noted the King's desire to limit the overweening pride of his son and the impact Prince Henry would make on the citizenry of London. 'The King would not allow him on this occasion, nor yet on his going to Parliament, to be seen on horse-back.' Foscarini gives two possible explanations for James's behaviour: 'the reason is expense or, as some say, because they did not desire to exalt him too high'.[53] Carleton, writing to Edmondes after the event, confirms the relative restraint of the festivities, and reiterates the need to conserve funds as the reason. A horse-back entry would have constituted a pointed visual parallel to the royal entry ritual which usually appertained only to reigning monarchs. The people of London had witnessed only two such

---

[50] Goodman, I, 251.
[51] Wilson (1653), p. 52. Arthur Wilson's patron was the staunchly Protestant third Earl of Essex who had been a member of Prince Henry's household and who was to command the Parliamentary forces in the Civil War.
[52] Parry (1981), p. 94; Williamson, p. 43.
[53] CSPV, XI (1603–7), 507.

entries in the recent past: the celebration of James's accession in 1604 and the state visit of Christian IV of Denmark in 1606.

In the event, Prince Henry entered the City of London by water, with the Thames's great importance as England's main trade route and source of the City's wealth bestowing symbolic weight onto the occasion.[54] Nevertheless, a water-borne procession effectively reduced the size of the audience, distanced the Prince from the spectators, and avoided the use of triumphal archways. James also circumvented the possibility of Prince Henry being displayed to the London populace in solitary splendour by travelling with him the short distance by water from Whitehall.[55] Here James was deliberately flouting tradition, evidence perhaps that he was concerned about his son's popularity.

Perhaps the surest way in which James sabotaged his son's performance was, however, by not informing the City about the Prince's entry by water until just six days before the event was to take place.[56] The account of the festivities organized by the City, 'London's Love to the Royal Prince', smarts with references to the lack of available time to make sufficiently splendid arrangements: 'London's Cheefe Magistrate the Lord Maior, with his worthie Bretheren the Aldermen, having very short and sudden intelligence thereof; after some small consultation, [. . .] they determined to meete him in such good manner as the brevitie of time would then permit them'.[57] The strength of feeling involved is indicated by further references within the text. Corinea, the personification of the Province of Cornwall, addressed the Prince thus during his water progress: 'The shortnes of time hath ben no meane bridle to their [the City officials'] zealous forwardness, which else would have appeared in more flowing and aboundant manner. Neuerthelesse, out of this little limitation, let me humbly entreat you to accept their boundlesse love.'[58] Without pointing its finger at the King, the City publicly denied responsibility for the relative moderation of the proceedings.

If James was unwilling to give his son any opportunity to inflate his warrior-hero self-image, why did he allow the investiture to go ahead at all? At first he was reluctant for it to take place, preferring to hang on to Prince Henry's revenues which were proving very useful in the payment of Crown debts. However, a worsening financial situation necessitated a shift in policy and Salisbury, the Lord Treasurer, drew up a plan which linked the granting of a subsidy by Parliament to the investiture of the Prince of Wales. Parliament had strong affection for Prince Henry, taking great pride in what he represented and, with some qualifications, agreed to the proposals.[59]

---

[54] Knowles, p. 166.
[55] Nichols (1828), II, 361.
[56] Strong (1986), p. 153.
[57] Nichols (1828), II, 317.
[58] Nichols (1828), II, 320.
[59] Williamson, pp. 60–3.

Why should James have so wished to circumscribe the public image of his son? Prince Henry was his heir and the production of a legitimate male successor was closely related to the question of the royal prerogative in James's interpretation of the theory of the Divine Right of Kings.[60] The reality of their relationship differed, however, from the political ideal. James's attitude to his son was, perhaps, partly motivated by a natural desire not to be eclipsed by him in his own lifetime. Yet James's wish to constrain Henry was greatly exacerbated by the political conflict which centred around King and Prince. The militarism of Prince Henry, noted already, was in direct opposition to the peace policies of his father.[61] Furthermore, Henry's promise of active intervention in Europe held much greater popular appeal for many than James's less glamorous policies which aimed at peaceful reconciliation. The Prince's court attracted both an older generation of Elizabethan militant Protestants, who bore the mantle of Sidney, and energetic young men, eager for military honour. Thus it gained a reputation for discipline, virtue and chivalric ideals in marked contrast to the lax, pleasure-house image of his father's court.[62] James, who understood the relationship between ceremony and power, needed to curb his son's popularity by controlling the level of his public display.

Jonson's entertainment, *The Barriers*, dramatizes the antagonism between Henry's militarism and James's pacificism.[63] The masque was staged on 6 January 1610 and marked Henry's first formal bearing of arms as a prelude to his creation. This was at a time when James himself was wavering towards military intervention in Europe, heightening the tension between a son hungry for action and a dilatory father. The performance was set against a backdrop of international tension over the succession to the Duchy of Cleves. Henry IV planned to march on Cleves in May 1610 as the prelude to a campaign against the Habsburgs and James was considering getting involved by sending a force of English and Scots soldiers already serving in the Netherlands, perhaps with Prince Henry making his military debut. James was, however, still wary of abandoning his peace policies and of bestowing upon his son an opportunity for the attainment of prodigious glory.[64]

---

[60] G. R. Elton, 'The Divine Right of Kings', in *Studies in Tudor and Stuart Politics and Government*, ed. by G. R. Elton, 4 vols (Cambridge: Cambridge University Press, 1974–92), II (1974), pp. 193–214.

[61] The conflict is traced by Williamson, p. 171. On the peace policies, see Strong (1986), p. 83.

[62] Parry (1981), p. 93. On Henry's court, see my chapter 6. For an example of corrupt images painted of James's court, see Thomas Park, ed., *Nugae Antiquae: being a miscellaneous collection of original papers [. . .] by Sir John Harrington and others*, 2 vols ([London (?): [n. pub.], 1804), I, 348–53.

[63] Stephen Orgel and Roy Strong, *Inigo Jones: The Theatre of the Stuart Court* (London: University of California Press, 1973), pp. 159–64.

[64] Parry (1993), pp. 93–107. For an account of the Cleves crisis, see S. R. Gardiner, *A History of England from the Accession of James I*, 2 vols (London, [n. pub.], 1883), II, 93–101.

In *The Barriers* entertainment Prince Henry cast himself as Moeliades, an 'Anagramme [which] maketh *Miles A DEO*', thus styling himself as God's knight.[65] In that role Prince Henry is called forth by the Lady of the Lake to revitalize chivalry which had fallen into decay at the English court.[66] Moeliades, or Meliadus, is guided to his tent and there Merlin bestows upon him a shield bequeathed to him by the fates. Merlin then presents Prince Henry with a series of paradigms of kingly behaviour. The first group emphasizes a defensive role in kings, a role which is symbolically in keeping with the gift of the shield (line 165). It is, however, in the description of the second group of warrior kings, from Richard, Coeur de Lion, to Henry V, that the fire and enthusiasm of Merlin's speech is located (lines 225–98).[67] Merlin catalogues a litany of war heroes culminating in a eulogy to James, shifting attention briefly from the Prince as dramatic subject on the stage to the traditional focus of the court masque, the monarch seated in the audience.[68] The final example held up for Prince Henry to emulate must, of course, be his own father: James whose golden reign has joined the 'Rose and Thistle'. Yet the praise rendered to James for restoring the Navy at the climax of Merlin's speech is equivocal (lines 349–56). Jonson was in fact pointing to an area in which there had been recent and public conflict between King and Prince and thus highlighting the gulf between the pacifist King and the military tastes of his son. James had allowed the Navy to decline alarmingly since the death of his predecessor partly because of cost but also because he was more interested in policies of peace than preparing for war. By the time the decision came to revitalize the Navy, it was Prince Henry who provided the motivating force.[69] Thus, even in its apparent praise of James, *The Barriers* dramatizes the conflict between the war-hungry Prince and the peace-loving King.

Further evidence of a power struggle can be gleaned from another of the court entertainments, *Tethys' Festival*, the masque for Prince Henry's creation (1610). This entertainment has convincingly been shown to be largely

---

[65] William Drummond, 'Teares, on the Death of Moeliades', quoted in Strong (1986), p. 141.

[66] The decline of chivalry was a commonplace topic in chivalric literature. See Mulryne (1989), p. 174. The Arthurian subject is indicative of Prince Henry's control over Jonson's masque. Jonson usually scorned such subject matter as outdated; see Parry (1993), p. 94.

[67] All line references to *The Barriers* and *Oberon* are from C. H. Herford and Percy and Evelyn Simpson, eds, *Ben Jonson*, 11 vols (Oxford: Clarendon Press, 1925–54), VII (1941; repr. 1963).

[68] Strong (1986, pp. 169–70) suggests that Prince Henry, who was taught perspective by Salomon de Caus, may himself have been responsible for this new way in which perspective was used to focus the eye on the central masquer.

[69] Simon Adams, 'Spain or the Netherlands? The Dilemmas of Early Stuart Foreign Policy', in *Before the English Civil War: Essays on Early Stuart Politics and Government*, ed. by Howard Tomlinson (London: Macmillan, 1983), pp. 79–101 (p. 84); CSPV, XII (1610–13), 264; Williamson, p. 49.

concerned with curbing his aspirations.[70] Even *Oberon* (New Year 1611) which places its focus much more squarely on James than *The Barriers* does, retains significant elements of the tension described in the earlier masque. The pacifist James is uncomfortably cast as King Arthur but the final compliment in the closing speech is paid to Prince Henry:

> That all that shall tonight behold the rites
> Performed by princely Oberon and these knights
> May, without stop, point out the proper heir
> Designed so long to Arthur's crowns and chair. (lines 365–8)

It is as if Henry is already breaking free from the restraining influence of his father.

The conflict between King and Prince may have been on the verge of damaging exposure at the time of Prince Henry's fatal illness. There is evidence to suggest that he intended to act in direct opposition to his father who wanted a Catholic bride for his son as part of his marriage alliance policy. As a prelude to his campaign, Prince Henry had intended to accompany his sister on a tour of Germany and select for himself a Protestant bride, thereby forestalling his father's plans in an act of supreme defiance and independence.

In view of the crisis towards which events were fast careering, it is perhaps unsurprising that Henry's sudden death engendered a certain amount of suspicion of poisoning.[71] The King himself was not immune from the charge and in an elaborate display of objective enquiry, James appointed the lords of the Privy Council to supervise a semi-ritualized opening of the body. Intriguingly the doctors in attendance included the personal physician of the Count Palatine.[72] The autopsy reported no traces of foul play but the rumours of poisoning persisted.[73]

Death certainly removed the threat his son had become to James's peace policies. Thus, ironically, it was only after Henry's demise that James could unequivocally celebrate the Prince's life. Although he had spent the last half-decade trying to contain his son's ambitions, it was now politically expedient for James to place his son centre stage: he needed to fulfil the expectations of the nation and to manage its grief. Prince Henry could not have ordered a more splendid funeral if he had been in charge of the arrangements himself. He was represented in effigy as if he had been a reigning monarch and was finally permitted the progress through the streets of London that he had been denied at his investiture. It is heavily ironic that Prince Henry achieved such status only in his funeral. James would allow Prince Henry to benefit from a power-conferring ritual performance only when his death had rendered that power

---

[70] Williamson, p. 82.
[71] Williamson, pp. 166–9; Akrigg (1962), p. 133; Strong (1986), pp. 54–5.
[72] Cornwallis, p. 75; Peck, I, 204.
[73] See, for example, the assertions made in Wilson (1653), pp. 62–3; CSPV, XII (1610–13), 470; Nichols (1828), p. 487.

The Theatre of Death

impotent. The large presence of Protestant nobles in the funeral procession meant that Prince Henry was honoured in the international context that his ambitions deserved but at the same time the premature truncation of those ambitions was underlined. For the moment the illusion of political consensus created by the funeral procession was useful in assuaging the pangs of thwarted ambition in Prince Henry's followers. James could willingly permit the presence of the German princes in the ceremony since their plans could no longer threaten his hopes for peace.

Through the funeral pageantry James was able to reinscribe his relationship with Henry. The magnificent funeral was the final gift of the loving and devoted father to his cherished and obedient son. Death once more allowed James to idealize his family relationships and restored Prince Henry as obedient son to his natural father.[74] The obsequies of Prince Henry is another clear example of James mobilizing bias in his favour through funeral pageantry and modifying the ritual traditions of royal funerals to suit his purposes.

The day of the funeral passed without disruption. Foscarini reports that the huge procession 'passed in perfect order and filled the whole road, more than a mile long, from the palace of St. James to the Church of Westminster, so that as the head of the procession entered the Church the tail had not yet left the Palace. The crowd was marvellous. All the houses filled with ladies and the nobility.'[75] James had gained an audience whose size and composition justified the care he had taken in organizing Prince Henry's funeral.

The Funeral Effigy as Monument

Although no monument to Prince Henry was built, plans for one were made. On 29 December, Foscarini reported, 'a rich tomb of marble and porphyry is being prepared, and many statues, it will take a long time and cost much. Meantime, the leaden coffin has been covered with velvet richly embroidered with gold and pearls.'[76] Interesting is Foscarini's comment that the projected tomb was to incorporate many statues. Images were once again the legitimate province of tomb-makers. These statues would, however, never be carved and neither would the Prince be commemorated with a tomb effigy. We have seen how the magnificent display of the funeral accomplished the aims of honouring the dead Prince's memory, providing a focus for the nation's grief and reinscribing James's relationship with his son. The success of the funeral pageantry took the urgency out of the need to provide a tomb, while the added cost no doubt contributed to the lack of will to see the project through. Further, the post-

---

[74] On the appearance of Prince Henry in portraits by William van de Passe idealizing the King's family after the Prince's death, see Goldberg, pp. 90–7.
[75] CSPV, XII (1610–13), 468.
[76] CSPV, XII (1610–13), 469.

funeral display of the funeral effigy, a practice established at least since 1607 when, ironically, Prince Henry himself had taken his uncle, the King of Denmark, on a visit to the tombs and effigies at Westminster Abbey, precluded the need for a monument.

After the funeral services the funeral effigy of Prince Henry continued to be displayed in its hearse in the Abbey church. Although it only remained there for ten days, the effect would be preserved forever because an engraving of hearse and effigy was produced, the first of its kind.[77] Upon its removal, the effigy, 'decked and trimmed with cloathes, as he went when he was alive, robes, collar, crowne, golden rodde in his hand, &c. [...] was set up in a chamber of the [...] Chappell at Westminster amongst the Representations of the Kings and Queenes his famous predecessors, where it remaineth for ever to be seene'.[78] Prince Henry would remain on display until well into the eighteenth century. George Vertue visited the Abbey in 1724/5 and wrote, 'Prince Henry, his Effigie was finely done especially the head is repaird in plaster, in a very good taste.'[79] Thus, James continued his policy of exaggerating the honours accorded to his son now that he was safely dead. Without exception all the other effigies in the Abbey chapel were of kings and queens.

It is not clear exactly how the royal effigies were displayed, whether upright or recumbent, and if lying down, upon what? I have not come across any direct evidence as to what became of Prince Henry's hearse after the ten-day period of display in the Abbey. It was normal practice, however, for the hearse to be taken down at this stage and its constituent materials divided up and distributed amongst the heralds as part of their fees. This would occur at the funeral of Henry's mother, Queen Anne, five years later and it is reasonable to assume that the Prince's hearse was dealt with in the same way.[80] In any case, the hearse was probably not constructed from long-lasting materials. The figures on James's hearse would, for example, be made of plaster of Paris and white calico drapery.[81] It would seem, then, that the hearse was not transferred to the chapel with the funeral effigy and that the latter was displayed alone.

The framework of the Prince's effigy was jointed, as the bill of account recording the work of Richard Loons, King's Joiner, makes clear:

> Item for makinge the bodye of a figure for the rep^{r}sentation of His Highnes w^t several joints both in the arms legges and bodie to be moved to sundrie accions first for the Carriage in the Chariot and then for the standinge and the settinge uppe the same in the Abbye with my attendance on the same work.[82]

---

[77] Sandford, p. 529; Harvey and Mortimer, p. 61.
[78] Nichols (1828), p. 503.
[79] Harvey and Mortimer, p. 61. Damage was done to the effigy between 1786 and 1872.
[80] See chapter 9.
[81] See Maclagan, p. 34.
[82] P. R. O. Lord Chamberlain's Records, Series I. vol. 555, cited by Hope, p. 555.

The Prince's effigy was not the first to be constructed with joints; Elizabeth of York's effigy had been built with elbow joints, apparently to facilitate dressing. However, this was the first time that specific reference was made to the function of the jointed structure.[83]

The joints found at the hips and toes have suggested to some that the effigy was designed to be displayed upright once the catafalque had been removed.[84] Martin Holmes concludes, however, that the joints are too few and not ideally situated for the figure to take up a life-like position. He convincingly argues that their purpose was rather to facilitate taking the figure to pieces to aid dressing and relocation, such as when the effigy was moved from the funeral chariot to the hearse in the Abbey.[85] Holmes has further identified an effigy head found at the Museum of London as that belonging to the representation of Prince Henry. If his identification is correct, the head was not designed to fit onto the figure in any way.[86] The sculptor responsible for the head was Abraham van der Doort, a Dutch numismatist, who had been official curator of the Prince's considerable collection of coins and medals. It is not clear why he was chosen in preference to the more obvious candidates, John and Maximilian Colt. The latter had been sculptor to the Crown since 1608 and prepared funeral effigies for both Anne of Denmark and James.[87] Van der Doort approached the design as a medallist rather than a sculptor, seeing the subject in terms of its profile rather than in its full-face aspect. He also seems to have worked in isolation, failing to consult the craftsmen responsible for constructing the remainder of the effigy, and thus the finished head could not be fixed to the body in any way. The only solution was to put the head in place when the figure was lying down on a firm flat surface.

Cornwallis provides evidence that supports this theory, elaborating on the placing of Prince Henry's effigy on the funeral chariot for the procession, 'it was laid on the back in [sic] the coffin, and fast bound to the same, the head thereof being supported by two cushions, just as it was drawne along the streets in the funerall chariot'.[88]

If the Holmes identification is accepted, then the Prince's effigy must have been displayed lying down, with the head carefully positioned but not secured in any way. This would certainly have aided the thieves who stole the effigy's

---

[83] Harvey and Mortimer, pp. 46, 60.
[84] The headless funeral effigy of Prince Henry still survives at Westminster Abbey but is in relatively poor condition and is not on public display.
[85] Martin Holmes, *A Carved Wooden Head of Henry Frederick, Prince of Wales*, transcript of a lecture given by Martin Holmes in 1986, held in the library at Westminster Abbey (Box: Royal Funeral Effigies), pp. 1–11 (p. 9); Gittings, p. 223.
[86] Canon Anthony Harvey of Westminster Abbey does not accept Holmes's identification of the head and points out the effigy head was probably made from plaster as James I's would be. See Harvey and Mortimer, p. 61.
[87] Harvey and Mortimer, p. 60.
[88] Cornwallis, p. 85; Peck, I, 205.

creation robes in 1616.[89] The horizontal posture of the funeral effigy, while being less striking than an upright display, would, however, have produced a strong visual parallel of a recumbent tomb effigy. Thus both visually and functionally the funeral effigy took over from the monument and tomb effigy.

---

[89] Holmes, p. 11. The head itself appears to have been stolen shortly before George Vertue's visit to the Abbey in 1725, although he remembered seeing it on a previous occasion (Holmes, p. 4).

CHAPTER NINE

The Funeral of Anne of Denmark (1619)

The Vulnerability of Ritual: Anne's Lying-in-State and Funeral Procession

The Queen consort, Anne of Denmark, died of dropsy on 2 March 1619 at Hampton Court. She was unpopular with her husband and also with many of her people, not least because of her Catholicism which had been very publicly aired when she refused to take communion at her coronation.[1] Her death did not provoke the intense focused emotion caused by the death of her eldest son five years before and her funeral lacked the cohesive unity displayed at his. James had no need to work to create a display of political consensus at Anne's funeral as she was not a key political figure. The funeral was marred by factional interest and the desire to cut costs, and it functions as a clear example of the potential vulnerability of funeral pageantry.[2]

On 9 March, after the body had been disembowelled, embalmed and leaded, it was taken from Hampton Court to Denmark House for the lying-in-state ceremony.[3] Although it was conveyed by barge and under cover of darkness, the transfer was effected with 'great solemnity'. Twelve barges, together with other vessels, were assembled on the river at Hampton Court. 'Many Countesses and divers other great Ladyes were commanded to repayre to Hampton Court to give their attendance upon ye Corpse.' The encoffined corpse was brought down in a procession comprising these noblewomen together with heralds Norroy and Richmond who marshalled the women into the waiting barges, according to their rank. The water-borne convoy arrived at the stairs of Somerset House at 8.00 p.m. where it was met by the Earls of Pembroke and Arundel, accompanied by other members of the Privy Council. The corpse, attended by these gentlemen, was then conveyed inside.

Three chambers had been prepared for the lying-in-state of the body at Somerset House. In the bedchamber there was 'a certain frame in the manner of a bed', nine feet long, nine feet high and seven feet in breadth. Four pillars

---

[1] Ethel Carleton Williams, *Anne of Denmark* (London: Longman, 1970), pp. 52–6, 82–3, 111, 164–5.
[2] On the vulnerability of French royal funeral processions, see Giesey (1960), p. 9.
[3] Sandford, p. 526. Denmark House was the name given to Somerset House, after Anne of Denmark to whom it was assigned under James. When it was erected in the 1540s it had been named after Lord Protector Somerset; see Smuts, p. 54 n. 1.

The Funeral of Anne of Denmark

supported the canopy which was topped with plumes of black feathers. The coffin was placed in this magnificent bed of state to await the funeral.

More than two months was to pass before the funeral took place on 13 May 1619, much longer then the period of one month that had become traditional practice by the time of Elizabeth's obsequies.[4] The indelicacy of the continued delay was noted by Chamberlain who reported on 17 April that, 'The day of the Quene's funerall is not yet set down, though yt be more then time yt were don.' The funeral, already postponed once from its original date, just after Easter, to 29 April, would not take place until 13 May. By that time the noblemen and other mourners, who had been informed by Lancaster that their presence was required, would already have been long in the capital.[5]

With the continued delay the court ladies involved in the lying-in-state ritual began to get indecorously impatient and 'grow wearie of watching'. There was 'talke of the Ladies watching and matching there by turnes in such sort as is neither comly nor convenient for the place or person they attend'. The hordes of people reported to be flocking to Denmark House to view the coffin further contributed to the progressively unseemly ambience of this lying-in-state ritual, but are also a testament to the Jacobean public's fascination with funeral ritual and display. Chamberlain comments, 'there is more concourse than when she was living'.[6]

Among those who were ill-convenienced by the continued delay in the staging of Queen Anne's funeral were London's theatre companies. As Chamberlain reported, the procrastination was 'to the great hindrance of our players, which are forbidden to play so long as her body is above ground'.[7]

What lay behind this protracted and undignified delay? Part of the reason was financial. When his wife died James directed that £20,000, or more if necessary, should be transferred from the Treasury to the Master of the Great Wardrobe, Lionel Cranfield, to pay for the ceremony. The money was not immediately forthcoming, however, and on 17 April Chamberlain reports, 'they are driven to shifts for monie, and talke of melting the Quenes golden plate and putting yt into coine: besides that the commissioners for her jewells and other moveables make offer to sell or pawne divers of them to good value'. Meanwhile servants were pilfering silver, plate and even vestments from the Queen's private chapel. Many of Anne's jewels were found to be missing when an inventory was finally taken.[8]

Time was required to settle the vexed question of how the funeral of a queen

---

[4] BL, Harley MS 5176 fol. 236.
[5] McClure, II, 220–36; Parry (1981), p. 256; CA, Nayler, p. 6.
[6] McClure, II, 224, 232.
[7] McClure, II, 222. Members of the Queen's own theatre company would also take part in the funeral ceremony, grouped in a section referred to as 'The Queens inferiour sorte of Servants' together with the gardeners, shoemakers and plumbers. CA, Nayler, p. 8.
[8] McClure, II, 232, 240; Williams (1970), p. 203.

The Theatre of Death

who was consort of a living monarch should be performed. It was, after all, the first since the funeral of Jane Seymour in 1537. Shortly after the Queen's death, 'the Erle of Worcester, Lord Privy Seal, the Erle of Pembroke, Lord Chamberlain of his Majestie's Household and the Erle of Arundell with divers more of the Privie Counsell repayred to Hampton Court for the ordering things according to his Majesties Commandment'.[9] These men summoned members of the College of Arms to give them advice on procedure. On 18 March, Garter, Norroy and the rest of the College of Arms debated the question of which banners should appear in the funeral procession. They were concerned that the difference between the funeral of a sovereign queen and a queen consort should be marked in Anne's funeral procession by the omission of some of the funeral hatchments. Anne would be honoured only with a coat of arms, crest, sword and shield; there would be no helmet or gauntlets.[10]

Although by 10 March the Privy Councillors had approved a plan, drawn up by the heralds with details of the numbers and identity of the mourners, on 17 April Chamberlain reports that there was a quarrel over who should take the role of chief mourner. 'Lady Arundell' he writes 'professes not to give place to the Countesse of Nottingham, that pretends yt in her husband's right, who upon surrendring of the Admiraltie had a privilege graunted him to be *promus comes* during his life: the Countesse of Northumberland and divers others are likewise saide to take the same exception to her, and will by no means go behind, so that to stint some part of the strife (yf yt be possible) the old marchioness of Northampton is sent for yf by any meanes she can supplie the place.' In the event the Countess of Arundel acted as chief mourner, although Chamberlain was unsure as to whether this was 'in her owne right, or as supplieng the place of the Lady Elizabeth'.[11]

When the funeral procession was finally performed it followed the usual form except that Prince Charles was included among the mourners: 'The Prince came after the archbishop of Caunterburie (who was to make the sermon) and next before the corps, that was drawne by six horses.'[12] The presence of the Prince broke the traditional heraldic regulations that restricted mourners to those of the same gender as the deceased.[13]

The processional display was, in Chamberlain's eyes at least, far short of impressive: 'It were to no purpose to make any long description of the funeral which was but a drawling, tedious sight, more remarqueable for number than

---

[9] CA, Nayler, pp. 1–22.
[10] CA, Nayler, p. 6.
[11] McClure, II, 232–3, 237. CA, Nayler, p. 20. The Countess of Arundel was Aletheia Talbot, wife of Thomas Howard, second Earl of Arundel; the Marchioness of Northampton was Helena, widow of William Parr, first Marquis of Northampton (d. 1571) and wife of Sir Thomas Gorges. See Williams (1970), p. 203.
[12] McClure, II, 237. A funeral car was specially constructed for the funeral at a cost of twenty pounds; see Harvey and Mortimer, p. 63.
[13] See chapter 1.

for any other singularitie [. . .] and though the number of Lordes and Ladies were very great, yet me thought altogether they made but a poore shew, which perhaps because they were apparelled all alike, or that they came laggering all along even tired with the length of the way and the weight of their clothes.'[14] Chamberlain's interpretation reeks of bias but he assembles considerable evidence to support the view that others, too, may have noticed failings in this display of funeral pageantry, despite the lengthy negotiations that had taken place. The sheer number of disparate groups involved made the funeral procession vulnerable to disruption and disputation.

Some Catholic Ladies, who had been nominated as mourners, refused 'to staine their profession with going to our church or service upon any shew of solemnitie, a straunge boldnes and such as wold not have bene so easilie digested in some times'.[15] More significantly, despite all their careful planning, James's advisors overlooked the representatives of the City when they drew up plans for the funeral convoy. Complaints must have been lodged and James set about making hasty reparation for the crime of offending the honour of the City. On Trinity Sunday, the Sunday after Anne's funeral, 'Paules Crosse mourned being hangd with blacke cloth and scutcheons of the Quenes armes, and all our aldermen and officers of this towne came thether in blacke [. . .] Because they were forgotten or neglected at the funerall, the King to please them would needs have yt don now.'[16] This is illustrative of the two-way operation of ritual performance. Anne's funeral could not simply take the form that James and his government wished it to take: they were constrained to stage a second ritual to meet and contain the outrage of the civic dignitaries who had come to expect a significant role in the proceedings of a royal funeral. The failure to include them in the original procession had destroyed the propensity towards co-operation which usually characterized ceremonial occasions.

James himself seems to have contributed directly to the subversion of his Queen's funeral. In accordance with custom, James was absent from the funeral itself, remaining at Newmarket and then Theobalds. When he did return to London, however, Chamberlain reports that he was dressed more like a wooer than a mourner, wearing 'a suit of watchet [pale blue] satten laid with silver lace, with a blew and white feather'. Chamberlain notes the indecorum of James's appearance juxtaposed with the black mourning worn by the foreign ambassadors newly arrived to offer their condolences. While black may have been considered an improper colour for a king, James could have worn the traditional royal mourning colour of purple. In any case, as Chamberlain sardonically remarks, he had donned black 'for the Archduke or Cardinal of Guise, or both'.[17]

---

[14] McClure, II, 237. For funeral procession participants, see Nichols (1928), III, 538–42.
[15] McClure, II, 233.
[16] McClure, II, 241.
[17] McClure, II, 329, 391.

Despite its cost, which was in the region of £30,000, Queen Anne's funeral procession completely failed to present an impression of order and unity. On this occasion, power was divorced from ceremony.

The Funeral Effigy and the Burial of the Viscera: A Shift towards Catholic Ritual Forms?

The only element of the whole funeral proceedings which attracted the praise of Chamberlain was the Abbey hearse in which Anne's funeral effigy was displayed. It was, he said, 'the fairest and stateliest that I thincke was ever seene there'.[18]

A design exists that has been attributed to Inigo Jones and claimed as his plan for Queen Anne's hearse. If it was indeed intended for the hearse, then it was highly innovative. Instead of depicting the usual recumbent effigy, it shows a seated figure, for which there was certainly no precedent in England. Neo-classical taste is applied to the traditional forms and the structure has a canopy, or baldachin, supported by mannerist caryatids rather then classical orders. The overall form was semi-architectural, carved in stone rather than the ephemeral wooden structure of the Elizabethan hearses. The unusual design was given a more monumental aspect by the decision to place the symbol of a golden tree laden with fruit, the sign of dynastic fertility that the Queen had carried in the Masque of Blackness, on the canopy above the enthroned effigy. Such a decorative feature would not have been out of place on a permanent tomb memorial.[19]

The Jones attribution of this design has not been proven, however, and more research needs to be carried out before a definitive connection can be made. In any case, the final form of the hearse that stood in Westminster Abbey appears to have been much more traditional.

The engraving reproduced in Wagner's *Heralds and Ancestors* (1978) depicts a conventional wooden hearse with a raised tower, capped by a pyramid structure, resting on top of the canopy. The hearse is decorated with numerous escutcheons and penons bearing the late Queen's arms. There are references among the payments made to 'a Crowne to sett on the top of the hearse'. The most unusual features are the neo-classical pillars that stand at the four corners of the outer wall, each bearing an heraldic figure. More familiar are the lion and unicorn, heraldic supporters of the royal arms of England and Scotland respectively. Less well-known and more striking are the two wildmen or 'savages' holding clubs, heraldic figures that traditionally bore the sovereign arms of

---

[18] McClure, II, 23.
[19] Peacock, p. 2; Parry (1981), p. 256; Gittings, p. 228; J. Harris, S. Orgel and R. Strong, *The King's Arcadia: Inigo Jones and the Stuart Court* (London: Arts Council of Great Britain, 1973), p. 99; Harvey and Mortimer, p. 65.

Denmark. Wagner attributes the hearse design to Maximilian Colt, still the King's Sculptor at this date. Certainly it was Colt that made the Queen's effigy. John de Critz was responsible for the decorative features and received payment for the lion, unicorn and wildmen besides numerous coats of arms.[20]

There is some evidence to suggest that the hearse was taken down a couple of months after the funeral. According to one account the heralds and the Dean of Westminster became involved in a dispute over who had the right to the valuable materials used in the construction of the hearse. The hearse was taken down on 12 July, 'and then, after good proof that it belonged to them [the heralds], was divided at the Office of Arms amongst us'. The heralds' claim, which was in line with tradition, was upheld by the Commissioners for the Earl Marshal, with the King's consent.[21]

According to another source, however, Queen Anne's hearse was still in place, by the Queen's grave, when Cromwell took control of the Abbey in 1642.[22] Even if accurate, this reference need not relate to the original hearse, however. A second hearse-like structure may have been constructed in the Abbey to facilitate the continued display of Anne's effigy. Anne of Denmark did not receive a tomb and while the dynastic security of the Stuart regime may have contributed to the decision not to erect a monument in her honour, it may be that, as I have argued with respect to Prince Henry Stuart, the funeral effigy was deemed to have taken over the commemorative role of a tomb monument. In any case, a 1634 glazier's bill for new leading for the windows next to where, 'the kings and queenes statues are,' confirms that the funeral effigies were on display at least well into the 1630s.[23]

The use of an effigy at the funeral of a Queen consort was in line with tradition. The first on record is that of Anne of Bohemia, the first wife of Richard II who died in 1394.[24] Effigies also survive of Katherine de Valois and Elizabeth of York. An account of the funeral procession of the latter describes the effigy lying upon the coffin in the funeral chariot 'clothed in ye very robes of estate of ye quene / having her very ryche crowne on her hed her here about her shoulder / hir scepter in her right hand / and her fyngers well garneshed w^t rynge of golde & pysous stones (& on every ende of ye cofres kneled a gentelman hussher by all the way to Westminster)'.[25] Jane Seymour, unsurprisingly, was the only one of Henry VIII's wives to have a representation carried at her funeral (1537), the

---

[20] Wagner (1978), pl. XV and p. 64; 7; Sandford, p. 64; J. Harris, S. Orgel and R. Strong, p. 99; Foxe-Davis, p. 433.
[21] Gittings, p. 225.
[22] Stanley (1869), p. 183.
[23] Parry (1981), p. 256; Llewellyn, *Royal Body* (1990), p. 228; WA, MS 41770. See my chapters 7 and 8.
[24] Hope, p. 544. The extension of this custom to his late Queen may have been Richard's decision, as he had a well-documented interest in portraiture; see Harvey and Mortimer, p. 37.
[25] CA, I Series XI, cited by Hope, pp. 545–6.

last occasion an effigy had been used for a queen consort before Anne's funeral.[26] Thus a medieval tradition was revived at this Jacobean royal funeral.

The odd juxtaposition between neo-classical hearse and medieval funeral effigy, noted in relation to Prince Henry's obsequies, was tempered on this occasion by increased naturalism in the appearance of Anne's funeral effigy (figure 14).[27] Comparison between the effigy and the royal portrait of Anne of Denmark which hangs in the National Portrait Gallery has revealed that the two representations accord well.[28] This supports the view that Anne's effigy, like earlier royal effigies, was fashioned from a death mask.[29] In addition, some trouble was taken to reproduce facial blemishes on Anne's effigy. A pimple on the left cheek of the wooden head was painstakingly sculpted by carving away the surrounding area. Similarly veins were represented on the face and breast.[30] Such textural details would not be noticed by spectators during the funeral proceedings but would be apparent to the visitors to Westminster Abbey who beheld Anne's effigy lying in its hearse. However, now that a post-funeral display function had been established for the funeral effigies, there was, perhaps, a greater desire to produce accurate portraits of deceased members of the royal family.

The sculptor, Maximilian Colt, had considerable experience in this field, having already carved the tomb effigies of Elizabeth I and Mary Stuart. The Queen Anne effigy shares stylistic features with the Colt tomb effigy of Elizabeth and the bare-breasted figure of Virtue that stands at one corner of the Colt tomb built for the first Earl of Salisbury (1614) at Hatfield.[31]

The clear increased naturalism of Anne's funeral effigy, a trend which was hinted at in Elizabeth's, also fits in with the broad shift of attitude towards the arts described in chapter 5. For some, however, the cultural influence of continental Renaissance and counter-Reformation suggested by Anne's effigy may indeed have triggered suspicions of an insidious Catholic influence at court.

Another aspect of Queen Anne's funeral proceedings may also have smacked of popery to those with a Puritan bent. After the body had been disembowelled the viscera were encased in an urn covered with black and white drapery. They were buried separately on 5th March eight weeks before the funeral, at a location provided by the Dean of Westminster in a little chapel on the left at the top of

---

[26] Hope, pp. 547–8.
[27] On Prince Henry's effigy and hearse, see chapter 8.
[28] Strong ascribes the National Portrait Gallery painting to William Larkin and dates it to c. 1612 because the Queen appears in mourning; see Roy Strong, *The English Icon: Elizabethan and Jacobean Portraiture* (London: Routledge and Kegan Paul, 1969), p. 323. On other portraits of Anne, see Harvey and Mortimer, p. 65.
[29] Howgrave-Graham, p. 168. See also my chapter 5.
[30] *Westminster Abbey*, p. 20.
[31] Harvey and Mortimer, p. 63.

the stairs going into the Henry VII Chapel. The charges for the funeral include an unspecified amount paid to Abraham Greene, 'Serjant Plumber', 'for one greate vessell to putt in the Bowells and inwarde partes wch were sent to Westminster'.[32]

Separate burial of the heart and viscera was, however, not foreign to English tradition. The practice dated back at least to the time of Henry I (d. 1135). Following Henry's death at the castle of Lions or Lihun, Normandy, his body was transported to Rouen where it was roughly disembowelled and embalmed. The corpse was then transported to England and eventually deposited at Reading but the entrails were separately buried at the church of St Mary de Pratis, near Rouen.[33]

Primarily separate burial seems to have arisen out of necessity due to the length of time between the death of a monarch and the funeral. The viscera constituted the main corrupting agent of the corpse and their removal was a key element of the embalming process.[34] The use of a viscera chest and its subsequent, often ritualised deposit permitted the unavoidable mutilation of the royal corpse to be accomplished with dignity.

However pragmatic the beginnings of the custom of separate burial, it seems to have become overlain with religious significance since it facilitated a multiplication of the number of churches associated with the deceased which could house shrines or chantries set up to pray for the soul of the deceased.[35]

The practice of embalming and separate burial of the viscera continued into the Tudor period. Shortly after her death, Mary I 'was opened by her Physicians and Surgeons, who took out her bowels, which were encoffin'd and buried solemnley in the Chappel, the heart being separately enclosed in a coffer with velvet, bound with silver'.[36] Mary's was the last full Catholic royal funeral and it may be significant that subsequently there is no mention of division of the body or multiple burial for any royal until the death of Queen Anne of Denmark. Elizabeth I had felt a horror of embalming and specifically requested that her body would not be opened. The delay before her burial necessitated by the elaborate preparations for her funeral probably made embalming essential but nowhere is there any mention of a separate, ritualized burial of the viscera.[37]

---

32 PRO Lord Chamberlain's Records, Series I. Vol. 556, cited by Hope, p. 556.
33 William of Malmesbury, *Chronicles of the Kings of England*, ed. by J. A. Giles (London: Henry G. Bohn, 1874); Hope, pp. 521–2. On the French royal tradition of multiple burial, see Giesey (1960), p. 20; J. Santiago, 'Les Funerailles Princières en France (Bourgogne et Orléans 1465–1468)' (unpublished thesis, University of Paris, 1981), pp. 40–2, 191; Boureau (1988), pp. 36, 57–9; and Appendix II.
34 Litten, pp. 33–43.
35 White (1978), p. 25. The heart of Arthur, Prince of Wales (d. 1502) was buried at Ludlow while his body lies in Worcester Cathedral. On the religious associations for medieval man, see Litten, p. 33.
36 CA, Briscoe MS II fols 314–15.
37 On the embalming of Elizabeth's body, see Litten, pp. 41–2.

The lack of ceremony may, however, have been in deference to the late Queen's wishes rather than in response to a post-Reformation discomfort with a ritual that suggested popish notions of purgatory and praying for the souls of the dead.

The separate burial of Anne's viscera was essentially, then, a practical consequence of the requisite embalming process but there may have been a recognition that its religious connotations would anger some. The nocturnal timing of the procession to transport Anne's bowels to Westminster suggests an attempt to mute any such resonance: it did not take place until 9.00 p.m. In addition their conveyance was effected by barge, keeping the procession out of the streets. The account-writer states that all was done 'without ceremony'. The barge was met by a small reception committee, headed by Richmond herald bearing his coat of arms on his arm.[38] The viscera were disposed of with dignity but minimal public ritual. In the context of James's reign, however, when so little attention was paid to the religious overtones of ceremony, it seems unlikely that such issues determined the ritual form on this occasion and there is no evidence to suggest that the interment of the viscera was ever attended with great public ceremony.

The separate burial of Queen Anne's viscera seems not, then, to be indicative of a concession to Catholic ritual. The changes to royal funeral ritual effected at the obsequies of Anne's husband, James, would, however, catholicize the royal theatre of death, rendering it barely distinguishable from its French counterpart.

[38] CA, Nayler, pp. 3–4.

CHAPTER TEN

The Funeral of King James I (1625)

The Church Service

The Image of the King: Sermon, Effigy and Hearse

James I died at Theobalds on 27 March 1625.[1] His funeral, which took place just over six weeks later on 17 May, was a highly theatrical affair, a carefully stage-managed synthesis of English and continental cultural influences with potent political intent.

The sermon preached at the obsequies is a useful starting point for an analysis of James's funeral because it equips us, as it did the original congregation, with a series of verbal clues to the visual symbolism constructed from the various cultural influences involved. It is perhaps fitting that the sermon should have played such a central role on this occasion because during the Jacobean period this genre had developed into an art form of which James himself had been particularly fond. The 1604 Canons had stated that sermons could only be preached on the catechism, the creed, the Ten Commandments or the Lord's Prayer. Funeral sermons were, however, exempt from this restriction.[2]

The sheer length of James's funeral address is indicative of its importance in the ritual proceedings; it lasted for two hours, as Prince Henry's had done.[3] The sermon was delivered by John Williams (1585–1650), Bishop of Lincoln and Privy Councillor since 1621. Williams, whose religious allegiances were middle of the road, was an uncontroversial choice. He was a Calvinist in doctrine but combined attendance at the sermons of the Puritan William Perkins with support for the discipline and ceremonies of the Church of England. He was, however, to oppose the Laudian programme of ceremonial change. Williams was, nevertheless, the epitome of Jacobean moderation and not a Presbyterian

---

[1] Theobalds was Lord Burghley's great house which had been presented to the Crown in 1607. James was having a banqueting house constructed on the site at the time of his death; see Harvey and Mortimer, p. 70.

[2] Babbage, p. 94; McClure, II, p. 616; Parry (1981), pp. 230–1; and my chapter 2. The Arminians disliked excessive preaching and attempted to suppress lectureships, emphasizing the sacraments instead; Tyacke, p. 186.

[3] CSPV, XII (1610–13), 486.

revolutionary. The ceremonies that Laud was advocating were arguably against the law.[4]

Given Williams's religious persuasions it is interesting that the concept at the heart of his sermon was the image of the king, indicating the extent to which image-making had been rehabilitated by the official church. The sermon was entitled *Great Britain's Solomon* and celebrated James as a reincarnation of the Old Testament King. Solomon had received a solemn funeral in Jerusalem but Williams declares, in a comment which acknowledges the controversial status of images, 'hee had no Statue at all caried before him. That was peradventure scarce tolerable among the Jewes.' James, argued the Bishop, would provide a statue for Solomon and 'Solomon shall then arise in King James his Vertues.' Thus Williams characterized James as a modern monarch in whom Old Testament virtue was reborn.[5]

The association between James and Solomon had been signalled at the very beginning of the reign. In the midst of his lament for Elizabeth, during the sermon he preached at Paul's Cross on 27 March 1603, John Hayward looked forward to her successor: 'as *Salomon* succeeding *David* (unto which two in Isreal I compare these two in England for wisedome, pietye, and love to Gods house) we have and shall have [. . .] the heigh and mighty, King *James*'.[6] By the time of James's death, the association had become routine. Those who attended James's body at Denmark House in the days before the funeral procession, had already witnessed a sermon on a text from the Song of Solomon, 'Behold King Solomon Crowned' (3.11) preached by John Donne on 26 April 1625.[7] In this sermon Donne used the corpse of the King as a paradigm of mortality to set against the immortality of Christ, signified textually in the name and person of Solomon. The polarity of Solomon and the King in Donne's argument contrasts with Williams's technique of fashioning James as an image of Solomon.

A physical representation of the statue of James as Solomon was present in the Abbey during the funeral in the form of the 'lively image and repraesentation [. . . that did] decke and adorn these present Funerals'. This 'lively image' was the funeral effigy lying now in the hearse at the centre of the choir (figure 22).[8] The identification with Solomon is part of James's personal royal image. The emphasis in Williams's sermon is all on the effigy as a representation of James the individual monarch with no reference to it representing the general

---

[4] Tyacke, pp. 209–10; Sommerville, pp. 220–1; Lockyer, p. 311.
[5] John Williams, *Great Britain's Salomon: A Sermon Preached at the Magnificent Funerall of the most high and mighty King, James* ([London (?)]: J. Bill, 1625), pp. 7–8; Peacock, p. 3.
[6] Hayward, p. 133. For other characterizations of James as Solomon in sermons, dedicatory epistles, poems and iconography throughout the reign, see Parry (1981), pp. 29–31, 231–2; Smuts, p. 25.
[7] Evelyn M. Simpson and George R. Potter, eds, *The Sermons of John Donne*, 10 vols (Berkley: University of California Press, 1953–62), VI (1953), 280–91.
[8] *Westminster Abbey*, p. 17. The effigy wore Parliamentary robes as James does in Paul van Somer's portrait.

The Funeral of King James I

Majesty of Kingship. The Gloriana-Majesty duality of Elizabeth's funeral effigy has been replaced.[9]

The sermon delivered by Archbishop Abbot at the funeral of Prince Henry Stuart thirteen years previously had similarly used the effigy as a prop but in a much less sophisticated fashion. Dr Abbot's text was taken from Psalms 82.6–7: 'I have said, Ye *are* gods; and all of you *are* children of the most High: But ye shall die like men, and fall like one of the princes.' The Archbishop, 'for ocular proofe and use of all', invited the congregation to cast 'their eyes to the present dolefull spectacle of their late ever-renowned Prince, who not long ago was as fresh, brave, and gallant as the best of them [. . .] who yet now for our sinnes lay thus low, bereaved of life and all being, was forced to prove the truth of this text, not onely to fall, but to fall as others'.[10]

Despite the pivotal role of the effigy in James's funeral sermon, it was the hearse, not the effigy, that caught the attention of most observers (figure 21). The impact of James's hearse was registered by the Venetian ambassador, Zuane Pesaro, who says that it was 'much esteemed for its architecture and decoration'. Chamberlain likewise commented that the hearse was the 'fairest and best fashioned that heth ben seen'.[11] Like that of Queen Anne, it was painted by John de Critz, Serjeant Painter to the King and this time it was definitely Inigo Jones, Surveyor for the royal household's Office of Works since 1615, who provided the design.[12] If his ideas on funeral architecture had been blocked at the time of Queen Anne's death, now he was given free reign to display his unrivalled knowledge of Italian Renaissance architecture and fortunately, Jones's drawings for the hearse of James I survive.[13]

The hearse design shows the influence of the cultural eclecticism of the Stuart court in the mid-1620s, drawing on Biblical, pagan and Catholic precedents in the fashioning of an architectural setting for James's funeral image. Jones based his design, octagonal in concept, on Bramante's *Tempettio*, commemorating the martyrdom of St Peter, but also looked back to the antique architecture which had inspired Bramante.[14] The base on which the catafalque stands and the three

---

[9] It may be that the shift towards naturalism in effigy production noted in chapters 5 and 9 contributed to this narrowing of the effigy's symbolic function.

[10] Nichols (1828), II, 502.

[11] CSPV, XIX (1625–6), 55; McClure, II, 614. This seems to have been Chamberlain's stock comment on hearses; see chapter 9.

[12] Harris and Higgott, p. 187.

[13] Parry (1981), pp. 77–8; Smuts, p. 125; Colvin, p. 309; Nichols (1828), IV, 1048; Harvey and Mortimer, p. 71. The drawings for the hearse are held at Worcester College, Oxford. It seems that the design was altered slightly in execution; see Whinney, p. 86.

[14] Jones may also have based his design for the domes of St George's Palace, in the *Barriers* and Oberon's palace on Bramante's *Tempettio*. It had frequently been illustrated in architectural handbooks including the *Archittetura* of Sebastiano Serlio (1475–1553?); see Orgel and Strong, pp. 214–17. Serlio's work was a major popularizer of Roman and modern Italian architecture in Europe; see David Thomson, *Renaissance Architecture: Critics, Patrons, Luxury* (Manchester: Manchester University Press, 1993), pp. 118–19.

steps leading up to it recall the Temple of Vesta at Tivoli, illustrated in the fourth book of Palladio's *Architettura* and visited by Jones during his second tour of Italy in 1613–14.[15] Jones was also working with a more recent tradition of funerary architecture and in particular echoes the catafalque designed by Domenico Fontana for the obsequies of Pope Sixtus V (1591), although he re-classicizes the design replacing its enriched order with the plain Doric order of Bramante. The Catholic Fontana design is modified into one which was both Protestant and monarchic, incorporating twelve statues of female figures standing on short pillars. Four of these figures Williams identifies in the sermon as representing Religion, Justice, War and Peace.[16] The statues were the work of the French sculptor, Henry Le Sueur, who came to London in 1625, and was the first sculptor with first-hand knowledge of Renaissance Italy to arrive in England.

While working on the design of the catafalque, Jones probably had access to Lelio Guidicioni's funeral book for Paul V and is likely to have been familiar with Antoine Canqué's translation of Xiphilinus in which he could have read the description of the catafalque constructed for the funeral of Pertinax.[17] In the realm of continental funeral ceremony the connection between classical obsequies and those of contemporary rulers had been made long before 1625. Several Renaissance treatises on ancient funeral rites appeared during the sixteenth century. Examples include L. G. Giraldi's *De Sepulchris et vario sepeliendi ritu, libellus* (Basel, 1539); T. Porcacchi's *Funerali Antichi di Diversi popli et nationi* (Venice, 1574); and C. Guichard's *Funerailles & diverses maniers d'ensevelir des Romains, Grecs, & autres nations* (Lyons, 1581). In 1567 the French expert on court ceremonial, Jean Du Tillet, attempted to establish a Roman origin for the French effigy lying-in-state ritual based on translations of Herodian. The latter included descriptions of the imperial funeral effigy which was treated as if it were still alive but sickening day by day until it was finally pronounced dead.[18] A similar preoccupation with classical precedent is revealed in the printed account of Cosimo I's funeral in Florence in 1574 when the catafalque is compared to the pyramid of Cestius.[19]

The connection does not seem to have been made in England, however, until James's reign. Henry Savile, in his translation of Tacitus's *Histories* (1622), commented that the obsequies of Charles IX resembled those of a Roman

---

Serlio was published in England as *The [. . .] Booke of Architecture* (1611) in a translation by Robert Peake.

[15] Peacock, p. 1; Harris and Higgott, pp. 53, 62.

[16] Peacock, pp. 2–3; Harris and Higgott, p. 187. It is worth recalling that the tombs for Mary and Elizabeth had no secondary statues; see chapter 7.

[17] Peacock, p. 4.

[18] The French translations of Herodian appeared in 1541. See Giesey (1960), pp. 147, 169–70.

[19] *Descritione della Pompa funerale Fatta nelle Essequie del Ser. ^{mo} Sig. Cosimo Gran Duca de Medici Gran duca di Toscana* (Florence, 1574), sig. Eii^r, cited by Peacock, p. 3.

emperor.[20] Then, commenting on James's funeral procession, the Venetian ambassador, Pesaro, remarked, rather confusedly, that the Bishops wore rochets and the choristers wore surplices 'after the ancient Roman fashion'![21]

In James's funeral service, the influence of classicism was apparent in the sermon. John Williams drew a parallel between the current obsequies and the posthumous celebration that Hadrian gave in honour of Trajan:

> After his death he triumphed openly in the Cittie of Rome, In Image, in a Lively Statue, or Repraesentation invented by Adrian for that purpose: soe shall this Salomon of Israel doe at this time in the Statue, and Repraesentation of our British Salomon. Truly me thinkes (Si nunquam fallit imago) the remembrance is very lively.[22]

James, like Solomon, will have an effigy to function as a public memorial perpetuating the glory of the defunct King. Yet Williams's words contain an equivocation and hint at the startling new direction the image symbolism will take at the climax of the sermon.

> For God hath provided another Statue yet to adorne the Exequies of our late Soveraigne. I doe not meane this Artificiall Representation within the Hearse, for this shews no more than his outward Body, or rather the Bodie of His Bodie, his Cloathes and Ornaments. But I meane that Statue which [...] walk't on foot this day after the Hearse, one of Myrons Statues, Qui paene Hominu[m] animas effinxerit, which came so neare to the Soules of Men, A breathing Statue of all his Vertues. This God hath done for Him, or rather for Us. For he hath made a lively Repraesentation of the Vertues of Salomon, in the person of King James: so he hath done a like Repraesentation of the Vertues of King James, in the person of King Charles Our Gratious Soveraigne.[23]

In this fascinating statement Williams at once deconstructs the funeral effigy and infuses the image symbolism with striking new significance. He openly comments on the artificiality of the effigy and even exposes the superficiality of the trappings of royalty. Robes, crown, orb and sceptre, the symbols of divine Majesty, are dismissed as mere 'clothes and ornaments'. There is no attempt here to suggest that any part of King James mystically lives on in the effigy. Attention is switched from the man-made statue to the living 'statue' of Charles who, as chief mourner, was seated at the head of the catafalque.[24] The charisma attached to the effigy is prematurely returned to the living monarch. Although perhaps not visible to the majority of the congregation now, all had seen Charles in the funeral procession, where he followed the chariot and effigy in his capacity as chief mourner. In a moment, at the close of the sermon, Charles

---

[20] Henry Savile, *The Ende of Nero and Beginning of Galba, Fower bookes of the histories of Cornelius Tacitus* ([London?]: [n. pub.], 1591; 5th edn, 1622), p. 4, cited by Peacock, p. 3.

[21] CSPV, XIX, (1625–6), 55.

[22] Williams (1625), p. 36.

[23] Williams (1625), pp. 75–6.

[24] For a list of the chairs and stools provided for Charles and the other mourners, see Nichols (1828), IV, 1035.

would take part in the performance of the offering ritual, receiving the hatchments of his father in a ritual enactment of the succession process. The shift of attention away from the effigy to the living monarch enacted the greater mystery of hereditary kingship which became infused with the ambiguity that was at the heart of the creation and display of power in the traditional funeral ritual. The features of the old King are reborn in those of the new. Charles is the living image or 'statue' of his father. Here indeed, 'art', as Henry Wotton had said of the statues which lined the high ways of ancient Athens and Rome, 'was a piece of state'.[25]

The Offering Ritual: the Adaptation of Royal Funeral Ritual to Divine Right Kingship

As we have seen, in England, as well as France, it was traditional for the new monarch not to display his royal person in public until after the funeral of his predecessor, not even to attend his obsequies.[26] At James's funeral the succeeding monarch was, for the first time, the protagonist in the offering ceremony at the heart of the church service.

> For the Kings Matie being principall Mourner with his Supporters assistants and traynebearers [. . .] did proceed to the Altar to offer for the defuncte and havenge offered his Matie did returne to his Chayre and after a little stay there his Matie did goe up agayne/ with Garter and the rest of the officers of Armes, his gentlemen ushers and his two supporters, no Trayne borne but the two Gentlemen of his bedchamber did followe behind him to lift it sometimes for ease and so did go up to the high altar and his Matie did offer for himselfe and havinge offered did there stay to receyve the hatchments where there was a chayre provided for his Matie when he should please to sytt [. . .] Theis things being done his Matie returned to his place at the upper end of the Hearse agayne and there rested till all the Lords had offered.[27]

The impact of the offering ceremonies must have been felt by all. Pesaro, for one, highlights the presentation of the banners in his description of the funeral ceremony and also identifies the catafalque as the centre of these ritual proceedings.[28] The classical Roman setting of the hearse transposed the offering ceremony, a ritual form that had long outlived its medieval chivalric origins, refashioning it in the context of the Jacobean Roman-chivalric revival.

The model for the revised offering form at the funeral of James had long been practised at the heraldic funerals of the aristocracy. The offering procedure

---

[25] Wotton, p. 106.
[26] See chapters 3 and 5.
[27] CA, Nayler, pp. 55–6. The use of 'altar' in this account of James's funeral and in BL, Lansdowne MS 885 fol. 124, indicates how much the term had been re-legitimized by the Arminian influence in the Church of England. The altar rail was destroyed in 1643 by Cromwellian soldiers; see W. R. Lethaby, *Westminster Abbey Re-Examined* (London: Duckworth, 1925), p. 258.
[28] CSPV, XIX (1625–6), 55.

closely parallels that of the Derby funeral, described in chapter 1, even down to the marking of the change in roles by an alteration in the King's escort. When Charles approaches the altar to offer on behalf of his dead father, his train is borne by two assistants. When he goes up again, in his own capacity, his train is not borne. It is as if Charles was not due the respect of a king until he had received the hatchments. Yet the achievements, as was pointed out earlier, appertained to the private person of his father, not to the public office of kingship. The offering ceremony of the aristocratic heraldic funeral enacted a legal inheritance that would not have been appropriate to a royal funeral in the later Middle Ages. Although hereditary succession was firmly established under the Tudors, the particular circumstances of their successions (the minority of Edward VI and the gender of Mary and Elizabeth) meant that it was not until the accession of Charles I that there was another dynastic succession of an adult male heir – the first for more than a century. The hybrid succession/offering ceremony seems to reflect the Stuart desire to build a dynastic monarchy with the ceremonial changes consciously being made so that the offering ritual would enact the hereditary succession to the throne.

Support for this interpretation of the modified offering ritual comes from the lack of a separate succession ritual at James's interment. At earlier royal funerals, the heralds had ritually confirmed the succession at the interment. At the funeral of Henry VII this ritual included a small-scale French-style symbolic lowering and raising of heraldic objects.[29] On this occasion, 'all the heraudes did off their cote armour and did hange them upon the rayles of the herse, crynge lamentably in French, "the noble King Henry is deade", and as soon as they had so done, evere heraude putt on his cote armure againe and cried with a loud voyce, "Vive le noble Henry le viijth".'[30] The repeated cries and manipulation of the insignia were omitted from subsequent English royal funerals with Garter King at Arms simply proclaiming the succession. At the close of the funeral service for Mary Tudor, just before the interment, Garter called in a loud voice, 'Pray for the soul of the most Puissant and Excellent Princess, Mary by the Grace of God, late Queen of England', giving her titles in full and then proceeded to 'declare the state of the Queen present'.[31] The symbolic enactment of the royal succession in the offering ceremony at James's funeral rendered these interment succession rituals and proclamations superfluous and they did not take place.

The new ritual brought royal funeral ceremony into harmony with early Stuart concepts of divine right kingship.[32] As we saw in the discussion of Elizabeth's funeral, the royal effigy ritual that had formed the symbolic centre

[29] Chapter 3.
[30] BL, MS 4712–18 v. 4. 309, cited by Dallaway, p. 140. The manipulation of the coats of arms is not mentioned in Briscoe. On the symbolism of the elevation of banners and emblems at French royal funerals, see Giesey (1960), pp. 132–9.
[31] Nichols (1848), p. 183. For Edward VI, see CA, Briscoe MS II fol. 314.
[32] See chapter 6.

of earlier royal funerals was incompatible with these ideas. Yet James's absence from England at the time of Elizabeth's death and, more importantly, his need to demonstrate the legality of his lineal succession, in the face of anticipated contention and civil unrest, determined that he would nevertheless accord his predecessor all the expected funeral rites. Neither of these constraints applied to Charles: he was free to modify the funeral ritual and bring it into line with Stuart political ideology. This explains the loss of the traditional emphasis on the effigy as representative of a general Majesty of Kingship noted in the sermon. Charles did not need the funeral effigy to fill a ceremonial interregnum and used it rather to enact a dynastic succession. Thus the effigy represented James as an individual Stuart king.

The seventeenth-century theory of the divine right of kings presupposed a sovereign who had a personal and an individual right, derived directly from God, to his throne. Some proponents of the theory attached the right to the office of kingship, instead of the personal claim of the individual king, rather in the manner of Plowden and his counterparts whose arguments had supported the legitimacy of the Tudor claim to the throne. Others, however, identified an hereditary component in the theory and equated it with the private right to succession of land under feudal law, enacted in the heraldic funeral ritual. It was the latter group that found favour with James and Charles as the Stuart claim was based on hereditary kingship. James, in his exposition of the divine right of kings, insisted that the right attaches to the person of the king, not merely to the office.[33]

The concept of hereditary right was not unanimously accepted by royalists until after the death of Charles I. It was essentially a Scottish concept, based on Roman law, and conflicted with English common law.[34] The new offering ritual at James's funeral could have been a part of a propaganda campaign in favour of the hereditary component of divine right kingship.[35]

Who was behind this deliberate re-shaping of the offering ritual at the funeral of James I? It was usually the Privy Council, with advice from the College of Arms, that organized royal funerals. The Privy Council was sworn in under the new King on 28 March, the day after James's death.[36] On the same day Charles appointed a Commission to take charge of the funeral proceedings. This comprised James Ley, Earl of Marlborough, the Lord Treasurer; Henry Montagu, Earl of Manchester, the Lord President; John Williams, the Bishop of Lincoln, the Lord Privy Seal; the Duke of Buckingham; Thomas Howard, the Earl of Arundel and Earl Marshal since 1622; William Herbert, the Earl of Pembroke, the Lord Chamberlain; and the Earl of Montgomery.[37] Williams,

---

[33] Lee (1990), p. 65; Lockyer, p. 253; Sommerville, p. 23.
[34] McIlwain, pp. xxxiii–xxxvi.
[35] Sommerville, p. 45.
[36] CSPD, I (1625–6), 1.
[37] Acts of the Privy Council (1625–6), p. 7; Dallaway, Appendix 49. Until 1621 there had

Montagu and Howard were all well-qualified to contribute to the fashioning of James's funeral occasion. If we are to believe Pesaro, however, it was not these men but King Charles who took the decision to participate in the funeral himself. Pesaro reports, 'it was doubtful whether his Majesty would take part personally [. . .] Difficulties arose, but finally the King decided to pay this last tribute of respect to his father's memory in person' and further remarks that 'since William the Conqueror the King had only thrice been present at funeral celebrations'.[38] The conscious break with ritual precedent seems then to have come from the top. This is another case of the deliberate adjustment of ritual performance to suit the demands of a particular performance situation and also illustrates Charles's personal role in shaping court culture.

As Prince of Wales, Charles had participated in the funeral of his mother, Queen Anne. There gender had precluded him from enacting the role of chief mourner but he had, in accordance with heraldic practice, received the banners in the offering ceremony.[39] Charles may also have received the hatchments at the funeral of his royal brother, Prince Henry.[40] Perhaps personal familiarity with the role prompted Charles to take it once again in the new context of the funeral of a reigning monarch.

In making this extraordinary break with traditional practice, Charles might have been influenced by the changes in funeral practice evident in the nocturnal funerals that were becoming increasingly fashionable with the aristocracy. As Gittings has convincingly argued, part of the attraction of nocturnal funerals lay in their freedom from the heraldic regulations involving age, gender and rank that restricted the choice of chief and assistant mourners.[41] At a nocturnal funeral a wife, for example, could act as chief mourner for her husband and vice versa. Another encouragement to change might have been provided by the presence at court of large numbers of Scottish nobles who did not come under the jurisdiction of the College of Arms and were free to choose the form of their funerals.[42]

The idea of placing the monarch at the centre of the funeral performance may also have owed something to the masque tradition, itself a reflection of divine right kingship, in which the monarch provided the focal point of the

---

only ever been one clerical member of the Privy Council, the Archbishop of Canterbury, but John Williams combined his duties as Lord Keeper with the bishopric of Lincoln; see Lockyer, p. 259. Interestingly, Henry Montagu had a particular interest in the antiquity of festivals and consulted Cotton when drafting a paper on the subject; see Sharpe (1979), p. 35.

[38] CSPV, XIX (1625–6), pp. 53, 55.
[39] Nichols (1828), III, 542.
[40] See chapter 8.
[41] Gittings, pp. 175, 195–7; and my chapter 7.
[42] Gittings, p. 183. For the nocturnal funeral journey of the Marquis of Hamilton whose corpse was conveyed from London by torchlight before being taken all the way to Scotland, see McClure, II, 604.

proceedings. The verbal trick which transforms the visual image of Charles into the image of his father is reminiscent of the *trompe l'oeil* of the court masque. In his funeral sermon, Williams builds on the Mannerist fascination with *trompe l'oeil* and the physiognomy of the great.[43] Certainly the masque techniques of intermingling verbal and visual content are paralleled in Williams's sermon. He offers, 'unto your thoughts, not only a statue of King Solomon, but withall, as the Graecians did in their Hercules, and Xenophon in his Cyrus, an Idea or Representation of all the perfections required in a King'.[44] John Peacock similarly argues that the interaction of sermon and hearse constituted a synthesis of form and motif that paralleled court masques.[45] Taken together all four components of the funeral service, hearse, sermon, effigy and offering ritual, operated in a composite discourse of performance which demonstrated the royal succession in the context of divine right kingship.[46]

Finally, the form and content of James's funeral service surely owed a great deal to the re-legitimization of the image and the re-ceremonialization of religion described in chapter 6. The concepts of both 'image' and 'ritual' had attained a degree of acceptance that meant even the moderate Calvinist Bishop John Williams was happy for them to be the pivots of his funeral sermon.

An Alternative Solution: Funerals, Lits de Justice *and Absolutism in France (1563–1610)*

The French monarchists similarly revised their programme of royal ceremonial in the late sixteenth century to bring it in line with their more absolutist version of divine right kingship. The process began during the reign of the weak and youthful Charles IX.[47] At the majority *lit de justice*, held in the Parlement of Rouen in 1563, rhetoric and rituals of homage were used to affirm the authority of the King.[48] The reformist Chancellor, Michel de l'Hôpital, enlisted juristic arguments to affirm the validity and authority of royal edicts passed during the early years of Charles's reign, when he had been a minor. He reformulated the medieval adage, recently re-expressed in Jean Bodin's 'le roi ne meurt jamais', inventing his own phrase to stress the continuity of the monarchy: 'le royaume

---

[43] Strong (1986), p. 194.
[44] Williams (1625), p. 66. One is reminded of Jonson's representation of James as both man and statue in *The Barriers*; see Goldberg. p. 40.
[45] Peacock, p. 4.
[46] On Jones's belief in the political functions of his masque and building designs, see Smuts, pp. 168, 290.
[47] Jennifer Woodward, 'The Theatre of Death: Politics, Ritual and Ideology in the Royal Funeral of Charles IX' (unpublished master's thesis, University of Warwick, 1992); and ibid., 'Funeral Rituals in the French Renaissance', *Renaissance Studies*, 9 (1995), part 4, 385–94.
[48] A *lit de justice* was the personal attendance of the king in Parlement, usually to enforce registration of an edict; see Salmon (1975), p. 348. It differed from a *séance*, or honorary visit of the king; see Hanley, p. 209.

n'est jamais vacant'. Applied to the royal funeral ceremonial, his remarks exposed the fictive nature of the ceremonial interregnum filled by the effigy, which never had and certainly now did not have any basis in law.[49]

In line with his subversion of the royal funeral symbolism, L'Hôpital made a case for establishing the majority *lit de justice* as the dominant succession ritual. Disruptive behaviour by the French Parlement at the funeral feast of Charles IX and the disputes over precedence in the procession would affirm L'Hôpital's conviction that the whole matrix of royal ceremonial needed revision. He sought to promote the ethos of absolute hereditary kingship which would become the dominant philosophy of the late Valois and early Bourbon kings. This philosophy required the display of the new monarch's royal person in a ritual act of power as soon after his accession as possible, overriding the delay in public display determined by the non-appearance of the successor at the funeral ceremony. The *lit de justice* was the French monarchists' answer to this need. Louis XIII appeared in a 'succession' or inaugural *lit de justice* the day after the news of Henry IV's assassination, and a good two weeks before his burial.[50] Marie de Medici thus ensured that her son's status as king was ritually affirmed before the funeral of his father took place. The ceremonial interregnum was lost and the effigy ritual deprived of symbolic significance. Where Charles IX's effigy had lain in state, served as if it were the King still alive, for forty days, the effigy of Henry IV was to be so displayed for a meagre seven days.[51] After Henry IV's funeral, the French abandoned the effigy ritual altogether.[52]

Although French absolutism went considerably further than English divine right kingship, the monarchies of the two countries were moving in the same direction and both placed increasing emphasis on the hereditary component of the Crown. Further, both countries recognized that the traditional funeral

---

[49] See my chapter 3. Note the similarity between l'Hôpital's pronouncements and James's theories of instantaneous succession, and see my chapter 5.

[50] Winwood, III, 158. The young Louis would also appear in the 'sleeping king' ritual at the beginning of the coronation proceedings. This ritual was unique to the coronations of Louis XIII (1610) and Charles IX (1561) and underlined the principle of hereditary succession by emphasizing the personal resemblance between these kings and their fathers. See Richard A. Jackson, *Vive le Roi! A History of the French Coronation from Charles V to Charles X* (London: University of North Carolina Press, 1984), pp. 131–53; and Woodward, pp. 71–4.

[51] For Charles IX's funeral, see Appendix II and Simon Goulart, *Mémoirs de l'Estat de France Sous Charles Neufiesme*, 2nd edn, 3 vols (Paris: [n. pub.], 1577), pp. 375–7; Bibliothèque Nationale, Manuscrits français 18536 fols 72–5. For Henry IV, see *L'Ordre de la Pompe Funebre Observee au Convoy et Funerailles du [. . .] Henry le Grand, Roy de France et de Navarre* (Lyon: Claude Morillon, 1610); *The Funeral Pompe and Obsequies of the most mighty and puissant Henry the fourth [. . .] solemnized at Paris and at St. Denis* (London: [n. pub.], 1610).

[52] Giesey (1960), p. 180. Benkard (p. 24) states that the last effigy made was for Louis XIII (1643). It was not used in the funeral ceremony.

ritual, with its ceremonial interregnum filled by the funeral effigy and non-appearance of the new king, did not best serve their philosophical positions. Each, however, found a different solution to the problem. Where the English modified the funeral offering ritual so that it enacted hereditary succession, the French promoted a new ritual, the *lit de justice*, to answer the needs of hereditary absolutism.

The Lying-in-State Ritual

I have demonstrated the way in which the changing attitude towards 'images' influenced the church service but it was in the lying-in-state that the full impact of this change was manifested. The casting of King Charles in the central role of chief mourner was not the only striking break with tradition in the funeral rituals of James I.

After James's death, his corpse was disembowelled and the viscera enclosed in a leaden vessel which was buried separately, following the procedure used at Anne's funeral. The coffin was richly hatched with gold and a Latin inscription placed upon the breast.[53] A few days later James's embalmed and encoffined body was transported from Theobalds to Denmark House. The procession which attended the body was in 'such manner as they do when the King removes'. On arrival at Denmark House the coffin was placed on a 'specially prepared frame of board like a large bed' in the Privy Chamber. The bed or hearse was covered with forty ells of fine Holland and sixty-nine ells of black velvet and had a canopy above.[54] The chamber itself was hung with black velvet decorated with escutcheons wrought upon cloth of gold.

Manuscript sources indicate that these elaborate preparations were made for the display of an effigy:

> Immediately a representation of his Matie was layd upon the said Pall over ye body in his robes of Estate and Royall Diademe and so it contynewed until the funerall. All Kinge James his Servants removynge from Whyte-hall to Denmarke House and King Charles his Servants from St. James to Whyte-hall. The Service contynewed in all poyntes as if his Maite had byn lyvinge.[55]

The Venetian Ambassador's report confirms that the effigy was served as if it had been living and indicates further that the public were aware that this ritual was taking place. Pesaro says, 'After arranging the house where the remains of the late king are laid, they put life-like figures there, and they observe the customary vigil, thirty to forty noblemen and cavaliers being always present day and night.'[56] Similarly, in a manuscript account held at the Bodleian, it is

[53] Nichols (1828), IV, 1037.
[54] According to Peacock (p. 2 n. 12) Jones may have designed a different, more old-fashioned catafalque for the lying-in-state at Denmark House.
[55] CA, Nayler, p. 28.
[56] CSPV, XIX (1625–6), 19–20.

recorded that, 'when the body is reported here at Whitehall [sic], all the officers are to attend and the state of the house [is] to be kept as in the kinges life tyme'.[57]

On the occasion of James's death, for the first time in English history the funeral effigy took the place of the coffin in the lying-in-state ritual, as it had done in France at the funeral of Francis I (1547).[58] As demonstrated elsewhere, there was no question of imitating the French-style effigy-centred ritual at the funeral of Elizabeth I in 1603, although it was known. The shift in religious and cultural climate during James's reign was considerable and, at court at least, religious images and ceremony were being rehabilitated. These changes facilitated the eventual adoption of the French ritual form on the occasion of James's funeral. It is not clear who was behind this modification in the ritual programme, although it is logical to attribute it to Charles, instigator of the other significant adaptations of ritual at his father's funeral. Certainly, his willing support of the effigy ritual is indicated by his removal to Whitehall to facilitate the continuation of the late King's household at Denmark House.[59]

The Funeral of Ludovick Stuart, Duke of Richmond and Lennox (1624)
Whoever was responsible for the adoption of the French-style effigy ritual, he would almost certainly have been witness to a recent English precedent. Ludovick Stuart, son of the King's cousin, Esmé Stuart, had died suddenly on 16 February 1624. Prince Charles probably attended the Lennox funeral himself, while Arundel and Pembroke, both members of the Commission appointed to take charge of the arrangements for James's funeral, were mourners.

Ludovick Stuart's funeral did not take place until 19 April 1624. Meanwhile, as Chamberlain reports, 'there hath ben a herse, with his statue on a bed of state above these six weekes at Hatton House, where there hath ben great concourse of all sorts'. When the funeral procession finally took place, it was 'performed with great charge [...] for there were about a thousand mourners one and other, besides sixe or eight horse all covered with velvet, and his picture or figure drawne in a coach by six horses clad in like manner, and his herse at Westminster (that stands yet)'. The hearse remained in Westminster Abbey at least until 30 April and the Duke's widow went on to erect a tomb in the Henry VII chapel, the royal necropolis.[60]

---

57 Bod., Ashmole MS 818 fol. 51.
58 See my chapter 3. The English would never, however, adopt the French custom of switching the effigy with the encoffined body and transforming the *salle d'honneur* into a *salle de deuil*; see Appendix II.
59 Bod., Ashmole MS, 818 fol. 51. The Countess of Bedford misinterpreted the continuation of the late King's household as indicative of Charles's decision to keep his own servants and dismiss his father's. She commented, 'itt is thought he will imploye his owne and dismisse his father's, because he hath caused the latter to be removed to Denmark House to attend the body, and lodged the former about himselfe at Whitehall'. See Walter Scott, ed., *A Collection of Scarce and Valuable Tracts*, p. 231, cited by Bland, p. 46.
60 DNB; McClure, II, 551 n. 449, 554.

As I have indicated, the distinctive use of the effigy at James's funeral owed a great deal to the changed cultural climate of the mid-1620s. The same was of course true for the Lennox funeral, but other more specific motives must have lain behind its use, particularly in the context of this unprecedentedly elaborate non-royal funeral.

Practical reasons have been postulated. Lennox's body had been buried hastily either because the embalmers were unable to preserve it or because his widow had vetoed the embalming process altogether. Frances Stuart, the Duchess of Richmond and Lennox, had a horror of embalming which she precluded for her own body in her will, proved in 1639. It is certainly true that Lennox's corpse was buried the night after his death, 'necessity not permitting to defer his burying, he was carried by his own servants, and accompanied with a great number of servants and gentlemen unto the Abbey Church of Westminster' where the service was taken by the Bishop of Lincoln.[61] Yet the fact that Lennox's corpse had already been buried does not in itself provide an explanation for an effigy being used at the funeral, and certainly not for why it was felt necessary or appropriate for the effigy to lie in state. Earlier 'bodiless' funerals had occurred, a recent example being that of Bishop Richard Parry (1623) whose body was similarly buried before his funeral.[62] On such occasions an empty coffin was used in the funeral, perhaps with a coronet, or, as in the case of Mary Queen of Scots, a crown 'representing' the deceased. Gittings nevertheless suggests that an effigy was used because Lennox's body was not available and cites the example of Gilbert, Earl of Shropshire (1616) as a parallel instance. At the Gilbert funeral, however, I suggest the account writer was probably using the term 'representation' to refer to a coronet borne on the coffin to 'represent' the defunct. The term 'representation' was adopted from the French in c.1325 and in French it could simply refer to a coat of arms or crown, rather than an effigy. The manuscript mentions only 'the representation borne by six gentlemen' and makes no direct reference to an effigy.[63] Pragmatism cannot, then, explain the decision to use an effigy at Lennox's funeral, and reasons must be sought elsewhere.

Bishop Williams preached the sermon on this occasion, too, and the text chosen gives us a hint as to why Lennox might have been accorded such exaggerated ceremony at his funeral: 'And Zabud the son of Nathan was principal officer and the King's friend' (I Kings 4.5). Lennox had long been a favourite of James. As a boy he had borne the crown in the 1584 opening of the

---

[61] The procession and hearse both exceeded Queen Anne's in splendour. See CA, I Series MS IV fols 16–29; McClure, II, 554; and Gittings, p. 167.

[62] BL, Harley MS 2129 fol. 89.

[63] BL, Harley MS 1368 fol. 35; Gittings, pp. 167–8. The OED does not give any examples of 'representation' referring to heraldic symbols on the coffin, giving only its effigial meaning in the funeral context, but the meaning 'to express or denote by means of a figure or symbol' was current from 1526; see also chapter 4.

Scottish parliament. He joined the Privy Council in 1603 immediately after James's accession and became a Gentleman of the Bedchamber. In 1614 he was made deputy Earl Marshal. A final measure of Lennox's high status can be inferred from the fact that his death caused the deferral of the opening of Parliament which should have taken place on the very same day.

James's high regard for Lennox may have been a contributory factor in determining the exalted obsequies that he received. The impetus seems, however, to have come from the Duchess. Chamberlain commented, 'all things are like to be performed with more solemnitie and ado than needed: but that yt so pleaseth her Grace to honor the memorie of so deare a husband, whose losse she takes so impatiently and with so much show of passion'.[64]

Why should the Duchess of Lennox have adopted the French style ritual, with the effigy lying-in-state, for the funeral of her husband?[65] Lennox's father, Esmé Stuart, had spent a considerable time at the court of Henry III. He brought a knowledge of French court culture with him when he returned to Scotland in 1579 and helped to shape James's court on French lines. On a visit in 1601 Sir Henry Wotton commented that James's court was 'governed more in the French than in the English fashion'.[66] Lennox himself also spent some time at the French court, although not at the time of a French royal funeral. His father died when they were together in Paris in 1583. Lennox then returned to Scotland but was to be in France once more as ambassador in 1601 and again in 1604–5. His brother Lord Aubigny, together with his friends Hay and Ramsey, all of whom had spent time at the French court, also fostered the French influence at the English court. Although a strong supporter of the King's ecclesiastical policy in Scotland, Lennox seems to have had some Catholic sympathies, opposing, for example, a commission for executing laws against papists and Jesuits in Scotland in 1588.[67] Family sympathies with Catholicism as well as with France may have been responsible for the Duchess's decision to honour her husband's funerals in the French style.

The Duchess may also have been planning an on-going dynastic memorial to her family. At the time of her own demise a wax effigy would be made in her image. Certainly her daughter, also Frances Stuart, was very clear about her personal desire for an effigy. On nearing her death in 1702 she added a codicil to her will ordering her executors to have one made. Her effigy was not of the supine type but an upright figure designed to be set up in Westminster Abbey and still on display in the Undercroft Museum today.[68]

---

[64] McClure, II, 551 n. 449.
[65] The use of an effigy at Lennox's funeral may owe something to Henry Stuart's funeral, the first post-Reformation use of an effigy for the funeral of a non-monarch. Henry's effigy did not, however, lie in state.
[66] Cuddy, p. 180.
[67] DNB.
[68] *Westminster Abbey*, pp. 20–1.

The extravagance of Lennox's funeral did not meet with universal approbation. Chamberlain reports that, 'divers noble men refused some offices or services they were appointed to, as esteeming them unfit for him or themselves. In effect I have not heard of such a titularie prince and subject, so magnificently enterred.'[69] Exaggerated funeral ritual was divisive since it subverted the function of displaying the hierarchy of society. It is interesting, however, that Chamberlain's only specific criticism focused on precedence disputes in the funeral procession. He does not discuss the propriety or otherwise of the use of the effigy. Nor was there to be any criticism of the effigy lying-in-state ritual at the funeral of Lennox's King a year or so later.

The Lying-in-State of James I's Funeral Effigy
A number of other factors may have contributed to the adoption of the effigy lying-in-state ritual at the funeral of James, and perhaps that of Lennox, now that cultural conditions were favourable for its acceptance.

I agree with Gittings that part of the motivation behind the use of the effigy-centred ritual at James's funeral was probably Charles's desire not to be outdone by his continental rivals in the realm of funeral pageantry.[70] Certainly, the funeral organizers did not neglect the need for James's obsequies to be celebrated where the English had strong overseas links. Thomas Locke wrote to Dudley Carleton, Ambassador at the Hague, on 12 April wondering how much money should be sent for the celebration of the King's funeral there. He remarks that for the Queen's funeral, presumably Queen Anne's, £100 had been sent. Mourning blacks were also sent to the Lady Elizabeth, Electress Palatine in the care of Sir Henry Fane, official bearer of the news of the King's death. The amount of cloth sent was sufficient to clothe the Princess, together with her entire family and household.[71]

In accordance with tradition, the leading continental courts also marked the occasion of James's death with ceremony.[72] The French court went into mourning and the Master of Ceremonies even encouraged foreign ambassadors in Paris to do likewise. The Venetian Ambassador, Morosini, made a formal visit to his English counterparts to pay his respects and express the Republic's esteem for the late King. The young Spanish King, kept at Aranjuez by Olivares, also ordered mourning garments.[73]

In the context of continental rivalry, there are a number of reasons why Charles, like the Lennox family, should have displayed a marked inclination towards things French. The Esmé Stuart influence on James's Scottish court had, for example, persisted when James organized his English court giving it a strong

---

[69] McClure, II, 554.
[70] Gittings, p. 223.
[71] CSPD Addenda, XXIII (1625–49), 3–4, 12; CSPV, XIX (1625–6), 13, 37.
[72] See my introduction and chapter 4.
[73] CSPV, XIX (1625–6), 14–15, 22, 24; Elliott, pp. 169–89.

French component from the outset. Significantly, in this context, James had revived the custom of dining in state at the English court, in accordance with Franco-Scottish court etiquette. Those in charge of the actual table service, the Carvers, Cupbearers and Sewers of the Privy Chamber, were able to exploit James's habit of debating while dining and their positions could be instrumental in building a successful career at court. George Villiers was a Cupbearer; Sir John Digby, later Vice-Chamberlain and Earl of Bristol, a Carver; and Sir Thomas Overbury, for a time Carr's favourite, a Sewer. The revival of this French fashion may have made the French effigy lying-in-state ritual an attractive option, giving powerful courtiers an opportunity to demonstrate through ritual their continued power at the potentially vulnerable juncture of royal accession. Buckingham, bringing his experience as a Cupbearer to the meetings of the commission, may have been influential in the decision to make the traditional continuation of the household effigy-centred. The performance of the acts of service to the royal effigy by leading courtiers and noblemen enabled the lying-in-state to create and display the continuity of monarchial power, as the French monarchists had done at the funeral of Charles IX (1574).[74]

Charles's imminent marriage with Henrietta Maria was set to bring French royal culture to the centre of the English court. The French style of James's lying-in-state may well have been influenced by an interest in and fashion for things French triggered by the marriage negotiations.[75] In 1610, at the age of nine, Henrietta Maria had been taken to cast water on the body of her father, Henry IV, as it lay in state at the Louvre and she attended his funeral at St Denis (figure 23).[76] Henrietta may have exercised an indirect influence on Charles's decisions about the arrangements for the lying-in-state ritual, through the agency of her marriage negotiators. She did not arrive in England in person until the proceedings were well underway.

Henry IV's funeral provided the English with a recent model of French obsequies and may have generated wider interest in the effigy-centred lying-in-state ritual on the part of the organizers of James's funeral (figure 23). 1610, the year of Henry's funeral, had seen the publication in Lyon of a French account of the funeral by Claude Morillon which soon after appeared in an English translation to be sold at Paul's Churchyard.[77]

---

[74] Cuddy, p. 184. See also my chapter 3.
[75] Smuts, p. 186; Lockyer, p. 297.
[76] *The Funerall Pompe and Obsequies of the most Mighty and Puissant Henry the Fourth* (London: [n. pub.], 1610), p. 3; Rosalind K. Marshall, *Henrietta Maria: the Intrepid Queen* (London: HMSO, 1990), p. 4; Harris and Higgott, p. 191.
[77] *L'Ordre de la Pompe Funebre Oservee au convoy et Funerailles [. . .] Henry le Grand* (Lyon: Claude Morillon, 1610); *The Funerall Pompe and Obsequies of the most mighty and puissant Henry the Fourth, King of France* (London: [n. pub.], 1610). On enthusiastic English participation in the wars of Henry IV, see Hugh M. Richmond, *Puritans and Libertines: Anglo-French Literary Relations in the Reformation* (London: University of California Press, 1981), p. 298.

The Theatre of Death

The translation of Claude Morillon's account of the obsequies may not have been the only English source for the effigy lying-in-state of Henry IV's funeral. André Favyn's *Le Theatre d'Honneur and de Chevalrie* (Paris: Robert Foüet, 1620), which was translated into English and published in London under the title *The Theatre of Honour and Knighthood*, included an account of the same funeral. Pollard has the publication date as 1626 but the printed date in the copy held at the Bodleian is 1623 with a pencil correction to 1626. If it was indeed printed in 1623, the detailed description of Henry IV's lying-in-state ritual with the serving of the effigy would have been available as a model for the James and Lennox funerals. In any case the translation is likely to have been in progress and intriguingly it was to be dedicated to Henry Montagu (1563?–1642), the Earl of Manchester, who was to be on the commission that Charles appointed to make the arrangements for his father's funeral.[78]

The French accounts of the funeral of Henry IV include one by Pierre Matthieu which incorporates the first known explicit articulation of the effigy symbolism.[79] His remarks were prompted by a dispute between the Bishops and Parlement as to who should accompany the effigy in the funeral convoy. Matthieu remarked that 'Autrefois l'effigie estoit possée sur le cercueil, pour esmouvoir le peuple à honorer le corps qui estoit dedans, et pour monstrer que le Roy ne meurt point.'[80] Matthieu writes from the point of view of one for whom the symbolic meaning of the effigy was no longer current. As I explained above, by the time of Henry IV's death, the symbolism of the royal funeral had been deliberately undercut by Michel de L'Hôpital. Some Englishmen were certainly aware of this French precedence dispute. It is referred to in a letter from a M. Beaulieu to the diplomat William Trumbull at Brussels with an account of the funeral procession of the French King which he had witnessed.[81]

Matthieu's stress on the fictive nature of the effigy rituals may well have been imported with the ceremonial forms themselves, making them more acceptable and appealing to the English. Conscious artifice, as we have seen, permeated the church service at James's funeral and attention was overtly drawn to that artifice through the medium of the sermon. It is not difficult to see that the French effigy lying-in-state ritual was pervaded with the same fictive quality. The

---

[78] André Favyn, *The Theatre of Honour and Knighthood* (London: [n. pub.], [1623 (?)]), p. 516.
[79] Giesey (1960), p. 179.
[80] Pierre Matthieu, 'Histoire de la mort de Henri IV', in *Archives Curieuses de L'Histoire de France Depuis Louis XI Jusqu'à Louis XVIII*, ed. by M. L. Cimber and F. Danjou, 30 vols (Paris: Bourgogne & Martinet, 1834–41), 1st series, XIV, 77, cited by Giesey (1960), p. 180 n. 10. No date for this source is given by Giesey but he suggests that Matthieu was writing in 1610 about earlier funerals.
[81] Winwood, III, 188–9. Beaulieu also reports that not all the ambassadors that were in Paris took part. *L'Ordre de la Pompe Funebre* (1610) mentions only those of Savoy, Venice and Spain. Again the absence of the others may be explained partly because of precedence disputes and partly because of religious differences.

The Funeral of King James I

exploitation of images and even the acts of homage to an image required by the effigy lying-in-state ritual would be more permissible in the eyes of those Englishmen who, unsympathetic with Laudian ceremonial reform, retained Protestant worries about the legitimacy of showing homage to the image of the Prince, if their basis in fiction were openly acknowledged.[82]

The degree to which the artifice involved in staging the effigy lying-in-state ritual for James was conscious is signalled in a striking manner. In the French tradition, after the lying-in-state, the royal effigy would appear in the funeral procession. The effigy of James that had been on display at Denmark House did not. The surviving funeral accounts make it clear that two effigies were prepared.[83]

> Paid to Maximilian Coult for making the body of the representacion with several joyntes in the armes leggs and body to be moved to several postures and for setting up the same in Westminster Abbey and for his attendance there
>
> xli – –
>
> [...]
> Item for making a representation suddenly to serve only at Denmarke house untill the funerall and for his attendance there at divers times
>
> xli – –

There has been some speculation that a reference to 'a paire of Bodyes' in the accounts of Anne of Denmark's funeral is evidence that two effigies were also supplied on that occasion. Janet Arnold has, however, suggested that these 'bodyes' refer to stays and this seems a plausible explanation. There are no references to two effigies in any descriptions of Anne's funeral. Besides the decision to use two effigies at James's funeral seems to be the result of an ad hoc decision made at short notice rather than a conscious emulation of precedent, witness the reference to 'making a representation "suddenly"' in the extract from the accounts above. James's Denmark House effigy had to be prepared at great speed in order to be ready for display so soon after the King's death, perhaps because of the awkward timing of James's death at a juncture when the court was beginning to prepare for the marriage of Prince Charles and Henrietta Maria.[84]

A death mask may have been used in the preparation of both effigies; the accounts for the funeral include an item 'for the moulding of the King's face'.[85] Maximilian Colt was entrusted with the prestigious task of making the two

---

[82] See chapter 5.
[83] PRO Lord Chamberlain's Records, Series I, Vol. 557, cited by Hope, p. 557.
[84] Harvey and Mortimer, p. 11.
[85] Hope, p. 557. Compare the preparation of Francis I's effigy. Howgrave-Graham (p. 160) marshals together some evidence which suggests that effigies were generally prepared with some urgency. The effigy of Anne of Bohemia was made in less than ten days, while the accounts relating to the funeral of Elizabeth of York state that the joiners received four pence for one day's work and eight pence for a whole night.

effigies. He and his servant travelled to Theobalds on the very day of the King's death to take the death mask 'for the better making of the effigy'.[86] Daniel Parkes provided two sets of periwigs and eyebrows.[87] The Westminster Abbey effigy had a more complex design with jointed limbs to facilitate the removal of the effigy from the hearse to the effigy 'chapel'.[88] The decision to make use of two effigies seems to have been made in the midst of debate over the funeral arrangements with the intention of facilitating the overall performance. It did not reflect historical precedent but constituted a flexible response to the exigencies of the particular situation.

The public use of two effigies also seems to affirm the fictive nature of the effigy rituals and to undermine any potentially mystical interpretation of the effigy preserving James's kingship prior to the public appearance of King Charles in the funeral and the ritual succession of the offering ceremony. The effigy lying-in-state ritual of James was emphatically theatrical in tone. Further, the royal theatre of death as a whole occupied, it may be argued, a liminal area in which the lines marking out the idolatrous were deliberately blurred, creating a space within which a *religion royale* could develop. In the context of the funeral, this *religion royale* was articulated through the sermon but also operated in the realm of the affective. The effigies in particular, whether in the lying-in-state ceremony, the procession or the church service, were employed to deliberately engage the emotions of the onlookers and to create a sense of a rightly ordered patriarchal monarchy through the process of sublimation.

Another element of the effigy lying-in-state ceremony indicates to what extent this *religion royale*, which would flourish during Charles's reign, was already apparent at James's funeral.[89] Six candlesticks were placed at the corners of the bed of state where James's effigy lay. In each a four foot taper of virgin wax burned through the night.[90] The effect was to render the scene yet more theatrical, flickering candlelight illuminating the features of the effigy and making its regalia sparkle. In addition the use of candles brought the ritual closer to the French model, where candles always burned beside the *lit d'honneur*.[91] We have seen that torches and candles were stripped from funeral symbolism at the time of the Reformation because of their connotations of popery and intercession for the dead. Similarly, as recently as 1614, Chamberlain had condemned the funeral of Northampton, where candles had burned around the corpse, as distinctly popish.[92] Now candles were being used at a royal funeral. To add to the Catholic resonance on the occasion of James's lying-in-

---

[86] Harvey and Mortimer, p. 70.
[87] The effigy head has been lost but Colt's statue of King James at Hatfield House probably provides a good indication of its form and quality; see ibid., p. 71.
[88] Hope, p. 558. For a discussion of Prince Henry's jointed effigy, see chapter 8.
[89] See chapter 6.
[90] Nichols (1828), IV, 1038.
[91] See Appendix II.
[92] Chapter 7.

state, the silver candlesticks used were a set that Charles had brought back from his abortive trip to Spain to claim the Spanish Infanta as his bride in 1623. It should be remembered that James's body lay beneath the effigy, thereby increasing the connotations of intercession and popery that would be keenly felt by some.[93] Candles might have been thoroughly re-legitimized in court ceremony, but for others they remained taboo. Thomas Warmstry was still referring to 'candles in the day time' as the 'embleme of a fruitless prelacy or clergy in the church' in the 1630s.[94]

Yet, however 'Catholic' some might perceive the trappings of the James's funeral rituals to be, the core of the church ceremony remained Protestant, as was underlined by the behaviour of the French ambassador who withdrew from the service during prayers, deeming them incompatible with his faith.[95]

The Protestant-Catholic mix in the funeral ceremonies is indicative of the confused religious signals that emanated from James's court, reaching a climax towards the end of the reign but discernible even in the early years as the programme of tomb construction discussed in chapter 7 indicated. Catholic ritual elements might enhance the theatricality of the *religion royale* but they inevitably carried with them signals of doubtful religious allegiance. For many the effigy lying-in-state ritual would remain an example of popish idolatry in contravention of the second commandment.

The English thus developed the effigy lying-in-state ritual and enacted a magnificent display of loyalty to the dead King. Apart from the French ambassador's behaviour, the service took place as planned: the funeral successfully enacted the transfer of monarchial power. This drama of succession was a 'closed' coterie ritual unseen by the majority of the citizens of the capital but despite being small in number, the congregation nevertheless embraced a broad range of social groups.[96] In addition, some elements of the funeral service were to be preserved in the public domain. Although the hearse was probably broken up and distributed amongst the heralds, to whom it belonged by way of perquisite, James's funeral effigy joined the royal effigy display in the Abbey and Williams's sermon was soon to be in print.[97] As far as I am aware this was the first royal funeral sermon to be published and is indicative of the highly conscious manner in which the royal theatre of death was being promoted to a wide audience.[98] In the main, however, the public impression of the proceedings would come from the most 'open' segment, the funeral processions. Processional rituals, as we have already discovered in the context of the obsequies of

---

[93] CA, Nayler, p. 28. There were, however, no candles on the hearse for the church service.
[94] Warmstry, *A Convocation Speech [. . .] against images, altars, crosses, the new canons, and the oath* (London: [n. pub.], 1641), pp. 2, 5–6, 10, 13–15, cited by Tyacke, p. 242.
[95] CSPV, XIX (1625–6), 55.
[96] On the general propensity of the Caroline court towards closed ritual, see Smuts, p. 238.
[97] Dallaway, p. 260; McClure, II, 616.
[98] Abbot's funeral sermon for Prince Henry does not appear to have been printed; see Nichols (1828), II, 502.

Anne of Denmark, were more vulnerable to disruption than church services and, if disruption occurred, it was very public. The funeral processions of James I did not run smoothly.

The Funeral Processions of James I

The first procession, which conveyed James's body from Theobalds to Denmark House, took place at around 9.00 p.m. on a Monday night. The size and content of the procession are indicative of its public nature, illustrating just how acceptable and fashionable nocturnal processions had become. 'The convoy was well accompanied by all the nobilitie about the towne, the pensioners, officers, and household servants, besides the Lord maior and aldermen.' The procession was attended by guards on foot and horseback and followed by many lords in coaches. The whole cavalcade was lit by the light of numerous torches which, according to Mr Neve, numbered 3,600. The way-maker attended the heralds all the way to give directions and the Officers of Arms and gentleman ushers uncovered their heads in every town and village. Such ceremonious behaviour further stresses that the procession was expected to attract attention. Circumstances were not on the side of magnificent display, however: 'the shew wold have ben solemne but that yt was marred by fowle weather, so that there was nothing to be seen but coaches and torch'.[99]

The participants themselves, rather than the elements, would disrupt the second procession, which bore the body and effigy to Westminster Abbey. Disputes arose amongst the servants of the new and old Kings, even those of the highest rank. There was, for example, a quarrel between the Duke of Lennox and the Viscount of Andover over who should take the role of the Master of the Horse in the funeral procession. Charles decided in favour of the former, but feelings rankled.[100] At a less exalted level, petitioners vied for the limited number of places available in the procession. The Privy Council received a number of written claims from individuals and groups wishing to be included in the list of the King's servants. Those accepted would be assured a position in the funeral procession and, more importantly, the receipt of a mourning cloak, a garment of quality cloth of considerable value, particularly to the poorer members of the community.[101] Petitioners included servants of the late Queen Anne who felt they should be treated as a part of James's household.

[99] McClure, II, 609; Nichols (1828), IV, 1038 n. 2; CSPV, XIX (1625–6), 10.
[100] CSPV, XIX (1625–6), 21.
[101] Non-participants seem to have been given mourning cloth as well since the Council received other petitions which were solely requests for a portion of the King's blacks. This implies that the practice was to distribute a portion of mourning cloth to the poor; see CSPD, I (1625–6), pp. 4, 15. All the people took a piece of black cloth from the church after the funeral service of Mary Tudor (Nichols (1848), p. 183). On the impact of royal funerals on the London economy, see Loach on the funeral of Henry VIII (1547), p. 68.

Charles tried to use the funeral to quell fears that there would be increased toleration of Catholics under his rule. Catholic noblemen were barred from James's funeral and were not included in the list of titled nobility to which mourning blacks would be distributed. The Venetian ambassador, Pesaro, reports that this was 'to make a mark of them [. . .] They [Charles and his advisors] will show vigour about religion, to the satisfaction of the general.'[102] There were, however, many other indications of a drift towards greater sympathy with Catholicism which countered the political signals given out at the funeral.[103] In any case, the ritual forms of aspects of the funeral would reek of popery to some, despite the ban on involvement of Catholic personnel.

Disputes continued to dog the organizers even during the procession itself. Pesaro, the Venetian Ambassador, prepared very costly mourning outfits for himself and his household, spending around 1,000 crowns, as he was constantly to remind the Senate in the hope of receiving financial recompense.[104] In the event, he did not take part in the procession having been, he alleged, told by Lewkenor, the Master of Ceremonies, that none of the foreign ambassadors would be in attendance. Spectating on the day, Pesaro saw the French ambassadors in position. He was furious and took the matter up with the Lord Chamberlain whilst the procession was still in progress. Pesaro pursued the matter vigorously until Lewkenor was finally suspended from office in October 1625.[105]

Pesaro was certainly deprived of a major opportunity for personal display, if the preparations made in anticipation of the funeral are a fair indication of the crowds that turned out on the day. Fifty men were employed 'to make way and keep the streets for the proceedings clear' and special provision was made for some of the spectators. At Whitehall, for example, scaffolds, licensed by Arundel, were erected within the tiltyard and it is reasonable to assume that the streets of the procession route were 'railed' in order to separate participants from spectators, as was normal practice for processional occasions. Certainly there is evidence that such structures were erected for the funeral of Queen Anne.[106]

Anyone watching the whole procession pass would have had a long day. The funeral cortège was so extensive that it was 5.00 p.m. before all the mourners were inside Westminster Abbey. Between 5,000 and 9,000 participated in the procession.[107] The sheer scale of the enterprise may have contributed to the performance falling short of the desired ideal: a paradigm of social order.

---

[102] CSPV, XIX (1625–6), 4, 30.
[103] See my chapter 6.
[104] CSPV, XIX (1625–6), 5, 31.
[105] CSPV, XIX (1625–6), 54, 64, 193; Acts of the Privy Council of England (1625–6), pp. 195–6.
[106] Gittings, p. 221; CSPD, I (1625–6), 19; McClure, II, 234.
[107] Chamberlain's estimate is much the highest at 9,000; see McClure, II, 616; while Pesaro sets the number at 5,000; see CSPV, XIX (1625–6), 55. There were 2,000 participants in Prince Henry's procession and 1,600 in Elizabeth's.

Chamberlain reports 'in summe all was performed with great magnificence, but the order was very confused and disorderly'.[108] Ironically where, in 1603, genuine worries about civil disorder had been met with an undisrupted funeral procession, in 1625 what should have been a smoothly-staged ritual occasion was disturbed.

Chamberlain estimated that the whole event cost £50,000.[109] It may be true that by the mid-1620s some English noblemen were cutting back on funeral expenses but the same cannot be said of Charles's expenditure on the funeral of King James.[110] The arrival of Queen Henrietta Maria necessitated the outlay of a further £5,000 on blacks for herself and her train.[111] The wedding had already taken place in Paris, with the Duke de Chevreuse acting as proxy for the King, but, in addition to the costs of the obsequy, a total of £60,000 was to be borrowed from the City to fund the English celebrations of the marriage and the double coronation ceremony.[112] Coke's report on behalf of the King to the Commons on 8 July 1625 stated that 'the ordinary revenue is clogged with debts and exhausted with the late King's funeral and other expenses of necessity and honour'.[113]

The church service and lying-in-state ceremony may have been a ritual success, but these were coterie performances, observed only by the privileged few. The problems experienced with the much more public procession ritual might have led to questions being asked as to the efficacy of such grand funeral rituals and whether they constituted value for money. Would the English abandon the royal funeral ceremony, as the French did after the funeral of Henry IV where the procession had been dogged with disputes and the effigy ritual had been stripped of its symbolism and totally devalued?

'Royal' Funerals post-1625

Certainly, Charles was dissuaded from giving Buckingham a state funeral and tomb when he died in 1628 but this was at least as much attributable to the unpopularity of the favourite as to cost-cutting measures. Buckingham was interred by night to avoid a public demonstration. Charles's only gesture was

---

[108] McClure, II, 616. Chamberlain also reports that James's funeral 'was abridged' but it is not at all clear what he means by this statement; ibid., p. 608.
[109] McClure, II, 616. Frederick John Varley, *Oliver Cromwell's Latter End* (London: Chapman & Hall, 1939), p. 27, puts the figure lower, at £30,000 but does not cite his source.
[110] Smuts, p. 200; Gittings, pp. 195–7; Stone (1965), p. 577.
[111] CSPD, I (1625–6), p. 70. On the general distribution of mourning to the family at the funeral, see CA, Briscoe MS I fol. 2.
[112] CSPD, I (1625–6), 12, 33; Marshall (1990), p. 22.
[113] CSPD, I (1625–6), 56.

The Funeral of King James I

to insist that the magnificent monument erected by Buckingham's wife was located in the Henry VII Chapel at Westminster Abbey, the royal necropolis.[114]

Charles himself would of course never be accorded a full royal funeral ritual.[115] He was deposited simply and quietly in Henry VIII's vault at Windsor, avoiding the possibility of a Westminster tomb becoming a focus for pilgrimage and dissent.[116] Yet the elaborate form of the royal funeral complete with effigy ritual was set to survive into the middle of the seventeenth century and in a surprising context: the funerals of Robert, Earl of Essex (1646) and Lord Protector Cromwell (1658). Essex's effigy lay in state at Essex House prior to the funeral procession and remained in Westminster Abbey, displayed in a hearse, for one month after the funeral.[117]

Kinnersly, Master of the Wardrobe, was in charge of the funeral arrangements for Oliver Cromwell. His body lay in state at Somerset House, in a chamber hung with black velvet, and was the focal point of a ritual that was modelled on the funeral of Philip II of Spain (d. 1598). An effigy also lay in state in the same chamber but was located somewhere other than above the body. The effigy was on display until 1 November when it was transferred to the Great Hall. Once in the Great Hall, the effigy, royally dressed in a gown of crimson velvet with a sceptre in its hand and a crown upon its head, was displayed in a *standing in state* ritual. The term *standing in state* is ambiguous but probably refers to the effigy lying in an upright position like the effigy of Henry IV in figure 23. There were 'four or five hundred candles, [...] so placed around near the roof of the hall, that the light they gave seemed like the rays of the sun: by all which he was represented to be now in a state of glory'.[118] The effigy remained in this chamber until 22 November, All Souls Day. The total lying-in-state period was a month, in emulation of the royal form of the ritual.

Cromwell's funeral demonstrates that elaborate funeral ritual, while it may have been in decline as far as the aristocracy as a whole was concerned, was still deemed valuable by the ruling elite in the mid-seventeenth century.[119] It also underlines the way in which funeral ritual practices had come to be divorced

---

[114] Smuts, p. 42; Parry (1981), p. 144.

[115] Fritz, p. 70.

[116] Bland, p. 54. Charles I had no funeral service as the Constable of the castle prevented Bishop Juxton from reading the service; see Litten, p. 159.

[117] *The True Mannor and Forme of the Proceeding to the Funerall of the Right Honorable Earle of Essex* (London: [n. pub.], 1646), pp. 15, 24. Gittings (p. 231) discusses how the College of Arms was revived by Parliament to arrange this funeral.

[118] Firth, C. H., *The Memoirs of Edmund Ludlow: 1625–1672*, 2 vols (Oxford: Clarendon Press, 1894), II, 47–8. Cromwell's effigy standing-in-state appeared as a frontispiece to Carrington's *History of the Life and Death of Oliver, late Lord Protector* (1659), the year after his death; see Karl Pearson and G. M. Morant, *The Portraiture of Oliver Cromwell with Special Reference to the Wilkinson Head* (London: Biometrika Office, UCL, 1935), pl. VIII.

[119] On the decline of the College of Arms, see Fritz, pp. 75–7; Wagner (1967), p. 237; Litten, pp. 189–94.

from religious allegiance, at least in the minds of those in political power.[120] The 'civill respects' which were excluded from the prohibition on funeral ceremony found in the Commonwealth's *Directory for the Publique Worship of God* (1644) in effect allowed the trappings of Catholic funerals to be used at the funeral of the leader of the Puritan revolution for political ends.[121] Having resisted coronation during his lifetime, Cromwell was crowned in death in order to facilitate the succession of his son.[122]

Cromwell's funeral procession imitated that of James I but was even more elaborate and costly.[123] It was clearly intended to attract large crowds. The churchwardens' accounts of St Margaret's, Westminster include £12 received 'for 240 foot of ground in the old church yard lett to build scaffolds at the Lord Protectors funerall, at the rate of 1s the foot'.[124] Yet the possibility of an ambivalent and potentially disruptive response to the proceedings was acknowledged by the deployment of soldiers to line the processional route, the first time that such action had been taken. Despite these precautions, the funeral car was despoiled whilst the funeral service was in progress. During the church service that followed the effigy once again provided a focal point for the ritual proceedings, displayed as it was in the traditional hearse. Both hearse and effigy remained in position at Westminster Abbey until the fall of the Commonwealth while the coffin was interred in the same building.[125]

Commentators disagree as to whether or not Cromwell's body had been placed in the coffin. Varley holds that Cromwell's body had been separately buried before his funeral, apparently because of unsuccessful embalming. Consequently the coffin was found empty when it was exhumed on 29 January 1661 and thus the body escaped violation. Litten, however, convincingly argues

---

[120] The main source for Cromwell's funeral is Frederick John Varley, *Oliver Cromwell's Latter End* (London: Chapman & Hall, 1939). Edmund Ludlow (1617?–92), who became alienated from Cromwell after he had been proclaimed Protector, gives a very negative view of the funeral proceedings saying, for example, that the people threw dirt at his escutcheon which had been hung over the great gate at Somerset House in emulation of royal funerals. See Firth (1889), III, 48.

[121] *A Directory for the Publique Worship of God Throughout the Three Kingdoms of England, Scotland and Ireland* (London: [n. pub.], 1644). This was largely a translation of the 1566 *Book of Discipline*. See Rowell, p. 82. On the elaborate funerals of the New England Puritans, see David E. Stannard, *The Puritan Way of Death: A Study in Religion, Culture and Social Change* (Oxford: Oxford University Press, 1977). See also my chapters 2, 5 and 6.

[122] Gittings, p. 230.

[123] Varley, p. 29; C. H. Firth, ed., *The Clarke Papers: Selections from the Papers of William Clarke*, 4 vols (London: Longmans & Green, 1891–1901), III (1899), pp. 167–8. For the funeral expense accounts, see BL, Harley MS 1372 fol. 2 and 1438 fols 8–10, cited by Dallaway, p. 280. Also see E. S. De Beer, ed., *The Diary of John Evelyn*, 5 vols (Oxford: Clarendon Press, 1955), III, 224.

[124] Cox (1913), p. 174.

[125] Cromwell's family adopted the Abbey as its necropolis. See Stanley (1869), pp. 183–4. The hearse was claimed by the Abbey monument keepers in 1658. See WA, MS 6371.

that the coffin did contain Cromwell's body, founding his position on the evidence provided by Heath and Pepys. According to the latter, Cromwell, Ireton and Bradshaw were all dug up on the evening of 30 January 1661 and on the following day dragged to Tyburn to be strung up, their faces turned toward Whitehall. Later they were decapitated and buried under the gallows, near Connaught Square. Cromwell's head was spiked on the roof of Westminster Hall where, tradition has it, it remained for twenty-five years until the wind blew it to the ground and a sentry wrapped it up and took it home.[126] Intriguingly, the funeral effigy was similarly subjected to vengeful attack, being hung by a rope from a window of Whitehall palace on 14 June 1660.[127] Ironically, such treatment harks back to the magical and idolatrous practices of medieval England so condemned by the reformed church.

Supine funeral effigies would continue to be used for some time to come but not for royal funerals. An effigy appeared in the funeral procession and service of General Monk, Duke of Albermarle and Earl of Torrington (d. 1670), a prime mover in the restoration of Charles II. It was the King who gave the funeral for his erstwhile friend.[128] The last time that a supine effigy was borne above a coffin was at the 1735 obsequies of Edmund, Duke of Buckingham.[129] For the funeral procession of Charles II (1685) and subsequent sovereigns, the effigy was replaced by an imperial crown, borne upon a velvet cushion before the coffin, in a fashion reminiscent of the funeral of Mary Queen of Scots. Similarly a crown replaced the effigy in the lying-in-state ceremony. The reasons posited for the change are various and cannot all be dealt with here, but the shift to a constitutional monarchy was surely significant. The perpetuity of kingship symbolized by the effigy was clearly no longer appropriate in post-Civil War England.

Royal funeral effigies continued, however, to be made but their purpose was now restricted to the post-funeral display in the Abbey. Charles II sat for his own upright funeral effigy and intended that it should be set up near his tomb as soon as possible after the funeral had taken place. Arguably he meant it to be his sole monument and it continued to stand over his burial vault in the Henry VII Chapel until at least 1723. There was never any intention of using this upright effigy in a lying-in-state ceremony, the funeral procession or the church services.[130]

---

[126] In 1787 an actor named Russel is reputed to have sold the head to a museum and then it was sold on to Josiah Wilkinson who used to take it to parties. Wilkinson's grandson presented the head to Cromwell's old college, Sidney Sussex, Cambridge. The head has been subjected to rigorous examination and close comparison with Cromwell's death mask. It appears to be authentic; see Pearson and Morant.

[127] Varley, p. 42.

[128] Hope, pp. 559–63; Harvey and Mortimer, p. 13.

[129] A similar effigy had also appeared at the funeral of his brother, Robert, Marquess of Normanby.

[130] CA, Briscoe MS I fols 1–4; Fritz, pp. 66, 70, 75; *Westminster Abbey*, p. 20. Antonia Fraser

Subsequently, even the post-funeral display of the funeral effigy was dropped. James II abdicated, William III chose to dispense with an effigy for Mary II and Anne made no provision for an effigy for herself during her lifetime. The Dean and Chapter of Westminster Abbey paid to have effigies made for these monarchs to complete the Stuart series. George I died overseas and was buried in Hanover. With the accession of the Hanoverian dynasty, the practice of effigy construction was discontinued, a recognition, perhaps, that their popularity could never match that of the Stuarts.

Posthumous Images of King James

James, like Prince Henry, did not receive a tomb monument. Instead he was interred with Henry VII beneath Torrigiano's brass tomb and his Queen, Anne, was placed beside him. Although Inigo Jones appears to have put together grand plans for a Stuart mausoleum, they were never to be put into action.[131] While the Jones project may simply have been too costly, the reason for the non-erection of a tomb monument was not parsimony on the part of Charles, as the trouble and expense taken with the funeral arrangements indicate. As in the case of Prince Henry Stuart, the continued display of the funeral effigy precluded the need for a tomb effigy and monument. James's funeral effigy joined the earlier royal funeral effigies in the Abbey. The very fact that a separate Westminster Abbey effigy was constructed is illustrative of the importance attached to post-funeral display at this juncture. It is possible that James's Westminster Abbey effigy was also designed specifically with the intention of upright display, given that it featured 'several joyntes in the armes and leggs and body to be moved to several postures and for setting up the same'. If so, in the event the designers do not appear to have achieved their aims. The effigy of James that survives at the Abbey has been identified as the Denmark House effigy. It seems to have been brought to Westminster to replace the procession effigy which had been 'broaken by the often removeing of the representation'.[132] It may be that the use of two effigies at James's funeral added impetus to the shift towards a commemorative function for the funeral effigy, perhaps marking a key stage in the transition to the memorial waxwork that would replace the funeral effigy.[133] As Weever reports, both tombs and funeral effigies functioned

    incorrectly states that an effigy of Charles II was used in his funeral, *King Charles II* (London, 1979), pp. 458–60. See also Tanner (1935), pp. 170–1. The effigy of Mary II was similarly only displayed in the Abbey; see Lois G. Schwoerer, *The Revolution of 1688–9, changing perspectives* (Cambridge: Cambridge University Press, 1992), p. 146.

131 The designs envisage a huge fortress with a rusticated basement bearing a circular domed building with side chapels; see Strong and Orgel (1973), p. 136 and pl. 242; and Parry (1981), p. 259.

132 Hope, p. 559.

133 Harvey and Mortimer, pp. 69–70.

The Funeral of King James I

as a tourist attraction in early seventeenth-century London: 'What concourse of people come daily to view the lively Statues and stately Monuments in Westminster Abbey'.[134]

In addition to the funeral effigy, Charles was to provide other posthumous representations of his father. Within a few years of his father's death, Charles commissioned a set of images of James to adorn the ceiling of the Banqueting House at Whitehall. The paintings, executed by Rubens, glorify the life of James, using allegory to justify the divine right rule of the Stuart kings. One of the panels shows James passing judicial sentence in a scene deliberately imitating a formula for depicting the Last Judgement. Thus, directly above his head, Charles's father was metamorphosized into an image of God. The central panel depicts the Apotheosis of King James, an iconographic strategy closely associated with Counter-Reformation baroque artists.[135] Once again, in the court coterie setting, the *religion royale* of the Caroline court was in evidence.

There would be other images of James, visible to all. In 1625 an equestrian statue of James was erected outside the Royal Exchange at Aldersgate. Charles donated £4,000 towards the renovation of St Paul's so that a giant Corinthian portico could be constructed at the cathedral's main entrance. The portico was to support brass statues of himself and his father. Hubert le Sueur also made bronze statues of James and Charles for Winchester Cathedral in 1638.[136] Thus, without erecting a tomb, Charles used images of his father to promote the Stuart dynasty in the public arena.

---

[134] Weever, p. 41.
[135] Parry (1981), pp. 33–7, 52; Smuts, p. 237; Per Palme, *The Triumph of Peace: A Study of the Whitehall Banqueting House* (Stockholm: Almqvist & Wiksell, 1956), p. 242.
[136] Mercer, p. 253; Whinney, p. 87; Smuts, p. 127; Harris and Higgott, pp. 238–9, 250. A statue of James was also erected in the quadrangle at the Bodleian Library, Oxford.

Epilogue

The theatre of death documented during the course of this book embraced both tradition and innovation. The core ritual processes survived the Reformation virtually unchanged but the overlay, the trappings that enriched funeral performance were more dependent on cultural change. To a large extent, the distinction between the resilient and the vulnerable elements of heraldic funeral ritual rests on the degree to which they flouted the iconophobic decorum of the reformed religion. The choreography of the offering ritual was relatively uncontroversial, the bearing of torches, provocative, the banners of the saints, outlawed. The ephemerality of ritual movement makes it far more ambiguous, and thus a less obvious target of reform, than the physical ritual objects produced by the visual arts. Surprisingly, however, the central feature of the monarch's obsequies, and the most overtly idolatrous, the life-size effigy with its wax death-mask portrait of the deceased, was not abandoned until long after 1625, the temporal limit of this study.

Justifications for the use of the effigy, as for the more general construction of portrait tomb monuments, depended on the convenient differentiation made between the civil and the religious. Carved images could be legitimately produced for the commemoration of the dead but not as foci for intercessionary prayer. Such equivocations restored ambiguity to the representational aspects of the funeral ritual and permitted the affective stimulation necessary to involve spectators and participants and to encourage the homogenous behaviour and resultant display of consensus, deemed so crucial to the enactment of a smooth succession. Thus the royal effigy ritual was maintained despite the Reformation. For the same reason the government allowed the practice of bell-ringing to survive and torchlit processions to be revived.

Ironically, the insistent verbal affirmation of the civil aspect and the concomitant denial of a religious dimension to funeral ceremony, permitted the traditional medieval chivalric blend of the secular and the religious to persist in unvocalized, movement-based essence of the ritual. Through ambiguity the expectations of individual onlookers, participants and organizers could be mediated and the ritual could achieve its goal of social cohesion. This polysemic quality meant that, for example, the expectations of a 'traditional' royal funeral ritual, complete with effigy, could be used to smooth lineal succession at the funeral of Elizabeth. There were no fixed 'meanings' attached to the effigy ritual and thus no obvious incompatibility between the ritual, which involved the absence of the new king, and James's declared instantaneous succession.

Eventually, the widening religious rift experienced nationally at the beginning of the seventeenth century played its part in undermining the ambiguity central to the function of funeral ritual. The balance between the religious and the secular shifted and the funeral, particularly the royal funeral, became a High Church ritual. Instrumental in effecting the change was a new emphasis on language. At the funeral of James I the iconographic resonance of the effigy was overtly articulated through the sermon and enlisted in the cause of the *religion royale* that had been created to demonstrate and uphold succession according to the divine right of the Stuart kings. The traditional funeral was deliberately and adroitly modified so that the offering ceremony ritually enacted the succession of Charles I in person and the whole process was made explicit by Bishop John Williams in his sermon.

As at all times the funeral ritual movements, symbols and accoutrements were inevitably deployed in ways that were in keeping with prevailing religious and cultural conditions. The effigy lying-in-state ritual which constituted an effective propaganda exercise displaying the posthumous glory of the divinely ordained King in 1625, would have been unacceptable in 1603. In the meantime, however, the rise of Arminianism had blurred the definition of idolatry, creating a liminal space in which the modified lying-in-state ritual could be performed. Changes in ritual respond to changes in religion and culture. Situational adjustment can only operate within the bounds of what is acceptable in the broader cultural context. Ultimately, as this book demonstrates, ritual forms, like drama, are dependent on cultural conditions.

The situational adjustments made to the royal funeral ritual in 1625 were governed by political ambition. Yet the government did not have a completely free rein. Ironically, by making the message of the funeral performance verbal and politically specific, organizers of James I's obsequies diminished the ambiguity of the ritual. In a similar fashion, by recruiting the Westminster Abbey royal funeral effigies for his 1606 propaganda exercise occasioned by the visit of the King of Denmark, and by staging a second funeral for Mary Queen of Scots, reinstating his natural mother as a legitimate royal ancestor, properly commemorated with her counterparts in the royal necropolis, the Henry VII Chapel, James used funeral ritual for political gain. At the same time, however, he laid himself, and the ritual processes themselves, open to appropriation, critical assessment and even satire.

One group of people in Elizabethan and, especially, Jacobean society that appropriated royal funeral symbolism were the playwrights. The royal theatre of death was re-presented in the drama of the period. In this context it is worth noting that the heraldic model had long been emulated at the funerals of the rising middle class, particularly the civic dignitaries. The pages of Henry Machyn's diary (1550–63) are packed with accounts not only of funerals of noblemen but also those of mayors, aldermen, merchants, citizens and their wives.¹ It is important to recognize the homogeneity of funeral ritual experience across this social spectrum. Although differences in rank were acknowledged in the degree of pomp and magnificence of a particular occasion, the basic forms remained the same. On 14 May 1616 both the procession and church service of Sir Geoffrey Ellwas, Alderman of London and member of the Merchant-Taylor's, were attended by people of the parish as well as guild members. Thus, contemporary audiences brought their experience of heraldic funeral processions and church services to the playhouses and that experience could be exploited by the dramatists.²

The opening scene of Shakespeare's *Henry VI Part I*, set in Westminster Abbey, deconstructed the royal funeral ritual process, demonstrating the fallacy of the charade of co-operation enacted by the aristocracy at the obsequies of Henry V.³ The play was written in a period fraught with speculation over the vexed question of the succession, a question that Elizabeth persisted in leaving unanswered.

More subtle cross-fertilization of theatre and ritual occurs in *The Revenger's Tragedy* where, arguably, Vindice's instrument of revenge on the murderous Duke, the dressed up skull of Gloriana, is a visual pun on the funeral effigy of Elizabeth, refurbished by James for the royal visit made by the King of Denmark in the previous summer.⁴ Both Duke and, by implication, James, are masters of courts reeking of corruption and debauchery.⁵ Less biting in its funeral symbolism is the anonymous *Second Maiden's Tragedy*, a play which throughout is

1 Nichols (1848), pp. 116, 245–7, 294 (refer to index for many other examples). See also Duffy, p. 143.
2 The attitude of the worker in early seventeenth-century London who experienced a proliferation of funeral pageantry would have been very different from that of the fifteenth- or sixteenth-century feudal peasant witnessing the obsequies of the provincial aristocrat on whom he depended. See Strickland, p. 23.
3 *Henry VI Part I*, or at least a version of it, was written and performed by 8 August 1592, the date of entry in the Stationer's Register of Thomas Nashe's *Pierce Penilesse*, a work which refers to the play. It is possible that Shakespeare began to write the Henry VI sequence soon after the publication of the second edition of Holinshed's *Chronicles* in 1587. E. A. J. Honigmann has suggested that *I Henry VI* could have been written as early as 1589; see his *Shakespeare's Impact on His Contemporaries* (London: Macmillan, 1982), p. 88. Michael Hattaway thinks the play was written before the other two parts of the sequence at some date between 1589 and 1591; see his edition of the play (Cambridge: Cambridge University Press, 1990). Gloriana, the 'most royall Queene or Empresse', was the name Spenser gave to Elizabeth in his epic poem *The Faerie Queene* (1596). The identification of Elizabeth with Gloriana had also received at least one explicit airing on the stage prior to *The Revenger's Tragedy* in Dekker's play *Old Fortunatus* (Rose: 1599).
4 *The Revenger's Tragedy* was performed at the Globe Theatre by the King's Men in the season of 1606–7. For discussion of the dating of this play, see R. A. Foakes's edition (Manchester: Manchester University Press, 1966), p. lxix; and Lawrence J. Ross's edition (London: Edward Arnold, 1966), p. xii.
5 I take the view, argued so persuasively by Richard Dutton, that topical allusion, often politically controversial, was the norm rather than the exception for much of the drama of the period. See his *Mastering the Revels: the Regulation and Censorship of English*

Epilogue

preoccupied with issues of idolatry and the controversy over the rehabilitation of religious imagery and ceremony, both features of the increasingly influential Arminianism.[6] The absurd homage played out to the dressed up corpse of the Lady in Act V Scene ii is not so far from the formal lying-in-state ritual that would be played out to James's effigy while it lay in state at Denmark House some fifteen years later. Both performances are theatrically self-conscious but both also have an equivocal status and must have seemed idolatrous in the minds of at least some members of a contemporary audience. They show how dangerously close the emergent Caroline *religion royale* was to the ritual of the Catholic Church.

The liminal space occupied by both the royal theatre of death and the theatre itself in iconoclastic post-Reformation Britain was created by the very ambiguity of the symbols through which they primarily operated. The theatre can explore the potential idolatry involved in symbolic representation with great irony. In *The Second Maiden's Tragedy*, the Tyrant's homage to the Lady's body is clearly idolatrous but the audience is also compromised by the very act of observing the scene. On a deeper level all stage representation mirrors creation and thus contravenes strict Calvinist interpretations of the second commandment. Ultimately Calvinists questioned the legitimacy of using symbols whether in stage drama or in the context of religious ritual, including heraldic, and presumably even royal, funerals. Perhaps the extremists' ultimate quarrel was more with the ambiguous than with the idolatrous. That which cannot be pinned down to a specific meaning is dangerous and always potentially subversive.

It has become almost customary to offer a modern parallel at the close of any study in cultural history. The continuing relevance of funeral ritual in the world political arena has been recently demonstrated by the obsequies of Kim Il Sung, dictator of North Korea, one of the last remaining bastions of communism. Crowds gathered in the streets of Pyongyang to witness the ceremonies, which were held on 19 July 1994. In an arresting analogy to the Renaissance royal effigy ritual, the key element of this funeral procession was a ten foot portrait of the dead leader, his face alive with smiles. This portrait was surely designed to provide a focus for the grief of the nation, whether genuine or meticulously orchestrated. The comparison with Renaissance royal funerals can be taken further. The Pyongyang ceremonies were carefully organized to enhance Kim

---

Renaissance Drama (London: Macmillan, 1991). See also Leonard Tennenhouse, *Power on Display: The Politics of Shakespeare's Genres* (London: Methuen, 1986), pp. 2, 10, 15. For an opposite view, see Smuts, p. 81.

6 *The Second Maiden's Tragedy* was written between the end of May 1610 and 31 October 1611, the date of the licence on the MS prompt book. See Anne Lancashire, ed., *The Second Maiden's Tragedy* (Manchester: Manchester University Press, 1978), pp. 14–15.

Jong Il's image as the inheritor of his father's legacy. The son and heir bowed repeatedly in front of his father's coffin, before it was driven off through the streets of the capital behind the smiling portrait. There was a two-day delay in the funeral proceedings, perhaps because Kim Jong Il wanted more time to secure his position. In the event, however, the funeral preceded any public pronouncement of his succession. The ritual demonstration of the succession in the funeral was, therefore, valuable propaganda. Further, the official television portrayal of the obsequies was able to transmit an alternative version of events, much in the manner of the variant written and pictorial accounts of Mary Stuart's funeral. Kim Jong Il's stepmother, Kim Song Ae, who was listed as present at the funeral ceremony, was edited out of television footage of the mourning ceremonies. In a final parallel, Kim Il Sung's body was embalmed in Moscow at a cost of £200,000 and put on display to preserve Kim Jong Il's lineal link with his popular predecessor in the minds of the Korean people. So far Kim Jong Il's position seems secure but the funeral and ritual succession may have only postponed a power struggle.

This late twentieth-century North Korean funeral, like the funeral of James Staurt, was overtly political in its messages, but as part of a tightly-controlled communist regime, it has so far proved more resistant, perhaps, to the subversive effects of lost ambiguity.

In the three years since the completion of the doctoral thesis upon which this book is based, the situation in North Korea has deteriorated. Economically the country is in a desperate state, the border with the South remains tense and the nuclear program is a source of considerable anxiety in the West. Kim Jong Il survives so far but his position is by no means secure. It is perhaps unlikely that he will receive the orchestrated adulation accorded his father in 1994.

Finally, a few thoughts about the current status of funeral ritual in this country. The last decade has seen an increasing recognition of the worth of the funeral ritual, a reaction against the sanitized and de-ritualized hospital death and the often tawdry, commercialized and impersonal service provided by the new brand of chain funeral parlours. Some funeral directors are letting their customers take a more active role in planning the obsequies of their loved one, and some are providing highly individual ritual accoutrements. One firm, for example, has recently introduced a line of coffins decorated in psychedelic colours for the benefit of the 1960's hippies now approaching old age, while another sells fully-biodegradable coffins for the environmentally-aware. For those who want to select from a wide range of funeral products, coffins, cremation urns, memorial tablets and headstones, the country now boasts a number of funeral supermarkets, following the example set by French companies.

So much for the funeral appurtenances; what of the ritual itself? In our increasingly atheistic world, there has been some move towards developing non-religious ceremonies that nevertheless meet the ritual requirements of the social group that has lost one of its members. The humanist society has long provided services to meet this need.

Finally, with such items as the psychedelic coffins on offer for defunct hippies, how far are we away, I wonder, from the creation of a company that designs and organizes theme or period funeral rituals to order: Viking ship burials, Victorian processions with swathes of black crepe, or a Renaissance 'royal' funeral, complete with a life-size effigy of the defunct? Whatever form the funeral rituals of the future take will depend on the cultural trends of the time. The funeral directors of the twenty-first century will no more be able to dictate arbitrarily the form of a contemporary funeral than the organizers of the Renaissance royal funerals could impose ritual forms on participants and audience with no regard for their expectations.

APPENDIX I

The Funeral Procession of Elizabeth I (1603)

There follows a transcription of Henry Chettle's 'The Order and Proceedings at the Funerall of the Right High and Mightie Princesse Elizabeth Queene of England, France and Ireland, from the Pallace of Westminster, called Whitehall: To the Cathedrall Church of Westminster 28th April 1603', as printed in *A Third Collection of Scarce and Valuable Tracts*, 3 vols (London: F. Gogan, 1751), I, 51–4. The extra information included in the square brackets is from CA, Vincent MS 151 fols 521–35.

First the Knight Marshals man to make way
240 poor women (4 x 4)
Several Gentlemen Esquires and Knights
2 porters
4 trumpeters
Rose, Pursuivant at Arms [Philip Holland]
2 Serjeants at Arms
The Standard of the Dragon [borne by Sir George Bourchur]
2 Querries leading a Horse
Messengers of the Chamber (4 x 4)
Children of the Almonry
Children of the Woodyard
Children of the Skullery
Children of the furnes of Pastry
The Skalding house
Caterie
The larder
Grooms
Wheat Porter
Coopers
Wine Porters
Conductors in the Bakehouse
Bell-ringer
Master of Spice-bags
Cart-takers, chosen by the bord
Long cartes
Cart-takers:
Of the Almery
Of the Stable
Of the Woodyard
Skullery
Pastrie
Skalding-house
Poultrie
Purveyors of the Poultrie
Boyling house
Larder
Ewry
Confectionary
Wafery
Chaundry
Pitcher-house
butterie
seller
Pantrie
Bake-house
Noblemen and Ambassadors Servants
Grooms of Chamber
4 trumpeters
Blewmantle [Mercury Laten]
1 Serjeant at Arms
The Standard of the Greyhound [borne by Mr Philip Herbert, brother of the Earl of Pembroke]
2 Querries leading a Horse

210

The Funeral Procession of Elizabeth I

Yeomen of the Servitors in the Hall (4 x 4)
Cart-takers
Porters
Almondrie
Herberger
Woodyard
Skullery
Pastrie
Poultry and Skalding house
Purveyors of the Poultrie
Purveyors of the Acatrie
Stable
Boyling-house
Larder
Kitchen
Ewrie
Confectionarie
Waferie
Purveyor of the Wax
Tallow Chandler
Pitcher-house
Brewers
Butterie
Purveyors
Seller
Pantrie
Garneter
Bake-house
Counting-house
Spicery
Chamber
Robes
Wardrobe
Earls and Countesses Servants
4 trumpeters
Portcullis [Samuell Thompson]
1 Serjeant at Arms
[The Standard of the Lion borne by Mr Thomas Somerset]
2 Querries leading a horse trapped with velvet
Serjeant of the vestry
Children of the chapell in surplerses
Gentlemen of the Chapell in copes

Deputie Clarke of the market
Marshall of the Hall
Clarkes Extraordinaire
Cofferer
Diet
M. Cooke for the household
Pastrie
Larder
Skullerie
Woodyard
Poultrie
Bake-house
Acatrie
Stable
Serjeants
Gentleman Harbinger
Serjeants of the:
Woodyard
Skullery
Pastrie
Caterie
Larder
Ewry
Seller
Pastrie
Bake-House
Master Cooke of the Kitchen
Clarks of the Querrie
Second and Third Clarkes of the Chaundrie
Second and Third Clarkes of the kitchen
Supervisors of the Dresser
Surveyors of the Dresser
Surveyor of the Dresser for the Chamber
Musicians
Apothecaries and Chirurgions
Sewers of the Hall
Sewers of the Chamber
Groom Porter
Gentlemen Ushers and Waiters
Clarke, Marshall and Almoner
Chiefe Clarke of the Wardrop
Chiefe Clarke of the Kitchen
2 Clark Controllers

Appendix I

Clarke of the Green Cloath
Master of the Household
Cofferer
Rouge Dragon [William Smith]
1 Serjeant at Arms
Banner of Chester [borne by Lord Zouch]
[Clarkes of the Councell]
[Clarkes of the Privy Seale]
Clarkes of the Signet
Sir John Popham [Lord Chief Justice]
Clarkes of the Parliament
Doctors of the Physick
The Queen's Chaplaines
Secretaries for the Latin and French tongue
Rouge Crosse [Thomas Knight]
2 Serjeants at Arms
Dukes Second Sonnes
Banner of Cornwall [borne by Lord Herbert, eldest sonne to Earle of Worcester]
Aldermen of London
Solicitor, Attorney and Serjeant
Master of the Revels and Master of the Tents
Knights Bachelor
Lord Chiefe Baron and Lord Chiefe Justice of the Common Pleas
Master of the Jewell House
Knights and Ambassadors and Gentlemen Agents
Sewers for the Queen
Sewers of the Body
Esquires of the Body
Lancaster [Francis Thinne] and Windsor
Banner of Wales, [borne by Viscount Bindon]
Banner of Ireland
Master of the Requests
Agents for Venice and the Estates
Lord Mayor of London
Sir John Fortescue [Master of the Wardrobe]
Sir Robert Cecil, principall Secretary
Controller and Treasurer of the Household
Barons
Bishops
Earles Eldest Sonnes
Viscounts
Earles
Marquesses
Bishop Almoner and Preacher [Anthony Watson, Bishop of Chichester]
Lord Keeper
The French Ambassador
Archbishop of Canterbury
4 Serjeants at Arms
Great Banner
Somerset [Robert Treswell] and Richmond [John Raven]
Yorke [Raph Brooke] with the helm and crest
[Chester, James Thomas with the target]
Norroy King at Arms [William Segar] with the sword
Clarenceaux King at Arms [William Camden] with the Coate
Gentlemen Ushers with white rods
The lively Picture of her Highnesse whole body, crowned in Parliament Robes, lying on the Corps balmed and leaded, covered with velvet, borne on a chariot, drawn by four horses, trapt in Black Velvet
6 Banner Rolls on each side
Gentlemen Pensioners with axes, their points downward
Footmen
A Canopy borne over the Chariot by four Noblemen
2 Earles assistant to her
Earl of Worcester, Master of the Horse leading the Palfrie of Honour
2 Esquires and a Groom, to attend and leade him away
Gentleman Usher
Garter King of Arms [Sir William Dethick]
Lady Marchionesse of Northampton [Chiefe Mourner], assisted by the Lord Treasurer and the Lord Admiral.
Her Traine supported by the Master Vice-Chamberlaine [Sir John Stanhope]
14 Countesses assistant

The Funeral Procession of Elizabeth I

Gentlewomen of the Privy Chamber
Countesses
Viscountesses
Earles daughters
Baronesses
Maids of Honour of the Privy Chamber

Captain of the Guard with all the Guard following, five by five in a rank, their Halberds downward
Farewell
   Henry Chettle

APPENDIX II

The Funeral Rites of Charles IX of France[1]

After a long and painful illness, Charles IX died at half past three in the afternoon on 30 May 1574, the day of Pentecost, at the château de Vincennes. Dressed in a pourpoint camisole, the body remained on view for one day before being delivered up to the surgeons for the autopsy.

Under their supervision, the heart and entrails were removed and the body embalmed. The heart was to be buried separately in the church of the Celestines in Paris, before the main funeral rites. The body, encased in a coffin made of wood and lead, was placed once again in the chamber where the King had died. There the coffin was displayed on a bed of richly embroidered red satin and attended by officers of the King's household and forty-eight monks of the four mendicant orders who commenced the religious rites: the vigils, prayers and masses said for the dead King.[2]

Meanwhile the adjacent room was transformed into a 'salle d'honneur'. When ready, an effigy of the King, 'après le vif et naturel', was placed in state within on a bed of honour, draped in cloth of gold with an ermine border. The effigy was dressed in a red satin camisole, a tunic of blue satin embroidered with fleurs-de-lis and a royal mantle of purple velvet, again embroidered with fleurs-de-lis and having a collar of ermine.[3] Around the neck of the effigy hung the Order of St Michel, and on its head, over a red satin bonnet, was the imperial crown studded with jewels.[4] Its feet were clad in golden slippers with red satin soles.

On a richly embroidered velvet pillow to the right of the effigy lay the royal sceptre. While on the left, on a similar cushion, lay the hand of justice. At the foot of the bed were two little stools bearing a golden cross and a silver fount of holy water. On either side two further stools were provided for the heralds-at-arms who continually watched over the body.

---

[1] This account is based on Bibliothèque Nationale, Manuscrits français 18536, reproduced by Simon Goulart in his *Mémoirs de l'Estat de France Sous Charles Neufiesme*, 2nd edn, 3 vols (Paris: [n. pub.], 1577), III, 374–86. Also referred to are BN, (fr) 4317 and 18523, in particular for the order of the convoy.

[2] The four mendicant orders, the Carmelites, Augustines, Capuchins and Jacobins, were specialists in death. See Santiago, pp. 81–4; and Ariès, p. 83.

[3] The 'purple' robes are severally referred to as being red, scarlet or vermilion by various writers. See Giesey (1960), p. 56.

[4] The Valois kings adopted the closed imperial crown in imitation of Charles V. See Bryant, p. 109; and Guenée, p. 147.

A sumptuous canopy of gold and silver tapestry studded with pearls was suspended over the bed. Silver gilt candlesticks supporting white candles stood on altars on either side of the bed. Two more large candles at the foot of the bed provided the only remaining light in the room. The walls were lined with chairs draped in gold, upon which were seated the cardinals, prelates, gentlemen and officers who were continually present in the chamber.

The effigy lay in state for forty days. During this period, meals were served to the effigy at the usual hours of dinner and supper, exactly in the manner practised when the King had been alive. The table was set by the officers of the commissary; the service carried by the gentlemen servants, the bread-carrier, the cup-bearer and the carver; the usher marching in front of them followed by the officers of the cupboard who spread the table with the reverences and samplings that were customarily made. After the bread was broken and prepared, the meat and other courses were brought in by the usher, steward, bread-carrier, pages of the chamber, squires of the cuisine and *garde-vaisselle*. The steward presented the napkin to the most dignified person present to wipe the hands of the King. A cardinal proceeded to bless the table and bowls of water for washing the hands were presented at the seat of the King, just as if he had still been living. The three courses of the meal were acted out with all the usual forms, ceremonies and samplings, not omitting the presentation of the cup at the times and junctures when the King had been accustomed to drink at each of his meals. The repast concluded with the offering of water to wash and the saying of grace, the only addition to the normal sequence being the *De profundis* and the *Inclina Domine aurem tuam*. Assisting at the meal were the same people who had been accustomed to speak or respond to his majesty during his lifetime, and also others who were usually present.

Towards the end of the forty-day period the *salle d'honneur* was transformed overnight into a chamber of mourning. Triumph metamorphosed into lugubriousness. The gold and silver canopy was replaced by one of black velvet, twelve feet square in dimension, and decorated with gold cord and black silk embroidered with gold thread. Beneath the canopy, the effigy had disappeared. In its place, on an elevated platform, lay the coffin covered with a black velvet mortuary drape which had a large white satin cross in the centre, overlain with a cloth of gold. Around the bier was erected a barrier, seven feet wide, bearing fourteen large candles, each made with ten pounds of white wax, their flames burning continuously day and night.

The imperial crown rested on the centre of a square of cloth of gold at the head of the coffin, framed by the sceptre and hand of justice. A golden cross lay at the foot of the bier. The earlier arrangement of stools for the fonts of holy water and the heralds-at-arms was preserved. Two altars, one high and one low, were placed on either side of the coffin. Both were covered in black velvet drapes with white satin crosses. Services of high and low mass were performed at these respective altars from dawn until midday.

The encoffined body remained in this chamber of mourning until it was

Appendix II

transported in a processional convoy from the Bois de Vincennes to the Church of St Antoine des Champs, on the 10 July 1574.[5] This procession was headed by the five hundred poor, dressed in mourning, each carrying a torch bearing the royal arms and led by an escort of twenty men holding black batons to guide the poor and keep order. There followed a host of men-of-arms, servants, officers and gentlemen, the premier steward bringing up the rear of this group. Next came the guard of honour preceded by the premier squire carrying the Banner of France, its brilliant colours of blue and gold hidden beneath black crepe; and six pages mounted on chargers, tired in black velvet horse-cloths which trailed right to the ground. A group of church dignitaries, heralds-at-arms and twenty-four archers preceded five knights carrying the *pièces d'honneur* – two spurs, escutcheon, coat of arms, helmet and gauntlets – all draped in black. Then came the parade horse, entirely covered with a violet cloth embroidered with fleur-de-lis. The body followed, carried on a funeral chariot; while the rear of the procession comprised knights of the Order of St. Michel and four hundred archers of the guard, marching with their ensigns furled.[6] The effigy made no appearance in this part of the procession.

As the convoy approached the church of St Antoine, the twenty-four town-criers of Paris took their places in front of the poor. Representatives of the estates of Paris, together with a number of presidents of the court and councillors, lined the route leading to the church, bowing their bared heads in reverence as the coffin passed their ranks.

That evening a service was held in the church attended by officers and domestic servants of the deceased King. The church itself was hung with black drapes, garnished with escutcheons and brilliantly illuminated by the light of numerous candles.

On the morning of the 11 July, following the celebration of mass, the portals of the church were closed to allow the effigy to be laid on the funeral chariot which was then positioned at the entrance of the church. There the ranks of the prevosts of the merchants, the aldermen and other municipal officials and the bourgeois of Paris, who had come that morning in procession from the *Hôtel de Ville*, filed past the corpse and effigy aspersing both with holy water.[7] Then Pierre de Condy, Bishop of Paris said the subvenite and aspersed the corpse and effigy himself signalling the commencement of the procession to Notre Dame.

---

[5] BN 18536 has St Antoine des Champs but is probably inaccurate. More likely the church was St-Antoine-des-Quinze-Vingts, which was traditionally the final station of the funeral convoy before its entry into Paris; see Giesey (1960), p. 37. The church was located outside the city walls to the east of Paris, just north of the present-day Gare de Lyon. There may be confusion with Notre-Dame-des-Champs, a church in the south of Paris to which Francis I's body was taken.

[6] The Order of St Michel was created by Louis XI in 1469. See Boureau (1988), p. 112, n. 24.

[7] François Bonnardot, ed., *Régistres des Délibérations du Bureau de la Ville de Paris*, 18 vols (Paris: Imprimerie Nationale, 1883–1953), VII (1893), 9.

The Funeral Rites of Charles IX

The vanguard was formed of the archers and cross-bowmen of Paris whose job was to keep the crowd in its place and the route clear. Then came the various mendicant orders and the parish curates; then the five hundred poor; followed by the twenty-four town-criers ringing their bells constantly and calling on the people to pray for the soul of the 'trèshaut, très puissant, et très magnanime Charles par la grace de Dieu Roy de France très chrétien neuf[e] de ce nom. Prince clément et victorieux grand zélateur de paix et justice'. Next came the watch and the police; the advocates, notaries and other officials of Châtelet; then the families of the princes, cardinals and gentlemen, all in mourning.[8] Next came the chaplains of Notre Dame and St. Chapelle, marching with the Rector of the University. There followed two files marching side-by-side: the collegians and other religious on one side and the university on the other. The first part of the procession was completed by a group of one hundred Swiss guards; followed by two hundred gentlemen; the officers of the King's household; the First Esquire carrying the pennon; and finally the trumpeters and hautboy-players.[9] The funeral cart bearing the coffin came next, escutcheons fixed to its sides, with the mortuary drape now enriched with eight large embroidered coats of arms. Thus the cart was called a *chariot d'armes*.[10] It was drawn by six chargers with black velvet cloths reaching right to the ground. Then came the six knights bearing the *pièces d'honneur*, the coat of arms borne by the knight-in-chief.

A group of archbishops and bishops, wearing copes and mitres of white damask, separated the coffin escort from the focal point of the convoy: the effigy, which was appearing for the first time since the overnight transformation of the *salle d'honneur* into the *salle de deuil*. The cardinals of Lorraine, Bourbon and Aix, marching three-abreast, immediately preceded the parade horse, which was led by two valets on foot.[11] Next, side-by-side marched the Master of the Horse carrying the Sword of France, the Bishop of Paris and the Grand Almoner, accompanied by a chaplain bearing a cross.[12]

The effigy followed on a litter, borne according to established privilege by the *hanouars*, the salt-carriers of the city of Paris.[13] The *hanouars* were, however, all but totally screened from view by the golden mortuary drape trailing almost

---

[8] For a detailed discussion of the various styles of mourning appropriate to different ranks, see Santiago, pp. 116–69.

[9] A corps of one hundred Swiss guards became part of the royal household in 1497; see Boureau (1988), p. 112, n. 25.

[10] Giesey (1960), p. 12; see also Ariès, p. 118.

[11] BN 18532 puts the ambassadors here; but I have followed BN 18536 and 4317 placing them later in the convoy. The ambassadors also appeared in the later position at the funeral of Francis I. The Cardinal of Aix is not mentioned in BN 18523.

[12] The sword of France was also carried in front of the king as he left Rheims Cathedral after his coronation; see Bryant, p. 111 and Duchésne, p. 232. There was a kind of mysticism surrounding the sword; see Giesey (1960), pp. 68–9, 134 n. 30. The Bishop of Paris and the Grand Almoner are only mentioned in BN 18523.

[13] For more information on the role of the *hanouars* in the funeral convoy, see Giesey (1960), pp. 61–6.

Appendix II

to the ground, on which the effigy lay.[14] The corners of this mortuary drape were held by the four presidents of the Parlement of Paris dressed in their traditional scarlet robes.[15] Gentlemen of the Chamber accompanied them. The Duke of Aumale marched on the immediate right of the effigy, while on the left marched the Marquis of Nomchy who was representing the Duke of Mayenne.[16] Behind the effigy came the First Chamberlain who carried the Banner of France, and after him the Marshal of Retz.[17]

A canopy, which had in fact been provided by the town officials, was supported by the four *échevins* of Paris.[18] Rather than being held directly above the effigy, the canopy was carried a little behind so as not to obscure the effigy from view.[19]

Behind the canopy came the princes of deep mourning: the Duke of Alençon and the King of Navarre together with the Prince of Conde and his brother Francis of Bourbon, on horseback and wearing black robes of mourning with long trains.[20] They represented the mourning of the royal family.[21] Following them were the papal nuncio, and the ambassadors of the Empire, Scotland, Venice, Ferrara and Spain. The procession tailed off with a group of ushers of the royal chamber; gentlemen; knights and a royal guard of harquibusiers.

The entrance to Notre Dame was lit by two large candles and the wooden doors decorated with two large embroidered escutcheons. The nave, choir and transept were hung with black drapes embellished with more escutcheons. The main altar and lesser altars were also covered with black velvet. The whole church was lit with innumerable candles and lights; and for the reception of the effigy a *chapelle ardente*, hung with little bells and brilliantly illuminated, had been placed in the centre of the choir.

The seating arrangement for the service at Notre Dame was made according

---

[14] The *hanouars* are not mentioned in all the manuscript sources, but are included in BN 4315 and also in Bonnardot, VII, 193.

[15] BN 18523 erroneously has six presidents. This formation was imitated in the royal entry ceremony where the four presidents of Parlement bore the king's wax seal, see Bryant, p. 56. The seal was not displayed in the funeral ceremony; see Giesey (1960), p. 68.

[16] BN 18536 and 4317 put Aumale later in the convoy but they also omit the canopy and would seem to be less than accurate at this point. The Marquis of Nomchy is mentioned in BN 18523.

[17] The banner of France was deemed to be quasi-sacred, see Jackson, p. 33. BN 4317 and 18536 put Retz after Alençon, Navarre, the princes of blood and the ambassadors.

[18] The four *échevins* (aldermen in the municipal government) included the *prévôt des marchands* (the mayor of Paris); the registrar; the *procureur* (solicitor); and the *receveur* (tax-collector), see the glossary of terms in Salmon (1975), pp. 343–51. They are identified in Claude Malingré, *Les Antiquitez de la Ville de Paris* (Paris: Pierre Rocolel, 1640), p. 686, as Président Charron (*prévôt*); Jean le Jay; Jean de Bragelonne; and Robert Danés.

[19] Du Tillet, p. 343.

[20] BN 4315 mentions also a Duke de Longuet whom I have been unable to identify.

[21] See Giesey (1960), p. 14. BN 4317 and 18536 put Alençon and Navarre immediately behind the effigy.

to strict protocol. The princes of deep mourning were seated on high chairs in the choir; in front of them, on lower chairs, were the lesser nobles and then the knights of the Order. On the same side on still lower chairs were the two captains of the guard, and the captain of the hundred gentlemen. Opposite, seated on high chairs, were the ambassadors, the Rector of the University and Parlement of Paris. Before the high altar sat the Bishop of Paris with his assistants, and just to one side the cardinals seated on a long bench. Below them, on another bench were the gentlemen of the chamber who remained there throughout the whole of the service and vigils.

The following day, after the Bishop of Paris had celebrated the final mass, and the offertory had been reached, the princes of deep mourning were led one by one to the offertory chapel where they kissed the *platine*, took a white candle, decorated with five or six golden coats of arms, from one of the heralds-at-arms and were then led back to their seats by the master of ceremonies. Finally, the funeral oration, lasting about one hour, was pronounced by Monsieur de Saint Foy. Once the service was over, everybody retired to dine.

At one o'clock those involved in the procession together with the other court officials and the estates of Paris, gathered once more to march to the church of Saint-Denis. At the gate of Saint-Denis the municipal officials who had been carrying the canopy over the effigy delivered it up to gentlemen of the late King's household who would bear it to the doors of the church.[22] When the convoy arrived at a point between Paris and Saint-Denis called the *croix penchante*, the abbot of Saint-Denis, the Cardinal of Lorraine, came to receive the body and effigy of the King, and to bring them to the church which had undergone the same preparations for the funeral as had been made at Notre Dame: draped in black, and complete with a splendidly lit *chapelle ardente*.

The Cardinal of Lorraine officiated at vespers and again the next morning for the final high mass, assisted by various archbishops and bishops. The same ceremony that had taken place at Notre Dame, involving the princes of deep mourning proceeding to the offertory chapel, was observed. Monsieur de Saint Foy again pronounced the funeral orison.

After the service the Cardinal of Lorraine proceeded to the grave and vault prepared for the reception of the body which was carried to the graveside, still in its coffin, by the gentlemen of the chamber. After further prayers the coffin was placed in the grave at which point the most senior and principal herald-at-arms called out in a loud voice commanding all the other heralds-at-arms to come forward and deposit their coats of arms on the wooden railing built around and above the vault. They were followed by the captains of the guard carrying their ensigns. Next came eight knights bearing the *pièces d'honneur*, together with the crown, the sceptre and the hand of justice, all of which were laid right in the vault. At this moment the herald cried out three times in a loud voice 'Le Roy est mort'. Then, as the Banner of France was raised on high, the

---

[22] Bonnardot, p. 194.

Appendix II

herald cried three times 'Vive le Roy Henry troisième de ce nom a qui Dieu donne bonne vie'. Then all the objects were recovered from the barrier and raised on high. The objects in the grave were not recovered immediately. Traditionally, they were not displayed again in public until the coronation of the next king.

The ceremony at the graveside over, the party retired to the great hall for the funeral dinner. This room, too, had been draped in black. After grace had been said, Monsieur Aumale, representing the Grand Master, addressed the company saying that now, since their master was dead, the household would be dissolved, in token of which he broke his baton. The funeral ceremonies of Charles IX were over.

BIBLIOGRAPHY

Maniscript Sources

Bodleian Library (Bod.), Oxford
    Ashmole MS: 818, 836, 840, 845, 857, 1116
    Eng. Hist. MSS: c.480
    North MSS: c.4, c.29
    Top. Yorks MSS: d.7

British Library (BL), London
    Additional MS: 5408, 14417, 35324, 38141, 45131
    Cotton MSS: Julius B XII, Vespasian C XIV
    Egerton MS: 2642
    Harley MS: 1310, 1354, 1368, 1776, 2129, 3504, 3881, 4774, 6064
    Lansdowne MS: 23, 50, 82, 88
    Stowe MS: 152

College of Arms (CA), London
    Briscoe MS: I, II
    I Series MS: III, IV, XI, XIII, XIV, XV
    Nayler (Press 20F/ Royal Funerals): 1618–1738
    Vincent MS: 87, 151

Public Records Office (PRO), London
    SP 12/199   SP 14/1   SP 52/42   E351/3145
    SP 12/203   SP 14/71   SP 78/17

Westminster Abbey Library (WA), London
    Manuscripts: 6323, 6348, 6353, 6371, 6398, 6416, 6418, 31903, 41090, 41095, 41658, 41770, 47630
    Box: Royal Funeral Effigies

Bibliothèque Nationale (BN), Paris
    Manuscrits français (fr): 2691, 2762, 2968, 4315, 4317, 18523, 18536

Primary Sources: Printed

Acts of the Privy Council, ed. by J. R. Dasent, 32 vols (London: [n. pub.], 1890–1907) vols: 1558–70; 1587–8; 1601–4; 1625–6

Adams, Robert M., *Ben Jonson's Plays and Masques* (London: W. W. Norton, 1979)

A Directory For the Publique Worship of God Throughout the three Kingdoms of England, Scotland and Ireland (London: [n. pub.], 1644)

Bibliography

A Dirge for the Directory, written by one of King James ancient Protestants (Oxford: [n. pub.], 1645)
'An Extract relating to the Burial of King Edward IV', *Archaeologia* 1 (1777), 348–355
A Sermon at the Funeral solemnitie of the most high and mighty Prince Ferdinanndus, the late Emperour of most famous memorye, St. Pauls, 1564 ([London (?)]: [n. pub.], 1564)
Akrigg, G. P. V., ed., *The Letters of James VI and I* (London: University of California Press, 1984)
Alexander, Sir William, *An Elegie on the Death of Prince Henrie* (Edinburgh: Andro Hart, 1612)
Anglorum lacrimae: In a sad passion complayning the death of [. . .] Queene Elizabeth ([London (?)]: T. Pavier, 1603)
Arber, Edward, *An English Garner* (London: Constable, 1897), VIII
Ayre, John, ed., *The Works of John Jewel, Bishop of Salisbury,* 4 vols (Cambridge: Cambridge University Press, 1845–50), II (1847)
Bacon, Francis, 'Observations on a Libel', in *The Letters and the Life of Francis Bacon,* ed. by James Spedding, 7 vols (London: [n. pub.], 1861–72), I
Bacon, Francis, 'Post-Nati', in *The Works of Sir Francis Bacon,* ed. by J. Spedding and D. D. Heath, 7 vols (London: [n. pub.], 1892), VII
Bayne, Peter, ed., *Documents Relating to the Settlement of the Church of England* (London: W. Kent, 1862)
Birch, Thomas, *The Life of Henry Prince of Wales, Eldest Son of King James I* (London: A. Millar, 1760)
Bloxham, M. H., *Fragmentaria Sepulchralia: A Glimpse of Sepulchral and Early Monumental Remains of Great Britain* (Oxford: Oxford University Press, 1840–50)
Bolton, Edmund, *The Elements of Armories* (London: [n. pub.], 1610)
Bonnardot, François, ed., *Régistres des Déliberations du Bureau de la Ville de Paris,* 18 vols (Paris: Imprimerie Nationale, 1883–1953)
Boswell, John, *Works of Armory* (London: [n. pub.], 1597)
Botero, Giovanni, *The cause of greatnesse of cities. Three bookes with certain observations concerning the sea,* trans. by T. Hawkins (London: H. Seile, 1635)
Brantôme, Pierre de Bourdeille, Seigneur de, *Œuvres Complètes de Pierre de Bourdeille seigneur de Brantôme,* ed. by L. Lalanne, 11 vols (Paris: [n. pub.], 1864–1882), VII
Brathwait, Richard, *Remains after Death: [. . .] including divers memorable observances* (London: [n. pub.], 1618)
Browne, Sir Thomas, *The Major Works,* ed. by C. A. Patrides (Harmondsworth: Penguin Books, 1977)
Bruce, John ed., *The Diary of John Manningham* (London, Camden Society, 1868)
Calendar of State Papers, Domestic Series (CSPD): *Edward VI, Mary I, Elizabeth I, James I*: vols I (1547–1580); II (1581–90); VIII (1603–1610); IX (1611–18); *Charles I*: I (1625–6); and Addenda, XXIII (1625–49)
Calendar of State Papers, Foreign Series (CSPF): vols I (1558–9); X (1572–4); XXI (1586–88) parts I–IV
Calendar of State Papers, Scotland (CSPSc): vol. I (1509–1603)
Calendar of State Papers, Spain (CSPS): *Relating to English Affairs*: vol. IV (1587–1603)
Calendar of State Papers, Venice (CSPV): vols VII (1558–80); VIII (1581–91); IX (1592–1603); X (1603–07); XI (1607–10); XII (1610–13); and XIX (1625–6)

Bibliography

Camden, William, *The Historie of the most renowned and victorious Princesse Elizabeth, late Queene of England* (London: Benjamin Fisher, 1630)
Camden, William, *Remaines [. . .] Concerning Britaine* (London: [n. pub.], 1870)
Cardwell, Edward, ed., *The Two Books of Common Prayer, [. . .] of Edward Sixth: Compared With Each Other* (Oxford: Oxford University Press, 1841)
Carier, Benjamin, *A Missive to His Majesty of Great Britain King James*, ed. by N. Strange (Paris: [n. pub], 1649)
Chettle, Henry, 'The Order and Proceeding at the Funerall of [. . .] Elizabeth Queene of England [. . .] 28th April 1603', in *A Third Collection of Scarce and Valuable Tracts*, 3 vols (London: F. Gogan, 1751), I
Christmas, H., ed., *The Selected Works of John Bale* (Cambridge: Parker Society, 1849)
Cimber, M. L. [Lafaist, L.] and F. Danjou, eds, *Archives Curieuses de L'Histoire de France Depuis Louis XI Jusqu'à Louis XVIII*, 30 vols (Paris: Bourgogne and Martinet, 1834–41), VIII (1836)
Clapham, John, *Elizabeth of England: certain observations concerning the life and reign of Queen Elizabeth*, ed. by E. P. Read and C. Read (Philadelphia: University of Pennsylvania Press, 1951)
Clay, William Keatinge, ed., *Liturgies and Occasional Forms of Prayer set forth in the Reign of Queen Elizabeth* (Cambridge: Cambridge University Press, 1847)
Comper, F. M. M., ed., *The Book of the Craft of Dying* (London: Longmans, 1917)
Cornwallis, Sir Charles, *The Life and Death of Our Late Most Incomparable and Heroique Prince, Henry, Prince of Wales: A Prince (for Valour and Vertue) fit to be Imitated in Succeeding Times* (London: [n. pub.], 1641)
Corrie G. E., ed., *Sermons by Hugh Latimer* (Parker Society, 1844)
Corrie, G. E., ed., *The Works of Hugh Latimer* (London: Parker Society, 1844)
Cox, J. Charles, *Churchwarden's Accounts From the Fourteenth Century to the Close of the Seventeenth Century* (London: Methuen, 1913)
Dallington, Robert, *A Survey of the Great Dukes State of Tuscany, 1596* (London: Edward Blount, 1605)
Dallington, Robert, *The View of France* (London: S. Stafford, 1604)
De Beer, E. S., ed., *The Diary of John Evelyn*, 5 vols (Oxford: Clarendon Press, 1955), III
Dekker, Thomas, *The Whore of Babylon*, ed. by Marianne Gateson Riely (London: Garland Publishing, 1980)
Dekker, Thomas, *The Wonderful Year* ([London (?)]: [n. pub.], 1603)
Du Tillet, Jean, *Recueil Des Roys de France: Leurs Couronne et Maison* (Paris: Pierre Mettayer, 1567)
Duchésne, André, *Les Antiquitez et recherches de la grandeur et mageste des roys de France, receuilles tant des auteurs anciens que des meilleurs écrivains de ce siècle* (Paris: Jean Petit-Pas, 1609)
Dyer, Thomas Firminger Thiselton, *Church-Lore Gleanings* (London: A. D. Innes, 1891)
Favyn, André, *The Theatre of Honour and Knighthood* (London: [n. pub.], [1623 (?)])
Favyn, André, *Le Théâtre d'Honneur et de Chevalerie*, 2 vols (Paris: Robert Foüet, 1620)
Ferne, John, *The Blazon of Gentrie* (London: Toby Cooke, 1586)
Firth, C. H., *The Clarke Papers: Selections from the Papers of William Clarke*, 4 vols (London: Longmans & Green, 1891–1901), III (1899)
Firth, C. H., *The Memoirs of Edmund Ludlow: 1625–1672*, 2 vols (Oxford: Clarendon Press, 1894), II

Bibliography

Foakes, R. A. and R. T. Rickert, eds, *Henslowe's Diary* (Cambridge: Cambridge University Press, 1961)
Foakes, R. A., ed., *The Revenger's Tragedy* (Manchester: Manchester University Press, 1966)
Forset, Edward, *A comparative discourse of the bodies natural and politique. Wherein [...] is set forth the true forme of a commonweale, with the dutie of subjects, and the right of the soveraigne* (London: [n. pub.], 1606)
Frere, W. H. and C. E. Douglas, *Puritan Manifestoes: A Study of the Origin of the Puritan Revolt* (New York: Lenox Hill, 1907; repr. 1972)
Frost, David L., ed., *The Selected Plays of Thomas Middleton* (Cambridge: Cambridge University Press, 1978)
Fuller, Thomas, *The Church History of Britain; from the Birth of Jesus Christ, untill the year 1648*, ed. by J. S. Brewer (Oxford: Oxford University Press, 1845)
Gee, Henry and William John Hardy, eds, *Documents illustrative of English Church History* (London: Macmillan, 1896)
Gilby, Anthony, *A pleasant dialogue* (London: [n. pub.], 1581)
Godefroy, Theodore, *Le cérémonial de France*, 3 vols (Paris: Abraham Pacard, 1619)
Goodman, Godfrey, *The court of King James the First*, ed. by John S. Brewer, 2 vols (London: [n. pub.], 1839)
Gorges, Sir Arthur, *The Olympian Catastrophe dedicated to the worthy memory of the most heroicall lord Henry*, ed. by Randell Davies (Kensington: Cayme Press, 1925)
Goss, John, ed., *Ballads of Britain* (London: Bodley Head, 1937)
Goulart, Simon, *Mémoirs de l'Estat de France Sous Charles Neufiesme*, 2nd edn, 3 vols (Paris: [n. pub.], 1577)
Goulart, Simon, *Admirable and memorable Histories containing the wonders of our time*, trans. by E. Grimeston (London: [n. pub.], 1607)
Greenhill, Thomas, *NEKPOKHOEIA; or, The Art of Embalming* (London: [n. pub.], 1705)
Griffiths, John, ed., *The Two Books of Homilies* (Oxford: Oxford University Press, 1859)
Guillim, John, *A Display of Heraldrie* (London: [n. pub.], 1610)
Hanham, Alison, *The Churchwarden's Accounts of Ashburton 1479–1580* (Exeter: Devon and Cornwall Record Society, 1970)
Harington, John, *A tract on the Succession to the Crown, a. d. 1602*, ed. by C. R. Markham (London: Roxburghe Club, 1880)
Harrison, William, *The Description of England*, ed. by Georges Edeles (Ithaca, NY: Cornell University Press, 1968)
Harrison, G. B., ed., *The Elizabethan Journals: 1591–1603*, 3 vols (London: Routledge & Kegan Paul, 1938)
Haton, Claude, *Mémoires*, ed. by Félix Bourquelot, Collection de Documents Inédits sur l'Histoire de France, 2 vols (Paris: Imprimerie Impériale, 1857)
Hatton, Sir Christopher, *Book of Seals*, ed. by Lewis C. Lloyd and Doris Mary Stenton (Oxford: Clarendon Press, 1950)
Hayward, John, *Gods Universal right proclaimed: A sermon preached at Paules Crosse, 27 March 1603* (London: [n. pub.], 1603)
Henry, Philip, *Diaries and Letters 1631–96*, ed. by M. H. Lee (London: [n. pub.], 1882)
Herford, C. H. and Percy and Evelyn Simpson, eds, *Ben Jonson*, 11 vols (Oxford: Clarendon Press, 1925–1954), VII (1941; repr. 1963)
Historical Manuscripts Commission, *Salisbury MSS* Series 9: VII; XIII; XV

Bibliography

Historical Manuscripts Commission, *Downshire MSS*: III (1611–12)
Hooker, Richard, 'Of the Rites of Buriall', in *The Works of Richard Hooker*, ed. by W. Speed Hill and others, 3 vols (London: Harvard University Press, 1977), II, 409–413
Hughes, Paul L. and James F. Larkin, *Tudor Royal Proclamations*, 4 vols (London: Yale University Press, 1964–9), II (1969)
Hutchinson, F. E., ed., *The Works of George Herbert* (Oxford: Clarendon Press, 1941; repr. 1972)
Ingram, R. W., ed., *Records of Early Drama: Coventry* (London: Manchester University Press, 1981)
James I, *Basilikon Doron* (London: John Norton, 1603)
James I, *Basilikon Doron* (Edinburgh: Robert Waldegrave, 1599; repr. Menston: Scolar Press, 1969)
Jebb, Samuel, *The History of the Life and Reign of Mary Queen of Scots* (1725)
King James His Welcome [. . .] With Elizaes Tombe and Epitaph (London: [n. pub], 1603)
Laing, W. and Laing D., *Funerals of the Scottish Queen plain 196 Collections Relative to the Funerals of Mary Queen of Scots* (Edinburgh: [n. pub.], 1882)
Lancashire, Anne, ed., *The Second Maiden's Tragedy* (Manchester: Manchester University Press, 1978)
Lant, Thomas, *The Funeral Procession of Sir Philip Sidney*, ed. by T. De Bry (London: [n. pub.], 1587)
L'Art de Vérifier les Dates des faits Historiques, des Chartes, des Chroniques, et autres anciens monumens, depuis la naissance de notre-seigneur, 3rd edn, 3 vols (Paris: Alexandre Jombert Jeune, 1783), I
Legh, Gerard, *The Accedens of Armory* (1562)
L'Ordre de la Pompe Funebre Observée au Convoy et Funerailles du Très-chrestien, Très-puissant et Très vicotieux Prince, Henry le Grand, Roy de France et de Navarre (Lyon: Claude Morillon, 1610)
Maclure, Millar, *The Paul's Cross Sermons, 1534–1642* (Toronto: University of Toronto Press, 1958)
Malingré, Claude, *Les Antiquitez de la Ville de Paris* (Paris: Pierre Rocolel, 1640)
Malmesbury, William of, *Chronicle of the Kings of England*, ed. by J. A. Giles (London: Henry J. Bohn, 1847)
Marlowe, Christopher, *Tamburlaine the Great*, ed. by J. S. Cunningham (Manchester: Manchester University Press, 1981)
Marston, John, *Antonio's Revenge*, ed. by Reavley Gair (Manchester: Manchester University Press, 1978)
Mausoleum, or the choisest Flowres of the Epitaphs written on the Death of the never-too-much lamented Prince Henrie (Edinburgh: Andro Hart, 1613)
Maxwell, James, *The Laudable Life and Deplorable Death of our late peerlesse Prince Henry* (London: Thomas Pavier, 1612)
McClure, N. E. M., ed., *The Letters of John Chamberlain*, 2 vols (Philadelphia: The American Philosophical Society, 1939)
McIlwain, Charles Howard, ed., *The Political Works of James I* (Harvard: Harvard University Press, 1918; repr. New York: Russell & Russell, 1965)
McMurray, W., *The Records of Two City Parishes* (London: Hunter & Longhurst, 1925)
Misson, M., *Memoirs and Observations of His Travels over England*, trans. by J. Ozell (London: [n. pub.], 1719)

Bibliography

Muret, Pierre, *Rites of Funeral, ancient and modern*, trans. by P. Lorrain (London: [n. pub.], 1683)

Nashe, Thomas, *Martins Months Minde* (London: [n. pub.], 1589)

Nashe, Thomas, *The Unfortunate Traveller and other Works*, ed. by J. B. Steane (London: Penguin Books, 1972; repr. 1985)

Nicolas, Nicholas Harris, *Testamenta Vetusta, being illustrations from wills, of manners, customs, & c., as well as the descents and possessions of many distinguished families, from the reign of Henry the Second to the accession of Elizabeth*, 2 vols (London: Nichols & Son, 1826)

Nichols, J., ed., 'The History of [...] Fotheringay', in *Bibliotheca Topographica Britannica*, ed. by J. Nichols and others, 10 vols (London: the author, 1740–1800), IV (1740)

Nichols, John, ed., *The Progresses and Public Processions of Queen Elizabeth*, 3 vols (London: the author, 1823)

Nichols, John, ed., *The Progresses, Processions and Magnificent Festivities of King James The First, His Royal Consort, Family and Court*, 4 vols (London: the author, 1828)

Nichols, J. G., ed., *The Diary of Henry Machyn* (London: Camden Society, 1848)

Palmer, Anthony, ed., *Tudor Churchwarden's Accounts* (Braughing: Hertfordshire Record Society, 1985)

Park, Thomas, ed., *Nugae Antiquae: being a miscellaneous collection of original papers [...] by Sir John Harington and others*, 2 vols ([London (?)]: [n. pub.], 1804)

Peacham, Henry, *The Compleat Gentleman*, 2nd edn (London: [n. pub.], 1634)

Peck, F., ed., *Desiderata Curiosa*, 2 vols (London: Thomas Evans, 1779), II

Perkins, William, *A Salve for a Sickeman, or a Treatise Containing the Nature, Difference, and Kindes of Death: as Also the Right manner of dying well* (Cambridge: University of Cambridge, 1597)

Person, D., *Varieties, or, A Surveigh of rare and excellent matters* (London: T. Alchorn, 1635)

Platter, Thomas, *Travels in England* (1599), ed. by C. Williams (London: [n. pub.], 1937)

Price, Daniel, *Spiritual Odours to the Memory of Prince Henry* (Oxford: Joseph Barnes, 1613)

Queene Elizabeth's Losse, and King James his Welcome (London: John Smythicke, 1603)

Ross, Lawrence J., ed., *The Revenger's Tragedy* (London: Edward Arnold, 1966)

Rye, William Brenchley, *England as Seen by Foreigners in the Days of Elizabeth and James the First* (London: John Russel Smith, 1865)

Sackville-West, V., ed., *The Diary of the Lady Anne Clifford* (London: Heinemann, 1923)

Scott, W. and J. Bliss, eds, *The Works of the Most Reverend Father in God William Laud*, 7 vols (Oxford, [n. pub.], 1847–60)

Scott, Walter, ed., *A Collection of Scarce and Valuable Tracts*, 2nd edn, 2 vols (London: Cadell & Davies, 1809)

Scott, Edward John Long, ed., *Letter-Book of Gabriel Harvey A. D. 1573–1580* (London: Camden Society, 1884)

Secret History of the Court of James the First, 2 vols (Edinburgh: John Ballantyne, 1811)

Segar, Sir William, *Honour Military and Civill* (London: [n. pub.], 1602)

Segar, Sir William, *The Book of Honor and Arms* (London: [n. pub.], 1590)

Sermons or Homilies appointed to be Read in Churches in the Time of Elizabeth (London: Prayer-Book and Homily Society, 1817)

Shakespeare, William, *Hamlet*, ed. by Philip Edwards (Cambridge: Cambridge University Press, 1985)

Bibliography

Shakespeare, William, *The First Part of King Henry VI*, ed. by Michael Hattaway (Cambridge: Cambridge University Press, 1990)

Shakespeare, William and John Fletcher, *The Two Noble Kinsmen*, ed. by Eugene M. Wraith (Oxford: Clarendon Press, 1989)

Sidney, Sir Philip, *The Old Arcadia*, ed. by Katherine Duncan-Jones (Oxford: Oxford University Press, 1985; repr. 1990)

Simpson, Evelyn M. and George R. Potter, eds, *The Sermons of John Donne*, 10 vols (Berkley: University of California Press, 1953–62), VI (1953)

Smith, L. P., ed., *The Life and Letters of Sir Henry Wotton*, 2 vols (Oxford: Clarendon Press, 1907)

Smith, Nicholas, *The History of Herodian, a Greeke Author, Treating of the Romayne Emperors* (London: [n. pub], [1550 (?)])

Smith J. C. and E. De Selincourt, eds, *Spenser: Poetical Works* (Oxford: Oxford University Press, 1912)

Speed, John, *Historie of Britaine* (London: [n. pub.], 1622)

Speed Hill, W., and others, eds, *The Works of Richard Hooker*, 3 vols (London: Harvard University Press, 1977–90)

Stow, John, *The Annales; or, General Chronicle of England begun first by Maister John Stow and after him continued [. . .] by Edmond Howes* (London: [n. pub.], 1615)

Strode, George, *The Anatomie of Mortalitie* (London: [n. pub.], 1618)

Tate, F., 'Of the Antiquity, Variety and Ceremonies of Funerals in England', in *A Collection of Curious Discourses by Eminent Antiquarians upon several Heads in our English Antiquities*, ed. by T. Hearne, 2 vols (London: [n. pub.], 1771)

The Geneva Bible (London: Robert Barker, 1605)

The True Mannor and Forme of the Proceeding to the Funerall of the right Honorable Earle of Essex (London: [n. pub.], 1646)

The Funerall Pompe and Obsequies of the most Mighty and Puissant Henry the Fourth, King of France and Navarre, solemnized at Paris, and at St. Denis, the 29 and 30 daies of June last past (London: [n. pub.], 1610)

Thiers, J. B., *Traité de l'Exposition du S. Sacrement de l'Autel* (Avignon: [n. pub.], 1777)

Thiers, Jean Baptiste, *Traité de l'Exposition du St Sacrament de l'Autel*, 4th edn, 2 vols (Avignon: [n. pub.], 1777)

Webster, John, *The Duchess of Malfi*, ed. by John Russell Brown (Manchester: Manchester University Press, 1974; repr. 1986)

Weever, John, *Ancient Funerall Monuments* (London: Thomas Harper, 1631)

Weldon, Sir Anthony, 'The court and character of King James', in *Secret history of the court of James the First*, 2 vols (Edinburgh: [n. pub.], 1651; repr. Edinburgh: John Ballantyne, 1811)

Williams, John, *Great Britain's Salomon: A Sermon Preached at the Magnificent Funerall of the most high and mighty King, James* ([London (?)]: J. Bill, 1625)

Wilson, Arthur, *The History of Great Britain Being the Life and Reign of King James the First, Relating to what passed from his first Accession to the Crown, till his Death* (London: Richard Lownds, 1653)

Winwood, Sir Ralph, *Memorials of Affairs of State*, ed. by Edmund Sawyer, 3 vols (London: [n. pub.], 1725

Wotton, Henry, *The Elements of Architecture* (London: [n. pub.], 1624)

Wyrley, William, *The True Use of Armourie* (London: Gabriell Cawood, 1592)

Bibliography

Secondary Sources

Adams, Simon, 'Spain or the Netherlands? The Dilemmas of Early Stuart Foreign Policy', in *Before the English Civil War: Essays on Early Stuart Politics and Government*, ed. by Howard Tomlinson (London: Macmillan, 1983)

Addleshaw, G. W. O. and F. Etchells, *The Architectural Setting of Anglican Worship* (London: Faber & Faber, 1948)

Akrigg, G. P. V., *Jacobean Pageant of The Court of King James I* (London: Hamish Hamilton, 1962)

Andrews, Michael Cameron, *This Action of Our Death: The Performance of Death in English Renaissance Drama* (Newark: University of Delaware Press, 1989)

Anglo, Sydney, ed., *Chivalry in the Renaissance* (Woodbridge: The Boydell Press, 1990)

Anglo, Sydney, *Spectacle, Pageantry and Early Tudor Policy* (Oxford: Clarendon Press, 1969)

Anselme, Saint-Marie, *Histoire de la Maison Royale de France et des Grands Officiers de la Couronne*, 2 vols (Paris: Estienne Loyson, 1674)

Antheunis, L., 'La Maladie et la Mort de la Reine Elisabeth d'Angleterre', *Revue d'Histoire Ecclésiastique*, 43 (1948), 148–78

Ariès, Philippe, *The Hour of Our Death*, trans. by Helen Weaver (London: Allen Lane, 1981)

Aston, Margaret, *England's Iconoclasts, I: Laws Against Images* (Oxford: Oxford University Press, 1989)

Atkinson, A. G. B., *St. Botolph Aldgate: The Story of a City Parish* (London: Grant Richards, 1898)

Axton, Marie, *The Queen's Two Bodies: Drama and the Elizabethan Succession* (London: Royal Historical Society, 1977)

Babbage, Stuart Barton, *Puritanism and Richard Bancroft* (London: SPCK, 1962)

Babcock, Barbara A., *The Reversible World: Symbolic Inversion in Art and Society* (Ithaca: Cornell University Press, 1978)

Barker, Richard, *The Reign of Chivalry* (London: David & Charles, 1980)

Barton, Anne, *Ben Jonson, dramatist* (Cambridge: Cambridge University Press, 1984)

Benkard, Ernst, *Undying Faces: A Collection of Death Masks*, trans. by Margaret M. Green (London: Hogarth Press, 1929)

Berger, Peter L., *The Sacred Canopy: Elements of a Sociological Theory of Religion* (Garden City, New York: Doubleday Anchor, 1969)

Bergeron, David M., 'Art within *The Second Maiden's Tragedy*', *Medieval and Renaissance Drama in England*, 1 (1984), 173–86

Bergeron, David M., 'The Wax Figures in *The Duchess of Malfi*', *Studies in English Literature*, 18 (1978), 331–9

Bergeron, David M., *Pageantry in the Shakespearean Theatre* (Atlanta: University of Georgia Press, 1985)

Bergeron, David M., *English Civic Pageantry 1558–1642* (London: Edward Arnold, 1971)

Bergeron, David M., 'Prince Henry and English Civic Pageantry', *Tennessee Studies in Literature*, 13 (1968), 109–16.

Blair, Claude, *European Armour: c. 1066 to 1700* (London: HMSO, 1958)

Bland, Olivia, *The Royal Way of Death* (London: Constable, 1986)

Bibliography

Bloch, Marc, *The Royal Touch: Sacred Monarchy and Scrofula in England and France*, trans. by J. E. Anderson (London: Routledge & Kegan Paul, 1973)

Bloch, Maurice and John Parry, eds, *Death and the Regeneration of Life* (Cambridge: Cambridge University Press, 1982)

Blomefield, Francis, *The History of [. . .] Thetford* (Fersfield: [n. pub.], 1739)

Blundell, Joe Whitlock, *Westminster Abbey: the Monuments* (London: John Murray, 1989)

Boase, T. S. R., *Death in the Middle Ages: Mortality, Judgement and Remembrance* (London: Thames & Hudson, 1972)

Bond, Francis, *The Chancel of English Churches* (Oxford: Oxford University Press, 1916)

Booty, John E., *The Book of Common Prayer 1559: the Elizabethan Prayer Book* (Charlottesville: University of Virginia Press, 1976)

Borsook, Eve, 'Art and Politics at the Medici Court I: The Funeral of Cosimo I De' Medici', *Mitteilungen des Kunsthistorischen Insitutes in Florenz*, 12 (1965–6), 31–54.

Bos, Sander, Marianne Lange-Meyers and Jeanine Six, 'Sidney's Funeral Portrayed', in *Sir Philip Sidney: 1586 and the Creation of a Legend* (Leiden: Leiden University Press, 1986), pp. 37–67

Boureau, Alain, *Le simple corps du roi: L'impossible sacralité des souverains français XVe–XVIIIe siècle* (Paris: Les Éditions de Paris, 1988)

Boureau, Alain, 'Les cérémonies royales françaises entre performance juridique et compétence liturgique', *Annales*, 46 (1991), 1234–64

Boureau, Alain and Claudio-Sergio Ingerflom, eds, *La Royauté Sacrée Dans le Monde Crétien* (Paris: École des Hautes Études, 1992)

Brigden, Susan, *London and the Reformation* (Oxford: Clarendon Press, 1989)

Bristol, Michael D., *Carnival and Theatre: Plebian Culture and the Structure of Authority in Renaissance England* (London: Methuen, 1985)

Brooke-Little, J. P., *Royal Heraldry: Beasts and Badges of Britain* (Derby: Pilgrim Press, 1987)

Brooks, Neil C., 'The sepulchre of Christ in Art and Liturgy', *University of Illinois Studies in Language and Literature*, 7 (1921), 7–51

Brown, E. A. R., 'Death and the Human Body in the later Middle Ages', *Viator*, 12 (1981), 221–70.

Bryant, Lawrence M., *The King and the City in the Parisian Royal Entry Ceremony: Politics, Ritual and Art in the Renaissance* (Geneva: Librarie Droz, 1986)

Burke, Sir Bernard, *A Genealogical History of the Dormant, Abeyant, forfeited, and Extinct Peerages of the British Empire* (London: Burke's Peerage, 1883; repr. 1969)

Burke, Peter, *The Fabrication of Louis XIV* (London: Yale University Press, 1992)

Burleigh, J. H. S., *A Church History of Scotland* (London: Oxford University Press, 1960)

Calderwood, James L., *Shakespeare and the Denial of Death* (Amherst: University of Massachusetts Press, 1987)

Cannadine, D. N., 'Conflict and Consensus on a Ceremonial Occasion: The Diamond Jubilee in Cambridge in 1897', *Historical Journal*, 24 (1981), 111–46

Cannadine, David and Simon Price, eds, *Rituals of Royalty: Power and Ceremonial in Traditional Societies* (Cambridge: Cambridge University Press, 1987)

Carpentier, Edward, ed., *A House of Kings: The History of Westminster Abbey* (London: John Baker, 1966)

Carroll, William C., ' "The Form of Law": Ritual and Succession in *Richard III* ', in *True Rites and Maimed Rites: Ritual and Anti-Ritual in Shakespeare and His Age*, ed. by

Bibliography

Linda Woodbridge and Edward Berry (Urbana: University of Illinois Press, 1992), pp. 203–219

Chamberlin, Frederick, *The Sayings of Queen Elizabeth* (London: Bodley Head, 1923)

Chambers, E. K., *The Medieval Stage*, 2 vols (Oxford: Clarendon Press, 1903)

Chambers, E. K., *The Elizabethan Stage*, 4 vols (Oxford: Clarendon Press, 1923; repr. 1961)

Chaunu, Pierre, 'Mourir à Paris, XVe –XVIIIe siècles', *Annales E.S.C.*, 31 (1976), 29–50

Church, William Farr, *Constitutional Thought in Sixteenth-Century France* (Cambridge, Mass.: Harvard University Press, 1941)

Clark, Peter and Paul Slack, eds, *Crisis and Order in English Towns, 1500–1700: Essays in Urban History* (London: Routledge & Kegan Paul, 1972)

Clay, William Keatinge, ed., *Liturgies and Occasional Forms of Prayer set forth in the Reign of Queen Elizabeth* (Cambridge: Cambridge University Press, 1847)

Cohen, Abner, 'Political Anthropology: the analysis of the symbolism of power relations', *Man*, 4 (2) (1969), 125–135

Collins, Arthur, *The Peerage of England*, 5th edn, 8 vols (London: W. Strahan, 1779), III

Collinson, Patrick, *The English Captivity of Mary Queen of Scots* (Sheffield: Sheffield History Pamphlets, 1987)

Collinson, Patrick, *The Birthpangs of Protestant England: Religious and Cultural Change in the Sixteenth and Seventeenth Centuries* (London: Macmillan, 1988)

Colvin, Howard, *Architecture and the After-Life* (London: Yale University Press, 1991)

Corlieu, A., *La Mort des Rois de France depuis François Ier Jusqu'à le Révolution Française* (Paris: Germer Ballière, 1873)

Cox, John D., *Shakespeare and the Dramaturgy of Power* (Princeton: Princeton University Press, 1989)

Cox, Angela, *Sir Henry Unton, Elizabethan Gentleman* (Cambridge: Cambridge University Press, 1982)

Cuddy, Neil, 'The Revival of the Entourage: the Bedchamber of James I, 1603–1625', in *The English Court from the Wars of the Roses to the Civil War*, ed. by David Starkey and others (London: Longman, 1987)

Cunnington, P. and Lucas, C., *Costume for Births, Marriages and Deaths* (London: Adam & Charles Black, 1972)

Curl, James Stevens, *A Celebration of Death: An Introduction to Some of the Buildings, Monuments and Settings of Funerary Architecture in the Western European Tradition* (London: Constable, 1980)

Dallaway, James, *Inquiries into the Origin and Progress of the Science of Heraldry in England* (London: B. & J. White, 1793)

Darrah, Josephine A., 'The Funeral Effigy of Henry VII at Westminster Abbey' (unpublished report to the Dean & Chapter of Westminster, 1986, WA, Box: Royal Funeral Effigies)

Davis, Nathalie Zemon, 'Some Themes and Tasks in the Study of Popular Religion', in *The Pursuit of Holiness in late Medieval and Renaissance Religion*, ed. by Charles Trinkhaus and Heiko A. Oberman (Leiden: E. J. Brill, 1974), pp. 307–36.

Davis, Nathalie Zemon, 'The Rites of Violence: Religious Riot in Sixteenth-Century France', *Past and Present*, 59 (1973), 51–91

Davis, Nathalie Zemon, 'The Sacred and the Social Body in Sixteenth Century Lyon', *Past and Present*, 90 (1981), 40–70

Bibliography

Dessen, Alan C., *Elizabethan Drama and the Viewer's Eye* (Chapel Hill: University of North Carolina Press, 1977)

Dewick, E. S., 'On An Inventory of Church Goods Belonging to the Parish of St Martin, Ludgate', *St Paul's Ecclesiological Society*, 5 (1905), 117–28

Dix, G., *The Shape of the Liturgy* (Dacre: London, 1945)

Dollimore, J., *Radical Tragedy: Religion, Ideology and Power in the Drama of Shakespeare and his Contemporaries* (Brighton: Harvester Press, 1984)

Dollimore, J. and A. Sinfield, *Political Shakespeare: New Essays in Cultural Materialism* (Manchester: Manchester University Press, 1985)

Dorsten, J. A. van, *Poets, Patrons and, Professors: Sir Philip Sidney, Daniel Rogers, and the Leiden Humanists* (London: Oxford University Press, 1962)

Dorsten, Jan van, Dominic Baker-Smith and Arthur F. Kinney, eds, *Sir Philip Sidney: 1586 and the Creation of a Legend* (Leiden: Brill, 1986)

Draper, John W., *The Funeral Elegy and the Rise of Romanticism* (New York: New York University, 1929; repr. New York: Octagon Books, 1967)

Duffy, Eamon, *The Stripping of the Altars: Traditional Religion in England c.1400–c.1580* (London: Yale University Press, 1992)

Dumoutet, E., 'Les Origines de la Fête et de la Procession du Saint-Sacrement', *La Vie et les Arts Liturgique*, 126 (1925), 343–7.

Dunlop, Ian, *Palaces and Progresses of Elizabeth I* (London: Jonathan Cape, 1962)

Durkheim, E., *Elementary Forms of Religious Life*, trans. by J. W. Swain (London: George Allan & Unwin, 1915)

Dutton, Richard, *Mastering the Revels: The Regulation and Censorship of English Renaissance Drama* (London: Macmillan, 1991)

Edmond, John Philip, 'Elegies and Other Tracts Issued on the Death of Henry Prince of Wales, 1612', *Publications of the Edinburgh Bibliographical Society*, 6, part 2 (1906), 141–158.

Elam, Kier, *The Semiotics of Theatre and Drama* (London: Methuen, 1980)

Elliot, John H., 'Philip IV of Spain: Prisoner of Ceremony', in *The Courts of Europe: Politics, Patronage and Royalty, 1400–1800*, ed. by A. G. Dickens (London: Thames & Hudson, 1977)

Elton, G. R., 'The Divine right of Kings', in *Studies in Tudor and Stuart Politics and Government*, ed. by G. R. Elton, 4 vols (Cambridge: Cambridge University Press, 1974–92), II (1974), 193–214

Englefield, W. A. D., *The History of the Painter Stainers Company of London* (London: Chapman & Dodd, 1923)

Farrell, Kirby, *Play, Death and Heroism in Shakespeare* (Chapel Hill: University of North Carolina Press, 1989)

Ferguson, Arthur B., *The Chivalric Revival in Renaissance England* (London: Associated University Presses, 1986)

Foxe-Davis, Arthur C., *A Complete Guide to Heraldry* (New York: Bonanza Books, 1978)

Frank, Grace, *The Medieval French Drama* (Oxford: Clarendon Press, 1954)

Fraser, Antonia, *King Charles II* (London: Weidenfeld & Nicolson, 1979)

Frere, W. H. and F. Proctor, eds, *A New History of the Book of Common Prayer* (London: [n. pub.], 1902)

Fritz, Paul, 'From "Public" to "Private": the Royal Funerals in England, 1500–1830', in *Mirrors of Mortality: Studies in the Social History of Death*, ed. by Joachim Whaley (London: Europa Publications, 1981), pp. 61–79

Bibliography

Frost, David L., *The Selected Plays of Thomas Middleton* (Cambridge: Cambridge University Press, 1978)
Froude, James Anthony, *The Reign of Mary Tudor* (London: J. M. Dent, [1910 (?)])
Fruen, Jeffrey, P., ' "True Glorious Type": The Place of Gloriana in *The Faerie Queene*', *Spenser Studies: A Renaissance Poetry Annual,* 7 (1986), 147–73.
Frye, Roland Mushat, *The Renaissance Hamlet, issues and responses in 1600* (Princeton, Guildford: Princeton University Press, c. 1984)
Fuller, Thomas, *History of the Worthies of England 1608–1661* (London: I.G.W.L. & W.G., 1662)
Fuller, Thomas, *The Church History of Britain from the Birth of Jesus Christ until the year 1648*, ed. by J. S. Brewer (Oxford: Oxford University Press, 1845)
Gardiner, S. R., *A History of England from the Accession of James I*, 2 vols (London: [n. pub.], 1883)
Geertz, Clifford, 'Centers, Kings and Charisma: Reflections on the Symbolics of Power', in *Culture and Its Creators: Essays in Honor of Edward Shils*, ed. by Joseph Ben-David and Terry Nichols Clark (London: University of Chicago Press, 1977), pp. 150–71
Geertz, Clifford, *Negara: the Theater State in Nineteenth Century Bali* (Princeton: Princeton University Press, 1980)
Geertz, Clifford, *Local Knowledge: Further Essays in Interpretative Anthropology* (New York: Basic Books, 1983)
Gennep, Arnold van, *The Rites of Passage*, trans. by Monika B. Vizedom and Gabrielle L. Caffee (London: Routledge, 1960)
Gent, Lucy and Nigel Llewellyn, eds, *Renaissance Bodies: The Human Figure in English Culture, c. 1540–1660* (London: Reaktion Books, 1990)
Giesey, R., 'Models of rulership in French royal ceremonial', in *Rites of Power: Symbolism, Ritual and Politics since the Middle Ages*, ed. by Sean Wilentz (Philadelphia: University of Pennsylvania Press, 1985)
Giesey, Ralph, *The Royal Funeral Ceremony in Renaissance France* (Geneva: Droz, 1960)
Gittings, Clare, *Death, Burial and the Individual in Early Modern England* (London: Routledge, 1984)
Gluckman, Max, *Essays on the Rituals of Social Relations* (Manchester: Manchester University Press, 1962)
Goffman, Erving, *The Presentation of Self in Everyday Life* (New York: Penguin Press, 1959)
Goldberg, Jonathan, *James I and the Politics of English Literature* (Baltimore: John Hopkins University Press, 1983)
Graham, Victor E. and W. Mcallister Johnson, *The Paris Entries of Charles IX and Elizabeth of Austria 1571, with an analysis of Simon Bouquet's 'Bref et Sommaire Recueil'* (Toronto: Toronto University Press, 1974)
Graham, Victor E. and V. McAllister Johnson, eds, *The Royal Tour of France by Charles IX and Catherine de Medici: Festivals and Entries (1564–6)* (Toronto: University of Toronto Press, 1979)
Greenblatt, Stephen J., *Sir Walter Raleigh: The Renaissance Man and His Roles* (London: Yale University Press, 1973)
Greenblatt, Stephen, *Renaissance Self-Fashioning From More to Shakespeare* (London: University of Chicago Press, 1980)
Greengrass, M., 'Mary, Dowager Queen of France', in *Mary Stewart: Queen in Three Kingdoms*, ed. by Michael Lynch (Oxford: Blackwell, 1988)

Bibliography

Guenée, Bernard and Françoise Lehoux, *Les Entrées Royales Françaises de 1328 à 1515* (Paris: Centre Nationale de la Recherche Scientifique, 1968)

Gurr, Andrew, *Playgoing in Shakespeare's London* (Cambridge: Cambridge University Press, 1987)

Gurr, Andrew, *The Shakespearean Stage 1574–1642*, 3rd edn (Cambridge: Cambridge University Press, 1992)

Gurr, Andrew, *King Henry V* (Cambridge: Cambridge University Press, 1992)

Haigh, Christopher, *Reformation and Resistance in Tudor Lancashire* (London: Cambridge University Press, 1975)

Haigh, Christopher, ed., *The Reign of Elizabeth I* (London: Macmillan, 1984)

Haigh, Christopher, *Elizabeth I* (London: Longman, 1988)

Haigh, Christopher, *English Reformations: Religion, Politics and Society under the Tudors* (Oxford: Clarendon Press, 1993)

Hale, J. R., *Renaissance Europe 1480–1520* (London: Fontana, 1971)

Hanley, Sarah, *The 'Lit de Justice' of the Kings of France: Constitutional Ideology in Legend, Ritual and Discourse* (Princeton: Princeton University Press, 1983)

Hardison, O. B., *Christian Rite and Christian Drama in the Middle Ages* (Baltimore: John Hopkins University Press, 1965)

Harris, John Wesley, *Medieval theatre in Context: an Introduction* (London: Routledge, 1992)

Harris, John and Gordon Higgott, *Inigo Jones: Complete Architectural Drawings* (London: Royal Academy of Arts, 1989)

Harris, John, Stephen Orgel and Roy Strong, *The King's Arcadia: Inigo Jones and the Stuart Court* (London: Arts Council of Great Britain, 1973)

Harvey, Anthony and Richard Mortimer, eds, *The Funeral Effigies of Westminster Abbey* (Woodbridge: The Boydell Press, 1994)

Haugaard, W. P., *Elizabeth and the English Reformation: the Struggle for a Stable Settlement of Religion* (Cambridge: Cambridge University Press, 1968)

Heinemann, Margot, *Puritanism and Theatre: Thomas Middleton and Opposition Drama under the Early Stuarts* (Cambridge: Cambridge University Press, 1980)

Hertz, Robert, *Death and the Right Hand*, trans. by R. and C. Needham (Glencoe, Ill: Free Press, 1960)

Hibbert, Christopher, *The Virgin Queen: The Personal History of Elizabeth I* (London: Viking, 1990)

Hind, Arthur M., *A History of Engraving and Etching from the Fifteenth Century to the Year 1914*, 3rd edn ([New York (?): Houghton Mifflin, 1923; repr. New York: Dover Publications, 1963)

Holleran, James V., 'Maimed Funeral Rites in *Hamlet*', *English Literary Renaissance*, 19 (1989), 78–93

Holmes, Martin, *A Carved Wooden Head of Henry Frederick, Prince of Wales*, transcript of a lecture given by Martin Holmes in 1986, held in Westminster Abbey Library, Box: Royal Funeral Effigies

Höltgen, Karl Joseph, 'The English Reformation and Some Jacobean Writers on Art', in *Functions of Literature: Essays presented to Erwin Wolff on his Sixtieth birthday*, ed. by Ulrich Broich, Theo Stemmler and Gerd Stratman (Tübingen: Max Neimeyer Verlag, 1984)

Honigmann, E. A. J., *Shakespeare's Impact on His Contemporaries* (London: Macmillan, 1982)

Bibliography

Hope, W. H. St John, 'On the Funeral Effigies of the Kings and Queens of England, with special reference to those in the Abbey Church of Westminster', *Archaeologia*, 40, part 2 (1907), 517–70

Howard, Maurice, 'Power and the Early-Tudor Courtier's Houses', *History Today*, 37 (May, 1987)

Howarth, David, *Lord Arundel and his Circle* (London: Yale University Press, 1985)

Howell, Roger Jr., 'The Sidney Circle and the Protestant Cause in Elizabethan Foreign Policy', *Renaissance and Modern Studies*, 19 (1975), 31–46.

Howgrave-Graham, R. P., 'Royal Portraits in Effigy: Some New Discoveries in Westminster Abbey', *Journal of the Royal Society of Arts* (29 May 1953), 465–74

Huizinga, J., *The Waning of the Middle Ages: A Study of the Forms of Life, Thought and Art in France and the Netherlands in the Fourteenth and Fifteenth Centuries* (London: Edward Arnold, 1924)

Humphreys, Sarah C. and H. King, eds, *Mortality and Immortality: the Anthropology and Archaeology of Death* (London: Academic Press, 1981)

Huntington, Richard and Peter Metcalf, *Celebrations of Death: The Anthropology of Mortuary Ritual* (Cambridge: Cambridge University Press, 1979)

Jackson, Richard A., *Vive le Roi! A History of the French Coronation from Charles V to Charles X* (London: University of North Carolina Press, 1984)

Jacquot, Jean, *Les Fêtes de la Renaissance*, 3 vols (Paris: Centre Nationale de la Recherche Scientifique, 1956–75)

James, M. E., 'Ritual, Drama and the Social Body in the Late Medieval English Town', *Past and Present*, 98 (1983), 3–29

James, Mervyn E., *Society, Politics and Culture: Studies in Early Modern England* (Cambridge, Cambridge University Press, 1986)

Johnson, A. H., *The History of the Worshipful Company of Drapers*, 5 vols (Oxford: Clarendon Press, 1914–22)

Johnson, Paul, *Elizabeth I: A Study in Power and Intellect* (London: Weidenfield & Nicolson, 1974)

Jones, Norman L., *Faith by Statute: Parliament and the Settlement of Religion 1559* (London: Royal Historical Society, 1982)

Kantorowicz, Ernst H., *The King's Two Bodies: A Study in Medieval Political Theology* (Princeton: Princeton University Press, 1957)

Kay, Dennis, 'William Juxon's Elegy on Prince Henry (1612)', *Notes and Queries*, 230 (1985), 60–1.

Kay, Dennis, *Melodious Tears: The English Funeral Elegy from Spenser to Milton* (Oxford: Clarendon Press, 1990)

Keen, Maurice, *Chivalry* (New Haven: Yale University Press, 1984)

Kernodle, George R., *From Art to Theatre: Form and Convention in the Renaissance* (Chicago: University of Chicago Press, 1944)

Kertzer, D., *Ritual, Politics and Power* (London: Yale University Press, 1988)

King, John N., *English Reformation Literature: The Tudor Origins of the Protestant Tradition* (Princeton: Princeton University Press, 1982)

King, John N., 'Queen Elizabeth I: Representations of the Virgin Queen', *Renaissance Quarterly*, 43 (1990), 30–74

Kipling, Gordon, *The Triumph of Honour: Burgundian Origins of the Elizabethan Renaissance* (Netherlands: Leiden University Press, 1977)

Knecht, R. J., *The French Wars of Religion 1559–1598* (Harlow: Longman, 1989)

Bibliography

Knecht, R. J., *French Renaissance Monarchy: Francis I and Henry II* (Harlow: Longman, 1984)
Knowles, James, 'The Spectacle of the Realm: civic consciousness, rhetoric and ritual in early modern London', in *Theatre and Government Under the Early Stuarts*, ed. by J. R. Mulryne and Margaret Shewring (Cambridge: Cambridge University Press, 1993)
Kolve, V. A., *The Play Called Corpus Christi* (London: Edward Arnold, 1966)
Landwehr, John, *Splendid Ceremonies: State Entries and Royal Funeral in the Low Countries* (Leiden: A. W. Sijbhoff, 1971)
Langston, Beach, 'Essex and the Art of Dying', *The Huntington Library Quarterly*, 13 (1950) part 2, 109–29
Lebrun, François, *Les Hommes et la mort en Anjou aux XVIIe et XVIIIe Siècles: Essai de démographie et de psychologie historique* (Paris: Mouton, 1971)
Lee, Maurice, *Great Britain's Solomon: James VI and I in His Three Kingdoms* (Urbana: University of Illinois Press, 1990)
Lee, Maurice, Jr., *James I and Henry IV: An Essay in English Foreign Policy 1603–1610* (London: University of Illinois Press, 1970)
Lethaby, W. R., *Westminster Abbey Re-Examined* (London: Duckworth, 1925)
Letters to Howgrave-Graham from Mrs B. Johnston, Holyrood House, 14 October 1955 and E. M. McGory at the Headquarters of the Scottish Ministry of Works, 8 November 1955, Westminster Abbey Library, Box: Royal Funeral Effigies
Lever, J. W., *The Tragedy of State: A Study of Jacobean Drama* (New York: Methuen, 1971)
Lewis, Gilbert, *Day of Shining Red: An Essay on Understanding Ritual* (Cambridge: Cambridge University Press, 1980)
Litten, Julian, *The English Way of Death: The Common Funeral Since 1450* (London: Robert Hale, 1991)
Littré, Emile, *Dictionnaire de la Langue Française*, 7 vols (Paris: Gallimard, 1963–4), VI (1964)
LLewellyn, Nigel, 'Claims to Status through Visual Codes: Heraldry on post-Reformation Funeral Monuments', in Sydney Anglo, ed., *Chivalry in the Renaissance* (Woodbridge: The Boydell Press, 1990)
Llewellyn, Nigel, 'The Royal Body: Monuments to the Dead, For the Living', in *Renaissance Bodies: The Human Figure in English Culture, c. 1540–1660*, ed. by Lucy Gent and Nigel Llewellyn (London: Reaktion Books, 1990)
Llewellyn, Nigel, *The Art of Death: Visual Culture in the English Death Ritual c. 1500–c.1800* (London: Reaktion Books, 1991)
Loach, Jennifer, 'The Function of Ceremonial in the Reign of Henry VIII', *Past and Present*, 142 (February, 1994), 43–68
Loades, D. M., *Politics and the Nation 1450–1660: Obedience, Resistance and Public Order*, 3rd edn (London: Fanta, 1986)
Lockyer, Roger, *The Early Stuarts: A Political History of England 1603–1642* (London: Longman, 1989)
Long, John H., *Shakespeare's Use of Music: the Histories and Tragedies* (Gainesville: University of Florida Press, 1971)
Lukes, Steven, 'Political Ritual and Social Integration', *Sociology*, 9 (1975), 289–308
Lukes, Steven, *Essays in Social Theory* (London: [n. pub.], 1987)
Lynch, John, *Spain 1516: From Nation State to World Empire* (Oxford: Blackwell, 1991)
Lynch, Michael, ed., *Mary Stewart: Queen in Three Kingdoms* (Oxford: Blackwell, 1988)

Lytle, Guy Fitch and Stephen Orgel, ed., *Patronage in the Renaissance* (Princeton: Princeton University Press, 1981)
Macfarlane, Alan, *The Origins of English Individualism: The Family, Property and Social Transition* (Oxford: Basil Blackwell, 1978)
Maclagan, Michael, 'Genealogy and Heraldry in the Sixteenth and Seventeenth Centuries', in *English Historical Scholarship in the Sixteenth and Seventeenth Centuries*, ed. by Levi Fox (Oxford: Oxford University Press, 1956)
Marcus, Leah, *The Politics of Mirth: Jonson, Herrick, Milton, Marvell, and the Defense of Old Holiday Pastimes* (Chicago: University of Chicago Press, 1986)
Marshall, Rosalind K., *Queen of Scots* (Edinburgh: HMSO, 1986)
Marshall, Rosalind K., *Henrietta Maria: the Intrepid Queen* (London: HMSO, 1990)
Mathieu, Remi, *Le système heraldique français* ([Paris (?)]: [n. pub.], 1946)
MacCaffrey, Wallace, *Elizabeth I* (London: Edward Arnold, 1993)
McCoy, Richard C., *The Rites of Knighthood: The Literature and Politics of Elizabethan Chivalry* (Berkley: University of California Press, 1989)
McManners, John, 'Death and the French Historians', in *Mirrors of Mortality: Studies in the Social History of Death*, ed. by Joachim Whaley (London: Europa Publications, 1981), pp. 106–130
McMullen, David, 'Bureaucrats and Cosmology: the Ritual code of T'ang China', in *Rituals of Royalty: Power and Ceremonial in Traditional Societies*, ed. by David Cannadine and Simon Price (Cambridge: Cambridge University Press, 1987)
McMurray, W., *The Records of Two City Parishes* (London: [n. pub.], 1925)
Mercer, Eric, *English Art 1553–1625* (Oxford: Oxford University Press, 1962)
Moore, Sally F. and Barbara G. Myerhoff, eds, *Secular Ritual* (Amsterdam: Van Gorcum, 1977)
Moore, Sally Falk, *Law as Process, an Anthropological Approach* (London: Routledge & Kegan Paul, 1978)
Morin, Edgar, 'L'Homme et la mort dans l'histoire', *Annales* (1952), 223–238
Morley, John, *Death, Heaven and the Victorians* (London: Studio Vista, 1971)
Morris, Harry, *Last Things in Shakespeare* (Tallahassee: Florida State University Press, 1985)
Morris, Colin, *The Discovery of the Individual 1050–1200* (New York: Harper & Row, 1972)
Muir, Edward, *Civic Ritual in Renaissance Venice* (Princeton: Princeton University Press, 1981)
Mullaney, Steven, *The Place of the Stage: License, Play, and Power in Renaissance England* (London: University of Chicago Press, 1988)
Mulryne, J. R., *Thomas Middleton* (Harlow: Longman, 1979)
Mulryne, J. R. and Margaret Shewring, eds, *War, Literature and the Arts in Sixteenth-Century Europe* (Basingstoke: Macmillan Press, 1989)
Mulryne, J. R. and Margaret Shewring, eds, *Theatre and Government Under the Early Stuarts* (Cambridge: Cambridge University Press, 1993)
Muret, Pierre, *Rites of Funeral*, trans. by P. Lorrain (London, 1683)
Myherhoff, Barbara, 'A death in due time: Construction of self and culture in ritual drama', in *Rite, Drama, Festival, Spectacle*, ed. by John J. MacAloon (Philadelphia: ISHI, 1984)
Needham, Rodney, 'Percussion and Transition', *Man*, n.s. 2, no. 4, (1967), 606–14
Neill, Michael, ' "Feasts Put Down Funerals": Death and Ritual in Renaissance Comedy',

in *True Rites and Maimed Rites: Ritual and Anti-Ritual in Shakespeare and His Age*, ed. by Linda Woodbridge and Edward Berry (Urbana: University of Illinois Press, 1992), pp. 47–74

Neill, Michael, ' "Exeunt with a Dead March": Funeral Pageantry on the Shakespearean Stage', in *Pageantry in the Shakespearean Theatre*, ed. by David M. Bergeron (Atlanta: University of Georgia Press, 1985), pp. 153–93.

Neill, Michael, 'Monuments and ruins as symbols in *The Duchess of Malfi*', *Themes in Drama*, 4 (1981), 71–87

Nicolas, N. H., *Testament Vetusta* (London: [n. pub.], 1836), I

Norbrook, David, 'The reformation of the masque', in *The Court Masque*, ed. by David Lindley (Manchester: Manchester University Press, 1984), pp. 94–110.

O'Connell, 'The Idolatrous Eye: Iconoclasm, Anti-Theatricalism, and the Image of the Elizabethan Theater', in *English Literary History*, 52 (1985), 279–310

O'Day, Rosemary, *The Debate on the English Reformation* (London: Methuen, 1986)

Orgel, Stephen and Roy Strong, *Inigo Jones: The Theatre of the Stuart Court* (London: University of California Press, 1973)

Orgel, Stephen, *The Illusion of Power, Political Theater in the English Renaissance* (London: University of California Press, 1975)

Orrell, John and Andrew Gurr, 'What the Rose Can Tell us', *Times Literary Supplement*, 9–15 June 1989, p. 636

Outram Evenett, H., *The Spirit of the Counter-Reformation* (Cambridge: Cambridge University Press, 1968)

Palme, Per, *The Triumph of Peace: A Study of the Whitehall Banqueting House* (Stockholm: Almqvist & Wiksell, 1956)

Parry, Graham, *The Golden Age restor'd: The Culture of the Stuart Court, 1603–42* (Manchester: Manchester University Press, 1981)

Parry, Graham, *The Seventeenth Century: The Intellectual and Cultural Context of English Literature, 1603–1700* (London: Longman, 1989)

Parry, Graham, 'The Politics of the Jacobean Masque', in *Theatre and Government Under the Early Stuarts*, ed. by J. R. Mulryne and Margaret Shewring (Cambridge: Cambridge University Press, 1993), pp. 87–117

Parsons, Leila, 'Prince Henry (1594–1612) as a Patron of Literature', *Modern Language Review*, 47 (1952), 503–7.

Peacock, John, 'Inigo Jones's Catafalque for James I', *Architectural History*, 25 (1982), 1–5

Pearson, Karl and G. M. Morant, *The Portraiture of Oliver Cromwell with special reference to the Wilkinson Head* (London: Biometrika Office, UCL, 1935)

Peck, Linda Levy, *Northampton: Patronage and Policy at the Court of James I* (London: Allen & Unwin, 1982)

Peck, Linda Levy, *The Mental World of the Jacobean Court* (Cambridge: Cambridge University Press, 1991)

Peter, John, 'How the Stones of the Rose Give Drama a New Shape', *Sunday Times*, 28 May 1989, p. C7

Phillips, John, *The Reformation of Images: Destruction of Art in England, 1535–1660* (Berkeley: University of California Press, 1973)

Phythian-Adams, Charles, 'Ceremony and the Citizen: the Communal Year at Coventry 1450–1550', in *Crisis and Order in English Towns 1500–1700: Essays in Urban History*, ed. by Peter Clark and Paul Slack (London: Routledge & Kegan Paul, 1972)

Bibliography

Pigman, G. W. III, *Grief and the English Renaissance Elegy* (Cambridge: Cambridge University Press, 1985)

Pollard, A. W. and others, eds, *A Short-Title Catalogue of Books Printed in England, Ireland and Scotland and of English Books Printed Abroad 1475–1640*, 3 vols (London: The Bibliographical Society, 1986–1991)

Pomeroy, Elizabeth W., *Reading the Portraits of Queen Elizabeth I* (Hamden, Conn.: Archon Books, 1989)

Puckle, Bertram, *Funeral Customs: Their Origins and Development* (London: T. Werner Laurie, 1926)

Pullan, L., *The History of the Book of Common Prayer*, 2nd edn (London: Oxford Library of Practical Theology, 1900)

Ragon, Michel, *The Space of Death: A Study of Funerary Architecture, Decoration and Urbanism*, trans. by Alan Sheridan (Charlottesville: University of Virginia Press, 1983)

Richmond, Hugh M., *Puritans and Libertines: Anglo-French Literary Relations in the Reformation* (London: University of California Press, 1981)

Rolfe, C. C., *The Ancient Use of Liturgical Colours* (Oxford: Parker Society, 1879)

Rosand, David, 'The Portrait, the Courtier, and Death', in *Castiglione, the Ideal and the Real in Renaissance Culture*, ed. by W. Hanning and David Rosand (London: Yale University, 1983)

Routh, C. R. N., *They Saw it Happen: An Anthology of Eye Witnesses's Accounts of Events in British History [. .]. 1485–1688* (Oxford: Blackwell, 1956)

Rowell, G., *The Liturgy of Christian Burial: An Introductory Survey of the Historical Development of Christian Burial Rites* (London: Alcuin Club, 1977)

Russell, Conrad, *The Crisis of Parliaments: English History 1509–1660* (Oxford: Oxford University Press, 1971; repr. 1984)

Rutter, Carol Chillington, *Documents of the Rose Playhouse* (Manchester: Manchester University Press, 1984)

Salmon, J. H. M., *The French Religious Wars in English Political Thought* (Oxford: Clarendon Press, 1959)

Salmon, J. H. M., *Society in Crisis: France in the Sixteenth Century* (London: Ernest Benn, 1975)

Sandford, Francis, *A Genealogical History of the Kings of England and Monarches of Great Britain* (London: T. Newcombe, 1677)

Santiago, J., 'Les Funerailles Princières en France (Bourgogne et Orléans 1465–1468)' (unpublished thesis, University of Paris, 1981)

Scarisbrick, J. J., *The Reformation and the English People* (Oxford: Blackwell, 1984)

Schechner, Richard and Willa Appel, eds, *By means of Performance, intercultural studies of theatre and ritual* (Cambridge: Cambridge University Press, 1990)

Scholes, Percy A., *The Puritans and Music in England and New England: A Contribution to the Cultural History of Two Nations* (New York: Russell & Russell, 1962)

Schramm, Percy E., *A History of the English Coronation*, trans. by Leopold G. Wickham Legg (Oxford: Clarendon Press, 1937)

Schwoerer, Lois G., *The Revolution of 1688–9, Changing Perspectives* (Cambridge: Cambridge University Press, 1992)

Seyer, Samuel, *Memoirs historical and topographical of Bristol*, 2 vols (Bristol: [n. pub.], 1821–3)

Bibliography

Sharpe, J. A., *Early Modern England: A Social History 1550–1760* (London: Edward Arnold, 1987)

Sharpe, Kevin, *Sir Robert Cotton* (Oxford: Oxford University Press, 1979)

Sheils, W. J., *The English Reformation 1530–1570* (London: Longman, 1989)

Sheils, W. J., *The Puritans in the Diocese of Peterborough 1570–1610* (Northampton: Northampton Record Society, 1979)

Shennan, J. H., *The Parlement of Paris* (Ithaca: Cornell University Press, 1968)

Shepherd, Simon, *Marlowe and the Politics of Elizabethan Theatre* (Brighton: Harvester, 1986)

Sheppard, Edgar, *The Old Royal Palace of Whitehall* (London: Longmans & Green, 1902)

Smuts, M., *Court Culture and the Origins of the Royalist Tradition in Early Stuart England* (Philadelphia: University of Pennsylvania Press, 1987)

Sommerville, J. P., *Politics and Ideology in England, 1603–1640* (London: Longman, 1986)

Spencer, Theodore, *Death and Elizabethan Tragedy: A Study of Convention and Opinion in the Elizabeth Drama* (New York: Pageant Books, 1960)

Spinrad, Phoebe S., *The Summons of Death on the Medieval and Renaissance English Stage* (Columbus: Ohio State University Press, 1987)

Spottiswoode, Jane, *Undertaken With Love* (London: Robert Hale, 1991)

Stanley, A. P., *Memorials of Westminster Abbey* (London: Murray, 1869)

Stanley, A. P., 'On the Deposition of the Remains of Katherine de Valois, Queen of Henry V, in Westminster Abbey', *Archaeologia*, 46 (1881), 281–96

Stannard, David E., *The Puritan Way of Death: A Study in Religion, Culture and Social Change* (Oxford: Oxford University Press, 1977)

Starkey, David, 'Representation Through Intimacy: A Study in the Symbolism of Monarchy and Court Office in Early Modern England', in *Symbols and Sentiments*, ed. by Ioan Lewis (London: Academic, 1977), pp. 187–224

Starkey, David et al., eds, *The English Court from the Wars of the Roses to the Civil War* (London: Longman, 1987)

Stein, Arnold, *The House of Death: Messages from the English Renaissance* (Baltimore: John Hopkins University Press, 1986)

Stone, Lawrence, *The Family, Sex and Marriage in England 1500–1800*, 2nd edn (Harmondsworth: Penguin Books, 1979)

Stone, Lawrence, 'The Anatomy of the Elizabethan Aristocracy', *The Economic History Review*, 28 (1948), 12–13

Stone, Lawrence, *The Crisis of the Aristocracy 1558–1641* (Oxford: Clarendon Press, 1965)

Stone, Lawrence, 'Death and Its History', *New York Review of Books*, 22 (1978–9), 22–32

Stoye, John, *English Travellers Abroad, 1604–1667, their Influence in English Society and Politics* (London: Cape, 1952)

Strickland, Ronald, 'Pageantry and Poetry as Discourse: The Production of Subjectivity in Sir Philip Sidney's Funeral', *English Literary History*, 57 (1990), 19–36

Strocchia, Sharon T., 'Death Rites and the Ritual Family in Renaissance Florence', in *Life and Death in Fifteenth Century Florence*, ed. by Marcel Tetel, Ronald G. Witt and Rona Goffen (London: Duke University Press, 1989)

Strong, Roy C., *Portraits of Queen Elizabeth I* (Oxford: Clarendon Press, 1963)

Strong, Roy, 'Sir Henry Unton and his Portrait: An Elizabethan Memorial Picture and Its History', *Archaeologia*, 99 (1965), 53–76

Strong, Roy, *Tudor and Jacobean Portraits*, 2 vols (London: HMSO, 1969)

Bibliography

Strong, Roy, *The English Icon: Elizabethan and Jacobean Portraiture* (London: Routledge & Kegan Paul, 1969)

Strong, Roy and Julia Trevelyan Oman, *Elizabeth R* (London: Secker & Warburg, 1971)

Strong, Roy, *Henry, Prince of Wales: England's Lost Renaissance* (London: Thames & Hudson, 1986)

Strong, Roy, *The Cult of Elizabeth* (London: Thames & Hudson, 1977; repr. 1987)

Strype, J., *Ecclesiastical memorials relating chiefly to religion and the reformation of it*, 3 vols (London [n. pub.], 1721)

Sutherland, N. M., *Princes, Politics and Religion (1547–1589)* (London: Hambledon Press, 1984)

Tambiah, Stanley J., *Culture, Thought and Social Action* (Cambridge, Mass.: Harvard University Press, 1985)

Tanner, L. E. and J. L. Nevinson, 'On Some Later Funeral Effigies in Westminster Abbey', *Archaeologia*, 85 (1935), 169–202

Tanner, Lawrence E., *The History of the Coronation* (London: Pitkin, 1953)

Tanner, Joan D., 'Tombs of the Royal Babies in Westminster Abbey', *Journal of the British Archaeological Association*, 16 (1953), 25–41

Taylor, Jane H. M., ed., *Dies Illa: Death in the Middle Ages* (Liverpool: Francis Cairns, 1984)

Taylor, Lou, *Mourning Dress: A Costume and Social History* (London: George Allen & Unwin, 1988)

Tennenhouse, Leonard, *Power on Display: The Politics of Shakespeare's Genres* (London: Methuen, 1986)

Terrasse, Charles, *Germain Pilon* (Paris: Henri Laurens, 1930)

Tetel, Marcel, Ronald G. Witt and Rona Goffen, eds, *Life and Death in Fifteenth Century Florence* (London: Duke University Press, 1989)

The Dictionary of National Biography (London: Oxford University Press, 1917; repr. 1949–50)

Thisleton Dyer, T. F., *Church-Lore Gleanings* (London: [n. pub.], 1891)

Thomas, Keith, *Religion and the Decline of Magic: Studies in Popular Beliefs in Sixteenth-Century England* (London: Penguin Books, 1971)

Thomson, David, *Renaissance Architecture: Critics, Patrons, Luxury* (Manchester: Manchester University Press, 1993)

Tonkin, Elizabeth, 'Masks and Powers', *Man*, n.s. 14 (1979), 237–48

Trevor-Roper, Hugh, *Queen Elizabeth's First Historian: William Camden and the Beginnings of English 'Civil History'* (London: Jonathan Cape, 1971)

Turner, Victor, *Dramas, Fields and Metaphors, Symbolic Action in Human Society* (London: Cornell University Press, 1974)

Turner, Victor, *The Anthropology of Performance* (New York: P. A. J. Publications, 1987)

Tyacke, Nicholas, *Anti-Calvinists: The Rise of English Arminianism c. 1590–1640* (Oxford: Clarendon Press, 1987)

Vale, Malcolm, *War and Chivalry: Warfare and Aristocratic Culture in England, France and Burgundy at the End of the Middle Ages* (London: Duckworth, 1981)

Varley, Frederick John, *Oliver Cromwell's Latter End* (London: Chapman & Hall, 1939)

Véry, Francis George, *The Spanish Corpus Christi Procession: A literary and folkloric study* ([Valencia (?)]: [n. pub.], 1962)

Vimont, M., *Histoire de la Rue Saint-Denis de Ses Origines à nos jours*, 2 vols (Paris: Palais-Royal, 1936)

Bibliography

Vitry, Paul and Gaston Brière, *L'Eglise Abbatiale de Saint-Denis et ses Tombeaux* (Paris: D. A. Longuet, 1908)

Vovelle, Michel, *Mourir Autrefois: Attitudes Collectives devant la mort aux XVIIe et XVIIIe siècles* ([Paris (?)]: Editions Gallimore, 1974)

Wagner, A. R., *Heralds and Ancestors* (London, [n. pub.], 1978)

Wagner, Sir A., *Heralds of England: A History of the Office and College of Arms* (London: HMSO, 1967)

Waters, R. E. C., *Parish Registers in England* (London: F. J. Roberts, 1887)

Watt, Tessa, *Cheap Print and Popular Piety 1550–1640* (Cambridge: Cambridge University Press, 1991)

Westminster Abbey: The Chapter House, the Pyx Chamber and Treasury, the Undercroft Museum (London: English Heritage, [n. d.])

Whaley, Joachim, ed., *Mirrors of Mortality: Studies in the Social History of Death* (London: Europa Publications, 1981)

Whinney, Margaret, *Sculpture in Britain 1530 to 1830*, revised by John Physick (London: Penguin Books, 1964; repr. 1988)

White, F. O., *Lives of the Elizabethan Bishops of the Anglican Church* (London: Skeffington, 1898)

White, W. J., 'Changing Burial Practice in Late Medieval England', *The Ricardian*, vol. 4 no. 63 (1978), 23–30

White, W. J., 'The Death and Burial of Henry VI', *The Ricardian*, vol. 6 no. 78 (1982), 70–80 and vol. 6 no. 79 (1982), 106–17

Whiting, Mary Bradford, 'Henry, Prince of Wales: "A Scarce Blown Rose" ', *Contemporary Review*, 137 (1930), 492–500

Wickham, Glynne, *Early English Stages 1300–1600*, 3 vols (London: Routledge & Kegan Paul, 1959–81)

Wickham, Glynne, 'Romance and Emblem: A Study in the Dramatic Structure of *The Winter's Tale*', in *The Elizabethan Theatre III*, ed. by D. Galloway (London: Macmillan, 1973), pp. 82–99

Wilentz, Sean, ed., *Rites of Power: Symbolism, Ritual and Politics since the Middle Ages* (Philadelphia: University of Pennsylvania Press, 1985)

Williams, Robert, *The Fireside Book of Death* (London: Robert Hale, 1990)

Williams, Ethel Carleton, *Anne of Denmark* (London: Longman, 1970)

Williams, Mary C., 'Merlin and the Prince: The Speeches at Prince Henry's Barriers', *Renaissance Drama*, n.s. 8 (1977), 221–230

Williams, Neville, *The Life and Times of Elizabeth I* (London: Weidenfeld & Nicolson, 1972)

Williams, Raymond, *Marxism and Literature* (Oxford: Oxford University Press, 1977)

Williamson, J. W., *The Myth of the Conqueror: Prince Henry Stuart: A Study of Seventeenth Century Personation* (New York: A. M. S. Press, 1978)

Willson, D. Harris, *King James VI and I* (London: Cape, 1950)

Wilson, Jean, ed., *Entertainments for Elizabeth I* (Cambridge: D. S. Brewer, 1980)

Wilson, Elkin Calhoun, *Prince Henry and English Literature* (Ithaca: Cornell University Press, 1946)

Wilson, E. C., *England's Eliza* (Cambridge, Mass.: Harvard University Press, 1939)

Woodbridge, Linda and Edward Berry, eds, *True Rites and Maimed Rites: Ritual and Anti-Ritual in Shakespeare and His Age* (Urbana: University of Illinois Press, 1992)

Woodward, Jennifer K. A., 'The Theatre of Death: Politics, Ritual and Ideology in the

Royal Funeral of Charles IX' (unpublished master's thesis, University of Warwick, 1992)

Woodward, Jennifer K. A., 'Funeral Rituals in the French Renaissance', *Renaissance Studies*, 9 (1995), part 4, 385–394

Woolf, D. R., 'Two Elizabeths? James I and the Late Queen's Famous Memory', *Canadian Journal of History*, 20 (1985), 167–91

Wormald, Jenny, *Mary Queen of Scots: A Study in Failure* (London: George & Philip, 1988)

Wormald, Jenny, 'James VI and I: Two Kings and One?' *History*, 68 (1983), 187–209.

Yates, Francis A., *Astraea: The Imperial Theme in the Sixteenth Century* (London: Routledge & Kegan Paul, 1975)

Young, Karl, 'The Dramatic Associations of the Easter Sepulchre', *University of Wisconsin Studies in Language and Literature*, 10 (1920), 5–130

Young, Karl, *The Drama of the Medieval Church*, 2 vols (Oxford: Clarendon Press, 1933)

INDEX

The numbers refer to pages followed by illustration references.

Abbot, George, Archbishop of
    Canterbury 125–6, 177
achievements and hatchments 16, 21–2,
    33, 35, 47–9, 51, 61–3, 80, 153, 181,
    183, 217, 219
Acts of Supremacy 40, 58
All Saints' Eve 59
All Souls' Day 41, 199
altars 32, 38, 45, 49–50, 125, 180 n.27
ambassadors at funerals 92, 102, 195, 213,
    218
Andrewes, Lancelot, Bishop of
    Winchester 127
Anne of Bohemia, effigy of 90, 171, 193
    n.85, fig. 12
Anne of Brittany fig. 8
Anne of Denmark, funeral of 136, 163,
    166–74, 186, 190, 193, 196–7, 202
    art collector 118
    German relatives 155
    hearse of 177
    journey to London 98
    players 167 n.7
    servants of 196
    tomb effigy of 164
Anne, Duchess of Somerset 18 n.17, 150
Anne, Queen 202, fig. 14
Annales School 3
Ariès, Philippe 3
Arminianism 9, 123, 125, 127, 205, 207
arms, royal 16, 25, 39, 51–2, 115, fig. 6
Arthur, Prince of Wales 173 n.35
Aubespine, M. De L' 74
Aubrey, John 140
averil 36

Bacon, Sir Nicholas 53, 58, 94 n.37
Bandinelli, Baccio 132
banners and bannerols 22–3, 25 n.46, 27,
    35, 40, 51, 75, 80–1, 87, 204, 213
Barriers, The 120 n.12, 159, 160 n.67, 161
Basilikon Doron 94, 97
Bath, Countess of 45 n.46
beadsmen 44, 58

Beaton, James, Bishop of Glasgow 68, 72
Beauchamp, Edward Lord 100
Beauchamp, William de, funeral of 51
bells, bell-ringing and bell-ringers 55,
    58–60, 144, 204, 211, 218
Belphoebe 89–90
Bentham, Bishop of Coventry and
    Lichfield 45
Berkeley, Lady Isabel, funeral of 19 n.19,
    44, 46, 55
Berkeley, Lady Katherine, funeral of
    17–18, 30, 36, 41, 47
Bernini, Gian Lorenzo 122
Bible, Authorised Version (1611) 123
Bilson, Thomas 115
Bird, William 146
Blackwood, Adam 68 n.5
Bodin, Jean 95, 184
Bolton, Edmund 19, 25–6
Bothwell, James Hepburn, Earl of 73
Bourbon, Jeanne de, funeral of fig. 9
Bramante, Donato 177
Brandon, Charles 100
Bristol 152
Browne, Sir Thomas 60, 142
Burghley, Northamptonshire 99
burial cries 63, 181, 219

Calvinism 45 n.41, 54, 123, 125–8, 145
    n.90, 175, 207
Camden, William 87 n.1, 133, 140
candles and candlesticks 44–6, 49, 194–5,
    199, 215, 218
canopy, funeral 23, 29, 81, 85, 113 n.136,
    167, 170, 186, 213, 215, 218
    Corpus Christi 112
Carey, Robert 96
Carleton, Sir Dudley 118, 122, 157, 190
Carlisle, James Hay, Earl of 121
Carr, Robert 136
catafalque *see* hearse
Catherine of Aragon 78, 83 n.87, 105
    n.89, 140 n.67

243

Index

Cecil, Sir Robert 53, 97, 100–2, 111, 113, 124, 133–4, 136–7, 158, 213, fig. 17
  tomb of 172
Cecil, Thomas, Lord Burghley 137
Cecil, William, Lord Burghley 52–4, 57, 71, 79, 101 n.66, 113, 118, 124 n.32, 132
censing *see incense*
chairs and stools for mourners 179 n.24
Chamberlain, John 141–3, 145, 168–9, 177, 190, 194, 197–8
chancel 38, 81
chantries 50
chapelle ardente 45, 83, 218–19
Charles I, King of England, funeral of 199
  as art collector 122–3
  at funeral of James I 33 n.88, 179, 186–7, 195, 198, 205
  at funeral of Lennox 187
  at funeral of Queen Anne of Denmark 183
  as Prince 121, 152
  court of 122
  marriage of 193
  policy towards Catholics 128
  prohibition on nocturnal funerals 146
Charles II, King of England, 146, 201, 202 n.130
Charles V, Emporer 8, 75 n.44, 214 n.4
Charles VI, King of France, funeral of 62, fig. 10
Charles VII, King of France 84 n.94
Charles VIII, King of France, funeral of 64
Charles IX, King of France, funeral of 6, 8, 13, 48, 64, 114, 178, 214–20
  lit de justice of 184–6, 191
Charles, Cardinal of Lorraine 219
Chastel, Pierre Du 64
chasuble fig. 7
Chettle, Henry 87 n.2, 211
chief mourner 30, 33–4, 48, 102, 179, 183, 186, 213, fig. 2
chivalry 50–52, 180, 204
Christian IV, King of Denmark 130–1, 158, 163, 205
church service 28–35, 175–84, 198
church topography 137 n.53
choreography 10, 33, 49, 204
civil funerals 57, 106, 110, 200, 204
Clapham, John 89–91, 101
clergy *see priests*
Cleves, Anne of, funeral of 34

Clifford, Lady Anne 34, 115
collective effervescence 10, 91
College of Arms, regulations of 19, 26, 77, 139, 143, 145, 183
  attendance at funerals 25, 33, 44, 196
  decline of 145 n.93
  fees to 142
  organisation of funerals 75, 168, 182
  records of 150
Colt, Maximilian 109, 132, 136, 151, 164, 171–2, 193
communion table 28, 38, 49–51, 54
Coronation Portrait of Elizabeth I 89–90
coronation ceremonies, German 64 n.11
Cornwallis, Sir Charles 119, 151, 164
Corpus Christi 2, 24 n.42, 111
costume *see mourning dress*
Cosimo I, Duke of Florence, funeral of 178
Cosimo II, Grand Duke of Tuscany 119
Cottington, Sir Francis 121, 128
Cotton, Sir Robert 97
Counter-Reformation 126, 172, 203
court masques 157–62, 184
Cranfield, Lionel 167
Critz, John de 89, 109, 133, 171, 177
Cromwell, Oliver 171, 199–201
crosses and crucifixes 45 n.41, 58, 81, 111, 123 n.25, 144
cross-fertilization of ritual 8, 62, 65
cultural materialism 6 n.21, 10
Cure, Cornelius 135, 137 n.51
Cynthia 89

Dacre, Lord, funeral of 31, 47–8
Dallington, Sir Robert 122, 136
Darnley, Henry 136
Davison, William 70
death mask 82, 88, 90, 108, 193, 204
Dekker, Thomas 88 n.6, 91 n.24, 135
Denmark, Anne of, funeral of 34, 48
Denmark House 166, 176, 186–7, 193, 196, 202, 207
Denton tomb 107
Dethick, Sir William 18, 78–9, 83, 85, 138, 150
Devereux, Robert, second Earl of Essex 75
Devereux, Robert, third Earl of Essex 155, 199
Directory for the Publique Worship of God (1644) 200
Dissolution Acts (1536 and 1539) 44

244

Index

divine right of kings 69, 127, 159, 180–2, 185, 205
dole 36
Doort, Abraham van der 164
dubbing ceremony 50–1
Duchess of Malfi, The 107 n.101, 135 n.37
Duffy, Eamon 38
Dugdale, Sir William 139
Durkheim, Emile 10, 91
drums 18

Easter sepulchre 45 n.44, 111
Edmund, Duke of Buckingham 201
Edward the Confessor 65
Edward II, King of England, funeral of 66
Edward III, King of England, funeral of 66
 effigy of 88, 108
Edward IV, King of England, funeral of 21, 31 n.74, 61, 114
 has father reinterred 138
Edward VI, King of England 132, 181
Edward, the Black Prince 21 n.30
effigy, royal funeral 1–2, 8, 66–6, 82, 85, 87, 103–11, 129–31, 162–5, 170–4, 175–80, 182, 184–8, 194–5, 199–202, 204–5, 209, 213–14, 218
 episcopal 104, 150
 Roman 105
 standing in state ritual 199, 201
 tomb 104, 106–11
Egyptian symbolism 151
Elizabeth I, Queen of England, funeral of 17, 21, 87–117, 187, 211–13, fig. 15
 and Mary Queen of Scots 69
 and Sir Philip Sidney's funeral 76
 corpus fictum 96 n.45
 embalming 103
 funeral effigy of 87, 91, 98, 129–31
 images of 133
 mourning dress 19
 on use of torches 46
 pays for funerals of others 52
 political philosophy 57
 portraits of 89
 Procession Picture 113 n.136
 sermon for 176
 tomb effigy of 131–4, 172
Elizabeth of Bohemia 29 n.69, 136, 140, 148 n.4, 168
Elizabeth of York, funeral of 32, 66, 129
 effigy of 1 n.4, 171, 193 n.85
 tomb of 136

Ellwas, Sir Geoffrey 206
embalming 66 n.17, 78, 103, 143, 173, 188
escutcheons 22–3, 29, 49, 51, 186, 218

feast, funeral 35–6, 82, 84
Ferdinand, King of France 8 n.25
Ferne, John 23, 26
Fletcher, John 155
Fontana, Domenico 178
Forset, Edward 95 n.41
Foscarini 119, 151–3, 157, 162
Fotheringay 74, 78, 104, 132, 139
Framlingham 120, 138
France, absolutism 184–5
 effigies 131 n.15
 funeral supermarkets 208
 multiple burial 173 n.33
 royal funerals 5, 61–6, 192
 wars of religion 64
Francis, Duke of Alençon and Anjou, funeral of 114, 218
Francis I, King of France, funeral of 5, 64, 187, 193 n.85
Francis II, King of France 80

Gardiner, Steven, Bishop of Winchester 104
Geertz, Clifford 3, 10–11
George I, King 202
Gerbier, Balthazar 118
Gheeraerts, Marcus 89
Giesey, Ralph 5
Gilby, Anthony 48, 58–9
Giraldi, L. G. 178
Gittings, Clare 4, 188
Glencairn, William, Earl of 142 n.76
Gloriana 89–91, 133–4, 177, 206
Gluckman, Max 11
Goodman, Gabriel, Dean of Westminster Abbey 130
Goodman, Godfrey 134, 157
Gorges, Sir Arthur 156
Griffin, Bishop of Rochester 58 n.104
Grimes, Sir John 145
Grindal, Edmund, Archbishop of Canterbury 56, 59
Guest, Edmund, Bishop of Salisbury 106
Guichard, C. 178
Guise, Cardinal of 169
 arms of 80
 Duke of 68, 71–2, 140, 155 n.44

Index

Hamilton, Marquis of 183 n.42
Hampton Court Conference (1604) 123
hanouars 217–18
Harington, James 79, 89
Harington, Sir John 101, 135
Harrison, William 37, 39
Harvey, Gabriel 95
hatchments *see achievements*
Hatton House 187
Hatton, Sir Christopher 141
Hawkins, Sir Thomas, tomb of fig. 19
Haydocke, Richard 110, 122
hearse and catafalque 29, 32, 35, 37, 45, 48–9, 63, 81, 139, 151, 164, 170–1, 175–80, 186–7, 199–200, figs 3, 4, 5
Henrietta Maria, Queen 121–3, 128, 191, 193, 198
Henry I, King of England, funeral of 65
Henry II, King of England, funeral of 65, 113
Henry II, King of France, funeral of 8 n.25, 48
Henry III, King of England, funeral of 66
Henry III, King of France
   and Mary Queen of Scots 71
   exclusion from Paris 72
Henry IV, King of France, funeral of 116 n.150, 149, 185, 191–2
   at funeral of Charles IX 218
   conversion of 102
   death of 154
   effigy of 199, fig. 23
   military campaigns 159
Henry V, King of England, funeral of 21 n.30, 66
   effigy of 91
   image of 160
Henry V by William Shakespeare (1599) 2
Henry VI, King of England, succession of 62
   body of 138 n.60
Henry VI Part I by William Shakespeare (1592) 206 n.3
Henry VII, chapel 41, 130–1, 136, 139, 148, 163, 173, 187, 199, 201, 205
Henry VII, King of England, funeral of 46, 61, 181
   arms of 80
   builds chapel 131
   effigy of 1 n.4, 88, 90–1, 108–9, fig. 13
   lying-in-state 116–17
   regulation of funerals 52
   tomb of 136
Henry VIII, King of England, funeral of 9, 44, 114
   children of 150
   effigy of 91, 108 n.110
   tomb of 132, 199
   will of 99–100
Henry, Lord Cobham 53
Henry, Lord Hunsdon, funeral of 52
Henry Stuart, Prince of Wales, funeral of 148–65, 175, 177, 189 n.65, 195 n.98
   art collector 118, 121, 160 n.68
   effigy of 130, 171, fig. 22
   household 119
   investiture of 157
   marriage of 140
Henry Unton Memorial portrait (1596) 6
heraldic funeral 6–7, 15–36, 51, 204
heraldry 25, 27, 40
Herbert, George 126 n.42
Herodian, The Historie of 114
Hilliard, Nicholas 121, 133
Holmes, Martin 164
homilies 39 n.12, 46, 103
hoods *see tippets*
Hooker, Richard 54
Hopital, Michel de l' 184, 192
horse of honour 87, 92, 213
Howard, Henry, Earl of Northampton 98–9, 119, 123, n.28, 124, 136, 140, 144, 194
Howard, Lord Thomas, Lord Admiral 98
Howard, Philip, Earl of Arundel 120
Howard, Thomas, Earl of Arundel and Surrey
   and Prince Henry Stuart 119–20, 124, 149, 182, 187, 197
Howard, Thomas, Duke of Norfolk 31 n.74
Huntingdon, Earl of, funeral of 19, 45 n.46
   at Sir Philip Sidney's funeral 75

iconoclasm, iconomachy and iconophobia 39, 103, 133 n.23, 207
idolatry 39 n.12, 46, 57 n.99, 204
images and iconography 13, 49, 103, 111, 115, 126, 134, 137, 162, 179, 184, 186, 193, 202–3
incense and censing 44, 45 n.41
individualism 4
Injunctions (1547) 54

Index

Injunctions (1599) 38
Innocents 44 n.35
interment 34 n.91, 35, 79
intercession 46
Islip chapel 130, 194
Islip, John, Abbot of Westminster fig. 11

James I, King of England, funeral of 1, 33 n.88, 44, 175–203, 205, 208, fig. 21
    and Mary Queen of Scots 69
    and Queen Anne's funeral 169
    and Prince Henry Stuart 148, 152–3, 157–62
    court of 159 n.62
    effigies of 190
    exploitation of funeral ritual 129–47
    political philosophy 94, 127
    posthumous images of 202–3
    royal entry 98 n.55
    statues of 194 n.87
    succession of 86, 99 n.62, 181
James II, King of England 202
James, Isaac 120
James, Mervyn 24, 46, 50,
Jewel, Archbishop 39 n.12, 54
Jones, Inigo 120–1, 122 n.19, 151, 177, 202
Jonson, Ben 159

Kantorowicz, Ernst 5, 91, 93
Katherine de Valois, effigy of 108, 131, 171
Keen, Maurice 50
Keeper of Monuments, Westminster Abbey 130
Kim Il Sung 207–8
King's Evil 97
king's two bodies 5, 93
Knollys, Lady Catherine 52 n.74

Lant, Thomas 75, 77
Laud, William, Archbishop of Canterbury 125–7
Laudian Anglicanism 125, 175, 193
Legh, Gerard 26
Leicester, Robert Dudley, Earl of, funeral of 86
    and funeral of Sir Philip Sidney 75, 77
    art collector 118
Lennox, Margaret 136
Lewkenor, Master of Ceremonies 197
lit de justice 184–5
lit d'honneur 194
liturgy, burial 42, 47

Lomazzo 110, 122
Lord Mayor 77, 92, 196
Louis XI, King of France 84 n.94
Louis XII, King of France 8 n.25
Louis XIII, King of France 121, 155 n.44, 185
Louis XIV, King of France 137 n.54
Lowe, Sir Thomas 143
Lucy, William, Bishop of St David's 127
Luther, Martin 55
lying-in-state ceremony 64, 85, 113–17, 149, 166–70, 178, 186–96, 198, 201, 205, 215

Machyn, Henry 37, 45, 58, 205
Manchester, Henry Montagu, Earl of 182, 183 n.37, 192
Manningham, John 103
Mantua, Duke of 121
Margaret, Duchess of Norfolk 138
Marlborough, James Ley, Earl of 182
Mary I, Queen of England, funeral of 58 n.104, 181, 196 n.101
    effigy of 107, 109, 129, fig. 14
    embalming of 173
    lack of tomb for 132
    papal envoy to 128
    succession of 181
Mary II, Queen of England 202
Mary, Countess of Northumberland 143
Mary, Duchess of Suffolk 150
Mary Queen of Scots, funeral of 67–86, 140, 188, 201, 208, fig. 16
    as Catholic martyr 73, 137 n.55
    head of 74 n.38
    second funeral of 138–40, 205
    succession of 94
    tomb and tomb effigy 133 n.23, 134–7, 172, fig. 20
    vault of 148
Mattieu, Pièrre 192
Mauncey, James 137 n.51
mausoleum 202
Medici, Catherine de 64, 71
Medici, Marie de 185
Medici tombs 136
Mendoza, Bernardino de 72
Melville, Sir John 79, 82
Middleton, Marmeduke, Bishop of St David's 48
Middleton, Thomas 130

247

Index

Monk, General, Duke of Albermarle and Earl of Torrington 201
Montagu, Richard 127 n.47
Montague, James, Bishop of Winchester 125
Montaigne, George, Archbishop of York, Bishop of Coventry and Lichfield, Dean of Westminster 127, 139
Montgomery, Henry Herbert, Earl of 182
Moore, Sally F 13
Morillon, Claude 191–2
Morosini, Venetian ambassador 190
mourning dress 18–19, 33, 100 n.63
mourning cloth 196 n.101
Mytens, Daniel 119 n.6, 121
mystification 10, 28

Nassau, Count Lewis of 155
Neile, Richard, Archbishop of York 126–7
Neville, Richard, Earl of Salisbury, funeral of 31, 48, 52
Neville, Sir Thomas 48
night-burials 140–3, 183
Norfolk, Duke of, funeral of 44
Northampton, Helena, Marchioness of 102, 168 n.11
Notre Dame, Paris 68 n.5, 216
Nottingham, Countess of 168

Oberon 160 n.67, 161
offering ceremony 30, 37–8, 46–51, 61, 180–4
Office of the Dead 41
organ music 81
Ormskirk 15
Overbury, Sir Thomas 191
Overall, John, Bishop of Coventry and Lichfield, and later of Norwich 125

Palatine, Elector 29 n.69, 140, 154–5, 161
Palladio, Andrea 178
Parker, Matthew, Archbishop of Canterbury 56
Parkes, Daniel 194
Parr, William, Marquis of Northampton 52 n.74
Parry, Richard, Bishop of Asaph, funeral of 188
Parsons, Robert 100
Passe, William van de 162 n.74
Paulet, Sir Amias 74
Paulet, William, Marquis of Winchester figs 3, 5

Paul's Cross 96, 169, 176
Peacham, Henry 119, 122
Peake, Robert 178 n.14
Pembroke, William Herbert, Earl of 119, 182, 187
pennons 22, 25 n.46, 29
Pepys, Samuel 131, 201
Percy, Henry, Earl of Northumberland 124
performance, funeral ritual as 9
Perkins, William 175
Pertinax, funeral of 178
Pesaro, Venetian ambassador 180, 183, 186, 197
Peterborough 77–8
Peterborough cathedral 68, 138–9
pews and pewing 54
Philip II, King of Spain 73, 199
Philip IV, King of Spain 121
pièces d'honneur, see achievements
Platter, Thomas 117, 130, 132
Plowden, Edmund 93, 96, 182
Pope, Lady Elizabeth 107
Popham, Sir John, Chief Justice 101, 213
Porcacchi, T. 178
Prayer Book (1552 and 1559) 42–4, 55, 123
Price, Daniel 124
priests 44, 48
primers 56
procession, funeral 15–28, 47, 87, 92, 139, 149, 160–70, 196–9, 200
  parish 24 n.43, 53, 54 n.79
proclamations of royal succession 95, 99 n.62
Prynne, William 123, 127 n.47
psalm-singing 55, 81
pulpit 28, 38
purgatory 40, 41 n.22
Puritan funerals 146, 200 n.121
quarantaine 114

Reformation 9, 37–60, 103–6, 132, 194, 204
religion royale 97, 113, 127–8, 194–5, 205, 207
regularization 13, 64
representations 84, 150, 188
Revenger's Tragedy, The 206
Rheims 72
Rich, Henry, Earl of Holland 121
Richard II, King of England 19, 52

248

Index

Richard Plantagenet, Duke of York 138, 150
Richmond, Duchess of 143
Ridley, Nicholas, Bishop of London 106
Roman funerals 105, 141–2, 151 n.23, 178–80
rood cross 40, 51
rood screen 37–9, 50–1, 54
royal entry 157
Rubens, Peter Paul 119, 203
Russel, Bridget, Countess of Bedford 79, 86, 187 n.59
Rutland, Countess of 86
Rutland, Edward, Earl of 80

St Denis 66, 67–8, 131 n.15, 191, 219
St James' Palace 149
St Martin's, Ludgate 44
St Paul's 19, 28, 106, 203
saints, banners of 40, 49
salle d'honneur 64, 214–15
salle de deuil 215
Savile, Henry 178
Scaramelli, Venetian Ambassador 90, 100, 102, 116, 137
second funerals 139
Second Maiden's Tragedy, The 137 n.56, 206–7
secularization 49–52
Segar, William 80, 114, 141
semiotics 17, 28
Septimus Severus 114
Serlio, Sebastiano 177 n.14
sermon 38, 175, 184, 194–5, 205
Seymour, Jane, funeral of 168, 171
Shakespeare, William 1, 155, 206
Sidney, Sir Henry 58, 76, 80
Sidney, Sir Philip, funeral of 18, 75–7, 79, 156, fig. 1
  death of 153 n.34, 155, 159
Sixtus V, Pope 73, 77, 178
Solomon, King 176, 184
Somerset House 199, 200 n.120
Spanish Infanta 100, 195
Spenser, Edmund 89, 135
Stafford, Sir Edward 71–2, 114
standards 22, 92, 211
Stanley, Edward, Earl of Derby, funeral of 7, 15–36, 61
Stewart, Henry, Lord Darnley 80
Stone, Nicholas, 120
Stone, Lawrence 4

Stow, John 88, 91, 109
streets, with funeral blacks 19
  scaffolds in 197, 200
Stuart, Arabella 100, 102, 136
Stuart, Esme 187, 189–90
Stuart, Frances, Duchess of Richmond and Lennox 188–9
Stuart, Lodovick, Duke of Richmond and Lennox 119, 136, 145, 187–90, 192, 196
Stubbs, John 104 n.85
sublimation 11, 27 n.61, 60
Sueur, Henry Le 178, 203
Sylla, funeral of 105, 114 n.141
symbols and symbolism 8–9, 11, 27, 111, 175, 179, 205, 207

Talbot, Aletheia, Countess of Arundel 168
Talbot, Francis, fifth Earl of Shrewsbury 33, 35–6, 58
Talbot, Gilbert, seventh Earl of Shrewsbury 118, 137
Tethys' Festival 160
Theobalds 169, 175, 186, 194, 196
Theodosius I 114 n.142
Thirty-Nine Articles 58
Throckmorton, Sir Nicholas 113
Tillet, Jean Du 178
tippets and hoods 19–20, 33, 52
torches and torchlight 44, 46, 60, 78, 140–3, 183 n.42, 194, 204
Torrigiano, Pietro d'Antonio 108, 202
Trajan, funeral of 179
trental mass 49
Trew Law of Free Monarchies 94
trumpets and trumpeters 18, 64, 92, 211
Tudor, Margaret 100
Turner, Victor 2 n.5
tympanum 39, 50–1

Ulric, Frederic 155

Villiers, George, Duke of Buckingham 145, 182, 191, 198
  art collector 118
  foreign policy 128
viscera, separate burial of 67, 170, 186, 214
visual codes 10

Walsingham, Sir Francis 71, 74–6, 114, 142 n.80

249

Index

Warmstry, Thomas 126, 195
Warwick, Countess of 142
Webster, John 107 n.101, 156
Weever, John 105–6, 131, 142, 143 n.83, 146, 202
Western Rising (1549) 55
Westminster Abbey 30 n.71, 39, 41, 66, 87, 115, 129–31, 133, 140, 163, 170, 172, 187–9, 193–7, 199–202, 205, 211
Wharton, Lord Thomas 47
Whitehall Palace 29 n.69, 201, 203, 211
Wigenstein, Count 155

Winchester, Bishop of, funeral of 35
Winchester Cathedral 203
William III, King of England 202
Williams, John, Bishop of Lincoln 175, 179, 182–4, 188, 195, 205
Williams, Raymond 13
Wilson, Arthur 141, 157
Wotton, Henry 2, 122, 151, 180, 189
Wren, Matthew 127–8
Wriothesley, Thomas 53, 83 n.87
Wryley, William 26
Wyseman, Raphe & Elizabeth, tomb of fig. 18